THE COMPLETE NZ Fisherman
Saltwater & Freshwater Fishing

Geoff Thomas

David Bateman

Copyright © Geoff Thomas, 1997
Copyright © David Bateman Ltd, 1997

First published in 1997 by David Bateman Ltd, 30 Tarndale Grove, Albany, Auckland, New Zealand

Reprinted 1998, 2001

ISBN 1 86953 369 0 (hardback)
ISBN 1 86953 504 9 (paperback)

This book is copyright. Except for the purpose of fair review, no part may be stored or transmitted in any form or by any means, electronic or mechanical, including recording or storage in any information retrieval systems, without permission in writing from the publishers. No reproduction may be made, whether by photocopying or by any other means, unless a licence has been obtained from the publisher or its agent.

Cover design by Shelley Watson
Design by Errol McLeary
Typeset by TTS Jazz, Auckland
Printed in Hong Kong through Colorcraft Ltd

CONTENTS

ACKNOWLEDGEMENTS 7

1 **INTRODUCTION** 9

2 **THE FISH WE CATCH** 12
The food chain 12   *Types of fishes* 17   *Swimming* 18
Anatomy of fish 19   *Attracting fish — the senses* 20   *Organs* 24

3 **GETTING STARTED** 26
Balanced tackle 26   *Rods* 27   *Reels* 31   *Handlines* 35   *Fishing lines* 36
Spooling reels 37   *Care of nylon lines* 39   *Terminal tackle* 40   *Accessories* 44
Casting techniques 45

4 **FISHING FROM THE SHORE** 50
Wharf fishing 50   *Structures* 52   *Rock fishing* 56   *Beach fishing* 65

5 **SMALL BOAT FISHING** 70
Preparation 70   *Safety equipment* 73   *Harbour and estuary fishing* 74
Coastal fishing 80   *Fishing over a reef* 83   *Fishing over sand or mud* 87
Fishing with jigs 88   *Targeting big fish inshore* 92   *Deepwater snapper* 98
Big kingfish tactics 99   *Fishing the deepwater reef* 104   *Saltwater fly fishing* 107
Tips for big fish bait 110

6 **GAMEFISHING** 113
Using ocean currents to find gamefish 118   *Lure fishing* 121   *The strike* 130
Using baits 142   *Tackle* 145   *Land-based gamefishing* 155

7 **FLOUNDER FISHING AND NETTING** 157

8 **KITE FISHING AND LONGLINES** 161
Kite fishing 161   *Longlines in boats* 164

9 **CRAYFISH, SHELLFISH AND SQUID** 167
Crayfish 167   *Shellfish* 169   *Squid* 170

10 **HISTORY OF TROUT AND SALMON** 173

11 **TROLLING AND HARLING** 180

12 **SPINFISHING AND JIGGING** 197

13 **FLY FISHING** 204
Trout and the angler 204   *Reading the water* 204   *Trout food* 208
Fishing streams and rivers 211   *Fishing Taupo rivers* 218   *Dry-fly fishing* 220
Fly fishing on lakes 222   *Fly fishing tackle* 240   *Fly patterns* 241
Catching a trophy trout 242   *Bait fishing* 250

14 **SALMON FISHING** 256
History 256   *Life cycle* 257   *Canterbury salmon fishing* 258   *Fishing the surf* 258
River fishing 260   *Harbour fisheries* 263   *Rules of salmon fishing etiquette* 266

15 **COARSE FISHING** 268
Tackle 268   *Bait* 269   *Stillwater fishing* 270   *Fishing rivers* 272

16 **EEL FISHING** 275

17 **WHITEBAIT** 277

18 **TACKLE MAINTENANCE** 281

19 **FISH HANDLING** 284

20 **THE MOON AND WEATHER** 287

21 **KNOTS** 291

Glossary 300
Index 303

ACKNOWLEDGEMENTS

Warm thanks are due to the many fine anglers who have contributed through sharing time on the water, reminiscences and valuable knowledge. I wish to acknowledge the specific assistance from Nigel Wood, Glenn Maclean, Phil Sutton of NIWA, Ross Millichamp, Malcolm Bell, Steve Reed, Gavin Pegley, George Western, Paul Barnes, Philip and Sidey Smith, Bruce Duncan, Jason Wootton, Bruce Martin, Bill Hall, Bruce Smith, and Russell Murray; with special thanks to Peter Pakula. The *New Zealand Herald* kindly consented to material from my weekly column being reproduced.

    The value of any book on the outdoors is directly related to the quality of its illustrations, and it is a real bonus to have photographs by Rex Hudson, Rob Tucker, John McCombe, underwater photographs by Roger Grace, John Batterton and special contributors acknowledged where appropriate. Some even came from my own camera.

    Most of the drawings are by John Morgan, who is also a fisherman; with others by Mandy Hague and Linda Wong.

    It is a luxury to have an editor who is an accomplished angler and accordingly Mike Bradstock contributed with some technical as well as editorial expertise.

CHAPTER ONE
INTRODUCTION

Wherever you live in New Zealand, you are not far from water. It may be a stream or lake, a harbour or other part of our huge coastline. There will be fish to catch — eels, perch, trout, whitebait, rays, kahawai, mullet, snapper, red cod, moki, gurnard, trevally, herrings, mackerel, kingfish, dogfish, salmon, tuna, mussels on the rocks or flounders in the shallows. The list goes on and on.

The sport of fishing continually changes and evolves. Fish which were scorned a generation ago are now recognised for their sporting and table qualities. New materials and technology make our efforts more efficient. Fishermen have access to more water, whether by trailer boat probing offshore or long-range launch cruising to remote fishing grounds. We are indeed fortunate in the quality and variety of fishing available to us.

Success on the water comes from a combination of experience, confidence and patience; and the willingness of those people who regularly catch fish to pass on their knowledge is the key to this book. But do not be restricted by the advice and tips offered. Apart from any legal requirements, there are few rules. It is rather like cooking, where recipes need not be adhered to strictly. But an understanding of the best approach to take and which ingredients complement others, will lead to success. An ability to be adaptable combined with some lateral thinking will put fish in the box.

Fishing should also be fun and to this end technical and instructional material has been complemented with anecdotes, which are both entertaining and informative. Some relate true incidents while others just possibly may be fantasy.

No honest study of fishing in this country would be complete without reference to management. Freshwater fisheries are in good shape under a restructured system, but the same cannot be said for all saltwater fisheries. In many cases the fishing we have is in spite of management, not as a result of it. Political squabbles contribute little to the future of our fisheries, and a serious effort is needed from all parties to ensure that where resources are threatened the pressures are reduced and stocks allowed to rebuild.

The mystery of fishing is one which will always be with us.

This book is dedicated to all anglers — past, present and future. Enjoy it!

Opposite: The promise of a bright day on the ocean — a charter launch heads for the gamefishing grounds off the Bay of Islands.

Following spread: The magic hour on a cold, frosty morning in the first light of dawn. A solitary fly fisherman at the mouth of the Te Wairoa Stream on Lake Tarawera.

CHAPTER TWO
THE FISH WE CATCH

Get together a rod, reel and a few hooks and sinkers and you are ready to go fishing. Right? Wrong. But take the trouble to learn and understand a little about the fish you hope to catch, and you are halfway there.

The most important aspect of getting started in fishing is knowing where fish live and why, what they like to eat, and when they can be caught. An appreciation of the fish and the environment they live in will also help ensure that the sort of fishing we enjoy will still be available for future generations of anglers.

All fishermen have their favourite spots, and this local knowledge is the key ingredient to successful fishing. Other important factors like tides and weather also influence fish behaviour and while much can be learnt from books and talking to more experienced anglers, nothing compensates for time spent on the water.

The food chain

Saltwater

The sea is incredibly rich and plays host to a remorseless cycle of eat-or-be-eaten. Just about all fish are part of the food chain which starts with plankton. There are two basic types of plankton: plant plankton — myriads of tiny plants called algae, which drift in the oceans and coastal waters — and animal plankton, which feed on plant plankton and animals smaller than themselves. They in turn are consumed by baitfish and many species of juvenile fish.

Krill, the tiny red shrimp-like creatures which drift in dense concentrations, are also a type of large animal plankton. They can sometimes be seen as a dark red stain on the water, and are important food for salmon and whales. Pigments in the krill produce the deep crimson colour in the flesh of salmon which is so highly valued by anglers.

Plankton flourishes better in cooler waters, and the great traditional fisheries of the northern hemisphere are all found above the 40th parallel.

New Zealand is situated across comparable latitudes, and we are fortunate in having both cool and warm currents reaching our coastline, providing suitable conditions for a wide range of both local and migratory fishes.

Where currents strike an obstruction, like the continental shelf surrounding land, the resulting upwelling carries nutrients from the ocean floor to the surface. Together with the sunlight these nutrients encourage the growth of plant plankton at the base of the food chain. In turn, animal plankton flourishes, providing food for fish.

Where tides carry plankton-rich water in and out of harbours, and where ocean waves wash back and forth, a regular supply of plankton is delivered to filter-feeders like mussels and barnacles clinging to rocky shores, and pipis on sandy shores. In fact, wherever there is water movement, some forms of marine life will be found.

But it is not only tiny fish that eat plankton — the largest creatures in the ocean live solely on it. These include manta rays, basking sharks and whale sharks, which are the biggest among the fishes, and many species of whales.

Most fish are also opportunists and few restrict their diet to a single type of food the way the specialist weed-eaters do (e.g. parore and drummer). Fish learn by trial and error what is edible, and without hands their only method of investigating something is to try and eat it. A fish may

A tight mass of fish all facing the same way with their noses on the surface, creating a rippling effect, signals a school of fish feeding on plankton.

eject a morsel several times before swallowing it. This is why the angler must resist the overpowering urge to strike when a kingfish or marlin is checking out his live bait, and give the quarry time to go through the ritual of taking it into its mouth, perhaps spitting it out, and then picking it up again.

But fish do build up a set of preferred food items, and a prior understanding of this will help the novice angler. Many of their favourite foods may be available only for brief periods. Large masses of food may suddenly appear, causing fish to switch diets. At other times fish cannot afford to be choosy, and must eat whatever nature will provide. While predators may prefer slim-bodied, soft-finned fish like pilchards because they are easy to swallow, when food is scarce they will eat deep-bodied, spiny-finned prey. But there are also regular patterns, and baitfish which hatch in spring become large enough to interest predators by mid-summer. Fishing then slows down when the predators become glutted.

Kahawai will prey on small sprats and whitebait, but will also join trevally and maomao feasting on concentrations of plankton.

The observant angler can tell by the behaviour of certain school fish what they are feeding on, and will amend his approach accordingly. For example, splashes on the surface spread over a wide area and moving across the water indicate fish like kahawai feeding on small baitfish. Conversely, a tight mass of fish all facing the same way with their noses on the surface, creating a rippling effect, signals that they are feeding on plankton. There may be a number of different species in the school, and they will ignore a lure which resembles a baitfish but will snap up a small, pink krill imitation.

It is safe to assume that, except in very shallow water, wherever there are small fish larger fish will not be far away.

Freshwater

New Zealand is a long, narrow country punctuated with mountain ranges and forests. With no part of the landmass more than about 100 kilometres from the coast, the weather is unpredictable and changeable. This can be the bane of coastal fishermen, but the resulting high rainfall provides a rich supply of clean, fresh water, a resource we are only beginning to appreciate as water quality in other places is continually eroded. Our lakes and rivers are the envy of many, particularly trout fishermen from overseas. Trout have been used as indicators of water quality in other countries, and the world-class reputation of our trout fisheries is an indication of the quality of water we still enjoy.

We are blessed with a wide variety of waters holding good populations of trout and, in some places, salmon. Trout and salmon were introduced by sporting-minded settlers in the late 19th century and early this century. Indeed, where ever they occur in the southern hemisphere is because they were introduced.

Lakes and rivers are not as fertile as the sea, but each is a delicately balanced ecosystem with a similar food chain. Their particular types of animal plankton, such as water fleas, feed on algae and in turn are eaten by the larvae of fish and aquatic insects. Young trout and salmon feed on these, and also directly on animal plankton. In some fisheries the food is so rich, and the water temperatures and chemistry so well suited to trout, that phenomenal growth rates are recorded, with trout reaching double figures within two years.

Management also has a strong influence on the health of fisheries in popular areas like the central North Island lakes where angling pressure continues to grow.

As on the sea, the successful angler will learn to read the signs on a lake. The direction of the wind is one of the most important. Wind-blown algae which builds up along a shoreline can be a clue to fish location. Smelt grazing on the algae will attract trout that can ambush them in the murky water.

Shelter

Many fish will be found close to some form of shelter, e.g. a wharf pile, reef, weed bed, or rocky shoreline. Food will be delivered twice a day by the tidal currents, and if there is no current there will be few fish.

Some species are also attracted to floating objects like marker buoys in harbour channels, and flotsam like logs and debris floating at sea. This habit has long been exploited by Asian fishermen who anchored rafts of bamboo along the coast, returning to catch gamefish by trolling or netting around the rafts. The use of artificial structures to attract fish has developed into a sophisticated practice in many parts of the world.

Once seaweeds and barnacles become established, small fish and other marine life arrive quickly. More than a hundred crabs have been found hidden in weed attached to a single Japanese glass float drifting at sea. It is always a marvel that such tiny creatures can be found out in the vast ocean, clinging to such a precarious object as a floating coconut or piece of wood. Big-game fishermen will change course to troll their lures close to any floating debris, knowing there may well be mahimahi, tuna or other highly prized species lurking underneath.

In New Zealand experienced anglers are well aware of the way kingfish hang around channel marker buoys in harbours. Kingfish tend to congregate around the anchor line rather than the actual buoy, with smaller specimens near the surface and larger ones underneath.

Security in numbers

Security also comes in numbers, and small fish like pilchards, anchovies, whitebait and smelt rarely swim alone in deep water. Such individuals would be quickly snapped up by a roving speedster like a kingfish or tuna or, in a lake, by a hungry rainbow trout.

Instead, the individual is lost in a huge school comprising thousands or millions of fish. These flow and dance in the current like a living being as they feed on tiny organisms, binding together in a tight mass when attacked. That is one reason why nature has painted these fish in such brilliant silvery colours: a predator becomes confused by the shimmering mass and cannot pick out individuals. From above, the dark blue backs of the baitfish blend with the colour of the sea, to confuse airborne predators like seabirds.

For the same reason, small fish which live in coastal, greener water closer inshore often have green rather than blue backs, e.g. yellow-eyed mullet, jack mackerel and piper. If you dive under the water and look back up at the surface, you will see how it resembles a thick silvery layer of mercury, forever sliding and moving. It takes little imagination to assume the position of a predator hunting baitfish, and understand why the bellies of the pelagic fishes in particular are so flashy and bright. They would indeed be difficult to separate from the backdrop of the water's surface. Some fish also have patterns of spots, bars or mottled lines on their flanks to break up their outline. Others have a stripe through their eye or a spot on their tail which makes it harder for a predator to tell which end is the front.

There is always a reason for everything in nature — the pretty fish were not designed just for our enjoyment. But to marvel at the beautiful shapes and colours of the many fishes is a pleasure that we alone can experience.

Other species enjoy a different relationship with the plankton/baitfish/big fish chain. These are the scavengers, which like hyenas following groups of lions, are nature's vacuum cleaners. Red cod is one of our more adept scavengers, and snapper, one of the most versatile feeders around the New Zealand coastline, can often be found underneath schools of feeding kahawai, trevally or mackerel, scavenging for injured baitfish or pieces which drift down.

Many fish also gather in schools to spawn. This varies with different species in terms of the timing and the places where they congregate. Blue moki, for example, travel long distances each year to gather in deep water off Cape Runaway in the eastern Bay of Plenty, to carry out their annual

The brilliant silver flanks and belly of baitfish like these pilchards are designed to blend with the shimmering underside of the surface of the sea.

spawning ritual in mid-winter. Anglers know that these fish will be in prime condition, with extra fat to sustain them through the rigours of breeding.

Snapper also begin to form up into schools during late winter, ready for spawning in spring and summer in inshore areas where they are readily accessible to the greatest predator — man. Immediately after spawning, the snapper feed ravenously and are easily caught.

The gleaming colours of freshly caught snapper vary from burnished silver flecked with blue spots to the bronze and red shading on a specimen which lives among the kelp.

Types of fishes

For the purposes of angling, fishes can be divided into two main groups: those which are streamlined for fast swimming, and those which are poor swimmers.

Pelagic fishes

The first group includes the pelagic fishes, which live off the bottom of the sea. They are commonly blue and silver in colour, and many migrate over long distances and are often fast-growing with a comparatively short lifespan.

These include the great gamefish like tuna and marlin, which visit our coast every summer, and also flyingfish and small species like pilchards and needlefish.

The pointed nose, fins which fit neatly into slots, powerful sickle tail and metallic-looking, streamlined body of the tuna make it the perfect swimming machine. Tuna cleave the water like a supersonic jet fighter slicing through the atmosphere, and are like a machine for converting food into energy. They have small stomachs, a high rate of metabolism and a rich flow of blood through the muscle tissue, and consequently a high content of red flesh.

Pelagic fish that live year-round in our waters include mackerel, kahawai and adult trevally. Some of these migrate widely along our coasts during each year.

Bottom dwellers

Fish that live on or near the bottom include poor swimmers like the stargazer and conger eel, which rely on camouflage or ambush for their own security and to secure their prey; and better swimmers, such as tarakihi and snapper, that spend most of their time close to the bottom. Fish that swim near the bottom are also called demersal fish, and those that actually sit on the bottom or live in crevices, such as conger eels, stargazer, and blue cod, are called benthic fish. Some demersal fish may form schools, for example snapper and tarakihi. There is a huge variety of fish that can be found on or near the bottom.

Hapuku or blue cod do not require food as often as the tuna. Their gut cavities and mouths are much larger in relation to their body size, and they take longer to absorb their food.

From the angler's point of view, one rule of thumb that can be applied is that the closer to the bottom a fish lives, the better it will be to eat. Think of the delicate, white meat found in gurnard, tarakihi, blue cod, flounder, hapuku and other species.

Swimming

Water has 700 times the resistance of air, and fish move through it by contracting the muscles in succession along each side and pushing against the water. The fast wriggling motion ends with a swish of the tail fin, which provides rapid turning and breaks down drag and turbulence rather than directly aiding propulsion. This comes from the tail itself, the one-third of the body behind the vent.

Long, thin fish like eels and frostfish move with sinuous snake-like undulations, while the parrotfishes scull along with their pectoral fins, using them for propulsion as well as manoeuvring.

With fast-swimming fish the pectorals act like aerofoils and some species have developed special features. The pectorals of sharks, which have no air bladder, are rigidly fixed in a horizontal position to aid buoyancy. Flyingfish have large wing-like pectorals enabling them to glide above the water to escape from predators. On most fish, however, the pelvic and ventral fins appear to be used for lateral stability, to prevent them from moving sideways.

Some, like rays, have wide delta-shaped 'wings' which are used to 'fly' through the water. Gurnard have soft fleshy rays under their colourful fan-like pectoral fins which they use for 'walking' along the bottom, and some fish, such as red cod and ling, have a fleshy tentacle called a barbel under their mouth for locating food hidden in mud or sand.

The poorer swimmers are generally adapted to living on the bottom, and often hide among rocks, e.g. scorpionfish and tiny blennies, or in sand, e.g. flounders and sole. These more sedentary species do not have the need for high-metabolism muscles for high speeds. Others live in both worlds — on the bottom and in midwater — like snapper and trevally. The variety is endless and fascinating.

The speeds at which some fish can swim has been measured by allowing the line from a hooked fish to run freely over a small pulley connected to a speedometer. Other methods have also established speeds for various species. The fastest fish recorded is the wahoo, a tropical gamefish which exceeds 110 kph; while other speedsters are marlin, clocked at 80 kph, and mako sharks at 56 kph. Trout reach 40 kph in bursts, while mullet and eels can only manage a sedate 13 km/hr. These fish have different attributes which attract the angler.

Nature combines symmetry with function. The broad, flat tail of a trout delivers power for short bursts of speed up to 40 kph.

Anatomy of fish

The two groups of fishes are the bony fishes and those with cartilage instead of bone.

Cartilaginous fish include the sharks and rays which have a number of unique characteristics including a skeleton of cartilage, up to seven gill openings, small rough scales that do not overlap, and rigid fins that cannot be folded back. They also lack an air bladder.

Bony fishes have a hard skeleton of bone, a single gill opening on each side, and some fins which can be raised or lowered and are strengthened by fin rays. Most also have an air bladder. Bony fishes (also called teleosts) are the most common types of fishes (Fig. 1).

All have eyes, ears, gills, fins and internal organs. As in warm-blooded animals, the backbone supports the body and is divided into individual

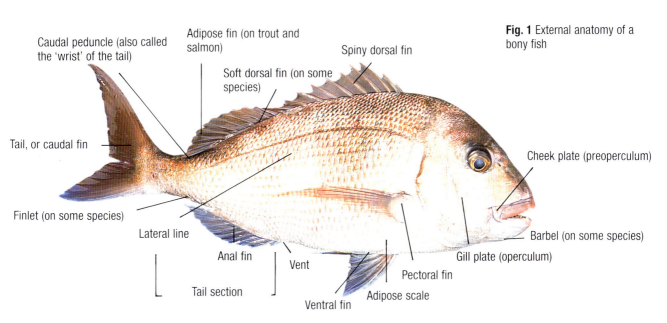

Fig. 1 External anatomy of a bony fish

vertebrae supported by muscles. The spinal cord runs through a hollow centre. The spines of the vertebrae help support the fins and the muscles which operate them, and rows of ribs protect the gut cavity.

Different fishes also have different fin arrangements. Rays on the fins of fast-swimming fish are small, while on slow-moving species they often are developed into long bony spines or soft, trailing rays. Some fish that wriggle or swim with undulating motions have continuous fins around the body, e.g. eels and flatfish.

The shape of the tail fin also varies, from the widely forked tails of fast, long-distance swimmers like marlin and tuna, which chase their quarry, to the broad fan-shaped tail of a hapuku which provides explosive initial speed for ambushing its prey but also creates more drag.

As well as the vertical fins, which vary in size and length, most fishes have two sets of paired fins — the pectorals, behind the gills, and the ventrals, on the underside. Sharks have large pectoral fins which keep the head up, but fish with a swim bladder have pectorals set higher up the side where they can be used as paddles or brakes. Fins may have soft rays, or sharp spines for defence, or be totally rigid as on sharks.

All fish have a layer of mucus or slime which protects against infection and reduces friction against the water. Many fish like blind eels (hagfish) exude extra slime when stressed, a habit which anglers often find unpleasant.

Fish also have scales, which usually overlap but are flexible to allow the body to move when swimming, and provide protection for the body. Scales vary in size and shape, from the almost invisible scales of eels to the large scales of parrotfishes, e.g. spotties. Some have spines on the rear edge while others are smooth and round. The scales of sharks, called denticles, are constructed exactly like minute teeth, giving the skin a rough texture.

Some fish, like seahorses and pipefish, have developed a rigid bony covering, providing protection for the poor swimmers which rely on tiny fins for propulsion.

Attracting fish — the senses

While fish have ears, they do not 'hear' in the sense that we do, but rely on picking up vibrations transmitted through the water, which of course is much denser than air and conducts both sound and vibrations differently. This is important to anglers because so much fishing involves attracting fish.

Apart from the obvious places where fish are found, like sprats hanging around wharf piles or a school of surface-feeding fish indicated by much splashing and birds diving, fish can be attracted to the angler's bait or lure by sending out signals through:
- The use of berley, which is a mixture of attractive odours and food particles designed to draw fish to the area being fished and excite them, making them easier to catch.
- Vibrations created by the action of a lure being dragged through or across

Predators slashing into baitfish provide a beacon for fishermen who can cast or troll lures, jig under the activity or put out live baits.

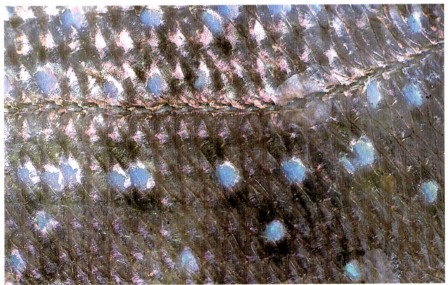

Left: Scales provide protection while the lateral line is a highly developed system for detecting vibrations and changes in water pressure and currents.

the water. This may be a wobbling type of small trout lure, a snapper jig bounced on the bottom, a popper which splutters across the surface to attract kingfish, or a large plastic-skirted lure designed to hook the great gamefish.
- The struggles of a live baitfish.

Lateral line
All fish have a lateral line along each flank, but it is more highly developed in the bony fishes. The lateral line system consists of a series of tubes beneath the skin which protrude through the scales as pores, extending along the body and on to and around the head and jaws. These tubes are sensitive nerve endings with which the fish can detect changes

in water pressure, currents, and vibrations sent out by artificial lures, injured fish, and live baits. The lateral line also helps fish to co-ordinate their swimming in schools.

Hearing

Fish have a keen sense of hearing, because water conducts sound about five times faster than air. They have no external ears, but pick up sound directly through the bones of the head, and can hear over a frequency range of 30 to 30,000 hertz (vibrations per second). Responses vary greatly from species to species. A trout may spook at the lightest of steps on the bank above, while a kingfish or marlin can be attracted by the throb of a propeller.

Sight

Most fish have no eyelids. They may rest motionless in the water but never close their eyes and are easily roused. The vision of many fish is best described as near-sighted as they have eyes on opposite sides of the head so they cannot focus on an object together. Others, like flounders and stargazers, have the eyes side by side on top of the head, giving them excellent binocular vision.

Fish see both brightness and colour, and shallow-water fish have excellent colour vision. Water filters out colour, and red is the first to fade in the depths, followed by yellow and finally blue. In deep water fish respond to flashes of light reflected off other fish, so a lure's brightness and action is more important than its colour. This is one reason why barracouta is a favoured bait for hapuku — the skin retains its brightness, and a long, thin strip hooked only through one end will provide movement, the other signal the eyes are well tuned to pick up.

It also explains why fish are attracted to lures that do not resemble any natural food. Trout will try and eat wobbling lures like cobras and flashy lures like tobys or veltics, yet there is nothing like these that swims in the lake or river.

Fly fishermen also have a saying: "The darker the night, the darker the fly." Common sense suggests the reverse, but at night a black fly presents a better silhouette to a trout looking upward than does a light-coloured one. The vibrations of the fly moving through the water are a factor also, and colour only becomes relevant as the amount of light increases.

Fish view the outside world through a 'window' in the surface of the water: a hole in the surface which is about twice as wide as the depth at which the fish is swimming. But what the fish actually sees is distorted by refraction (the bending of light rays entering the water), and the fish can also see objects above the water that are far back from the window. Anglers stalking trout know full well the importance of keeping a low profile, and not casting a shadow over the fish with the line.

In the world of the fish, a mirror surrounds the window — a large area of water surface through which the fish cannot see. Images of underwater objects are mirrored on the underside of the surface film. Thus lures and flies fished sub-surface are 'doubly' visible.

The lens of the eye bulges beyond the head to provide all-round vision. On flat fish like this eagle ray both eyes are on the top of the head.

The distance which fish can see underwater is determined by water clarity. In a lake, fish may see only a few metres, while gamefish can see more than 30 metres in clear oceanic waters.

Smell

The sense of smell is important to fish, and sharks and eels can detect the odour of blood over long distances. In fact fish can detect odours in concentrations so small that it almost defies belief — concentrations as low as a few parts per trillion.

Smell alerts fish to the presence of predators and prey, and baitfish will emit a chemical from the skin that warns other baitfish of the danger.

The use of smell by salmon seeking their natal river is well known. They will return unerringly to a small tributary after tracking it from many miles out to sea.

Fish will distinguish the smell of different foods — an attribute which many anglers use to their advantage by adding fish oil or smelly fish scraps to berley.

Taste

The sense of taste is not as important to fish as it is to people, and few fish detect taste with much sensitivity. One exception is the catfish, which uses its sensitive whiskers to check food before eating it.

Temperature

While fish are cold-blooded and their body temperature matches that of the surrounding water, they can detect changes as small as one-tenth of a degree through nerves in their skin. This susceptibility to changes in temperature is one of the most important variables determining where fish will be found.

Some fish, mainly fast swimmers such as tuna, expend so much energy their body temperature is higher than the surrounding water. These fish are extremely temperature sensitive and each species has a critical water temperature below which it will not be found, e.g. about 18 degrees Celsius for skipjack and 20 degrees for yellowfin tuna.

The powerful jaws and crushing teeth of big snapper can inflict painful injuries. Use pliers to remove hooks from such fish.

Touch

Fish can also sense touch through their mouth, but it is not a major factor for fishermen. Snapper are accustomed to crunching the hard or spiny shells of sea urchins (kina), crayfish, crabs and mussels, so a hook protruding from a bait is probably of little consequence to the fish. It is more important to the angler that the hook point is clear and able to penetrate, rather than obscured.

The diet of trout includes a variety of natural sensations, including the tough carapace of a freshwater crayfish (koura), a knobbly snail, a slippery smelt or a gob of slimy weed containing tiny organisms. The feel of a lure or fly probably causes little alarm to a hungry trout, but the sudden pull of the line undoubtedly delivers a strong message.

Organs

Fish have most of the same organs as other animals — e.g. stomach, intestine, liver, gall bladder, heart and kidney (Fig. 2). The kidney is very different from that of a mammal: it is the line of dark material looking like congealed blood, lying under the backbone and stretching the length of the gut cavity. Its main function is to regulate the salt levels of the body — retaining salts in freshwater and shedding excess salt in seawater. The heart is situated underneath the gills.

Most fish also have a swim bladder — a shiny, membranous gas bag under the backbone at the centre of gravity of the fish. This can be adjusted to the exterior water pressure through the inner ear, allowing the fish to remain neutrally buoyant at any depth because the weight of the fish is cancelled out by the buoyancy of the swim bladder. When fish are quickly brought up from the depths this bladder expands, making it impossible for the fish to dive again. This is why hapuku hooked on a line float up freely when nearing the surface. If such a fish is to be released, the bladder can be punctured by inserting a hollow needle where the stomach bulges out. This releases the air with an audible hiss, enabling the fish to return to the bottom safely.

Fish which live at great depths have an oil- or fat-filled bladder, or their bodies contain lots of extra fat for buoyancy, because gas-filled swim bladders don't work so well at such great depths. In sharks the large liver, which is full of oil, also provides buoyancy.

Fish require a constant supply of oxygen, but instead of breathing air they exchange carbon dioxide for oxygen by passing water over the gills. While air is 20% oxygen, water contains less than 2% dissolved oxygen. Water is drawn into the mouth and pumped out over the gills, which contain myriads of very fine blood vessels with walls of a thin, fragile membrane. Fast-moving pelagic fish have a continuous intake of water, but sedentary, bottom-dwelling fish have large heads and gill covers to pump the supply needed.

The gill filaments are delicate and easily damaged, which is why some fish with a rich blood supply like tuna and kahawai bleed easily from the gills. If fish are to be released unharmed, it is imperative that the gills are not touched.

The teeth found in different fishes vary enormously. Some are designed to grasp and hold prey; others are long and sharp, as in predators like barracouta; and there are often teeth on the tongue (e.g. trout) and throat (e.g. blue cod) as well. The forward-pointing teeth of spotties and parrotfish can pull food organisms off rocks and weed, while the crushing teeth and powerful jaws of the snapper can easily injure an unwary finger. Sharks have rows of teeth for cutting and tearing flesh, whereas mullet have virtually no teeth because they swallow vegetable matter along with mud and sand which is ground up in a muscular stomach.

For anglers, it is important to recognise which fish may inhabit the water they are fishing and to use appropriate tackle — fine, light line for small fish in clear water, and wire leaders for sharks and barracouta.

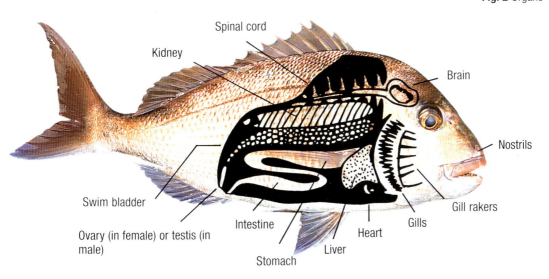

Fig. 2 Organs

CHAPTER THREE
GETTING STARTED

A visit to a fishing tackle shop can be rather daunting, as the variety of gear, tackle and prices appears to be endless. But staff at specialist shops will help with sound advice, and joining a fishing club or discussing your plans with experienced anglers will also help avoid costly mistakes.

If possible, borrow some gear to test before deciding what to buy. The sort of questions you need to consider are — what type of fishing will you be doing? Will you be casting from a beach, from a wharf, or in a small boat? Where will you be fishing? What types of fish are you likely to catch? What sort of baits or lures will you need? Will it be a combination?

Buy the best quality tackle your budget allows and choose well-known brands. There is nothing more frustrating than losing fish through gear which will not function properly, or continually having to return to a shop for repairs. Cheap tackle is made from cheap materials, and just will not last. The oft-repeated maxim: "You get what you pay for" is never more appropriate than when it comes to selecting fishing tackle.

Balanced tackle

When I was a skinny-legged boy crouching enthralled on a small jetty on the Panmure estuary many years ago, my tackle consisted of a nylon handline wound on a stick, plus the heavy armament — a thick green cord handline with a solid mono leader and a heavy sinker. This was always hurled out as far as possible and left while the schools of spotties and sprats under the jetty were dealt with. Bait for the small fish was usually fresh shrimp tails, and a few minutes fossicking around the rocks along the shoreline with a muslin net yielded enough for an afternoon's fishing. The big line would carry half a sprat, and occasionally a large trevally, kahawai or even a small snapper would commit suicide, creating a boy's proud smile that no video game could match.

The thought of balanced tackle was a million miles away, but there were so many fish around that the basic tackle proved deadly.

Today, the tackle department resembles a well-stocked retail shop and everything seems more complicated. But today's tackle produced from space-age materials and technology is very efficient and almost foolproof.

Once the decision is made to invest in a rod/reel combination, the trick is to match the rod, reel and line, because all need to work in unison. Some rods and reels are designed specifically for trolling or casting, others for straylining and still others for general fishing.

A rod designed to handle 4 to 6 kg line will perform poorly with 15 kg line on a heavy reel. Most tackle manufacturers display ratings on rods

Sprats, a boy, and a wharf — where it all starts.

and reels, with recommended line weights. Some optimistically advise a range of line weights for a particular model of rod, and my experience suggests leaning towards the lighter end of the scale.

The exception is when fishing over foul ground when some fishermen load their reels with heavier line than necessary for greater protection from abrasion.

Rods

The modern fisherman can choose from a wide array of rods, most designed for specific purposes. The materials used for rod construction continue to change with the relentless advances in technology, but for most people price is the overriding factor. The various materials are:

Natural wood — basically out of date and rarely used, except for custom-built trout fly rods made of split cane.

Solid fibreglass — considered by some to be almost out of date, solid

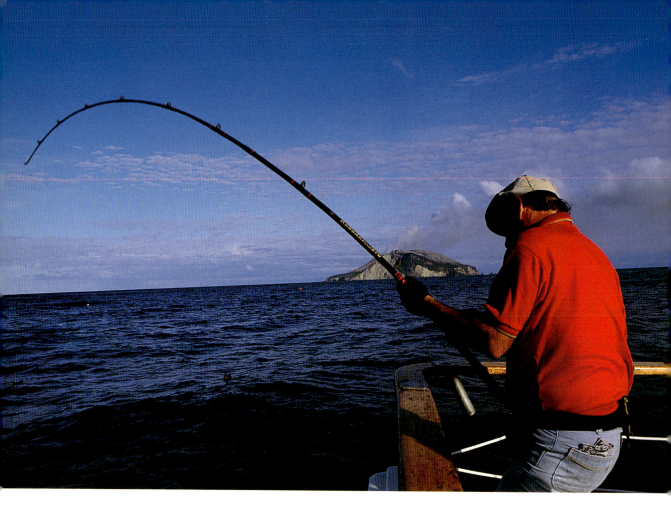

If casting unweighted baits for straylining big snapper, the rod will have a softer tip section to aid the cast, but plenty of strength in the middle section to stop a big fish diving into the reef.

glass has actually improved despite its bottom-end reputation. The emphasis placed on fast-taper rods for versatility has given solid glass rods a stronger position in the market, and these are now available in a huge variety of actions — from the common 'stump-pullers' that we know to fast-tapered multi-purpose rods for both jigging and gamefishing. Solid glass blanks are made by extruding the blank as a bar then grinding it to the required taper. The manufacturing techniques have improved considerably and solid glass rods are actually very pleasant to fish with — not the handicap that many consider them to be. Solid glass makes for a very strong rod which is crush resistant and generally very robust, but also heavy. Consequently it is unusual to find solid-glass rods exceeding 2 metres in length.

Hollow fibreglass — the most common type, made by wrapping sections of glass cloth impregnated with resins around a tapered steel form called a mandrel, then curing it in an oven. Rods can be made in a huge variety of lengths and thickness of the walls.

There are two main types of material used to make hollow fibreglass blanks — E glass, in both light and heavy options, and S glass. S glass incorporates magnesium to further stiffen the glass fibre, and is approximately 15% stiffer for its weight because it requires less cloth for a given action. This offers the angler a more resilient or powerful rod combined with less weight.

Graphite — this is the American name for what the English call carbon fibre. Of all the modern rod-building materials, none has the power-to-weight ratio of graphite. It provides the ultimate in sensitivity and power, and offers superb casting characteristics because it can recover from bending very quickly.

Invented in 1965 by the Royal Aircraft Establishment at Farnborough, it is made by heating a synthetic fibre called polyacrylonitrile to 2500 degrees then stretching it. The resulting filaments have exceptionally high strength and stiffness: they are 5-10 times as stiff and 3-9 times as strong as titanium, steel and aluminium.

Used in rods, graphite is twice as strong as fibreglass, much stiffer and only half to three-quarters the weight. It is unaffected by heat, cold or moisture. Early graphite rods had poor impact resistance, but new superior high-impact resins have improved this, while also providing better stiffness and performance.

Graphite/glass combinations — combining the best characteristics of both in terms of strength and action with price.

Other space-age materials continue to be developed, including boron and kevlar, which have serious deficiencies in strength, stiffness and ability to flex. They are occasionally used in small quantities, combined with other materials.

Action and power

Before making a selection, an understanding of the variables will help.

Action refers to where a rod bends, and is determined by the degree of taper in the shaft. Power or strength is the amount of force needed to bend the rod, and is determined by the thickness of the shaft walls and overall diameter. Sensitivity is the ability of the rod to transmit vibrations from the line through the tip and down to the hand. It is determined by the type of material used and by the action. A fast-action rod is more sensitive than a slow-action rod of the same material.

The big question facing the prospective purchaser is: how does all of this affect me, and what sort of rod do I need? It depends on the type of fishing you contemplate.

If casting from the shore, you need a long rod of 3 to 4.3 m designed to hold the line high over the breakers and to cast an 80 to 100 g weight and bait with line of 4.5 to 9 kg breaking strain. It will have a long butt for two-handed casting, and fairly fast action. 'Soft' rods which flex all the way down to the butt are not appropriate in this situation, but come into their own as effective shock absorbers when ultralight tackle is being used.

For jigging from a boat, a 2 m rod with a fast action, carrying line of 4.5 to 15 kg will be used. If casting unweighted baits for straylining big snapper, the rod will have a softer tip section to aid the cast, but plenty of strength in the middle section to stop a big fish diving into the reef.

Dropping ledger rigs for blue cod in the Marlborough Sounds does not require such a specialised outfit, so rod length will be determined more by what is practical to use. A short rod is easier to handle in a boat, and because casting is not required, a short, solid fibreglass rod is fine. The trend is now towards shorter rods with fast actions for boat fishing. They are less cumbersome in the confines of a craft, and shorter rods give more leverage to the angler, making his efforts more efficient.

Rod fittings

The other variables to check when selecting rods are:

The butt end — does it have a gimbal nock for seating the rod in a belt-mounted gimbal or other type of fighting belt? When fighting strong fish while standing up or from a chair, such fittings are virtually essential. The crossed slots on the end of the rod lock into a pin in the bottom of the gimbal; this prevents the rod from twisting. The same function applies when game rods are locked into rod holders while trolling. But if the rod is to be used for general bait fishing, the sharp points on the nook can be a nuisance, and a rubber cap should be fitted over the end. On light rods a nylon gimbal nock is fine, but on heavier rods it should be made from graphite or metal.

The grips — these should fit the angler's stature and should not be too narrow or hands may cramp in a long battle. Moulded rubber called duralon or hyperlon has replaced cork on just about all rods except trout fly rods, and is comfortable to use but can become compressed in small-diameter rod holders. The length of the grips is more important — is the reel too far out when the rod is held in the fighting position? The main consideration is that the outfit should feel comfortable.

The reel seat — or winch fitting — should be robust enough for the job. To save weight, fly rods and light casting rods will have graphite or nylon components, which are fine and resist corrosion. Avoid overtightening the locking ring, as it can crack under extreme pressure. But heavier work requires heavier reels, and quality rods will be fitted with full alloy reel seats, with two locking rings. This is one area where skimping is not advised.

Rod guides — these can be made out of many different materials, from the cheaper chrome-plated stainless steel to tungsten carbide and various ceramic materials. They are all good. What is important is that the guides should suit the intended purpose, which will be the case on all reputable brands of rod. For distance casting, the first guide will be a wide one, set far enough away from the reel that the line is not compressed as it whips off the spool. Ceramic guides, with smaller openings, will not be used here. Weight is another factor, which is why quality fly rods will have fine single-foot metal guides.

The guides must be positioned so that the line does not touch the rod when it is fully curved under load. Cheap rods will have fewer guides.

One-piece guides are better than guides with several parts. The ceramic inner rigs of some guides can become cracked or chipped, or even pop out of the frame. Check regularly for damage which will quickly tear the fishing line as it passes over it under pressure: a piece of pantyhose rubbed inside the rings will soon catch on any nicks. If your line suddenly develops wispy tendrils hanging off it, check the tip ring immediately.

Gamefishing rods may have roller guides, which require more maintenance, and many anglers are reverting to regular chromed steel guides at the tip as well as down the rod. When fighting a fish on stand-up tackle, the angle of the line at the tip may change direction suddenly and some fishermen do not like their line coming off the roller tip sideways.

Bindings — should be of good quality, with double bindings on heavy-duty rods and an underbinding to protect the rod from the guide foot and also prevent any movement.

Varnish — check the finish on the bindings of a new rod before buying. It should have a honey-like appearance from multiple coats which smoothly cover the bindings with no sharp edges or air bubbles. If cheap resin has been used it will develop cracks when the rod bends, letting in water and air to cause staining and corrosion of the bindings and guides.

Reels

There are six different types of reel, each with different advantages.

Closed-face reel

This is the type of reel that many children start fishing with. The name refers to the hood which covers the spool. Simple to operate, closed-face reels have a release button which allows line to run out through a hole in the centre of the spool cover. They are basically modified fixed-spool reels with a different bail-arm mechanism. Useful for learning to cast, these reels are very popular in Europe and North America for casting small lures in freshwater, but less popular in this country.

They are not robust, and are designed for fishing with light line of 4 to 6 kg. Such reels usually come factory-spooled with line in budget-priced sets with cheap fibreglass rods. They are best suited to wharf and estuary fishing, and are of limited value if any big fish turn up. Swivels should be used on all rigs to prevent the line twisting on the retrieve.

Centre-pin reel

This is the simplest type of reel, basically a spool mounted on a plate. They were once very popular. With the more advanced technology and materials of newer types of reels, these more basic ones are not used as much. Their main application is in fly fishing and trolling for trout, and for certain types of sea fishing.

Large models of centre-pin reels are now available with a simple drag system which makes them useful for fishing in deep water, mainly because of the direct-drive winding mechanism. They are popular in parts of the South Island for blue cod fishing in deep water.

Another useful centre-pin reel is the side-casting type which was developed in Britain but is widely used in Australia. This is a direct-drive reel where the spool can be rotated through 90 degrees and the line cast like a conventional fixed-spool reel. Because the line spills sideways off

> Don't lean rods against brick or stone walls, particularly gamefishing rods. The slightest abrasion of the tip ring will damage the line when a fish puts side strain on the rod.

the spool, a swivel must be used with the terminal tackle to prevent line twist.

The advantages of these reels are their ease of use and their ability to winch heavy fish up onto a high jetty or rocks.

The reel is mounted under the rod, within 25 cm of the end of the butt, and the rod should also have large guides, the first of them at least 1.2 m up from the reel. This is because of the large diameter of the reel, and because casting distance would be reduced if the line had to be compressed into a small guide.

This outfit is easy to cast with, but the heavy reel and rod is more cumbersome than other types and requires a little more brute force.

Fixed-spool reels

The most widely used and popular reels on the market, these are also called threadline reels, spinning reels, coffee grinders or eggbeaters. In various sizes they are used for surfcasting, straylining, spinning for trout and salmon, fishing from a wharf — in fact just about every type of fishing except big-game fishing and really deepwater fishing.

The term 'fixed spool' refers to the spool which remains stationary when casting while the line spills over the rim which is permanently facing forwards. When winding in, a wire bail arm picks up the line and threads it around the spool, which moves in and out to spread the coils evenly.

A drag with a slipping clutch allows line to be pulled off when a preset tension is reached. The tension or drag is set by turning a knob positioned either in the centre of the front of the spool, or at the rear of the reel.

These reels are mounted under the rod, are easy to use and to cast with, and in the hands of an expert can achieve long distances. Most models can be adjusted for left or right-handed operation by swapping over the handle. It is one of the few situations where a right-handed person often winds with the left hand, because the reels are so easy to use the stronger hand can take the weight of the rod and fish.

Some expensive reels with long, thin spools made from lightweight materials are designed specifically for distance casting. At the other end of the scale, super-cheap models are made from poor materials, e.g. with nylon bushes rather than ball bearings, and will not last long.

Some models are designed for particular fishing methods, like ones with the 'bait-feeder' mechanism which free-spools the reel when the bail arm is in the closed position, allowing line to run out when a fish grabs the bait. This is ideal for straylining with drifting baits. After allowing the fish to run with the bait, the angler strikes simply by winding the handle or flicking off the bait-feeder lever to engage the drag mechanism.

The speed at which the line comes off the reel determines the distance the bait or lure will travel, and generally the lighter the line the further it will cast. So a balance is needed between castable distance and line strength. As more line comes off the reel, the diameter of the line on the spool reduces. This increases the distance it has to travel over the lip of

Fixed-spool reels mounted under the rod are also called threadline or spinning reels, coffee grinders or eggbeaters. Modern reels like this D.A.M. have a counterbalanced handle for smooth operation.

the spool, increasing friction and reducing line speed, thereby slowing the cast.

The reel should be spooled to within about 2 mm of the lip for optimum performance. Some manufacturers add a mark to indicate how much line to put on the spool. If the spool is only half full to start with, an unnecessary handicap is introduced.

Some anglers like to carry a spare spool holding a different weight of line — giving a back-up in case of disaster and also providing greater tackle flexibility.

Because of the way they work, fixed-spool reels will impart a twist to the line if the drag is set too loosely or if swivels of the correct size are not used. If the drag is set too loosely, as the angler winds the line will not come in, because the clutch slips. Then each rotation of the bail arm merely imparts another twist to the line, which will spring off in long looping coils when the bail arm is flicked over ready for casting. Tightening the drag will prevent this.

Free-spool reels
Also called multipliers, overhead free-spool reels or revolving drum reels, these are mounted on top of the rod. They are the most difficult to cast because the free-spinning spool can easily over-run, causing backlash or 'bird's nests'. Improving technology has added magnetic or centrifugal anti-reverse functions to prevent such over-runs, but they are not foolproof and must be correctly adjusted — see the instructions, or check with your retailer.

However, once the technique has been mastered, longer casts will be achieved than with fixed-spool reels because of the smoother mechanism and reduced friction. These reels are preferred by tournament casters.

The free-spool overhead reel is more commonly used for boat fishing, and will have either a star drag or lever drag.

Most high-ratio free-spool reels have thumbing lips on the side of the spool to prevent possible friction burns caused by thumbing the line.

Overhead reels are also better for using with heavier line when boat fishing. They are geared so that for every revolution of the handle the spool will revolve by up to six times. This enables the angler to wind in line very quickly, which is a real advantage in some fishing situations. Deepwater winching requires a heavy, large reel with a low gear ratio, while high-speed jigging calls for a faster retrieve.

The amount of line recovered with each turn of the handle also depends on the diameter of the spool. A large reel with a 3:1 ratio can recover more line per turn of the handle than a tiny baitcaster with a 5:1 ratio.

Some models are designed specifically for casting, with light aluminium or graphite composite spools. Others, with heavy stainless steel spools, are commonly used for fishing from a boat, where the bait is simply dropped over the side.

Overhead reels have many advantages. They can be thumbed with a light pressure on the spool controlling the line, important when a fish is running with a bait.

The most durable overhead reels are made from one cast of alloy, which will be reflected in the price. Graphite or plastic reels are fine for lighter work. If cheap metal has been used, corrosion is likely, and regular maintenance will become even more important.

There are two types of overhead reels — those with star drags and those with lever drags:

A star drag is a star-shaped tension control, conveniently located between the handle and the reel casing. When tightened it increases pressure on a series of washers, allowing line to slip out only when the pull exceeds the pre-set level of tension.

Such reels also have a free-spool lever which bypasses the drag, and is used when casting, when lowering a bait to the bottom, or when setting a lure behind the boat.

A lever drag has a lever located alongside the handle to control tension and free-spooling. As the lever is moved forward, pressure increases evenly on a single, large metal plate that is forced against a similar-sized fibre washer. The advantage is that you can see at a glance what tension setting you are using. Another difference is price: lever drag reels are more expensive, being usually made from better materials. The resulting smooth drag system appeals to anglers chasing big fish, and today most gamefishing is done using lever-drag reels. In small sizes these reels are excellent for bottom fishing.

On all overhead free-spool reels the line must be evenly spread from side to side as it is wound onto the spool, to prevent a build-up on one side of the spool. This is done with the forefinger or thumb of the hand holding the rod. Some reels have a level-wind mechanism which does this automatically.

Baitcaster reels

These reels are tiny versions of the star-drag overhead reels with a free-spinning spool, and are designed for casting light lures on small, one-handed spinning rods which often have a pistol grip.

They are high-tech reels, finely machined and balanced, with a release button which can be operated by the thumb of the casting hand.

Baitcasters also have a level-wind mechanism as a standard feature, and are designed for using light lines on matching rods — a fun outfit for catching a variety of fish where a heavy sinker is not needed.

Handlines

In reality, unless long casts are required, a simple handline will do the job. Many famous anglers started their careers using a handline, and some still enjoy the close feel of fish hooked on a handline. It is more sensitive than a rod-and-reel outfit as the angler is in more direct contact with the fish.

Lines are often carried wrapped around a piece of stick or a plastic drink container, but today these are largely replaced by cheap, moulded plastic hand-casters. The round spool sometimes has a central crossbar which serves as a handle, so it can be held sideways to the direction of the cast with one hand while the other swings the weighted line. A small curtain ring can be used to connect the main line with a heavier leader which carries the sinker and will receive more wear and tear. Inserting a small stick into the ring helps add speed when the leader is swung round and round before releasing it, giving greater distance.

When fishing the line is stripped in and piled on the ground or on the deck, not wrapped onto the spool each time it is retrieved. Controlling this loose line can take a little practice, particularly in deep water where a long line is needed.

When fishing deep water some people pull the handline over the side of the boat so the gunwale takes some of the weight. This is fine with braided dacron or twine, but if nylon monofilament is used there is a danger that heat created by friction will weaken or even break the line.

When buying a hand-caster choose one with a large diameter. The larger coils formed in the line are less likely to tangle than small ones, and the line can be wound on faster.

Fishing lines

While there are certain specialist lines for particular fishing situations, most fishing in New Zealand is done with nylon monofilament lines.

The specialist lines are wire, lead-core lines and plastic-coated fly-fishing lines used by trout anglers; braided dacron, used by big-game fishermen; and the relatively new superbraids.

Nylon or mono is a product of the post-war plastics revolution. The first such lines were uneven with poor knot strength, but today there are no really bad lines in the competitive fishing tackle market. The best guide to quality is the price.

The term monofilament refers to the single strand of line which is created by extruding molten nylon through holes in metal discs. These filaments are dried in a series of fans, then subjected to a further process called drawing, in which the line is passed over rollers and stretched to several times its original length. This rearranges the molecules into a more regular and orderly structure, giving greater strength and elasticity.

There are also two new types of superior mono line: copolymer and cofilament. The first is made the same way, but is a blend of two or more types of nylon. Cofilament is more advanced and involves using two different types of nylon, one which forms a soft centre and the other a durable outer coating.

The breaking strain of line, which is the weight an unknotted piece will support before snapping, generally varies with the diameter. But some lines are now produced which have a breaking strain out of proportion to their diameter, in other words quite thin line which is very strong. This can be an advantage because thinner line is less obvious to fish and creates less drag in a current, it sinks faster, and you can get more of it on to a reel. But it can also be a disadvantage because knot strength varies and tying knots in thin line is more risky. Such specialist lines are better suited for casting lures and spinfishing than general bait fishing.

When fishing over rocky areas, abrasion is a major problem and thin lines just will not last. Some brands of nylon are designed specifically for such rough conditions, and you can find out about these at your specialist tackle shop, or from other experienced anglers.

Mono line is labelled with the diameter and breaking strain, and the latter is only really important if catching record fish is a possibility. Most manufacturers understate the breaking strain of their lines. Also, the rating is based on a dry line, but nylon lines absorb water and after a period in the water — up to 2 hours — the line strength decreases by as much as 20%. Line stretch also increases dramatically: up to 40% in extreme cases.

Line companies intentionally make line thicker and stronger than the listed rating, and some have tested at 70% stronger than the listed breaking strain. Diameter is important when calculating how much line a reel can hold.

Line designed for gamefishing or catching record fish will be marked 'tournament' or 'pre-test', which is meant to guarantee the line will break at or slightly under the rated strength. Such lines are more expensive than regular mono.

Colour is the other consideration, and a neutral colour which blends with the water colour is the best choice — clear, pale blue, pale green or grey. Some brightly coloured or fluorescent lines are designed for easy visibility when gamefishing or fishing in low light, so you can instantly tell the position of the fish. These are not recommended for general fishing.

Generally, soft or limp lines are suitable for spinning or casting, but they are prone to abrasion. Springy lines are hard wearing, suit large-diameter reels, and are good for trolling but not for casting.

Low-stretch line is better for bait fishing in rocky conditions, so you can stop a fish quickly. The same line can lose resilience after long periods of trolling, and may break on the strike or after a long fight with a big fish.

The knot strength of a fishing line is just as important as its breaking strain. Knot strength depends on the quality and toughness of the coating on the outside of the line, which varies. Some new brands have tested at close to 100%. The knots which test best for strength are the spider hitch, uni-knot, palomar and Trilene knots.

Line strength, knot quality and knot strength are all part of the system between the fisherman and the fish — and it will always fail at its weakest point.

The serious fisherman will also know the true strength of the line used as well as its knot strength, otherwise it will not be possible to set the drag correctly. The only way to be sure is to test the line yourself.

Spooling reels

The line should first be connected to the spool. A simple knot to use is the arbor knot (Fig. 3). Sometimes the empty spool will revolve inside the first loop and it's hard to get started. This can be solved by taking the tension off the reel and allowing a few loose turns to be wound onto the spool.

Another option is this more secure knot: wrap the line tightly round the reel spool three times, then tie the end to the main line with four half hitches pulled tight. Leave enough of a tag end to wrap around the spool again and tie off with three more hitches. This will not slip when you start winding.

Some people like to first lay on a cushion of dacron (the backing line for trout reels is fine) which has two benefits: it absorbs pressure from the stretched mono wound on tightly during a fight, which could later contract and damage the spool; and it adds bulk, reducing the amount of mono needed.

Line should be wound onto the reel under firm tension, which is con-

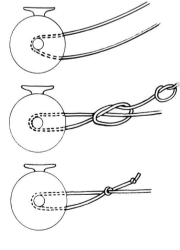

Fig. 3

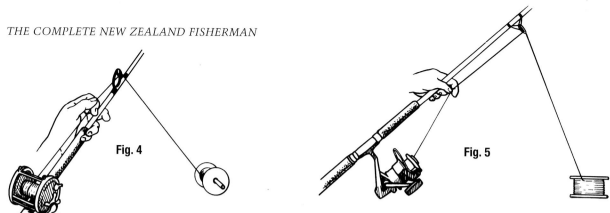

Fig. 4

Fig. 5

trolled by the thumb and forefinger of the hand holding the rod. It should be tight enough so it can't be compressed or moved with finger pressure, and laid neatly back and forth across the spool. This is done manually on an overhead reel if there is no level-wind mechanism. On a fixed-spool reel the line is spread evenly by the action of the spool. This applies when actually fishing, just as much as when spooling a reel with new line.

To ensure no twist is imparted to the line, it must come off the plastic spool correctly. With a free-spool reel, this means directly off the front of the spool (Fig. 4), which can revolve around a pencil or piece of dowel held by another person or locked between the knees of the operator. Don't forget to thread the line through at least the first guide if doing it alone, or the whole rod if a helper is holding the spool of new line. To provide a steady tension, the line can be run through the pages of a book, with extra weight placed on top of the first book to achieve the right tension. If you are working alone, the dowel can be wedged halfway down a bucket filled with water up to that level. The drag of the water adds tension as the spool revolves.

With a fixed-spool reel the line comes off the side of the spool of line (Fig. 5), which can be laid on the ground. It should come off the correct side of the spool to counter the rotation of the bail arm. This can be tested by winding a few metres onto the reel then stripping off a slack loop. If it twists then the spool should be turned over.

Setting the drag

The drag setting on a reel can be tested by pulling against a set of scales (Fig. 6) with the drag lever in the strike position for game reels, or a selected position on other reels. The rule of thumb is to set the drag on strike at about one third of the breaking strain of the line.

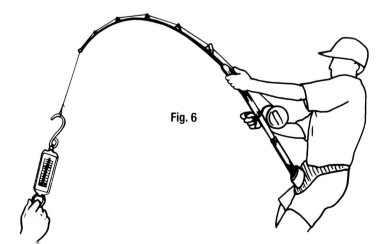

Fig. 6

To determine the line weight best suited for a rod, multiply by three the maximum weight that can be registered by pulling on the scales. For example, most 3.65 m surfcasting rods will pull a maximum of about 3 kg, so fishing with line of more than 15 kg breaking strain serves no purpose except to reduce casting distance.

Care of nylon lines

Monofilament line is resistant to many chemicals, and is not affected by water-repellent treatments like Tackle Guard. But remember that fish may not like the smell, so try and keep lines clean. The worst chemicals are acids and some insect repellents. Certain chemicals, fumes and ozone (produced by appliances with electric motors, such as refrigerators) can seriously weaken line. Bulk spools should be sealed in large zip-top plastic bags and stored in a dark cool place.

But the most damage is caused by ultraviolet radiation through excessive exposure to sunlight, by friction and by abrasion. Reels or spools of mono should not be left lying in direct sunlight for long periods. Friction can be caused by damaged or dirty rod guides, or by rubbing on the gunwale of a boat. Common sense dictates how to treat tackle, and end sections should always be checked for damage that may result from rubbing on shell-encrusted wharf piles, rocks, or kelp, and even sharp scales and fins on large fish. It is a simple matter to cut off the last metre or two and retie leaders and swivels.

Damaged line will feel rough to the touch, and may have tiny jagged white slivers sticking up. Your line should also be clear and shiny; if it has taken on a white, clouded appearance discard that section.

Mono line will also stretch, and if fishing in very deep water it may be necessary to strike a fish several times, winding in line between strikes, until it is firmly hooked.

How line is wound onto the reel is important, and it is not unknown for the spool of a reel to be crushed by the contraction of line which was wound on too tightly. Conversely, if line is wound on loosely, the coils on the spool can bite into the coils underneath, causing it to jam when line is let out again. It should be wound on with an even, firm pressure which is applied by running the line through the thumb and forefinger of the hand holding the rod, and distributed evenly across the spool. Some reels have a level-wind mechanism which does this automatically.

If the line is allowed to build up on one side of the spool until it collapses on itself, or is angled across the face of the reel so that coils are criss-crossed over each other, it will jam when pulled out quickly. Often these problems are not noticed until a fish is hooked and suddenly the line stops running out then breaks. By then, it is too late.

Nylon mono line will last for years, but if used regularly it should be replaced every season, or possibly every two years. The line itself requires minimal attention, but washing the salt away under a tap will help reduce corrosion of the spool.

Trolling with lures occasionally causes mono to twist because the lure is rigged slightly off-centre and rotates in the water. This can be prevented by ensuring the knot is tied to the centre of the ring on the swivel or the wire loop. One way to untwist line is to cut off the lure or leader, let out the line behind the boat, and drag it with only a swivel on the end to provide a little weight. However, this is not 100% effective and a better solution is to tie the line to a swivel attached to a tree or post, then walk backwards while paying out line under tension and running it through the fingers as the swivel spins.

However, if your line is badly twisted, cut off and replace the offending bits. It is one of the least expensive materials used in fishing, but is also your only direct link with the fish.

One of the single biggest handicaps people create for themselves is using tackle which is too heavy for the job. When it comes to line weight, the golden rule is to choose the lightest line you can fish with confidence. It will create less drag in waves and currents, will be less obvious to the fish, will require less sinker weight, and will give the bait more movement so it looks more natural.

Terminal tackle

This is the important bit at the business end of your fishing tackle. It is what the fish sees, bites and tries to break or rub off.

It usually incorporates a length of mono line, the trace or leader, which is heavier than your main line simply for added strength and protection; a weight; a swivel; and a hook or hooks.

When lure fishing, a lure replaces the baited hook at the end of the leader or is tied directly to the main line. Usually no weight is attached, because the lure either contains sufficient weight or is fished on the surface. Lures are cast and retrieved, trolled or jigged to attract fish.

Leader
The leader varies in length from half a metre for surfcasting to several metres for fishing in shallow water with lightly-weighted baits. It is usually attached to the main line with a swivel, but occasionally a special knot may be used so that the join can be wound in through the guides of the rod.

Swivels
These are designed to prevent the line from twisting, but are also used to connect line and leader, and to stop sliding sinkers. They come in a variety of shapes and materials for different purposes.

Basically, the smallest practical size should be used — a large swivel is less efficient because it resists turning. A rule of thumb is to match the diameter of the swivel's wire loop with the line. See Fig. 7 for examples of common types of swivel.

Box and barrel swivels (Fig. 7 — top two) are the most commonly used. Torpedo swivels (third row) are much stronger and are used for big strong fish, but do not turn as smoothly as stainless steel ball-bearing swivels

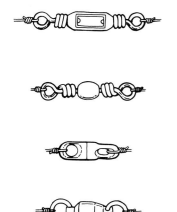

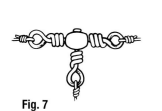

Fig. 7

GETTING STARTED

When used in conjunction with a bright light at night, squid jigs are good for catching fresh squid bait, or calamari for the frying pan! The sand eel lure is an unusual one which is effective on bottom-dwelling fish.

(fourth row). These swivels are used more by game fishermen, as they are inclined to clog up with silt and lock up when used for bottom fishing.

Snap swivels (fifth and sixth row) are designed for quickly changing lures or traces without retying knots; but some clips will fail under load and they should be used carefully.

The three-way swivel (bottom row) was developed for surfcasting and for attaching droppers for bottom fishing.

Sinkers

There is a bewildering array of different sinkers, but many will never be used by the average angler.

The most useful are the round ball or bean sinkers with a hole through them. These can be used in a variety of sizes in most situations, but remember that sinkers are solely intended to aid casting or to take a bait down to a desired level. Beyond that, they can be an impediment to actually catching fish. Always use the lightest sinker possible.

Specialist sinkers include wire-pronged sand-grip models for surfcasting in strong rips, torpedo-shaped sinkers for distance casting, and huge teardrop-shaped 'bombs' for deepwater hapuku fishing.

When fishing among rocks do not use sinkers with sharp angles or corners. Try disposable sinkers, made from a bag of sand or length of old anchor chain attached with light line that will break before your main line does.

Remember the weight of sinker used should match the line weight; in other words do not put a 200 g sinker on 4 kg line.

If in doubt about what weight to use — and it does vary with currents and depth — try several lines: one floating, one lightly weighted, and one with a heavier weight.

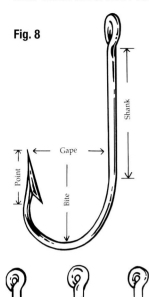

Fig. 8

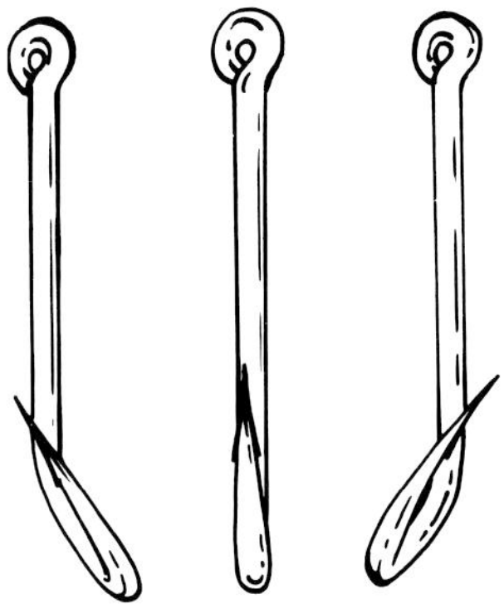

Fig. 9

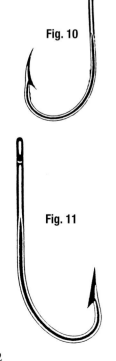

Fig. 10

Fig. 11

Hooks

The basic shape of hooks has changed little throughout history, but improved materials and technology have made them progressively more effective.

Whereas a hook sharpener used to be a vital piece of equipment, the advent of chemically-sharpened hooks has made life much easier for fishermen. These hooks have been immersed in a chemical bath which removes the rough edges left on the point in the manufacturing process. They are ready for use straight out of the packet. But older types of chromed hooks or stainless steel hooks should be checked, and often need a touch-up.

Only a few of the many varieties available are really necessary for most fishing.

The various parts of a hook (Fig. 8) are of academic interest to most anglers. The size of the gape and length of the shank are important, as is the type of hook used. Eyes which are turned up or down are designed to hold the hook straight and in line with the leader.

Hook sizes start with size 14 as the smallest, which are used for catching small sprats and piper. The hooks get bigger as the number becomes smaller, until size 1 is reached. Then the numbering system changes and the '/0' is added, which refers to hooks measuring at least 35mm from the bottom of the bend to the eye. Sizes then start increasing again, up to 14/0 which is a huge gamefishing hook.

Shark hooks are sized according to the gape, so a 10 cm hook measures 10 cm across from the point to the shank.

Another important factor is the strength, and hooks made from heavier-gauge metal are available. A 5/0 2X hook is a normal 5/0 in terms of size, but twice as thick in cross-section. The strongest types of game hooks are forged for extra strength, and are not circular but are flattened in cross-section.

Hooks also come in straight or offset types. Straight hooks are used for trolling, and for rigging long thin baits or whole fish baits (Fig. 9 — centre). Offset (also called kirbed) hooks are commonly used for bait fishing (Fig. 9 — left and right). They are said to be less likely to pull out of a fish's mouth, but on a straight-line pull, penetration may not be so good. It is a matter of personal choice.

Commonly used hook types are:
- Beak or octopus hooks (Fig. 10), with short shanks and long, inward curving points — fine for most bait fishing.
- French or Viking hooks (Fig. 11) may be used if big snapper with tough mouths are expected. These are strong, rigid hooks with flattened sides, straight spear and point, and a big barb set well down.
- Recurve hooks (sometimes called tuna circle hooks) have inward-curving points. These are used mainly on set lines, longlines, or in very deep water where fish virtually have to hook themselves. Penetration is very efficient, the hook being designed to rotate in the mouth of the fish as it turns away after taking the bait. The hook does not bite so deeply into

the flesh; but once hooked, usually in the corner of the mouth, fish rarely throw the hook.
- Wide-gap hooks are another variation (Fig. 12). They are similar in concept to recurve hooks, but with a wide, almost circular gap. These are popular with many surfcasters and boat anglers, as fish tend to hook themselves.
- Sliced hooks (Fig. 13) have raised barbs on the back or front of the shank, which help hold cut baits in place so they do not slide down and mask the point.
- Treble hooks are usually used on lures, but many experienced anglers replace them with single hooks, maintaining that singles give better hookup rates and are also easier to remove from the fish. Trebles require more care as fingers are easily impaled on spare points (Fig. 14).
- Live bait hooks (Fig. 15) have a short shank, an inward curving point, and are very strong — ideal for targeting kingfish.

Hooks in size 1/0 to 4/0 would cover most fishing situations, and the main thing is to use small rather than large hooks. Big fish can be caught on small hooks, but the opposite is less likely. The exception is when undersized fish are being hooked and need to be returned to the water. By increasing the size of hooks used, the angler will reduce the number of small fish hooked.

Stainless steel hooks are readily available, though more costly than plated hooks. They are strong and will not rust, but do need constant attention to the point, which becomes blunt easily. Like all hooks, they must be kept very sharp.

All hooks should be washed to remove salt after use, as most will rust. A little petroleum jelly (Vaseline) or fish oil added to the container will ensure they last longer.

Hooks invariably find their way into unplanned targets like hands, arms and legs. If it is a solid game fishing hook, heavy duty boltcutters and a doctor are needed. But small hooks like those on trout flies and light tackle fishing can be easily removed if the surface around the wound is relatively flat. Thread a piece of strong line around the hook and loop it around your hand. With the other hand press down on the shank of the hook, which clears the barb on the inside, and jerk the line sharply (Fig. 16). Ensure the angle of pull is in line with the angle of the hook point, and it will pop out surprisingly smoothly.

The treatment should be done as quickly as possible while the wound is still numb and before pain sets in, and the person administering it has to have the courage to jerk the line firmly. A half-hearted pull will only

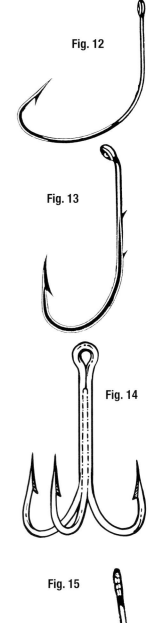

Fig. 12

Fig. 13

Fig. 14

Fig. 15

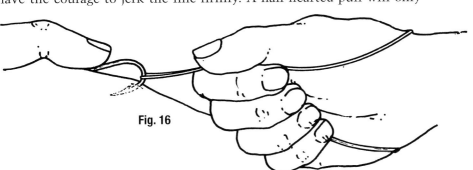

Fig. 16

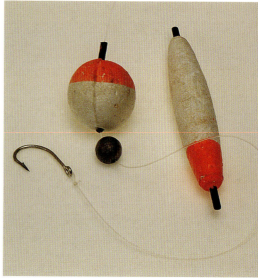

Floats in different shapes and sizes are used to present baits at pre-determined levels, and to indicate bites.

Above right: Bobby corks come in a range of sizes and shapes and are useful for fishing dead and live baits.

make the situation worse and both parties will lose confidence. But a sharp jerk will remove the hook without the patient feeling a thing.

Floats

Floats are used to present baits at pre-determined levels, and to indicate bites. They are usually used when fishing for small fish, and children fishing from a wharf will often use a rig with a sliding pencil float above a light trace weighted with split shot and one or two tiny hooks. The float should be three-quarters submerged, and is either fixed on the line with a rubber band or it slides against a stopper.

The other main use of a float is when fishing a live bait near the surface for predators like kingfish. This is usually a balloon but may also be a large manufactured float of cork or polystyrene, or a plastic drink container. Land-based game fishermen use them to keep a live bait away from the rocks, and as an indicator of the bait's position.

When bottom fishing, a cork will very occasionally be added to the leader to lift the bait off the bottom and keep it away from crabs, weed or rocks.

Accessories

The fishing tackle industry produces innumerable odds and ends — many of them gimmicks designed for selling to hopeful anglers rather than aiding the catching of fish. But some of them really are necessary, including something to carry the packets of hooks, swivels, sinkers, spare mono line, leader material and other bits and pieces. Good-quality moulded plastic tackle boxes are excellent for this, but if walking is involved, a backpack or even a plastic container with a secure lid can be used.

The plastic containers which 35 mm film comes in make a handy container for small hooks or swivels, and small plastic boxes with several compartments are commonly used for carrying hooks.

The baitcatcher is popular with children having fun catching sprats.

GETTING STARTED

The fish are attracted with bread in the water, then the baitcatcher is lowered with bread inside it.

A good-quality, sharp filleting knife for cleaning fish and cutting bait is essential; and another short, strong knife for cutting through bone is also useful.

A pair of good-quality rustproof scissors is very useful for trimming bait on hooks, cutting bait scraps off hooks, trimming knots, cutting lines, and other purposes.

A set of scales, and a landing net which will handle all but the biggest fish, can be added. A lot of fish are lost when being lifted out of the water — the line breaks or the hook tears out. A net with a long handle and wide mouth makes securing the fish simple and sure.

Gaffs, bait tanks, harnesses and gimbal belts and other items can be acquired as fishing develops and the need arises. Like learning about fishing, the equipment and tackle used is endless.

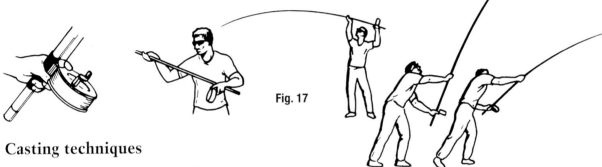

Fig. 17

Casting techniques

How to cast a side-cast outfit

Fig. 17 shows the technique — the catch is released and the spool is turned at right angles to the rod. For a right-handed caster the line is held with the forefinger of the left hand or gripped with the thumb against the rim of the spool. If unfamiliar with the gear, the angler can lower the rod tip and rest the sinker and bait on the ground so line does not run out while preparing for the cast.

The rod is then swung back, with the right hand gripping it about 65 cm above the reel. At this point the sinker or bait should be hanging about a metre below the rod tip. The cast is started by raising the right arm to its full extent and swaying the body back on the right foot. The rod is swung over by the left hand pulling strongly down on the butt, and at the same time the right arm pushes strongly and the body thrusts forward against the weight of the rod. As the rod swings over, the weight of the body passes to the left foot and the angler leans forward to complete the cast.

Just as the sinker or bait is about to fall into the water the finger or thumb clamps down on the spool to stop the flow of line; the spool is then turned back to the winding position and the slack line wound in.

How to cast fixed-spool outfits

The two alternative methods of holding the line while casting are illustrated in Fig. 18.

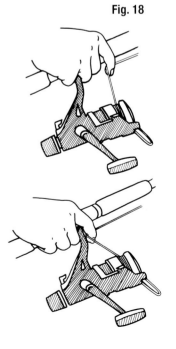

Fig. 18

THE COMPLETE NEW ZEALAND FISHERMAN

Fig. 19

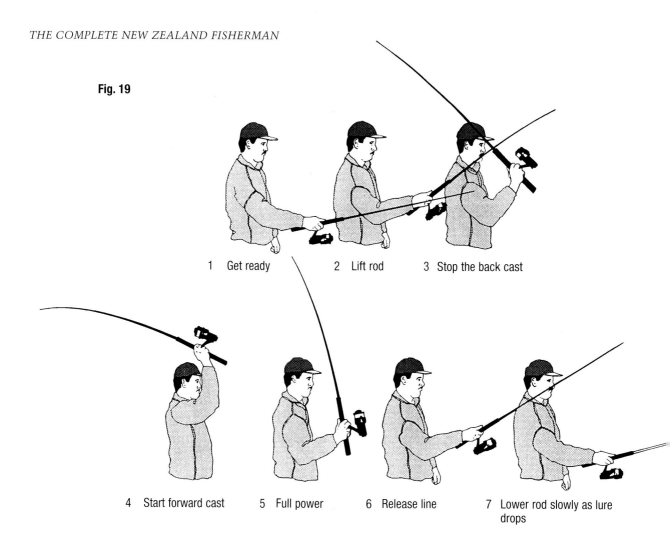

1. Get ready
2. Lift rod
3. Stop the back cast
4. Start forward cast
5. Full power
6. Release line
7. Lower rod slowly as lure drops

Spinfishing

When casting small lures or baits with a light rod, it is usually done with one hand (Fig. 19). The rod is held in the 1 o'clock position behind the caster's shoulder and flicked through to the 10 o'clock position. The key is the timing of the release. If the lure flies high in the air and lands at the angler's feet, it was released too early. Conversely, if it is propelled into the ground at high speed, it was released too late.

Surfcasting

This technique is illustrated in Fig. 20.

1. For a right-handed caster, your right hand should hold the rod with the foot of the reel between the second and third fingers, and the index finger controlling the line. Your left hand grasps the butt near the end of the rod, and the two hand positions should be about the width of the shoulders apart. Ensure that the drag is set tightly and will not slip. Your feet should be about the width of the shoulders apart, with most of the weight on the right foot and your toes at right angles to the direction of the cast. Your knees should be loose so they can flex during the

GETTING STARTED

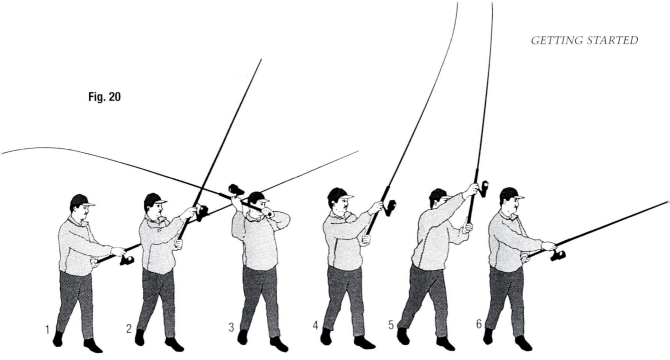

Fig. 20

cast. Point the rod at your target with the tip roughly parallel to the ground, and the sinker about a metre from the tip.
2. Lift and swing the rod back over your right shoulder.
3. The rod should be parallel to the ground, with the butt pointing toward the target and your left elbow raised.
4. Do not stop the movement. With experience you can swing the bait and sinker to create a pendulum effect, then push forward with the right hand and pull down with the left. The rod should be fully loaded in a powerful bend.
5. Lean forward into the cast, and continue pushing the right arm out and down. As the energy is transferred through the rod to the line the weight builds up momentum very quickly.
6. Release the line when the rod is at the 1 o'clock position, continuing your body swing and following the path of the line with the rod tip, allowing it to drift forward. This reduces the friction created by the line passing through the end ring, and you lower the rod as the line drops. You can then feather the line flowing off the reel to control the distance, ready to clamp down and stop it the instant the weight hits the water, to prevent an over-run. Then let extra line run out as the weight sinks.

For maximum distance the sinker and bait should be propelled outward at a trajectory of about 45 degrees.

The angler changes hands quickly and places the rod butt in the groin or between the legs. As soon as the sinker hits the water the line will fall slack, and to prevent free line springing off the reel the angler raises the rod and starts winding to snap the bail arm over and take up loose line until the weight of the sinker can be felt.

The cast should be one smooth, powerful movement with rapid acceleration. Timing is more important than sheer power; and a little practice will improve casting dramatically.

With all distance casting (side-cast, fixed-spool or free-spool reel), the explosive transfer of energy from the rod tip to the line may snap light line. Some people overcome this by attaching a shock tippet of heavier line. If the main line is 6 kg, a tippet of about 9 kg is fine. This should be twice the rod length, so that the heavy line is on the reel when the cast is made. It is best tied on with a double uni knot.

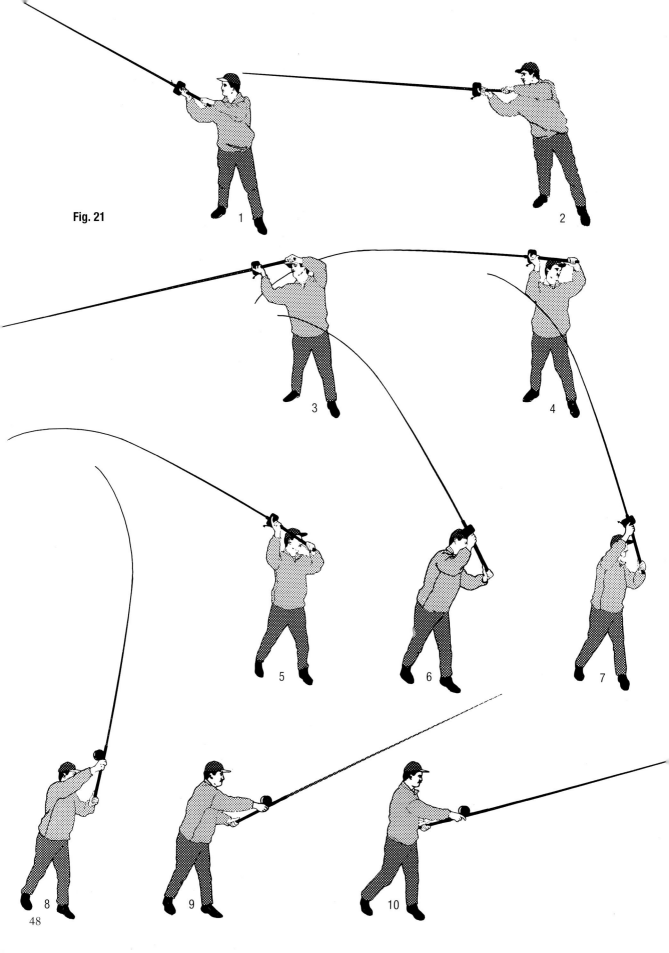

Casting an overhead reel

On a 3-4 m casting rod, the reel should be located 60-70 cm above the butt end.

Unlike the explosive cast with a fixed-spool reel, this cast is longer with a smooth acceleration, and the rods used have a fuller action, bending evenly all the way (Fig. 21).

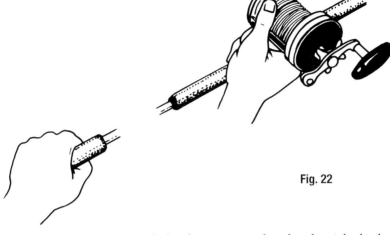

Fig. 22

Put the reel into free-spool mode by disengaging the clutch with the lever or button control, then press the thumb firmly on the spool where the line comes off (Fig. 22).

1. A right-handed caster should stand with the left foot forward, at an angle of 45 degrees to the line of the proposed cast. The weight is on the right leg, which is bent, and the hips twisted round to the right.
2. The left arm is stretched as far as possible and the rod tip pushed round as far behind the caster as he can reach — this gives maximum arc of swing. The sinker is about half a metre from the end of the rod, and can lie on the sand just below the rod tip.
3. The left hand brings the butt end to eye level with the elbow held high, and the cast commences with a full body pivot.
4. As the right hand comes up the left pulls down with a crisp action.
5. The body leans forward into the cast against the resistance of the rod and the left hand pulls down, using the right hand as a fulcrum.
6. Body weight is transferred to the left leg and the rod is bent to the maximum, ready to spring over in the opposite direction after describing a sweep.
7. The eyes should be watching where the sinker and bait will land, and as the rod comes over the thumb releases the spool. This is the critical point, and the timing is determined only by experience.
8. The full energy of the cast has been transferred to the weight which should then fly out at 45 degrees.
9. Lower the rod slowly to follow the path of the line, clamping the spool tight at the instant the weight hits the water — if it is allowed to continue revolving a backlash will occur.
10. With the reel in gear, slack line is taken up.

CHAPTER FOUR
FISHING FROM THE SHORE

If there is a boat in the family, the introduction to fishing is an exciting one; but most of us start by fishing from the shore — usually as a youngster dangling a mono line over the edge of a wharf, totally absorbed with the mysterious world under the shining surface of the green water. We then progress to surfcasting, boat fishing or serious angling from a rocky shore.

Whether it involves the simple crunch of clean sand underfoot or a precarious track to be negotiated to reach a favourite rock platform, fishing from the shore is one of the simplest of pleasures.

In some ways the land-based fisherman is handicapped, but in others he has a great advantage over those in boats. There is no launching involved, no anchors to pull up, and there is usually ample room. We are fortunate in the quality and diversity of fishing we have on our coasts.

Wharf fishing

Many children feel that jetties and wharves were invented just for them to fish from, and a lot of fish are caught there.

The water under the jetty on the Tamaki Estuary used to be sparkling green, and the plump paketi or spotties that lived there were suckers for a fresh shrimp tail. Kids didn't know much about catch-and-release in those days, and the pile of fish on the wharf grew quickly. The big spotties had patches of brilliant blue on their mottled brown and yellow flanks, and they seemed to pull harder than small fish do now.

The green handline was the prized possession and was always thrown as far as the heavy sinker would reach into the swirling water. The jetty was downstream from the old Panmure Bridge, close to a bend on the Panmure side, and the main current swept close enough for a young fellow to just reach it after about four swings of the heavy line. It took a special flick of the wrist to really make the sinker fly. Today's graphite rods and reels were a space age and a world away.

Occasionally a kahawai or a small snapper would take a liking to the chunk of sprat on the big hook, and the small boy's heart would thump as the thick line was pulled in hand over hand. A huge trevally once ate a wrinkled piece of brown smoked fish skin, and the struggle which followed would have done justice to a marlin fisherman. The boy won.

Long green and yellow kingfish often lay silently under the jetty on the edge of the current behind one of the pilings. They were like gods — great menacing shadows that could snap the line with disdain. And they ignored everything except pieces of fresh piper.

> Good quality Polaroid glasses and a hat are useful for cutting glare and increasing visibility on the water — as well as offering protection from the sun.

An incoming tide at dawn — a prime time for fishing the beach.

A man came down to the jetty once and shot a kingie with a .303 rifle and the story was told at school for many weeks. The big fish had 27 sprats inside it — a number which has remained imprinted firmly in my memory for some reason — but some school kids refused to believe that part of the tale.

The sandwiches carefully packed before leaving home were often forgotten in the absorption of catching fish, and when the tide slackened and the fish stopped biting the hot sun had curled the crusts. But fish blood and slime added a wonderful taste to sandwiches. Big fish were strung from the handlebars of the bicycle, attracting stares and waves during the long ride home to Pakuranga.

That was 35 years ago.

Today a similar scenario is acted out every weekend around New Zealand. Young and old fishing people, from all types of backgrounds and ethnic groups, patiently cast baits or lures from wharves, jetties and other

> One of the best baits for piper... is piper! A tiny cube of the shiny silver flank is highly visible, and really attracts other piper.

man-made structures. We are all familiar with the sight of immigrants enjoying the fishing around our cities like shoppers who have won a free trolley full of goods at a supermarket.

The expression "The fishing isn't what it used to be" is getting pretty hackneyed, and compared to most other countries, particularly those with dense populations, our fishing is rather good.

You can catch a lot of fish from jetties and wharves — but of course it hardly needs to be pointed out that some spots will produce better fishing than others. The basic rule is: the more remote the location, the better the fishing.

Bridges can also provide good fishing, and the techniques that apply to fishing from wharves also apply to bridges. If protection from traffic is assured and no risks are taken, a bridge can offer a variety of water as the angler can try different depths and currents.

Structures

The term 'structure' is widely used when discussing fishing, and means any fixed object which fish can relate to as a fixed reference point — from a natural one like a reef or clump of weed, to one man-made like a mooring chain or wharf pile.

All structures will attract fish and other marine life. Piles grow a coating of seaweeds and encrusting animals like mussels and barnacles, and these in turn provide habitat for shrimps, worms and other invertebrates. These tiny creatures attract small fish seeking food and shelter, which lure larger fish to the area. Many fishermen know that kingfish love to hang around structures, both to shelter from strong currents and because they provide points of reference.

This tendency to relate to structures is a common one in nature. Cows and sheep will often be seen standing around a single tree in a paddock, and for the same reason the greatest number of ants will be found near the edges of a concrete path or along cracks, rather than in the middle.

The decking on a wharf provides shelter and shadow. Small cod and spotties will be found around the pylons, and can be hooked with tiny baits near the bottom. Surface or mid-water baits will attract school fish like sprats, mackerel, piper, and occasionally trevally.

> Fish are more likely to venture into shallow water during periods of low light — at dawn and dusk, or even at night. Beach fishing can also be good after a storm when the huge waves have subsided and the water is still stirred up and discoloured. Fish will be feeding on organisms uncovered by the storm.

Bigger fish are usually caught on baits or lures cast out from the structure into deeper water or stronger currents, but as with all fishing, there are exceptions and kingfish or john dory may be found directly under the planks.

Tackle

Casting great distances is not usually an advantage when fishing from a wharf or bridge, as the current will bring fish past the point where the angler is fishing. Tackle used can be as simple as a spool of nylon with hooks and sinker attached for catching small fish, to an expensive game-fishing outfit for handling big fish like kingfish and sharks. By far the most common rig is a fixed-spool reel and rod which matches the line weight.

For small fish, light rods and line of 4 kg breaking strain are fine, and the terminal rig will be either a dropper rig for bottom fishing or a floating rig. On the latter the depth of the bait can be varied by sliding the float up or down the line which passes through a rubber band on top of the float and through an eye on the bottom. One of two split shot sinkers under the float will pull the float partly under, and also sink the bait.

A handline is fine for most situations and some experienced fishermen still use a simple but practical system with a nylon line wound onto a plastic milk container. The end can be tied to the handle for security, and when dropping the bait or casting any distance, the container is pointed at the water and the line slips off the end.

When aiming for larger fish like kahawai, snapper or trevally, the tackle should be stronger, and again it is advisable to use the best quality you can get. The rod will be somewhere between 2.1 and 3.6 m long, with a fixed-spool reel that can hold about 300 m of line between 6 and 15 kg. Shorter, stronger rods will carry the heavier line. At the business end will be a running sinker rig, although a dropper rig may be used occasionally, with only as much weight as is needed to hold in the current. Hooks used will be size 3/0 or 4/0, with a smaller keeper hook.

If seriously targeting kingfish the outfit will be a 15 or 24 kg stand-up game rod with matching overhead free-spool reel. A rod belt or gimbal bucket will increase the angler's chances, and the most important aspect is to stop the fish from wrapping the line around obstacles like mooring chains or wharf piles.

The fish

Small fish can be found at all tides and all times, though night fishing usually produces more action. Some game fishermen collecting live mackerel for bait will fill their buckets using sabiki jig flies after darkness has fallen.

Larger fish will venture into shallow water at dawn and dusk, and if this coincides with high tide the fishing will be at its best. Small fish can be found all year round, but trevally are more common in spring, and kahawai, kingfish, piper and salmon during summer.

Baits and lures

For small fish, sabiki flies are excellent. Tiny lures rigged on a series of side-traces off a main line, they vary in size and colour and resemble shrimps and other tiny aquatic creatures. Their shortcomings are the lightweight hooks and line, which will not hold a strong fish, and their tendency to tangle — particularly when there are several fish bouncing around on the same rig. The tiny, sharp hooks also tend to find their way into small fingers with frightening ease. Careful supervision is needed when young, inexperienced hands are holding the rod.

With a small sinker at the bottom, the flies are lowered into the water and gently jigged up and down. Try different depths for different species. Cutting off every second trace reduces the tangles, and a shred of bait added to each hook can also help.

> Sometimes piper will attack any bait, but they can be frustratingly selective also. In this case the minimum weight float should be used, or even no float, with two or three tiny baits allowed to drift in the current. If the piper are not on the surface, crimp a split shot onto the line to get the baits down. Use the smallest hooks available.

John dory love live baits fished on the bottom with a sinker either above or below the bait, which is on a short trace with a 3/0 or 4/0 hook through the skin of its back. A small treble hook can also be used. John dory can often be seen like shadowy ghosts swimming slowly around the piles under a wharf, and can also be snagged with a large treble hook above a weight. Another method, practised by local children on the Pukenui Wharf at Houhora, is to throw rocks on the seaward side of the dory, which is driven towards the shallows. A poor swimmer, the hapless fish can be captured by nimble hands in the shallow water.

Top baits for small fish include mussels and pipis, both of which are available at little cost in supermarkets. The tough rind and tongue are used and the soft parts can be mashed for berley. A handful of crumbled stale bread will also attract fish.

Small hooks and small baits are important — probably the single biggest handicap is the use of heavy tackle, large hooks and big baits. Try and slip the bait around the bend in the hook to conceal much of the metal, but leave the point clear. Small pieces of bonito and pilchard are fine, but come off easily. Other popular baits are dough balls (perhaps with cotton wool added for durability), kernels of canned corn, worms and maggots.

Baits for larger fish do not vary so much, but fresh is always best and the serious angler will throw out a pilchard or strip of mullet then try and catch a fresh piper or sprat to replace it.

Cut baits like bonito, mullet or fresh mackerel work better in strips rather than chunks. Whole or half pilchards can be used, but should be checked regularly as small fish will strip them. Shellfish like mussels and pipis can be also used, impaling them through the toughest part and tying the soft flesh to the hooks with cotton or a rubber band.

Kingfish are the ultimate quarry and they are commonly caught on some wharves in Northland, particularly at Mangonui, Houhora and Paua; and occasionally in other harbours throughout the North Island and northernmost parts of the South Island. A live bait is most effective: in order of preference piper, small kahawai, sprat and jack mackerel. The live bait is rigged with a hook through the back just in front of the dorsal fin. If hooked through the skin of the back in front of the tail the bait will try to swim away from the wharf. The hook should not be too large in comparison to the size of the baitfish, and a 4/0, 6/0 or 8/0 is fine. If the hook is kirbed the point should face upward when it lies along the back of the baitfish.

The hook is attached to a short, heavy trace of at least 30 kg mono connected to a good-quality swivel. Do not skimp on materials as tough fish like kingfish will exploit any weakness.

To keep the bait away from the wharf, a balloon is tied to the top eye of the swivel with cotton or dental floss and hopefully the wind and current will pull it away from the wharf.

The strike of a kingfish is spectacular and exciting, and the fish should be given time to swim away and swallow the bait. Keep the reel in free spool with the ratchet on until the fish strikes, then take the ratchet off and thumb the spool gently so there is little resistance. As the fish swims away steadily point the rod down, put it into gear, and lift smoothly but firmly. Use the rod, not the reel, to fight the fish, and only reel in line when dropping the rod. All actions should be smooth, not jerky, and you should use the rod to lead it to the wharf. A long-handled gaff is a great help in landing these magnificent fish and a long-handled net is also useful for smaller fish like kahawai and trevally.

If a live bait is hard to catch, a whole pilchard or piper, rigged with the hook inserted through the head from underneath with a small ball sinker sliding against the hook, can be cast out and slowly retrieved. Kingfish rarely take a stationary bait. As a last resort a strip from the belly of a bonito or kahawai can be used, cut in a long taper and hooked through one end.

Metal jigs and spinners like the ticer are effective on kahawai when cast out and retrieved. Generally, small rather than large lures are better, and if fish follow without striking try increasing the speed or varying the action by jerking the rod tip while winding.

Surface lures like poppers or Rapalas will occasionally hook kingfish, and should be retrieved fast with plenty of splashing. Hold the rod high, then drop the tip as the lure nears the wharf.

The big one

One of my fishing friends makes his own rods and knows how to use them. If fish could talk, Frank Perry would speak their language.

Whenever Frank wants a little action he goes to the Cornwallis Wharf on the Manukau Harbour, takes out a frozen yellowtail about 30 cm long, and tramples it on the deck until it is nice and squishy and leaking juices. He impales this messy bait on a large hook and casts it out past a marker to where a huge stingray lives in a hole. Franks knows he will never land the ray and has no desire to, but he enjoys the thrill of hooking it.

One bright Sunday afternoon Frank arrived at Cornwallis to find a particularly loud and unpleasant character giving unwanted advice to all the people who had been enjoying a quiet afternoon's fishing.

He started chatting to this fellow, who had an exceptionally red nose and large girth. Frank mentioned that he had occasionally hooked a big fish just out past the yellow marker — over there actually — but had never seen it.

"No trouble to me. This new rod can handle anything in the harbour," said the fellow, pointing to a shiny telephone pole with rings on it.

Frank produced a steel trace and shark hook, and suggested it might be an idea to attach it to the line on the new rod. He then trampled on a 30 cm yellowtail until it was squishy and leaking, and politely offered it as an attractive sort of bait for big fish.

The assistance was accepted and a loud commentary ensured that everyone present learned how to catch a big fish.

The cast was adequate and the squishy yellowtail landed close to the deep hole. The fisherman was busy recounting some of the many battles he had had with giant fish when the line started to pull off his big reel. Frank suggested it might be an idea to wind the drag up really tight and throw it into gear, to set the hook in the fish which had the bait.

"Of course, that's what you have to do!" exclaimed the fisherman.

As he flicked the reel into gear and hauled back on the telephone pole, the effect was quite remarkable. He was suddenly propelled across the wharf to the edge, where the railing caught him in the stomach and stopped him just as suddenly. The air left his prodigious body in a loud whoosh and the telephone pole, which was also caught on the rail, snapped with a crack like a rifle shot.

"Must have been a big one," mused Frank, as the fisherman was trying to find his feet and his breath.

Actually a lot of rays and kingfish are hooked from wharves, but they are rarely landed because the hapless angler cannot follow the powerful fish. I recall some Asian sailors catching a kingfish of 30 kg off a freighter at Queens Wharf once. They used anchor chain wrapped round a bollard to hold the poor fish.

Rubbish from ships attracts a lot of fish, and some enterprising wharfies once managed to subdue a giant stingray by winching it from under the wharf with the help of a crane and a steel hawser.

What was that about fishing being a genteel art?

To tell the truth

There is a fish that can be found in most harbours — and in many fish-and-chip shops. It is the humble parore, at times mistakenly called the black snapper. The parore has earned many unpleasant names through its propensity for consuming anything in the water. With so many people living in our big cities, all sorts of things find their way into the harbours and the parore hang around the overflows.

But as its natural and preferred dinner is vegetation, including weed and algae, the parore is rarely caught on a hook and line. Some imaginative youngsters often convince the parore that dough or cheese are worthwhile substitutes. Pieces of tuatua or mussel may also fool them.

The Australians respect the parore for the nuggety little fighter that he is, and they go to great lengths to get him onto a hook. They even make special rods and use special techniques to catch what they call luderick or blackfish.

Dave McLellan and I used to employ the same technique at the Birkenhead Wharf on Auckland's North Shore, on the hot summer days when the parore move into the harbour. They can also be found in most northern inlets and estuaries, and also around rocky parts of the coastline where they graze on sea lettuce.

Our preferred tackle was a slender glass trout rod and light spinning reel equipped with 3 kg line. We made floats out of cork and feather quills, crimping tiny split shot below the float then tying on special size 8 long-shanked hooks imported from Britain.

In the mangrove swamps at Cheltenham we found soft, slimy blanket weed. A 7 cm piece was suspended above the hook then wrapped around the shank in opposite directions. A handful of chopped weed mixed with wet sand and breadcrumbs tossed into the slow-moving current would get the parore in the right frame of mind.

The baits were floated past the rock wall and under the piles of the wharf. You had to walk along, following your float until it stopped then slipped under the surface. Sometimes the float would bob up again, but when it stayed under — you struck! The name 'bronze battler' is well earned, and the trout rods bent alarmingly, with at least one of us always busy fighting a tough parore during the hour either side of high tide.

Other fishermen could not resist asking the inevitable question: "What are you using for bait?"

"Why, seaweed," we replied innocently.

"Rubbish!" they scoffed, clumping back to their lifeless surfcasting rods.

Well, we told the truth. Perhaps that was the problem.

Rock fishing

Some of the best fishing will be found close to a rocky shoreline where breaking waves, foamy water and clumps of wavy brown kelp attract fish.

Fishermen in large boats will often anchor offshore, using an inflatable dinghy to access a likely spot and pulling the boat up onto the rocks. But the boat angler will seldom, if ever, leave the boat to fish from a beach: the fishing is never as good from the sand as it is from the rocks. Many top spots can also be reached by walking.

The shore-based angler is less intrusive, and big fish will come right in close if they are not disturbed. Every year many New Zealand fishermen land huge snapper and kingfish while fishing from the rocks, and as with most fishing they have usually travelled some distance to find a good spot. If a place is easily reached, and close to a city, the fishing will rarely be very good.

Our rocky coastline is nearly always surrounded by reef structures

> If you wet the line by making a short, easy cast before the power cast, you will not burn your thumb on the spool.

Whitianga fisherman Dave Bryant uses a robust sea-going kayak to reach remote fishing spots on the Coromandel coast.

Left: The ultimate prize for the rock fisherman, a 5 kg snapper.

which, like offshore reefs, are the preferred habitat of desirable species such as snapper, moki, cod, butterfish, trumpeter and other bottom dwellers.

Between the reef and the surface kahawai, maomao and trevally feed on tiny food particles and baitfish lifted to the surface by coastal currents which are forced upward when they encounter shallows. The best fishing will be found where currents meet a rocky coastline — the stronger the current, the better the fishing. And the greater the danger will be, also. Currents will confuse a coastal swell, combining with the effect of a shelving bottom and forcing the wave upwards as it nears the rocks.

To remove the smell of fish oil and smelly bait, wash hands with toothpaste.

A sign of a good spot to fish — snapper will be attracted to juvenile mussels which grow quickly after drifting spat become attached to weeds and rocks on the Northland coast.

Right: White water washing a rock ledge close to deep water indicates a prime fishing spot which can also be dangerous. Always check the tide and watch the waves and stay well above the highest breakers.

Reading the water

Even though New Zealand can boast thousands of kilometres of rocky coast suitable for fishing, not all of it produces good fishing. Huge areas of coastline, for one reason or other, are nearly devoid of fish life. This may have occurred through overfishing or pollution, both unfortunate side-effects of our society.

But the main factor will be the geography of the particular area. The water may be too shallow, or even too deep with no shelter beyond the foreshore. Other areas may have the right depth and good shelter for fish, but no current flow, for example small bays and inlets.

The ideal fishing platform is where the land drops steeply but levels out on a point or a headland with a good current flow, at least five metres of water close to the rocks, and a reef running out for perhaps 100 metres with deep water on at least one side. Weed beds and clumps of brown kelp will also be evident.

Fish like the security of kelp, handy access to deep water, and the plentiful food supply. Good spots can be located by studying hydrographic charts which show shallow areas, rocks, reefs and currents — all vital clues for the angler.

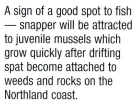

By sitting on a high vantage point and studying the beach, the surfcaster can pinpoint promising features. The best time to locate holes, sandbars and gutters is at low tide.

Topographic maps with land contours are also useful guides. If the land slopes gently to the sea this often continues underwater, making it too shallow. Conversely, steep cliffs usually indicate deep water with little cover for fish and poor access for anglers.

Fish can always be found where waves smash into narrow guts or crevices in the rocks and suck out food particles. Baitfish use the aerated white water for cover, and predators will often be found on the fringes. A lure cast out and retrieved, or a whole pilchard or piper drifted through the white water, will often be grabbed.

A congregation of terns fluttering and diving indicates school fish near the surface, with predators likely to be in the area and scavengers below — often within range of the rock-based angler. Shags swimming and diving also indicate the presence of small fish, and bigger fish will be not far away.

Tides are a major factor, with depth and currents varying four times during each 24-hour period. For example, the best rock fishing at Great Barrier Island is at low tide and for the first two hours of the incoming tide. But that may not apply in a different area.

Some fish, like parore, use high tide to reach weed which will be

> Heavy rain washes all manner of material and food into drains and streams, and good fishing can often be found where these flow into the sea, attracting scavenging fish.

The legendary author and angler, Zane Grey, once said, "Always remember that the might of the sea is invincible. Its power incredible. Never tempt it . . ."

An unwary angler can be caught by an occasional freak wave, often with tragic results.

Some basic safety rules should be observed:

- Never fish alone. When a person catches a fish, a second person should gaff or net it while a third watches the sea.
- Watch the sea at all times, and don't turn your back to it. Even when calm, an occasional large wave will appear.
- Check whether the tide is rising or falling.
- Watch before fishing to see how waves strike the rocks. Is there an escape route if an abnormally large wave appears?
- What would you do if a companion was washed into the sea? Do you have something to throw to him, and where could he come ashore safely?

uncovered at low tide, while predators may lie in wait for baitfish forced out of the shallows by a falling tide.

The biggest tides or spring tides coincide with the full moon and new moon; while the neap tides, or smallest, occur during the first and last quarters of the monthly cycle. These are all factors which the successful fisherman takes into account. Such an angler will be observant, and will understand what influences fish. Successful patterns are always repeated, and variables like the tide, weather and sea conditions, time of day and season will all be noted.

Successful angling is rarely the result of coincidence or luck.

Tackle

Popular outfits are 3 to 3.5 m surfcasting rods with large, fixed-spool spinning reels. The line will be heavier than is used for beach fishing, because distance is not so important.

But the rock fisherman has to contend with sharp shells, rocks and weed — and fish which know how to use their habitat and will head for the nearest rocks or kelp when hooked. So line of 10 to 15 kg breaking strain will be used on standard surfcasting tackle.

The serious angler will use more specialised tackle — a shorter rod of 2.3 to 2.7 m with a soft tip action for casting unweighted baits and a strong butt section for putting pressure on big fish.

Reels are a matter of personal preference and budget. Overhead reels give better control over big fish, as they have more sensitive and smoother drag systems and the line also follows the curve of the rod more closely. But they require more experience for casting. Quality fixed-spool reels are simple to cast and are capable of handling most fish.

Rigs

Terminal tackle includes a selection of hooks: from size 12 for baitfish to 4/0 and 9/0 offset hooks for large baits. When fishing for big snapper with floating baits, a heavy trace of 30 to 40 kg mono gives protection against their strong jaws. Some brands designed to resist abrasion are now available. For smaller fish a lighter trace will be used. A small ball sinker may be added directly above the bait to take it down through waves and currents, but unweighted baits are used predominantly from the rocks.

Where a weight is needed for casting distance, it can be rigged on a special rock-fishing rig with a section of light line designed to break when snagged. If casting onto sand, a regular surfcasting rig can be used.

Hooks will be rigged on a running rig, and occasionally on a dropper rig if a sinker is used.

Accessories

A boat gaff with a short handle is virtually useless, and even dangerous as the gaffer has to get into the water to use it. A suitable gaff will have a 3 m handle and can be tied to the rod for carrying. Telescopic versions are available and a long-handled net is also useful.

As walking is often required to reach top spots, a backpack is more practical than a plastic tackle box for carrying gear and food.

A safety line of about 20 m of strong rope, and a light cord for lowering bundles down a steep face, should be included. The latter is also useful for securing berley containers, or as a safety line for the rod.

Baits and berley

In most rock fishing situations the use of berley can make the difference between a good catch and no fish, because the fish will be widely spread over rough terrain including large rocks and forests of kelp. A single bait floating around in this environment is unlikely to be taken. But berley will attract fish to the area, often right at your feet, bring them on the feed, and keep them there.

A frozen block of minced berley in a lightweight container hung over the edge of the rocks is fine until a heavy wave smashes it and the entire contents drop into the water in one lump. A robust container is better, like a wire cage, onion bag or plastic milk container with holes punched in it. Place such containers in a gut where the wash will spread the berley. In areas with no wave action the container can be hung in the water, though the berley tends to sink and not disperse.

The secret to effective berleying is to dispense a little continuously, in a steady trail. Frozen berley is best thawed in a bucket of seawater and distributed by throwing half a cupful into the water every couple of minutes.

A simple, effective berley can be mixed on the spot by carrying grain pig pellets and a bottle of fish oil. This is mixed with seawater and any crushed shellfish available — mussels or sea eggs. Good berley can also be made from oily fish like bonito, pilchards and mackerel mixed with shellfish. Tying the frame of a kahawai or bonito through the gills and hanging it in the water is also effective. Waves will pound it, washing small particles off and dispersing them. Chunks of pilchards thrown into the berley trail will help attract larger fish.

Large slabs or strips of cut bait like bonito, mullet, kahawai or squid work well and can be cast easily. They should be rigged on a single large hook with the point exposed, and a small keeper hook above the main hook helps prevent the bait sliding down the hook.

A whole bonito head, or a half split longways, makes a good bait for big snapper, and has enough weight to cast easily. The blood and juices attract fish, and small ones can't pick it clean.

Pilchards rigged whole on two 3/0 or 4/0 straight-shanked hooks (Fig. 23) are effective when fished unweighted. The pilchard is virtually sewn onto the trace, with the lower hook passing through the body above and below the backbone then stuck through the head or the eyes. The second,

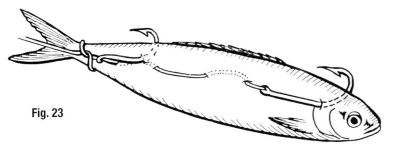

Fig. 23

> Always use the rod to lead a big fish to the rocks — not the reel. Wait for an incoming wave and use the power of the water to float the fish up to you. Never fight the power of the waves by pulling a fish against a receding wash. This doubles the strain on the tackle and often results in a lost fish.

> Check out promising spots at low tide when the contour of the bottom is revealed. Key features like beds of kelp, the abundance of natural food like crabs and sea eggs, and deep guts which are fish 'highways', can all be more easily spotted.

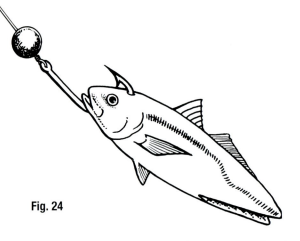

Fig. 24

> The best fishing will always be found immediately after a storm on the section of coast which has been exposed to the wild sea. Fish will venture into the security of dirty water to feed on creatures which have been dislodged or injured by the pounding waves. Best time to fish is just as the water starts to clear. Conversely, calm clear water and bright sunlight make for tough fishing; and the best time to fish is at periods of low light, such as dawn and dusk.

free-running hook is placed through the bait near the tail so that the eye of the hook is level with the base of the tail. A half-hitch pulled tight around the tail of the bait and the eye of the hook holds the pilchard securely for casting.

A large sprat or yellow-eyed mullet rigged this way is a favourite bait among some Northland fishermen who target big snapper off the rocks. Another enticing bait is a bunch of four or five pilchards threaded once through the eyes onto a large hook; but it should be cast carefully or they may fly off.

In Taranaki, where all good shore-based fishing is in rocky areas, sections of octopus tentacle are favourite baits because octopus is a favourite of snapper. The octopus is skinned and a tubular 10 cm piece of the white arm is threaded onto the hook and pushed up the shank to the eye. The point is then forced through the side, and a short piece left protruding below the hook. It's a tough bait which lasts well in rocky areas.

A butterfly bait is another effective bait for big fish. This uses a whole baitfish like a jack mackerel or koheru with the tail and a section of backbone cut out to just forward of the anal fin (Fig. 24) by cutting from the tail forwards on each side of the backbone, then snapping the bone. A single big hook (e.g. an 8/0 for a 200 mm bait) is forced up through the head so the point and barb are exposed just behind the eyes.

All large baits are cast out and allowed to sink. If left for long, the bait will finish up among weed or in a rocky crevice, pulled in by a crab or small fish, so it is important to keep in touch with the bait by taking up any loose line until the weight can be felt. The bait is lifted periodically to ensure it is not snagged, and so it is slowly retrieved to be cast out again or replaced with a fresh one.

When a take is felt, the reel is put out of gear or the bail arm opened to allow a couple of metres of line to run out. Then, when the fish runs off steadily, strike it firmly.

Whole shellfish like a mussel or sea egg can be used if they occur naturally in the area. Bore a couple of small holes in the shell with a nail thumped with a rock, or even a portable drill, so a large hook can go in and out of the shell. The holes allow juices to leak out, providing a further attractant.

The flesh of shellfish is used to target particular species, like pipis or

> Your monofilament line is the only link between you and the fish. This line is not indestructible. It is constantly being damaged — abraded, soaked and dried, stretched and unstretched, and weakened by the ultraviolet radiation from sunlight. Throw away terminal sections after every trip, and replace complete lines once a year if fishing regularly.

tuatuas for trevally, and mussels or crayfish for blue moki. Such baits are often secured on the hook with cotton or a rubber band wrapped round them.

Some anglers fish with the drags on their reels set lightly, allowing fish to run with the bait and swallow it before striking. A little slack line may make the difference if fish are shy. Others strike immediately a fish takes. Both systems work. At other times, when fish hit hard, they can be hooked instantly. It is a matter of preference. As always, those prepared to be adaptable will take home more fish.

Crabs as bait

Towards the end of winter the red and green crabs which live in the cracks among the rocks are changing their shells. It is a dangerous time for them, for during the moulting process they lose the protection of the hard carapace. But like crayfish, the old shell has to be replaced by a shiny, larger one to allow the owner to grow.

Life is perilous for crabs as they scurry around the rocks looking for scraps to eat, or scavenge among the rock pools left by the receding tide. When the incoming tide covers the pools, the hunters arrive, seeking out the crabs among the thick, brown clumps of weed and kelp. Crusty old snapper with teeth worn from chewing the brittle shells of kina and crabs, their flanks flushed a muddy crimson, love to gorge on the rock crabs when they can catch them. The wide shadows of rays gliding silently over the kelp forests send the crabs scuttling for cover. The powerful jaws of the stingrays and eaglerays are lined with flat dentures that easily grind the crabs. Crab cocktail is also a favourite dish of the slimy octopus which slips a long tentacle deep into the cracks where the crabs back up until they become wedged into the tightest crevice.

But when the crabs are between shells, waiting for their new covering to grow and harden, they are particularly vulnerable. Experienced anglers know this, and will seek out rocky platforms with currents sweeping past and channels leading out into deep water to provide access for the snapper and other predators which are wary of the shallows during the bright daylight hours. The keenest anglers will be there at dawn or dusk, particularly if a recent storm has smashed the kelp, leaving crustaceans helpless and the water still coloured by sediment. They know the big snapper they seek will be foraging close to the shoreline, within easy casting range.

Playing a fish from the rocks

Unlike an angler in a boat, the rock fisherman cannot follow a big fish: he can only let the fish take out line, and the more line the fish takes out, the less control the angler has. The only solution is to use the tackle to its maximum and be tough on the fish. The first searing run of a big fish must be stopped, and the rod held high to keep the fish away from rocks or weed.

If a fish does snag the line, it can be felt rasping on the obstacle, and if the fish is given slack line quickly it might swim out when it feels the weight gone. If this happens, work the fish to the surface before it can

> Crabs are a natural food of snapper and can be an effective bait. To rig a crab, insert a 6/0 hook into the body behind the back leg, and out again behind the front leg. Tie all the legs on that side onto the trace with a dozen turns of cotton.

> Permanent rod holders at popular rock fishing spots can be made by taking a 300 mm piece of galvanised pipe (diameter big enough to hold the rod butt) and bashing flat the bottom 100 mm. This is hammered into a rocky crevice and fixed in place with premix cement and sand.

Fish will stay alive in a rock pool and can be released if larger specimens are caught.

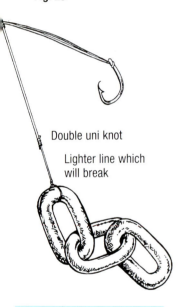

Fig. 25

Double uni knot

Lighter line which will break

Cheap sacrificial sinkers can be made from old spark plugs or a length of old anchor chain, attached with line which is lighter than the main trace so it will break first. Anchor links will also slide through most rocks and are less likely to get snagged (Fig. 25).

react. Otherwise the only alternative is to break the line.

As the fish is brought in, think about where you want to land it and steer the fish to that spot by using the rod and changing the angle of pull. This should always be done gently but firmly. A sudden jerk may break the line. Small fish can be lifted onto the rocks with the rod, but large fish should be gaffed or netted.

Locations for rock fishing

There are many great fishing platforms along the coast, from remote areas like Lottin Point near East Cape, to large peninsulas like Coromandel and Cape Karikari. Those lucky enough to visit islands like Great Barrier can also find good rock fishing, and the Northland coast offers many top platforms, ledges and protruding points with access to deep water. So too does much of the west coast.

For Aucklanders prepared to drive for an hour then walk for 20 minutes, there is often very good snapper fishing to be found at Takatu Point, at the end of Tawharanui Peninsula, a regional park north of Auckland. It was a favourite destination 25 years ago during the months of July and August when, after the long walk down the steep hill at the end of the peninsula, large slabs of kahawai or trevally were cast out into the deep channels and guts in the reef at low tide. These floating baits drifting down among the kelp were soon snatched up by snapper which had moved into the reef to forage for soft-shelled crabs. The snapper ranged from feisty youngsters of 1.5 kg to powerful red-sided moochers of 7 kg or more — many of them too strong for the 7 kg line which snapped when tangled among the thick strands of kelp.

While a marine reserve has been created along the northern side of the Tawharanui Peninsula, anglers can still hook the big snapper at the end of Takatu Point, after driving to Warkworth and taking the road to Matakana and Omaha then following the signs until the last 8 km of metal road is reached.

Beach fishing

Casting from a beach is the most relaxing form of saltwater fishing, with none of the concerns of launching or anchoring a boat, or climbing round steep rocks. When a fish is hooked the only issue is whether it will stay hooked, as there is no risk of snagging the line on an anchor rope or a long, waving strand of kelp.

There is no need for a complicated range of tackle, just a single rod and reel (or perhaps two), a small selection of hooks, swivels and sinkers, and a couple of other accessories.

From the vast expanse of Ninety Mile Beach in the Far North to the steeply sloping shingle beaches of the Otago coast, with the long surf beaches of the Bay of Plenty and the rugged splendour of Wellington's shoreline in between — the opportunities for surfcasting are endless.

Reading the water

Fish may be scattered in small numbers all the way along beaches, but it is the congregations of fish — like oases in a desert — that the angler seeks. These will always be associated with an unusual feature which breaks the monotony of the flat sea bottom, which in turn alters the

The New Zealand coastline is rich in prime fishing beaches, but Ninety Mile Beach offers solitude and endless fishing opportunities.

Always check that the line has not wrapped around the rod tip before casting, particularly at night.

A few useful items will make your beach fishing more enjoyable — a small bag for carrying terminal tackle items (if walking is involved, this may be a backpack), bait, perhaps lunch and a drink, and a beach spike. Commercially-produced spikes are readily available. Most of these are short, and hold the rod with the butt at sand level. A long spike of 1.5 metres is useful for holding the rod well up and keeping the line above the breakers on the shore. A length of 50 mm PVC pipe can be adapted by cutting one end at a sharp angle for driving into the sand. A large nail driven through the pipe about 300 mm from the other end will prevent the rod from sliding down inside it and resting on the reel. This nail can be used to hang the tackle bag above the sand — and the occasional sweeping wave.

rhythm of the waves. It may be a gutter, a hole or a sandbar, or a rocky outcrop.

Unlike other fishing environments, surf beaches change shape continually, moulded by wave action. The water thrown up onto a beach must return to the sea, but it meets incoming waves and is forced into currents of moving water which in turn gouge out gutters, build up sandbars and dig holes.

The waves also change the character of a beach. During a storm they will crash down, tearing away sand and eroding the beach. In periods of stable weather, waves will be more uniform and constructive, adding new sand and building up the beach.

Winds, tides and ocean currents influence the currents on a beach, which may flow along it or directly offshore, producing the rips which are so dangerous to swimmers. Calm, sheltered bays attract swimmers but offer the least good fishing, and it is the most dangerous features that anglers look for.

In spite of their fluctuating and dynamic nature, surf beaches are among the easiest scenarios for anglers to read and understand. Fish will be found in holes and gutters, along ledges and in strong currents. One of the best combinations is where clear, slow-moving deep water meets areas scoured by foamy currents. This usually indicates a deep gutter running through or along the edge of a sand bar. Such gutters are the beach's arteries, which fish travel along. Where a T-junction is formed by one gutter meeting at right angles another gutter or a long hole running parallel to the beach, the observant angler will find good fishing. If a pipi or worm bed is handy, it will be even better.

Predators follow baitfish into shallow water; trevally, gurnard and snapper look for shellfish and worm beds uncovered by scouring and pounding waves. Pebble beaches will not change as much as sandy ones, and local knowledge as to where deep holes or rocky reefs are located is the most important element. But the incoming waves will still behave like those on a sandy beach.

Some of the signs an observant fisherman will look for are:
- A separate line of white water breaking well offshore, indicating a shallow bar.
- An unbroken section of a wave — this indicates a localised deeper area.
- Currents and rips — usually easily identified by the movement of foam on the surface. Sometimes a beach will have two or more gutters running parallel to the beach — both should be fished.
- Holes or depressions in the seabed — these will be found in much the same way, but the wave variation is less obvious. A short section will flatten out for a short period and then build up again.

If there is little or no wave action, the prime fishing spots are more difficult to locate. The deep water will be a darker colour, which is better viewed from a high vantage point such as a rocky headland or a sand dune.

Small isolated rock structures offshore are prime locations for fish, and can be located by looking for breaking water at low tide, or whirlpool-type swirls on the surface.

Surfcasting tackle

The most popular rods are two-piece, 3.65 m fibreglass rods capable of casting 60 to 100 g weights and holding the line above the breaking waves. In some specialised fishing situations like Ninety Mile Beach anglers may prefer heavy rods 4.8 m long for casting up to 200 g. The extra power is supplied by mixing graphite material with the fibreglass, as a pure glass rod of this length would be very heavy.

Super-cheap rods should be avoided, and quality rods will have recommended line and casting weights written on them. The weight should be balanced to the performance of the rod, so that it loads the rod correctly, allowing it to impart rapid acceleration.

If the line used is too heavy it will reduce casting distance, and if too light the line may snap — 6 to 8 kg breaking strain line is right for most situations. It has little wind resistance and flows through the rod guides easily.

The most common reels are the fixed-spool type because of their economical price and uncomplicated function. Free-spool reels in the hands of an experienced caster can achieve greater distances, but they are difficult to master as the spool often over-runs, resulting in a 'bird's nest' or tangle.

Side-casting reels are very popular in Australia, but less so in this country. The positioning of side-cast reels on the rod is different from other reels, just 20 cm up from the end of the butt because the lower hand controls the line coming off the reel, not the upper hand as with the other two styles.

But with recent developments in fixed-spool reels, like longer, thinner spools, even newcomers to surfcasting are reaching impressive distances.

During the cast, line pours over the front lip of the spool and as the diameter of the spool decreases, the friction of the line passing over the lip increases. This reduces the speed of the line and so reduces distance. This effect can be minimised by filling the spool to within about 2 mm of the lip, and by using the lightest line which can be confidently cast.

Terminal tackle

Sinkers will be matched to the rod, so only a limited range of sizes is necessary. For fishing clear, sandy areas the tournament sinker, shaped like an elongated teardrop, is designed for minimum air resistance, improving distance. Where a strong current rolls the sinker along the bottom, a sand-grip type sinker is called for. These come in different shapes. The channel sinker, shaped like a tyre with points on each side, holds well but casts poorly; a tournament sinker with four wire legs is superior. With the legs locked into notches and bent outward they hold well, and when pulled hard the legs straighten out, releasing their grip on the sand.

In rocky or weedy areas the spoon sinker casts well, and rises up when retrieved so it should not become snagged. But if sinkers are inevitably going to become caught, a sacrificial weight can be used.

If holes and other hot spots are not easily located, a rig that will roll with the current can be used. This is a simple ball sinker above a swivel

---

When casting, it is the sinker which carries out the bait. Sometimes the bait swings around the sinker, creating drag and reducing the casting distance. This can be overcome by taping the bait and sinker together with paper masking tape. The single weight will travel further, and on hitting the water the tape comes unstuck, freeing the bait. Simply sticking the point of the hook into the sinker can achieve the same result, but it is more likely to pull free during the cast.

To break the line when snagged: if you have no alternative but to break your line, do not pull hard and bend the rod. This could damage or snap it. Hold the rod straight, wrap the line around a cloth in your hand and walk backwards. Or, lay the rod down after first slackening the drag off, then wrap the line several times around a cloth over your hand before pulling to break it.

Sand can damage reels. The drag mechanism should be tightened, then the reel should be cleaned with fresh water and wiped with an anti-corrosion spray. Finally, be sure to loosen the drag right off again before storage. Do not spray water under pressure onto reels, as it can enter the gears. Always use the recommended grade of lubricating grease.

and a short trace. When cast up-current this rig will roll along until directly offshore, then the angler can walk along keeping pace until it is washed ashore. This technique covers a wide area, and the line should be kept tight enough so that a bite can be detected.

For most beach fishing two styles of hook are adequate. Most popular are offset beak hooks in sizes 3/0 and 4/0, with an optional smaller keeper hook.

The second hook is the kahle or wide-gap hook. These unusual-looking hooks are favoured by many fishermen, particularly where wave or wind conditions makes it difficult to detect bites. They are designed for the fish to hook itself as it moves away with the bait in its mouth.

If targeting rays and sharks, which are common on some beaches, a short leader of light wire and a slightly larger hook are called for.

Standard brass swivels in sizes 4 and 6, both regular and three-way, complete the essential tackle items. Like hooks, the size of swivel should balance with the tackle used. Swivels which are too large won't work properly, and can hinder the cast by separating from the sinker, creating a slight pendulum effect.

Casting rigs

Apart from special situations like spinning at river mouths for salmon and kahawai, all beach fishing is aimed at presenting a bait to fish on the bottom.

When using a light main line, a shock tippet may used to prevent the line snapping at the rod tip when the cast is made. This tippet will be a length of stronger line (e.g. 10 kg for a 6 kg main line) connected with a double blood knot or double uni knot, and should be long enough to ensure the join is on the reel when casting. The knot must be a tidy one so it can travel through the rod rings. The other end of the tippet is tied to the swivel.

There are many different ways of rigging the trace, hooks and weight, some of them quite specialised. But the two most commonly used rigs are the standard running rig and the Australian rig.

In the running rig, the sinker is free running on the main line above the swivel and a metre-long trace of heavier line. When a fish takes the bait it can move off with it and the line runs through the sinker.

The Australian rig uses a 3-way swivel with the sinker at the end of a metre-long trace off the bottom of the swivel, and a separate, shorter trace carrying the hook running from the swivel's side eye.

Greater distance is always achieved with the sinker at the end of the trace. The length of trace affects casting as occasionally a swinging, pendulum effect can occur which reduces distance. Some people like to use a shorter main trace, with the bait or sinker hanging only about half a metre from the end of the rod before casting. It is a matter of trial and error.

When casting a surf rod or a spinning rod, if the weight flies high up in the air and drops close in front of the angler, the line was released too early in the cast. Conversely, if the weight rockets into the ground, it was released too late.

Bait and berley

Berleying is not generally associated with beach fishing, but it can be used effectively. Throwing handfuls of berley into the waves is a 'scattergun' approach, and it disperses by the time it reaches deep, fishing water — but it's better than nothing.

A more effective technique is to peg a container full of berley close to a hole or deep water at low tide, using a long tent peg or stick. The container could be an onion bag or plastic milk container with holes punched in it, filled with frozen, minced bonito or shellfish. A line to the beach ensures it can be retrieved later. Pace out the distance from the berley to high-tide mark and ensure it is within casting range. During the early stages of the rising tide, cast past the berley, as particles will be washing out and hopefully attracting fish. A new type of sinker, incorporating a wire berley cage with the weight in an aerodynamic design, is also useful for attracting fish.

Many commonly used baits like bonito and pilchard are too soft and will fly off during the cast, or will be washed off or eaten by crabs. Soft baits can be tied on with cotton. About a dozen tight winds around the bait and hook shank will suffice, and there is no need to tie it off. Such baits should be checked regularly.

Good tough baits include squid, octopus and cut baits of kahawai and mullet.

Shellfish is a prime natural bait on many beaches, and in Wellington both mussel and crayfish are used for blue moki. Such baits are also tied on with cotton. Tuatuas are easily found on surf beaches, and can be used fresh. But they are much tougher, and stick better on the hook if first salted heavily and kept in a punnet — either frozen, or in a dark place. Salted tuatuas may smell a bit, but they certainly catch fish.

> When striking a fish on a surfcasting rod, the stretch in the mono line will absorb much of the energy. The line should be wound in until tight, then the rod jerked back. This may have to be repeated two or three times before the fish is hooked.

The Australians respect the parore for the nuggety little fighter that he is.

CHAPTER FIVE
SMALL BOAT FISHING

Opposite: Hot kingfish action at White Island with four fishermen hooked up as live baits are drifted over a deepwater pinnacle.

New Zealand is a nation of boat owners, and whether a small dinghy or large runabout, most are used for fishing. The faithful 'tinny' or aluminium dinghy has accounted for more fish than a Minister of Conservation would care to consider. In fact a tinny is more efficient as a fishing machine than a large launch — except for offshore blue water fishing.

Some catch very large fish, but whether the quarry is cod, a feed of school snapper, kingfish or marlin, you will always be more successful if you are well prepared. Your fishing will also be more comfortable and safer if you are not tripping over tackle boxes, bait boards, bags of bait, rods, nets, gaffs and other equipment. It just takes a little planning and common sense.

Preparation

Though much fishing is done with lures, artificial baits will never replace the real thing in most saltwater fishing situations. Every boat needs somewhere to prepare the bait that is easily accessible to all on board and is easily cleaned. The day's catch can be cleaned on a bait board. It also protects parts of the boat from knives, and also protects knife blades from accidentally cutting into screw heads or stainless steel. The board is the only place that knives should be used on a boat.

The tinny usually has bench seats at the front, centre and stern. The centre seat is the obvious place for the bait board, as anglers at both ends can easily reach it without having to stand.

Commercially made boards of plastic, steel or wood are available; or they can be made from plywood. The important features are a raised lip to prevent liquids from spilling, slots for knives, and a stable support. Some fit into rod holders, clamp to a rail, or rest on a seat. Blood and grime should either leak directly overboard, or be collected in a plastic bag.

Live bait tanks
The ability to keep small fish alive is a real asset in any boat. While large launches will have bait wells built into the duckboard or transom, it can be a problem in a tinny. There are some easy systems which can be adopted — a floating cage or clothes basket hanging over the side is the simplest — but it poses a problem when a move to another location is called for. A portable live bait tank can be made cheaply using a large bucket and a small aquarium pump. Stronger portable pumps are also available and a lid for the bucket will prevent water slopping out during a rough ride.

> A 20 litre plastic bucket makes a good container for storing fishing equipment. The lid fits tightly, making it waterproof, and it doubles as a handy seat in a boat.

Rod holders

Rod holders must be securely fitted to the boat. Cheap fittings can be wrenched free, and valuable rods lost over the side.

In the smaller tinnies, where narrow gunwales enable only side-mount rod holders to be used, quality aluminium or steel ones can be screwed or pop-riveted to just about anywhere on the boat. In the middle of the boat, side-mounted holders can be angled out with the flare of the bow for the angler fishing there. At the stern, four can be fitted across the transom, with two at about 60 degrees on the outside and two vertical inside holders.

When fitting rod holders to an aluminium boat, a little silicone under each mounting plate will hold it in place while being riveted and also seal around the rivets.

In larger boats rod holders can be fitted just about anywhere from along the gunwales to across the transom, and even in the engine well. If the coaming along the top of the gunwales is wider than 100 mm, flush-mounted holders are best used as side-mount holders can infringe on cockpit space.

When fitting rod holders, consider which are to be used for trolling and which for bottom fishing. Trolling holders should be angled towards the stern, but not all at the same angle from the centreline of the boat or the line from the forward rod will touch the tip of a rod behind it.

Fish boxes

The days of simply throwing fish on the bottom of the boat are long gone — or they should be! The slime and blood leave the floor dangerously slippery, and the dorsal spines of many fish are sharp, hard and can inflict painful wounds. Fish treated this way also deteriorate quickly. A simple alternative is a large hessian sack secured over the side in the water, but even better is a plastic fish box with a cover, which can double as a seat.

Where space allows, a portable fish box can kept under the transom or under a seat. Some boats utilise under-floor space with fish boxes which have lift-out bin liners. Serious fishermen will keep their bait and fish separate, to keep the catch in top condition.

Storing rods

The days of one rod and reel for each angler also seem to have passed, and many fishermen feel inadequately prepared if they go to sea without a couple of different outfits.

In small dinghies rods can be stored across the transom — not in holders designed for trolling, but in cheap plastic holders specifically made for storing rods.

There is generally enough room on the transom on either side of the motor to accommodate three or four rods. These can be made from 220 mm lengths of 40 mm PVC pipe attached by saddle clamps. A bolt through the bottom acts as a gimbal nock and also prevents rods from falling right through the tube.

On larger trailer boats an overhead 'rocket launcher' of stainless steel or aluminium is usually fitted over the windscreen or cabin. Some

> Small clear plastic 35 mm film containers are useful for storing terminal tackle like hooks, swivels etc.

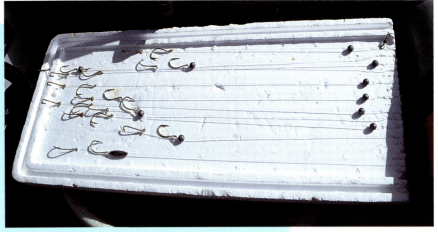

Having traces pre-rigged with hooks and a swivel is useful. Replacing lost traces, or changing to different weight traces takes time if they have to be rigged — particularly when the fishing is hot. Traces can be made in a variety of sizes, some with small ball sinkers above the hooks, and stored wound round a piece of flat polystyrene. The swivel end is jammed into a small slit on one side, and the hook stuck into the material. A piece of plywood can also be used, and is more durable.

thought should be given to the angle of the tubes. In some cases the tubes are set back at an angle to match the rake of the windscreen, often at 50 degrees. This may look smart, but it can severely restrict the overhead casting space in the cockpit. It is equally important to not place rods in the rocket launcher if the local petrol-filling stop has a roof over the forecourt!

An elastic bungy cord secured to each end and stretched over the reels is an extra safety precaution in rough seas.

Rods are also carried in the shelves along the side of the boat, below the gunwale. While this can be convenient if there is sufficient room, the rods and reels can be damaged. A cloth wrapped around each reel, or better still a proper reel bag, will provide some protection.

Modern boats may also have special rubber rod holders fitted along the sides. You can never have too many rod holders fitted to a boat.

Safety equipment

Of all the equipment carried on boats, everything is secondary to the safety equipment. Ironically, in many cases this receives the least attention.

The standard list includes mandatory lifejackets for everyone on board, a fire extinguisher, flares, a first-aid kit, a basic tool kit, anchor or anchors and warp, bailers, and either paddles or oars.

If lifejackets are not worn, they should be easily accessible. They can be kept in a canvas or plastic pouch secured behind a seat with velcro fasteners; or stored under the roof of the cabin, held in place by straps or bungi cord.

A plastic drum with a tight-fitting lid makes a useful dry storage container for tools, flares and other items. In small dinghies clothing and food can be kept in tough plastic bags to keep the boat tidy and the gear dry.

Where a bulkhead is available for attaching mounting brackets, a fire extinguisher can be kept — it should also be accessed easily.

A plastic bucket and scrubbing brush are handy for cleaning up the boat after a day's bait fishing. An old towel in the boat for wiping hands after baiting hooks helps to keep the rod and reel clean.

It is wise to have several bailers as in an emergency it could make all the difference if more than one person can bail at the same time.

Oars and paddles can be a problem as they are so long, but if simple brackets are made (Fig. 26), they can be kept out of the way. These brackets, one for the blade and the other for the grip, are made from 3 mm aluminium about 40 mm wide. This material can be bent into shape, and is strong enough to hold the oars securely.

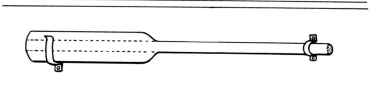

Fig. 26

Harbour and estuary fishing

New Zealand's thousands of kilometres of coastline offer rich fishing opportunities in harbours, estuaries, fiords, islands and sheltered bays. Such places are the mecca of the small-boat angler, for even in the wildest of weather conditions a sheltered spot can usually be found.

Mangrove inlets, estuaries and harbours are the nurseries for a wide range of fish species. To the small-boat angler, this means that at any time of day or tide, fish will be moving through a harbour or channel, and establishing where these fish are likely to be is the key to success.

Reading the water

Just as a trout fisherman studies a stretch of stream to try and determine where fish will be holding, so the inshore fisherman should study the area he intends to fish. The channels through which the tide flows are the main conduits in harbours, and fish will follow these as they move in to feed on the shallow banks at high tide, and when seeking shelter in the channels at low water. The fear most fish have of shallow water and bright conditions is the reason that night fishing in harbours can be very productive.

Fish will be found around man-made features like bridge piles, wharves, marker buoys or seawalls; and natural features such as points, reefs, islands, rocky outcrops or depressions scoured out by currents. Hydrographic charts are useful for identifying channels and markers.

Fig. 27 shows a harbour with wharves, a bridge, a seawall, a reef and a number of underwater formations. In areas with strong currents the fish will often be found upstream of many objects as the current is reduced by back-pressure.

Many predators will hunt downstream from large schools of baitfish like sprats or jack mackerel, and if an individual is injured or leaves the safety of the school, it will attract attention. This is why a live bait is so effective on all predators — they are constantly looking for weak or injured prey, anything which behaves differently from the main group.

> Measuring fish which are of dubious legal size is important to ensure the law is not unwittingly broken. A useful reference can be made by marking the butt section of a rod like a ruler, starting at the bottom of the rod. A marker pen will leave clear marks on the rod above the foregrip.

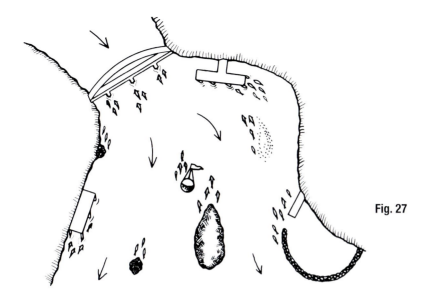

Fig. 27

When the tide starts flowing out in a harbour, fish which have been feeding on shallow banks will move back into deep channels. The small guts leading from banks into such channels are the places to fish.

Fish are also attracted to holes or depressions, to feed on bottom-dwelling organisms like shellfish and crabs, and for security. In these holes, fish tend to be found on the upstream edge where the current is less, and also along the edges.

As harbour currents flow around points of land, back-eddies are created and these are favourite feeding spots for nearly all types of fish. Tiny food organisms are drawn from the main current into a back-eddy, attracting small species like mullet and mackerel, which in turn attract predators like kahawai, kingfish and john dory. Other fish like snapper will be found on the bottom.

The Rapala in various sizes and colours is regarded as the best all-round trolling lure for inshore waters.

Trolling in harbours

Trolling lures in saltwater generally evokes images of trolling large lures in blue water for marlin and tuna. But smaller gamefish like kingfish and kahawai can also be caught on lures trolled in inshore waters. In fact,

An effective way of immobilising your boat and trailer is to remove a wheel and lock it away separately. The chances of a thief having a spare wheel with the corresponding size and stud pattern are remote.

Fig. 28

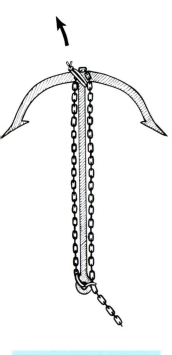

A grapnel anchor is usually used on a rocky bottom, but if a regular anchor is used it may become jammed in the rocks. One solution is to tie the chain firmly to the top of the anchor, or use a shackle; then run the chain back and tie it to the other end with a light line which will hold while the anchor is raised and lowered (Fig. 28). But when it becomes stuck, a heavy pull will snap the line and the angle of pull will switch to the end which is jammed. You can drive the boat over it and free the anchor.

trolling in harbours accounts for many memorable catches of kingfish each year.

The most productive lures are the bibbed minnow style, shaped and coloured roughly like a small baitfish. They have a metal or plastic bib or scoop just below the head, causing them to dive deep and to wobble, which simulates an injured baitfish. Skirted lures, bibless minnows and even metal jigs can also be successfully trolled past bridge piles and marker buoys, which are favourite haunts of kingfish. When a hookup occurs, head the boat for deeper, clear water as a kingfish will try and tangle the line around any object it can find. They can often be led away from any structures with a gentle, steady pressure. Once out in clear water the fight can be taken to the fish.

When boating a fish caught on a minnow-style lure, extreme care is needed as these lures usually have two sets of treble hooks which will easily snag an unwary hand as the fish struggles. A net or gaff is best, and when handling fish, a wet cloth or towel in the hand helps grasp it firmly.

When trolling for kingfish, star-drag or lever-drag overhead reels are best, with a capacity of up to 400 metres of 10 to 15 kg line. Fixed-spool reels are not suitable as their drag systems are not designed to handle the hard run of a kingfish strike. The drag should be set at about one third of the line's breaking strain — 5 kg of drag for 15 kg tackle. Rod choice is a matter of individual preference, but the short, stand-up gamefishing rods are ideal as they give greater control over hard-fighting fish.

Lures should be rigged on a trace of about 1.5 m of at least 24 kg monofilament, with a good-quality ball-bearing swivel connecting it to the main line. Wire traces are used only if barracouta are a problem.

Bibbed minnows are best trolled about 30 metres behind the boat. To check the speed first hold the lure beside the boat with the tip of the rod a few centimetres above the water. If the lure moves slowly from side to side in a lazy manner, increase the speed a little; if it jumps from the water every couple of seconds, slow the boat down. The lure should wobble with the fastest action, sending vibrations up the line; and most of these lures work best at between 5.5 and 6.5 knots.

Only two lures should be used; any more and they can easily become tangled through their erratic action. One can be set at 30 metres and the other at 40 metres behind the boat, to reduce the chance of a tangle.

Trolling for smaller fish like kahawai can be more productive — and a lot of fun. Lighter tackle is used, with 8 or 10 kg line and matching rods. Kahawai will take small bibbed minnows, but are also easily caught on the old-fashioned green plastic jigs which also come in white and paua shell varieties. But they can be frustratingly difficult to hook at times, particularly when seen splashing on the surface, because of the size of baitfish they are feeding on. Regular lures are too big, and are ignored. Try using a smaller lure, even trout lures like a small silver or blue toby, or a smelt fly like a size 6 Grey Ghost. Most kahawai lures are light, and a small ball sinker above a swivel connected to a metre-long trace will help.

Some fishermen even use trout trolling tackle like a lead-core or wire line, to get down deep when trolling for kahawai or kingfish.

SMALL BOAT FISHING

Fishing high-current areas

In all harbours and enclosed waterways there are areas which hold good numbers of fish but are not close to any obvious structure or feature. These are the deep holes, rocks and reefs on the bottom, or shellfish or worm beds. While there may be little current right on the bottom, the water between the fish and the angler can be moving fast — up to 5 knots in some harbours. The challenge facing the angler is to get a baited hook down to the fish and present it in as natural a way as possible.

Correct positioning of the boat is essential, as the baits will be fished 15 m or more behind. Tackle for this type of fishing is again a question of personal preference. It may be a sturdy handline, or a rod with either an overhead reel or a spinning reel. Fixed-spool reels are the least successful type when heavy weights are used. The rod and line must be strong enough to handle weights up to 2 kg or more, as used in the Kaipara Harbour at times. Often the best fishing will coincide with the biggest tides and strongest currents; but to reduce the weight needed many anglers will fish only through the period of slack tide — high or low. This is one situation where a short, sturdy rod can be used, with line of 10 to 15 kg or even stronger.

Some people like to use a ledger rig, with the sinker at the bottom and one or two hooks on side traces above it; while others prefer a running rig with the sinker above a swivel and long trace of 4 or 5 m. Sometimes a small sinker is needed above the bait as well, as the long trace can swing up in the current.

One useful technique is to drop the sinker into the current and allow it to drift out behind the boat, holding the bait in one hand while a further 15 m or so of line is fed out, before dropping the bait. When the bait hits the bottom it can move freely in the lesser current, while slowly being drawn back against the current towards the sinker by the pressure on the line of the stronger current in mid-water. Fig. 29 illustrates this technique.

As this method does not allow direct contact between rod tip and bait because of the belly of line in the water, a tuna circle (longline) or wide-gap (kahle) hook can be used so the fish hook themselves.

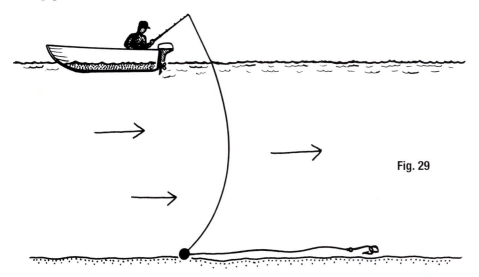

Fig. 29

> When bait fishing, a piece of rag tied to the trace below the swivel helps attract fish. It can be a thin strip of bright red or yellow cloth about 15 cm long, tied tightly around the trace. If it slips, tie a knot around the cloth with the trace.

> Old socks make good bags for carrying reels inside a tackle box — this prevents them bouncing around.

THE COMPLETE NEW ZEALAND FISHERMAN

A good baby squid bait. A half hitch around the head takes the weight. This is a tough bait which will resist the attentions of small fish. Ideal for straylining or bottom dunking.

Baits used in such areas should be tough enough so the current will not tear them from the hook. Shellfish, pilchards and bonito are all soft and if used can be combined with mullet, squid or kahawai; or these latter baits used alone.

Fishing low-current areas

In harbour or estuary areas where there is little current flow, or when tides are small, the location to be fished needs to be carefully considered. There may be a rocky outcrop off the shore, a marker buoy or a reef which attracts fish. Once the fishing spot is determined, the techniques are similar to coastal fishing where lightly weighted baits and berley are used to attract fish.

Wide, shallow flats in harbours often fish well at the top of the tide when the water is at its deepest and fish move onto the flats to feed. Tackle used can be lighter for this situation, as there is little need for heavy sinkers. Straylining and jigging rods with 6 to 8 kg line are ideal, particularly in conjunction with the weighted strayline rig. This has a trace of about a metre with a very light ball sinker running right to the hook, and is perhaps the best rig for snapper, trevally and gurnard. The trace will be heavier than the main line, about 10 to 15 kg line in most cases, and the sinker 10-25 g. If cut baits like mullet or bonito are used, a 3/0 or 4/0 hook with a small size 6 keeper hook is ideal, as in Fig. 30.

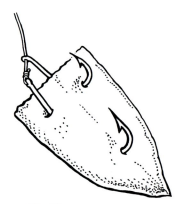

Fig. 30

Whole pilchards are also popular and can be rigged in many ways — two 3/0 or 4/0 hooks with straight shanks, as in Fig. 23, is one option. Different pilchard rigs are shown in the opposite photos.

In some harbours, it is a definite advantage to use a long trace. This allows the bait to move freely, and is more attractive to many fish. Some people will use a trace of up to 5 m long, and if the water is clear and shallow, the material used should be lighter. We sometimes do not use a trace, but just attach the hook to the end of the main line.

When tying knots in thin or light nylon, double the end and tie the knot with the doubled section of line. It gives a stronger knot.

Depending on the strength of the current, berley can be distributed from the surface, or from a dispenser either lowered with the anchor or separately. If on the surface, the berley will drift down slowly, so baits should be cast well back from the boat and allowed to sink in the same area. The amount of weight used will vary with the current, but the object

SMALL BOAT FISHING

Fixed two-hook pilchard bait.

Alternative two-hook pilchard bait, with a half hitch around the tail to take the weight. This can be rigged with fixed hooks, or the second hook can be sliding freely above the bottom hook on the trace.

'Pilchard sandwich' — a good bait for big fish! The first hook is threaded through the eyes of two pilies and the trace wrapped around the baits several times. The second hook, which is sliding, is inserted through both tails or on one side as shown. A couple of half hitches around the tails will take the weight for casting the bait.

Another version of a double hook bait, but with the head cut off. This allows the juices to flow freely, adding to the appeal of your bait.

Opposite: John Dory are poor fighters but are highly prized as table fish. They prefer live baits like small cod, sprats or mackerel but will also take jigs.

is to get the bait down to the bottom with as little weight as possible. The bait is usually fished with a light drag setting on the reel — often in free spool with only the clicker or ratchet on to warn of a strike, and the fish allowed to run with the bait before striking.

Low-current areas of harbours are one of the few places in sheltered areas where different fishing options can be covered — baits and berley set on the bottom for snapper, gurnard and other bottom fish, and a live bait on the surface for kingfish and kahawai. When fishing is slow, a jig or spoon can also be cast out and retrieved and this could easily yield a kahawai or trevally, or if allowed to sink, a snapper or john dory.

Coastal fishing

Unlike the sheltered waters of harbours and estuaries which offer just a few prime species, coastal waters around New Zealand offer a range of fish species unmatched in most parts of the world.

In the last two decades many recreational anglers have changed their approach to fishing. Rods like broom handles with super heavy line, big hooks and chunks of bait have given way to lighter tackle and more natural baits. Not only is this approach more sporting, but it is more successful.

With people giving more thought to their tackle and techniques, methods have developed which were unheard of in the past. Many fishermen have found that for a number of species, jigging a metal lure is more effective than using bait. Sinkers, always thought necessary to get a bait down to fish, have become lighter and lighter — and the effective technique called straylining has evolved.

Many of the recent innovations in sport fishing have occurred in coastal waters, that area out to a depth of about 50 metres. This is the domain of the small-boat angler. It is easily reached from launching ramps around the country, and good fishing is close at hand.

But the fish will never jump into the boat. The successful angler will study where fish are likely to be found, what species can be targeted and how they can be caught.

Reading the water

Fish will rarely be found on a flat sea floor. They require specific habitats which must provide the two essentials for survival — food, and shelter from predators. On the coast, this usually means a reef. It may be a structure extending out from land, or a self-contained one separated from the actual coastline, perhaps part of an island. To identify such prime spots, hydrographic charts are a good starting point.

Large reefs are a hazard to shipping and are always clearly marked on charts. They are also primary habitat for all coastal fish, from the smallest cod or maomao to the biggest kingfish or snapper. Reefs close to shore will not be shown in such detail on charts, but rocks which are exposed at certain tides and other navigational hazards will be shown.

Many such features can also be found by simply studying the land run-

It is frustrating to be continually untangling coils and twists in the trace which are formed by the bait and sinker spinning as they are raised and lowered. A stiff brand of mono will help prevent this problem. Some of the soft mono lines often retain a memory, which means basically that they twist and curl easily. For trace material in particular, a stiff mono which is also tough and resists abrasion is important.

A home-made jig fly or sabiki rig can be made by tying loops in a length of light mono to the desired length, then cutting off one arm leaving a single side trace (Fig. 31). The 'fly' is made from a small section of white, red or yellow plastic tubing slipped over a sprat hook, followed by a longer section of white tubing with a V-shaped cut in the tail protruding below the hook. Plastic beads can be added before the hook is tied on.

Fig. 31

ning down to the sea. Gently sloping hills running on to a sandy beach indicate that the sea floor will likely be flat, with little to attract or hold fish. Conversely, a sheer cliff dropping straight into the sea will mean deep water close to shore, providing good habitat for fish in close, but not much further out unless a reef can be found. A point of land which has steep hills behind, but levels out to a slope as it meets the sea generally signals a reef structure continuing offshore from that point — a good area to fish with a wide variety of marine life.

As well as the geography, there are other clues to the presence of fish. Abundant shags swimming and diving mean that small fish are present. And where there are small fish, bigger fish are usually not far away. Patches of white water, or washes, created by wave action between the rocks or in a gut or crack in the coastline, are prime fishing spots. The wave action flushes food from the rocks and weed. The security of the foamy water is also attractive to many species.

Electronic fish finders or depth sounders are regarded by many as essential for successful fishing, but thoughtful observation can also reveal clues. A change in the pattern of swells, or breaking white water, will indicate submerged rocks and reefs. Birds flying round or even sitting on the water are a sign of activity which may be over a reef, or at least indicate a school of fish in the area.

Even in Auckland you can find solitude on the water.

While reefs are the primary fishing areas, fish will also be found where holes are scoured out of the bottom, or a concentration of food organisms such as shellfish or worms is found on an otherwise featureless bottom.

A depth sounder certainly helps locate changes on the sea floor and of course schools of fish, which are the ultimate indicator of a good spot.

Many people identify landmarks which mark fishing spots, and as always local knowledge is the key factor in successful fishing.

Fishing over a reef

The widest variety of fish is found on or around reefs in coastal waters. Schooling maomao, kahawai, mackerel and trevally are often found on the surface, feeding on plankton carried up by upwellings created by currents hitting the reef and being forced upwards.

Sometimes these same fish are found in mid-water, along with cruising kingfish or sharks, while on the bottom lives a host of species like trumpeter, red and blue cod, snapper, tarakihi, wrasses, pigfish, parrotfish, porae, leatherjackets, eels, john dory, butterfish, moki and others. With such a variety available, targeting one individual species may seem difficult, but it can be done.

One of the most popular fish in many parts of the country is tarakihi,

Fishing along the edges of channels often produces better results than fishing in the middle.

> When fishing baits on the bottom a change in the terminal rig can often make all the difference. An old trick of some Auckland party boat skippers is to use both ledger and running rigs to determine which produces best on the day. Surprisingly, it can sometimes make a lot of difference.

which are more common in winter but may be found at any time. Unlike many reef fish, tarakihi have small mouths, which require small hooks of around 1/0 size. The tarakihi rig or coastal ledger rig, as in Fig. 24, is used to target these desirable fish. Note the sinker at the bottom.

The size of sinker is determined by the depth of water and strength of the current. If the main line is 10 to 15 kg breaking strain, a section of 4 kg line attached to the sinker as a sacrificial trace will prevent the whole terminal rig from being lost if the sinker becomes snagged on the bottom. And it will. Tarakihi are found over rocks and weed, and the baits must be presented on the bottom; the hook closest to the sinker will hook the most fish. The hooks can be attached to the main line; a heavier trace is not needed.

This rig is also used for catching cod, and a small cod of less than 15 cm can be rigged as a live bait for john dory. A useful quick rig is a coastlock swivel with a 6/0 hook attached to the eye of the swivel with a split ring. The clip of the coastlock swivel is connected to the top eye of the swivel holding the tarakihi trace. This can quickly be attached to the main rig, and with the small cod lightly hooked through the back, tarakihi fishing can continue, but if a john dory comes along it will make a welcome addition to the catch.

The snapper is one of the most popular fish in the North Island and the top part of the South Island, and while it may be caught on the small tarakihi baits, larger baits will be more successful.

As snapper are found in all depths, the rigs used vary with the depth of water being fished. The ledger rig in Fig. 32 with 3/0 to 5/0 hooks replacing the smaller tarakihi hooks will catch snapper in deep water. This rig is also the best to use when three or more people are fishing from the same boat because light rigs will often become tangled as they swirl around in the current.

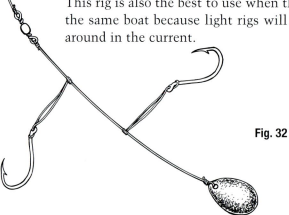

Fig. 32

Snapper are shy, wary fish, and a bait which is anchored to the bottom is less appealing than a bait which moves more naturally in the currents. This rig is more effective on school snapper up to 4 kg in weight than really big snapper. The trace used is heavier than for tarakihi, up to 24 kg breaking strain, as reef snapper feed on mussels, sea eggs and other shellfish and have powerful jaws which can easily crunch trace material.

Three basic types of rod and reel outfits are needed to fish a reef effectively. The first, classified as a heavy outfit, will be a rod of 1.5 to 1.8 m fitted with an overhead reel holding 15 to 20 kg line, with either a star drag or lever drag. This can be used for live-baiting for big fish, or for dropping a big ledger rig to the bottom for big snapper, trumpeter or dogfish. When big kingfish are expected, a 24 kg stand-up gamefishing outfit should be used.

The second outfit will be used for straylining or casting lures to surface feeding fish. The rod will be slightly longer, 1.8 to 2.1 m, and will have a soft tip for casting and a stronger mid section increasing to a powerful butt section. The reel is a fixed-spool spinning reel, with line of between 5 and 10 kg breaking strain.

The last outfit is a miniature version of the first: basically a small boat rod with an overhead reel holding lighter line for bottom fishing. It will probably be 8 to 10 kg line. This is the most commonly used outfit for tarakihi, cod and snapper fishing, and can be replaced by a handline.

A wide variety of baits will be used on a reef, and specialised baits are required for some species. For example, tarakihi feed on small crustaceans and other creatures, and the best bait for them is shellfish, either pipis or mussels, but they will also take small cubes of bonito. Pipis or tuatuas are soft baits which should be tied on with cotton wound several times around the bait and the shank of the hook. These can also be toughened by salting heavily and either stored in preserving jars, with alternate layers of salt, or frozen in plastic containers. Blue cod are not fussy feeders and will take jigs, cut bait or shellfish. But snapper do have preferences. They are opportunistic feeders, but at certain seasons exhibit preferences for mullet, pilchards or bonito — and at other times they will take any of these equally.

> It is important to keep in touch with your bait. Some fish will be hooked on a line which is untended, but if the line is kept tight and the bait moved occasionally you will catch more fish and also prevent the bait being dragged into a rocky hole by small fish or tangled among weed.

A cut pilchard bait when you do not want to use a whole pilie. The single hook is threaded through the eyes then inserted through the body sideways so the point protrudes on the other side. Fish will go for the guts first, so the hook should be placed in this area. This bait can be cast, but pilchards are soft and pickers or crabs will strip it quickly. Check these baits often.

Other top baits are mussel, kahawai, and fresh mackerel or piper. One of the best baits is undoubtedly a fresh slimy mackerel, filleted and offered in strips for smaller fish or whole when big snapper are around. Fresh piper cut in half or rigged whole like a pilchard is also a favourite of many Auckland snapper fishermen, while in Northland many people also use fresh sprats. With frozen commercial baits like pilchards and bonito now readily available, these are the most popular simply because of their convenience. Serious anglers will take a variety of baits with them including fresh and frozen baits, in case the fish are in a selective mood.

The phone rang, and a voice said, "It's Russell. What are you doing this afternoon? We are doing pretty well on kingfish at the moment." It was a Sunday in early March, and I was actually in the office, working on this book, when he called. Time was getting tight. "Sorry. Love to, but I really have to get on with this job."

Russell Murray is a very accomplished fisherman; one of Auckland's better anglers. He is one of those types who always catches fish. He never stops working at it, and will have two rods with livies out, a pilie cast well away from the boat, and still be busy catching piper or mackerel on jig flies. When he says he is doing well, it sort of tugs at the concentration.

Ten minutes later I called him back: "What time?"

"We want to be there at low tide and get the first two hours. That's the best time. See you at Half Moon Bay at 1.30. I'll get there earlier and put the boat in and get some bait. There are plenty of sprats at the wharf."

Nobody else was catching sprats, but he had a binful. The tiny pink jig flies sweetened with a chunk of pilchard had proved irresistible.

We dropped the anchor in about 4 metres of water off the end of Motuihe Island, 50 metres from a reef.

"Extra big tides, so the fish will be coming in," said Russell as he slipped the 4/0 hook through the lips of a sprat and dropped it over with a 1 m trace under a 56 g sinker. Another followed and soon we had four live sprats on the bottom, on 15 kg and 24 kg outfits.

"Hard strike them," said Russell, tightening the drag and engaging the clicker.

A berley bomb was dropped on a rope from the bow, and another at the stern; then tiny baits went over the back to try for piper, our favourite livies.

"We got a 42 and a 50 yesterday, and got blown away four times," he said. "That's about 19 kg and 24 kg. There are some big kings around here."

When the rod bends suddenly and the reel groans, it can be hard work just lifting the rod out of the holder. But you have to stop the big kings before they can reach the reef.

We did.

"I'll get there earlier and put the boat in and get some bait. There are plenty of sprats at the wharf." Russell Murray and Bill Penney soon had a bin full of livies.

Right: Russell Murray slips the 4/0 hook through the lips of a sprat.

Fishing over sand or mud

Fish are more difficult to find when fishing over a wide, flat area. Some features like holes, ledges or banks will attract fish; or they may just be travelling through the area with the tide.

A simple rig for this type of bottom fishing, as in Fig. 33, is a running sinker above the swivel connecting a metre-long trace to the main line. The trace material is slightly heavier than the line, but again, the line and weight used should be no heavier than needed to fish confidently.

One popular method of locating fish when the wind and tide are in the same direction is to drift, dragging the baits along the bottom. When fish are struck, landmarks can be taken or the location recorded using the satellite global positioning system, or GPS, so that the drift can be repeated. A simple method of marking the spot is to throw over a coloured marker buoy with line wrapped around it. The buoy spins on the surface as the weight drops to the bottom.

Alternatively, the anchor can be put down and the area fished from a stationary boat, but fishing is usually more productive when the baits are moving slowly along the bottom.

Relatively light tackle can be used, as there are no obstructions to tangle the line. A light rod of up to 2 m with a small overhead reel carrying 6 to 8 kg line is ideal. Fixed-spool reels can also be used if preferred.

The hook size will be determined by the type of bait used, but if in doubt, err on the small side. Baits will be salted pipis, or strips of mullet or bonito. Pilchards will also work, but can be damaged by dragging through the sand and need to be checked often.

> If you are catching only small fish, moving to the other side of the reef, bridge, hole or point you are fishing may change your luck dramatically.

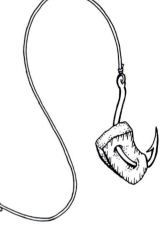

Fig. 33

> Baits can be pre-cut and stored in plastic ice-cream containers or big yoghurt containers for handy use, and frozen or refrigerated.

Fishing with jigs

Another effective method when the boat is drifting is jig fishing. While jigs can be fished on bait-fishing rods, this is one method where the right tackle really should be used. The rod should be light, strong and sensitive, about 2 m long with a firm or stiff action. Graphite rods are ideal.

If the rod bends too easily, the jig will not be worked correctly at the end of the line. Specialised jigging rods designed specifically for this type of fishing are available, and are rated for various line weights. Reels are overhead type, preferably with a quick-release free-spool lever which can be activated with the thumb. A pistol grip is an added advantage when jig fishing. A gear ratio which gives a fast retrieve, e.g. 4:1, helps make the fishing more efficient.

The jig is tied directly to the end of the line, with no trace or swivel used. If fishing light line, the end can be doubled for tying the knot to add strength, or a short double line can be tied with a spider hitch.

There are two golden rules when fishing with jigs:
- Wind and tide must be running in the same direction (or the boat will not drift);
- Use the lightest jig possible. As a rough guide to line weights, jigs of 30 or 40 g can be fished with line of 4 to 6 kg breaking strain, while 60 or 80 g jigs require 6 to 10 kg line. In water up to 30 m deep, which covers most inshore coastal waters, 40 or 60 g jigs are used. Deeper water

---

If fish are proving hard to catch with your regular rig, cut off the trace and tie the hook directly to the end of the line, with the sinker above the hook. You are taking a calculated risk by fishing with the main line at the business end, which may be 10 kg line or similar, if a big fish or a fish with sharp teeth is hooked. But the risk of losing one big one is outweighed by the extra fish you will catch.

Jigging for snapper

The technique of jigging for snapper was developed in Auckland, where the wide spaces and calm waters of the inner Hauraki Gulf proved ideal for this type of fishing. The roller-coaster ride which comes from drifting in places which are open to the ocean swells makes it more onerous.

The first anglers to use jigs regularly were a couple of experienced fishermen, Frank Perry and Bruce Riley, who never carried bait in their boats after discovering how deadly metal jigs were on snapper in the early 1970s.

Frank and Bruce were mainly interested in kingfish, and of course for kings you must have live bait. Their favourite method of catching small mackerel was to use the strings of tiny jig flies, called okan sabiki rigs, and one day they were fishing in the Sargent Channel, between Waiheke and Motuihe Islands.

"Every now and then we got what was obviously a heavy fish, which kept snapping off the jig flies," recalls Frank.

"So we made up some stronger gear, with flies on heavier line — and started catching snapper!"

They could not believe it, but Frank also remembers hearing a story at about the same time involving a fisherman who was catching snapper by trolling with a lead-core line — as used on the lakes for trout — and a spinner.

"Apparently he was trolling in the Motuihe Channel at slack tide so he could get down to the bottom.

"We started using jigs imported from overseas, and we caught huge numbers of snapper."

In fact they would tell people that jigging was almost as effective as using dynamite.

But the jigs were quite expensive, and so the enterprising pair started designing and making their own 60 g snapper jigs, which proved very popular.

The things people say

Frank Perry and Bruce Riley found snapper fishermen were a conservative lot and it was hard to change ingrained attitudes. It took a long time to convince other people to try using jigs — they just could not imagine how a chunk of bright metal could appeal to the shy snapper.

They attracted some strange comments from people fishing conventionally from anchored boats while Frank's tin boat drifted among them like a great shiny spider, with two or three anglers all lifting and lowering their long rods in a totally uncoordinated rhythm.

People would drop their anchors where they were catching fish, and often blocked their drift. But they usually moved after Frank let his scarred old tinny bounce off a couple of sparkling new glass boats.

Frank does not suffer fools lightly, and one morning as he and Bruce drifted along, bouncing their jigs off the bottom in a favourite stretch of the Sargent Channel, they heard a voice echo clearly across the calm water: "Look at those two silly bastards. What do they think they're doing? They'll never catch a snapper like that!"

At about that time they both hooked up to good fish, and they probably played them for a bit longer than was necessary. When their boat had drifted close to where the talkative bloke's boat was anchored, Frank turned to Bruce as he landed a beautiful 4 kg snapper and commented loudly: "Let's put these back and get some bigger ones." They released both fish, and Bruce and Frank had a quiet chuckle as the loudmouth nearly fell out of his boat trying to net one of the snapper which slowly swam past the back of his boat. But they didn't laugh — they were too busy playing fish again.

Frank is a bit older than Bruce, and his hair is fast disappearing. But Bruce carries a bit more weight. One day they were up to their usual tricks, pulling fish after fish out of the water while all around them bait fishermen holding slack lines watched enviously. Suddenly, when Frank hooked up, a voice could be heard drifting across the water: "Look, Dad, the old bloke's caught one."

Bruce thought this was a great joke, until he hooked up and the voice added, "Now the fat one's got one, too!"

But they did attract some abuse. "A lot of people would come up and ask, 'What are you using?' — and when we showed them they would accuse us of lying!" says Frank.

But not all anglers are so disbelieving. The real anglers are those people prepared to learn, and adapt. One such angler is Aucklander Sid Bartley, who pulled alongside one day when Frank and Bruce had 25 snapper in the box, and asked what he needed to catch fish like that.

"I told him you need an Abu 7000 and a good rod and it's not cheap. So Sid turned to his son and said, 'You won't get much when I die, but you'll get some good fishing tackle.'

"Today, he is one of the best jig fishermen in the Hauraki Gulf," says Frank.

But he maintains that Sid's wife, Eileen, is the best angler with a jig.

"She takes a good book, and doesn't put it down until some fish appear on the depth sounder. Then she picks up her rod!"

---

requires heavier jigs and stronger line.

Put the reel in free spool, and after casting ahead of the boat let line run out until the lure hits the bottom under the boat. As soon as it touches, clamp the thumb onto the spool and jerk the rod upward with the forearm, then drop it to let the jig flutter freely back to the bottom.

The jig should move across the bottom, diving up and then fluttering back down again. It is this erratic action which attracts fish. Sometimes the strike comes as it hits the bottom; sometimes when it is sinking. Any change in the action of the jig should produce an instant reaction from the

> Lower the jig slowly through schools of kahawai or mackerel to reduce strikes, if you want to reach snapper underneath.

Jigs come in a range of colours and sizes, and should have extra weight at the hook end to ensure they don't flip over and catch the line.

The addition of a strip of fluorescent pink or green plastic tubing on the hook often adds to the strike rate. It probably gives the fish a more pronounced target, and they hit the hook end rather than the middle of the lure.

A scrap of cotton cloth secured to the ring holding the hook on a jig can be soaked in fish oil to add some smell to the metal lure.

angler: strike quickly by holding the spool tightly with the thumb to prevent line slipping off, lift the rod and put the reel in gear for the fight.

The jigging action can vary from a slight 'jiggle' of the wrist, to a full sweep of the arm. When fish are not biting, experienced anglers will vary their action; but generally, the deeper the water the more movement is needed to give action to the lure.

As the boat drifts away, more line is let out with each jig movement to keep it on the bottom, and the angle increases until too much line is out for effective jigging. It is wound in and the process repeated.

Winding very slowly at the start of the retrieve can often provoke a strike also, and some people have hooked fish by 'trolling' the jig slowly behind the boat.

Experienced jig fishers use one hand, but with heavy tackle the second hand can help support the rod by grasping the foregrip above the reel.

Fish are located either on a fish finder, or by fishing in recognised productive areas like in channels, or alongside reefs. Don't try it over a reef or the jig will become snagged in the rocks.

Once fish are caught, the drift is repeated by motoring back to the starting point. Such drifts may be only a short distance or several hundred metres.

Jigging is always good under schools of feeding surface fish, which are easily located by watching for birds wheeling and diving. Bottom fish are usually found under such activity, but it can be a problem getting the jig down through the predators like kahawai and mackerel. One solution is

SMALL BOAT FISHING

The things fish will eat

"Snapper will eat anything put in front of them, provided it is on the bottom and it is moving," says Frank Perry.

To prove a point, he and Bruce have actually caught snapper on a spark plug rigged with a split ring and hook attached to one end, and the line to the other.

On another occasion, "We were going out and there was a very strong wind blowing. We thought we would drift too quickly and the jig would never get down, so I looked around the workshop for something heavy and all I could find was some sheet lead. I hammered it into a shape roughly 15 cm long, 2 cm deep, and half a centimetre thick, and drilled a hole in each end. It was too thick for a split ring so I tied a loop of heavy nylon on one end to hold the hook — and we went out and slaughtered them!"

He also quotes a lady friend who can remember her father going out fishing in front of Takapuna Beach about 50 years ago and catching snapper on bare hooks which he jigged up and down.

These two experts have caught nearly every species of fish found in the inner Gulf — on jigs. They are still doing it, but the hair is a little thinner and the waistlines a little thicker. There is also a lot more competition out there now, because the message has clearly worked.

Watch for the line looping itself around the rod tip when dropping the rod. A twist of the rod to one side will avoid this problem.

Some jig fishermen add a second hook at the top of the jig, secured by a split ring, as they feel that a lot of fish strike this end of the lure.

Always keep control of the line — don't allow any slack. Keep in touch with the jig at all times.

Give the rod an extra tweak at the top of the stroke. This takes up slack and adds extra movement to the lure.

Vary the action.

Try reeling in fast for about 6 m, then let the jig down again.

Always keep the jig moving. A stationary lure will not attract fish.

Fish over clean sandy or mud bottoms. You will catch fish on the bottom 90% of the time.

---

to work the area behind the moving school for snapper and other fish feeding on scraps which drift down.

The variety of fish which will take a jig is impressive — cod, john dory, stargazers, red mullet and wrasses, as well as snapper, trevally and kahawai. In the Hauraki Gulf some anglers have caught every larger species of fish found there by jigging.

The type of hook used is the subject of much discussion. Most jigs come fitted with treble hooks, but these can be a nuisance when netting fish as they tangle. When the action is hot, the angler wants to unhook the fish and get the jig back into the water as quickly as possible. In this case, single hooks are much easier to handle. Also, some fishermen maintain they get a better hookup rate with singles. It is a matter of choice. The important thing is to have sharp hooks.

Another addition to jigs which adds to their appeal, is a couple of red 'gill slits' painted at the top with nail polish. This simulates the flaring gills of a stressed baitfish escaping a predator.

Brent Pearson is happy with his pair of snapper which he hooked on jigs off Cape Runaway in the Bay of Plenty. Every year in October and November big snapper like these 11.4 kg (25 lb) and 17.3 kg (38 lb) trophies are taken there.

Tidal fluctuations have a powerful influence on fish behaviour. For example, snapper fishing is better during large tides — over 3 m — simply because there is more current flowing. But when fishing very deep water, many people prefer slack tide because it is easier to get their baits to the bottom.

Targeting big fish inshore

In many situations small boats are better platforms for catching big fish from than much larger boats. A 15 m launch is far more obtrusive than a 4 m dinghy when straylining for big snapper in close to the rocks. The inflatable tender from a launch can be used to get close to the rocks, or even to go ashore.

As with all fishing, local knowledge and experience are invaluable and in many places the boat must be positioned in exactly the right spot. Sometimes a few metres to one side can make all the difference, and experienced fishermen will reposition the boat several times until they are satisfied it is sitting correctly in relation to the wind and current.

Two prime targets in much of the country are kingfish and big snapper. Together, these magnificent fish have spawned more dreams than any other fish.

Big snapper

Fast growth in all fish requires a prolific supply of food which can be obtained with the least expenditure of effort. A lot of body weight, or conditioning, can be consumed by having to exert excess energy in chasing food. Conversely, fish will grow quickly if food is readily available, although quickly in the case of a fish like snapper can mean 30 or 40 years, which is the age of most record-sized specimens of 12 kg or more.

Most of the mega-sized snapper come from reefs with a lot of kelp, and water as shallow as 2 m. But deep water, about 15 metres or more, and a good current flow, are never far away. They are opportunist feeders and will eat mussels, sea eggs, crayfish, octopus, small fish, squid — just about anything they can find. It is the variety of their prey that is the key to their success. One study of trawl-caught snapper in the Hauraki Gulf revealed that their main food was brittle-starfish

There is a story about a good-sized snapper which was caught in a net in an arm of the Manukau Harbour. Its gut was found to contain several lambs' tails, and visions of lambs sitting on the edge of the tide with their tails dangling in the water were dispelled when a local farmer admitted dumping tails into the tide after docking.

The big snapper's preference for shallow, rocky areas gives small boats a real advantage, as larger boats cannot enter such areas safely, and are also more likely to scare the fish. Snapper found here are often dark red and bronze in colour, giving rise to the term 'kelpies'. Their teeth will be worn from crushing the tough shells of sea urchins and other creatures, and their forehead will be rough and knobbled from fossicking among the rocks. Snapper from deep water will have bright, shiny coloration and sharp teeth.

Big snapper tactics

Having finely tuned their instincts for survival, large snapper are shy and cautious creatures. They seldom venture from cover in the bright daylight, preferring to roam their patch and feed in lower light conditions — at night, or at dawn and dusk. This is also the time when most marine life is more active.

Early-morning change of light and the last two hours of daylight are the best times to target a prime fish. But they must always be approached carefully. When arriving in snapper territory, it's a good idea to travel the last 50 metres or so quietly, and lower the anchor with as little noise as possible.

The technique is basically straylining, which means fishing with floating or unweighted baits. This will also work well in any shallow water, and will account for a variety of species including school snapper, kahawai, trevally, small kingfish and mackerel. Berley is essential for successful fishing, and should be dispensed quietly. If a pre-mixed berley is

---

In shallow water small boats are better to fish from than big ones. The tender from a launch can be used.

You will catch fish on any tide. If one tide is unproductive, try after it turns.

When targeting snapper, two clues to look for are currents and the presence of baitfish like jack mackerel or piper. They seem to go together.

> A good tough bait for snapper in Auckland is calf liver, cut into bait-sized strips and soaked in tuna oil or fish oil. It will keep in the fridge like this, or can be frozen after a period of soaking.

> When fishing for kingfish, the live bait is not always presented under a balloon. On deeper reefs in the Bay of Plenty the favourite live bait is a mackerel or flyingfish. These are caught at night with scoop nets after they are attracted to the boat with bright lights. These are rigged through the nose, inserting the 6/0 game hook from under the chin. A short heavy trace of 50 or 100 kg mono and a sinker above the swivel completes the rig. Tackle is usually stand-up gear with 24 or 37 kg line.

used, it can be suspended on the surface. This way, the movement of the boat will jiggle the bag and keep the berley flowing, and also it is less likely to tangle when a fish is brought to the boat.

If a berley pot clamped to the transom is used, try and operate it quietly. An effective basic berley can consist of pilchards broken up by hand and bonito frames scraped over the side or in the engine well. The important thing is to have a steady, consistent flow of scraps of fish and oil — not so much that the fish are fed, but enough to draw them up the trail.

Smaller fish will appear first, and larger fish tend to hang back from the boat. While fresh bait like piper or mackerel can be caught on small hooks right at the stern, the snapper baits are cast well away from the boat.

A good straylining outfit is a rod which has a soft tip for casting unweighted baits, and strength in the mid and butt sections for fighting big, strong fish. Fixed-spool reels with the baitfeeder feature are designed specifically for this type of fishing.

With the reel in the baitfeeder mode, the fish can take line with little resistance. The soft clicker signals a strike, and fish can be struck by winding the handle or manually releasing the baitfeeder lever so that the preset drag is engaged. Strikes are often tentative and the fish should be allowed to nibble the bait. A short run may follow, and then stop. If the fish feels any resistance, it may drop the bait, so some anglers will grab the rod if it is in a holder and lift the bail arm so there is no resistance at all. When the fish is running steadily, strike it by pointing the rod in the direction of the fish, engaging the drag, and lifting the rod firmly.

Other strikes will be a sudden strong run where the fish can be struck at once. If straylining in deep water, there will be a belly in the line and this is often sufficient to allow the fish to run, so the reel can be fished with the drag on.

To ensure the hook is firmly embedded, an extra two or three good sharp strikes are often needed with big fish, as their mouths can be very hard.

Free-spool reels can also be used, and indeed are popular, but the technique for casting must first be mastered. These reels are fished in free-spool mode with the ratchet on.

Line weight will be at least 15 kg for big snapper, with a half metre trace for easy casting of 20 kg, 30 kg or even 50 kg mono to counter the crushing teeth of the fish.

Hooks will be strong, chemically sharpened hooks in sizes 7/0, 8/0 or 10/0 with smaller keeper hooks. Either suicide beak hooks or straight-shanked hooks are fine. The question of trace is a vexing one, for if too heavy it may scare the fish, but if too light the fish may cut it. It is a matter of experience and preference, but most agree that it's better to hook the fish then worry about landing it, than to not hook it at all!

Sometimes a small ball weight is added, running freely down against

Fig. 34

the hook, to take the bait down (Fig. 34). This is more relevant when you first arrive and the fish have not moved up the berley trail. If it is slow to start, try one bait close to or on the bottom. As the action heats up the weight can be removed. Or, if there is a strong current and choppy surface, a small weight may still be needed to get the bait down to the fish in mid-water.

Many fishermen would argue that a freshly killed slimy mackerel (lower) is the most effective snapper bait. It is much better than the common jack mackerel or yellowtail (upper).

Baits

People have their favourite baits, and to my mind there is no doubt about the number one bait for large snapper — fresh slimy mackerel. These handsome, bullet-shaped fish with marbled green backs and flanks can be caught on jig flies, small baits or small jigs. They will often be found with other mackerel when feeding on the surface, or a deep school can be located on a fish finder.

Freshly killed, in fact still quivering is even better, with the tail and a section of backbone removed in the butterfly fashion, this is a deadly bait. To prepare this bait, slice up one side of the backbone from the tail towards the dorsal fin, flip over and repeat on the other side. Then snap the backbone off and throw away the tail.

The bait is then rigged with a single hook through the head, inserted up under the jaw and protruding out through the brain cavity (Fig. 24).

If a two-hook rig is used, the main hook can be threaded completely through the eyes sideways, and then hooked through the back behind the head to lie sideways. The trace then passes through the eyes, and the keeper hook can be slipped through the nose from underneath. By wrapping the trace around the keeper hook two or three times, the weight will be taken at this point for casting.

Other prime baits are a whole fillet of kahawai, or a whole or half fillet of bonito. Long, thin baits are better than chunks, and should be hooked only once or twice at one end so that most of the bait floats freely. A 'tail' can be added by cutting a slit at the other end.

One bite from the powerful jaws of a large snapper destroyed this bait which was a whole 35 cm slimy mackerel.

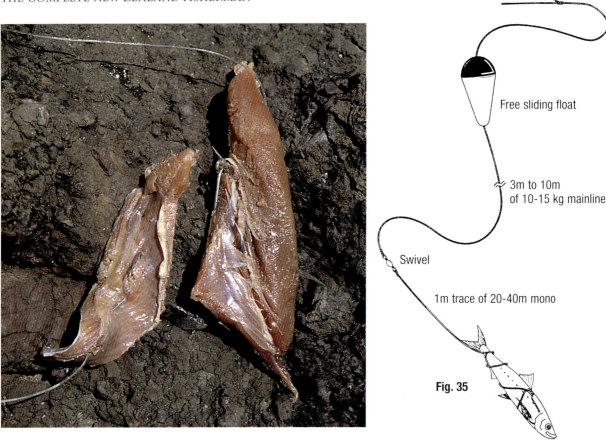

Long strips of skipjack tuna (bonito) with two 8/0 hooks threaded through them are top baits for big snapper.

Fig. 35

A good berley in deep water where there is a strong current is fresh shellfish like mussels or tuatuas. Just open shellfish and drop them over the side. They will sink straight down.

The belly strip from a bonito is another top bait, and is tougher than the fillets. Also, the head can be fished either whole, or split in half so that the blood and juices flow out. One thing big snapper love is a big, juicy, smelly bait. For this reason the gut of a bonito or mullet makes a useful bait, and it can be hooked through the strongest part of the stomach.

Flyingfish, koheru, mullet, big piper and jack mackerel are all top baits, whether fished whole, as butterfly bait or cut in half.

A bobby cork floating pilie rig (Fig. 35) is a deadly rig for floating a whole pilchard over a reef for big snapper. The depth can be varied by adjusting the stop knot. This can be dental floss, wool or a rubber band tied around your line. If the bobby cork has a large hole through it, rather than tie a bulky stopper knot which will not easily slide through your rod eyes, add a plastic bead between the float and the knot.

A single pilchard, however, is a bit small and a 'sandwich' of four or five of them threaded onto the bend of a large hook has accounted for a lot of good fish. A bundle of pilchards can also be rigged on the hook, and instead of dangling freely, the trace is wrapped around the fish several times and then wrapped over the heads and tails a couple of times, before being secured with the keeper hook.

Casting baits out at different angles from the side and stern of the boat also helps cover the water. Baits cast to the side will drift back with the current, so more line should be let out slowly to allow the bait to drift freely, but also remaining in contact with it.

SMALL BOAT FISHING

That is the key to successful straylining — to present a naturally drifting bait, but also remaining in direct contact with it so subtle takes can be detected.

Fighting the fish

Once the fish is hooked, you must stop it from reaching the sanctuary of a kelp forest or reef. As they are usually hooked close to such obstructions, this is not easy.

Big snapper are strong fish, and the first run will be a solid tearing rush as the fish feels the weight, panics, and heads for the nearest rock or ledge.

If you can keep the fish up near the surface, it increases your chances, but many fish are lost simply because of their strength and the terrain in which they are found. This is one situation where the tackle is tested to the limit. If in doubt as to how much drag to use, err on the heavy side.

If a fish successfully snags the line, it can be felt rasping on the rocks or weed. There are only two options — either keep pulling (on the line, not the rod) in the hope it will come free before the line breaks, or give it slack line and hope the fish will swim out into the open. Be hard on the fish until it is close to the boat, then handle it more gently as the line is shorter and has less stretch. As with all fish, a sudden jerk will snap the line or pull the hook out. Steady pressure maintained by the rod will usually beat the fish, and when beside the boat it should be led by the rod, not the reel.

A big snapper should be gaffed or netted. If gaffing it, aim for the throat if it is to be killed, or the lower jaw if releasing it.

When using a net, wait till the fish is lying on the surface on its side, and slip the net under its body from the head end. A net with a long handle and a wide mouth is very useful in this situation, as there is nothing more frustrating than trying to manoeuvre a big fish into a small net. Never try to net a fish which is still swimming upright under the surface.

> Fish often lie on the upcurrent side of a reef or large rock, in the pressure wave created by the current striking the obstacle. To fish such a spot, anchor your boat well upcurrent so your lines drop back to the front of the reef. You can fine tune the boat's position by retrieving or putting out the anchor rope.

When using a net, wait till the fish is lying on the surface on its side, and slip the net under its body from the head end.

Deepwater snapper

While most big snapper are caught in shallow water over reefs, many good-sized fish can also be taken from deep water. It could be up to 100 metres deep, and similar baits are used, except they are rigged on heavier tackle with weights to reach the bottom. Either a ledger rig, or a short trace below a weight, can be used.

The reefs close to Mayor Island produce a lot of big snapper during winter. Experienced anglers use whole slimy mackerel, hooked through the head, and dropped to the bottom. The amount of weight varies with the current, but at least 15 kg tackle is needed.

Increasing numbers of big snapper are being caught through education of anglers, and the advent of techniques and tackle aimed specifically at these fish. They are rarely caught by accident on small baits intended for small fish.

There are few prizes in the sea more worthy than a magnificent red-and-silver mega-snapper weighing over 11.4 kg (25 lb). The magic mark of 14 kg (30 lb) is rarely exceeded.

> If fishing a workup with birds diving and feeding, don't drive through the middle of the school of fish. Work the edges, or behind the school.

The first snapper I saw taken on a jig was caught by accident. It was about 30 years ago and we were fishing off the mouth of the Rangitaiki River, where it flows into the Bay of Plenty at Thornton.

It is a very fishy area. The brown river water attracts huge numbers of kahawai, particularly in late summer, and again in spring when the whitebait run. These in turn draw other predators like sharks and kingfish.

It is easy to find school snapper on the sand out off the surf beaches that run all the way to Whakatane, and straylining big baits off the Tasman Reef or Rurima Rocks a few miles offshore will always yield big, strong snapper, kingfish and other species. The tarakihi ground is not far away either.

After towing the 5 m runabout from Rotorua, we launched at the ramp inside the bar and headed out to spin or troll off the river mouth with tobys for the tough kahawai that haunt the breakers.

On this day I had a friend from the USA fishing with me and we were having fun tangling with big 3 to 4 kg kahawai on 4 kg spinning outfits. It was just a question of tossing the silver toby out, letting it sink down about a metre, then retrieving steadily.

I cast out then laid down my rod to net a fish for my companion, when my rod suddenly started jerking and bobbing. I grabbed it and struck what was obviously a powerful fish. It tore line from the reel and we had to follow it in the boat for nearly 20 minutes before a large silver shape gleamed in the brown water. A magnificent snapper surfaced, totally exhausted after a long fight on the light gear, the small toby dangling brightly from the corner of its jaw.

That snapper weighed 9 kg, and when cleaned was found to be packed with baby flounder, all around 10 cm long. It does not take much imagination to visualise the toby lure drifting down to the bottom and kicking up a puff of sand as it settled, perfectly simulating the action of a startled baby flounder in front of the prowling snapper. Today, snapper are caught routinely on jigs designed to simulate just that action.

The next encounter with jigs came when fishing with Rick Pollock on his first charter launch, *Toa Tai*, near White Island in the late 1970s. Rick learnt his fishing in the competitive world of charter fishing out of San Diego in southern California, and the Bay of Plenty was like virgin water to someone of his experience.

Big, flashy diamond jigs were commonly used in California, particularly to lure small kingfish —

SMALL BOAT FISHING

Big kingfish tactics

Kingfish are much faster-growing than snapper, and research indicates their life span is 15 to 20 years. Areas renowned for giant kings all have one common denominator — they have schoolfish like kahawai, maomao, mackerel or trevally living in the vicinity of a reef.

Lures and baits

While trolled lures, jigs and surface poppers account for many kingfish, there is no doubt that the really big fish are taken on live baits. Lures trolled around reefs or schools of fish, or outside the breakers on a surf beach will often take kingfish. When the kingfish are seen splashing and feeding on the surface they will take tuna lures such as purple squid imitations. They like fast-moving lures and will be attracted to poppers which sputter and splash across the surface like a fleeing baitfish.

This is an exciting way to fish, as it is very visual. The kings can be seen chasing the lure, and the sight of a massive green head and shoulders emerging to engulf it is one which anglers dream about. When casting

Lures have more movement if attached with a split ring and a loop knot (Fig. 36).

Fig. 36

I had a friend from the USA fishing with me and we were having fun tangling with big 3 to 4 kg kahawai on 4 kg spinning outfits.

small by New Zealand standards. A 15 kg fish there is a trophy, while at White Island it does not rate a mention.

Visiting American anglers brought boxes of jigs to Whakatane, and showed local fishermen how to use them. It soon caught on. But speed-jigging for kings is vastly different from bottom-jigging for snapper. Kings will ignore any jig that is not zipping past them at high speed. The technique is to drop the lure to the bottom, give it one huge heave to attract the attention of any fish in the neighbourhood, then wind as fast as possible, preferably using a reel with at least a 6:1 gear ratio.

Surface lures for casting like poppers have different head shapes designed to throw up spray and provide an erratic action, while the mackerel mauler style (upper) wobbles furiously under the surface when trolled.

New Zealand anglers are fortunate in having some of the best yellowtail kingfish in the world readily available in most parts of the country.

poppers a high-speed retrieve helps, holding the rod high for the retrieve and lowering it as the lure nears the boat. Kingfish will be found around channel markers in harbours and estuaries, where the best fishing is at slack water in the early morning when they rise to the surface. These fish can be hooked on poppers or a live bait, or sometimes a whole pilchard or piper will do the trick.

Dead baits will catch some kings, but the big fish will rarely show any interest. The baits must be moving continuously and are cast out, allowed to settle, then slowly wound in. The bait is rigged with a hook through the head from underneath. Sometimes a small ball sinker added above the head will be needed to give weight for casting, and to help it sink. To make such a bait more appealing, slashes can be made in the flanks to release blood and juices, and if the backbone is broken in a couple of places it will be more flexible. But compared to livebaiting, this is very much a last resort.

High-speed jigging is another method of lure-fishing for kingfish. The jig is dropped to the bottom, jerked upward to attract the attention of the fish, and then wound back to the surface as fast as possible. Special jig

SMALL BOAT FISHING

A quick rig for a whole dead piper. The hook goes through the skull from under the jaw. The spring from inside a ballpoint pen on the trace slides over the piper's beak, and a small lead ball adds weight. Good for kingfish, this bait must be moving — either trolled slowly, or cast and retrieved.

rods and reels geared for a fast retrieve are available, and while this can be productive it is a tiring method of fishing. Again, smaller fish will be hooked.

Live bait

The really big fish are caught on live baits, and the tackle will be no less than 15 kg if fishing in open water, and 24 kg stand-up gear around reefs and in shallow water.

The all-tackle world record kingfish of 52 kg (114 lb) was caught on 15 kg tackle by a Tauranga angler, Dr Mike Godfrey, while fishing live baits next to a school of kahawai. He landed one kingfish of about 35 kg, and then hooked the monster, which he was able to successfully land on such light line because he was fishing out over the open sand and there were no obstructions the fish could head for. Both of the huge kings took big kahawai, caught from the school of feeding fish and immediately returned to the water as a live bait. Even though there were hundreds, possibly thousands of kahawai in the vicinity, the predators were attracted to the baits because they behaved differently.

Mike just lowered his baits over the side, but in most situations the live bait should be fished under a balloon, well away from the boat to prevent the line tangling with other lines or the propeller — see Fig. 37. A live bait will try and swim under the boat for security, and so has to be kept away with a float, like a plastic bottle or balloon. The balloon is attached to the top eye of the swivel at the top of the trace with cotton or dental floss, so it will break off when a fish is hooked.

The bait is hooked through the back, just in front of the dorsal fin, with a game hook matched to the size of the bait. An 8/0 or 9/0 hook can be used on big baits like 3 or 4 kg kahawai; smaller kahawai or mackerel require hooks like a 5/0 or 6/0. Some people paint their hooks black or use black hooks which are less visible.

The length of trace varies depending on the depth at which the bait is fished. Normally about a metre of 50 or 80 kg mono is sufficient, but if you want to get the bait down deeper, a longer trace can be used. Alternatively, the balloon can be attached with a sliding knot or special plastic clip, allowing the line to slide through it. In this case the bait is hooked through the skin of the back just ahead of the tail. Hooked in this manner, the live bait will continue to swim downward. Another way of controlling the direction in which the bait swims is to cut off one lobe of

Fig. 37

the tail. If the upper lobe is removed, the bait will stay on the surface; if the lower lobe is cut off, it will swim down.

Kingfish swallow the bait head first, so the hook must be able to be pulled free of the bait when you strike. If hooked too deeply into the bait, the hook will be less effective, and it will injure the bait, reducing its swimming ability.

When pulled down to lie along the back of the baitfish, the hook should point upward. If it points down into the fish, it should be inserted from the other side.

A static bait will not catch big fish. If the bait is tiring and a kingfish appears but does not take it, replace the bait with a fresh one and it may do the trick.

Many big kingfish are also caught in deep water, by drifting the bait over a reef or pinnacle. The fish will congregate over such a structure, with smaller fish on the top level and big fish below. The bait has to be dropped through the small fish to reach the big ones, and a big bait is more likely to survive the trip.

While a live bait is always preferable, in this situation large fish will also take a dead bait if presented properly. The White Island rig of a swivel connecting a strong trace of about a metre with a 6/0 or 7/0 game hook at the bottom works well here. The ball sinker or sinkers, usually about 120 g, are either above the swivel or are suspended halfway down the trace, resting against a blood knot which has been created by cutting and retying the trace. The bait is usually hooked through the nose, or it can be hooked through the back.

The technique is to ensure the boat drifts over the spot to be fished, which is the skipper's responsibility. The advent of electronics like GPS and depth sounders makes this far more precise than in the past. The baits are lowered until they hit the bottom, then the reel is put in gear and the bait wound up for about five turns of the handle to keep it above the bottom. Then the reel is put out of gear again, and the angler fishes with the thumb pressed on the spool to hold it, while the boat drifts. The strike is usually a slow pressure increasing on the line, and a little line is run out to give the fish time to swallow the bait. Then it is locked in gear and the rod raised to strike it several times, winding between strikes, until the fish feels firmly hooked.

This deepwater fishing is similar to hapuku fishing, and in fact both species will be caught by this technique on the same reefs.

Stand-up game tackle of 24 kg is ideal, and should be fished with a rod bucket and a kidney harness.

Live baits can be caught by trolling small lures or flies, or casting and retrieving small jigs. If proving hard to catch, small fish may be found by allowing a jig to sink and retrieving it slowly in a jerky fashion. Like all fishing, you should vary the technique till the right formula is found. Live baits can be kept in a purpose-made tank all day, allowing the anglers to fish different areas. If a boat does not have a livebait tank, a simple arrangement with a bucket and small aerator pump will suffice; otherwise the fishing will be restricted to the area where the bait can be caught.

Live baits can be hooked in various ways so they swim unnaturally, increasing flash and vibration, and attracting the attention of predators. These may be small baits like piper or mackerel for kingfish, or kahawai and small tuna for bigger gamefish. Also, if one lobe of the bait's tail is cut off, it will swim erratically, heading down if the lower lobe is removed and up to the surface if the upper lobe is cut.

Top: Quick hook rig, up behind the lips, for casting or slow trolling.

Left: Standard position for drifting a kahawai for large kingfish or marlin which will swallow it head first. Often fished under a float.

Bait will stay on surface and swim away from you.

Bait will swim downward away from you.

When targeting big kingfish, big baits should be used — koheru, kahawai, slimy mackerel or flyingfish are prime baits. Big piper work well, but are more difficult to find.

Live baits can also be trolled slowly and are very effective on big kings. The bait is hooked through the nose or eyes, on a short trace with a sinker above the swivel, and the rig towed at about two knots.

The fight

The kingfish is one of the toughest fish that swims, but it is a dogged, dour fight, not spectacular like a marlin. The fisherman earns every inch of line gained, and if there are any underwater obstacles like mooring lines, weed beds or rocks, the kings will head for them faster than a big snapper. If the angler cannot stop the fish reaching such obstacles, the fight will be lost. But if in clear water, or once the fish has been lifted from the bottom, the tables are reversed and the angler can work the fish gradually to the boat.

A hooked kingfish can also be led out into open water by moving the boat slowly without putting any pressure on the fish and encouraging it to swim in the desired direction.

The artist responsible for many of the illustrations in this book, John Morgan, is a keen angler and his work reflects this interest. He loves fishing for kingfish with 10 kg gear or lighter, and likes to use 3 kg kahawai as live baits for big kingfish.

"Nine times out of ten you can lead them to clear water. We wait until we have clear sand on the sounder before striking. Sometimes it takes five minutes just going slowly and they hang on to the bait. The hardest part is resisting the urge to strike, but you have no chance at all if you hook them close to the rocks," he says. John has landed kingfish over 30 kg on 10 kg line, and takes some big fish on 6 kg gear.

Many kingfish are tagged and released, and such fish should be gaffed through the lip where they can be controlled, and released unharmed. Preferably, the fish should not be boated, but the tag placed and the hook removed with pliers.

If boating a big kingfish, gaff it in or near the head, so its explosive response will help direct it upward. The gaff-man can use the power of the fish to his advantage, and it will literally 'swim' into the boat. If gaffed in the middle of the body or near the tail, the reverse happens and it can be dangerous dealing with a big, powerful fish.

Small fish can be lifted into the boat by grasping the trace (not the line), or netted like a snapper.

Large powerful fish like trophy snapper and kingfish will exploit any weakness in the tackle. All elements should be of the best quality available — line, swivels, hooks and trace material. You will not often be connected to such fish, so you want everything going for you when you are hooked up.

Fishing the deepwater reef

When the weather and sea conditions are favourable, fishermen can venture offshore in search of large bottom-dwelling species like hapuku

Little things like changing the terminal rig can make all the difference. A group of Auckland fishermen were having difficulty finding snapper, and after trying several spots they decided to have a last attempt on the reef inside the Rangitoto lighthouse. They had been fishing in the Rakino Channel, with the standard running sinker rig — a ball sinker above a swivel, with a 1 m trace below the swivel. This is a popular rig for fishing channels where the current is running strongly, and the only variations are in the weight of sinker and length of trace. The deeper the water and faster the current, the heavier the sinker should be, and consequently the stronger the line used. Balancing the line strength with the weight used is also important.

But the running rig proved unsuccessful in the shallow water over the reef, in spite of a good trail of smelly berley which soon attracted small fish to the back of the boat. They switched to a simple rig with a small ball sinker sliding directly onto the hook (Fig. 34), and immediately started catching snapper. That change was all that was needed. Unfortunately all but four of the snapper were undersized, but they were carefully released after being held in a wet cloth while the hooks were removed.

On another evening just off Takapuna, a similar change ensured fish were hooked. Fishing started at low tide and small snapper were eager to grab the bait. So baits were changed from pilchards, which were sucked off the hook immediately, to tougher pieces of squid. But as the tide started running and the current quickened, the bites slowed. More line was put out but the increasing distance and angle made hooking the fish a problem.

The solution was simple, and obvious to many experienced fishermen. The sinkers were changed to heavier balls, and the bites increased. But as the current ran strongly it became too hard to keep the baits on the bottom without resorting to big, unwieldy weights. Time to go home.

Another example of changing the terminal rig to fit the conditions illustrates the importance of keeping an open mind and being prepared to try something different. On this occasion the scene was again that most popular of spots for Auckland snapper fishermen, the Motuihe Channel. It coincided with the largest tides for seven years, so the current running at half tide was really fierce.

A 2 m trace below a solid sinker worked fine until the tide flow lifted the sinker up off the bottom. The problem here is that a thinner line will reduce the drag against the current, but cannot be used in conjunction with a heavy sinker. So the line weight is increased from 10 to 15 kg, and a much heavier ball sinker added. This held on the bottom, but the 2 m trace was lifted by the current and the bites stopped because the bait was lying above the snapper.

The solution: a small sinker added to the trace, sliding down against the hooks. Immediately this rig was dropped, the bites started again.

Later, as the tide flow eased, the lower sinker could be removed and the main sinker reduced in size. At dead low tide, the 10 kg line with just a small sinker was employed again, and the catch rate increased. There is no doubt that the fishing will be more effective with lighter line and a minimum of weight — the angler has much more sensitive 'feel', and so can react to the bites and hook the fish more efficiently.

(groper), bass, bluenose, warehou, big tarakihi, trumpeter, and other fish found on deepwater reefs.

These reefs or pinnacles can be located by landmarks, with the help of a depth sounder, or by looking for other boats. In some areas such spots will be easily identified by the floats of commercial crayfish pots bobbing on the surface.

Straylining or jigging rods don't have a place in this type of fishing. The weight of the terminal tackle and size of fish encountered demand heavier tackle. A minimum requirement is a 4/0 sized overhead reel holding 500 m of at least 15 kg line, preferably 20 or 24 kg line. Rods are bal-

It's difficult getting berley to the bottom in very deep water, but small quantities can be delivered next to the bait by adding a film canister to the line above the swivel. The line runs through holes drilled in each end, and further holes in the sides will release the fish attractant. This can be a piece of kitchen sponge soaked in fish oil, or mashed berley. In shallow water, a small ball sinker can be slid down the line into the canister, keeping the terminal tackle tidy. However, in deep water the sinker needed to sink the rig will be too large to fit in it.

anced to the weight of line and are ideally short, with a fast taper. Long rods give a decided leverage advantage to the fish. Stand-up game rods for 15 or 24 kg tackle are well suited to deepwater bottom fishing — the ideal length and plenty of lifting power.

The rig used is a basic ledger rig (Fig. 38) with one, two or three hooks on droppers and a heavy sinker at the bottom. The trace matches the conditions, and the size of fish sought, and will be 50 to 80 kg mono, with tuna circle or recurve (longline) hooks. With the depth of water being fished, the mono line will stretch a further 20%, making it difficult to set the hook. The tuna circle style of hook will pull into the corner of the fish's mouth as it swims away with the bait.

Experienced fishermen have their favourite hapuku 'holes' — which may actually be pinnacles rather than holes — and they try and drop their baits right on the very spot. This requires precise anchoring in deep water, which is never easy. Another technique is to drift over the reef or pinnacle, e.g. when fishing live baits for kingfish. Even with modern aids like GPS, hapuku fishermen often rely on marks on shore to locate fishing spots (Fig. 39). The baits should be dropped well up-wind or up-current from the fishing spot, so that by the time they reach the bottom the boat has drifted into position.

Bites are difficult to detect and are usually signalled by a slow tightening of the line. The fish really has to hook itself, but as the line tightens, pump the rod and wind the reel, as many as 20 times. If the weight remains and moves it will be a fish, but if it cannot be moved, either it is a snag or a big fish like a bass has taken the bait and retreated into its hole. Such a fish can be almost impossible to shift, but sometimes giving it plenty of slack line will cause the fish to swim free, or free the line from a snag. Otherwise it has to be broken off. Wrap the line several times around a cloth held in the hand to break it, or secure the line to a cleat on the boat and motor away slowly.

Deepwater fishing is very much fishing the unknown, as until the fish hits the surface it is nearly impossible to tell what has been hooked. If the line starts to angle out and become lighter as the fish nears the surface, it

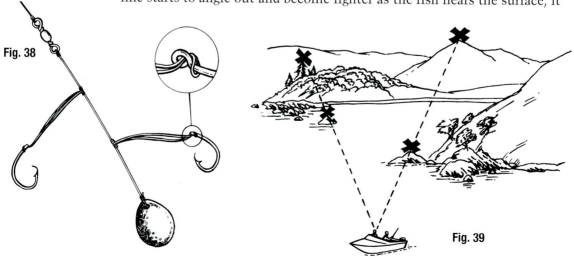

Fig. 38

Fig. 39

will be a hapuku or bass, as the swim bladders of these fish expand as the pressure changes, and they float to the top. Bluenose usually fight all the way, as do gemfish, hake and trumpeter.

Tarakihi are often found in such places, and can be caught by adding a short length of 10 kg mono to the top eye of the swivel holding the trace, with a 1/0 hook baited with a pipi or cube of flesh. In this way, a tarakihi may accompany a big hapuku to the surface on the same rig.

Common baits like bonito and pilchards are not suited for this style of fishing. Pilchards are too small, and bonito is too soft and can be stripped without the angler knowing. Fresh bonito is good if it can be obtained, but otherwise whole fillets or strips off a kahawai which has been scaled, or large chunks or strips from a barracouta are good baits. The shiny skin of a barracouta attracts fish, and it is tough and stays on the hook.

Strip baits are better than chunks, and can be hooked just once through one end. If the bait is threaded onto the hook it can clog up the gap and reduce its effectiveness. Other top baits are whole mackerel or flyingfish, hooked through the nose or through the back. Dead or alive, they catch fish.

This type of fishing is often done at slack tide, simply because it is much easier getting the bait to the bottom when there is no current.

Bay of Islands charter skipper Dave Morgan used a set line to catch this nice hapuku off Cape Brett.

Fishing droplines

Another technique for catching hapuku is to set lines on the spot, then return an hour or two later and haul them up. It is always a thrill when a thump signals a hooked fish as the line is retrieved.

Braided synthetic lines like kuralon make good main lines, with a sash weight or similar heavy anchor at the bottom. Tuna circle hooks are used on short side traces of monofilament, or on cord coated with tar to keep it rigid and sticking out at right angles from the mainline. This kind of rig is called a dropline.

Droplines are easily lost in strong currents if sufficient slack line is not allowed at the surface. The lifting power of waves will bounce the sinker off the reef, and the whole rig will be lost.

A small float, like a crayfish pot float, should be attached on the surface, followed by at least 10 metres of line before a large float like a small plastic container. The small float may be pulled under, but a big one is easier to spot, particularly if it has been sprayed with fluorescent paint.

Saltwater fly fishing

Trevor Clarke used to drive a charter boat for a living, taking visitors fishing on the famous waters of the Bay of Islands. On his days off, he went fishing.

He grew up in Southland, with a fly rod in his hand most of the time, and moved to Paihia to get into the tourist fishing business.

It was Trevor's trout fishing experience that helped him to a unique record in July 1994. He was fishing for snapper one day, anchored off Tapeka Point. The water was clearing after a fierce storm, and the snapper

The kahawai is a lightweight acrobat that offers fine sport on trout tackle. They readily take a fly and can be found in most waters.

were hungry. It was one of those dream fishing days — and Trevor was all by himself.

"The snapper were right up in the berley trail and I could just see the odd one near the surface. There were some big ones there.

"I had always wanted to catch a snapper on a fly rod, and I had my rod with me — but I didn't know what fly to use. So I put on a bug-eye nymph and cast it out, and a fish grabbed it," he said.

The snapper put up a tremendous battle on the light trout rod, and it took Trevor one and a half hours to subdue it because the tippet, the lightest part of his leader, was only 3 kg breaking strain.

He managed to bring it to the boat and net it, and was surprised and thrilled at its size.

Back at the wharf, the snapper was officially weighed by the Bay of Islands Swordfish Club at 7.27 kg, and was later ratified as a New Zealand record fly rod catch.

At that stage snapper had only been internationally recognised as game fish for two years by the International Game Fish Association (IGFA), the organisation which administers fresh and saltwater records. The saltwater fly rod sections for different line categories for snapper were vacant, and Trevor's catch would automatically have been a world record if he had had a second person in the boat to act as a witness as required under international rules. But because he was alone, it qualified only as a national record in the 4 kg line class.

Since then many world and New Zealand records for saltwater species caught on fly tackle have been set as more people take up what is one of the most challenging and thrilling methods of fishing.

We have chased small species like kahawai and trevally with fly tackle for more than 30 years, but I first encountered serious saltwater fly fishing when world champion Billy Pate visited to try for world records on mako sharks. He is the only angler to have caught all species of marlin on

Heavy duty saltwater fly tackle for gamefish: 12-weight graphite rods and Billy Pate reels with colourful flies tied on long-shanked hooks.

a fly rod — white, blue, black and striped marlin, and still holds the record for the prestigious tarpon on fly.

He set several records on that trip, and his exploits featured in some of the videos later produced.

Few people aspire to world records on the great game fish with a fly rod — it is simply too hard. However, for sheer fun on the water a fly outfit offers huge potential. Just about all species of fish will take a fly in some form, suggesting a propensity for eating anything put in front of them that belies the challenge so many fish pose to the fisherman. The biggest factor is actually getting the fly in front of the fish. It is obviously going to be impossible to target deepwater species like hapuku, but if fish can be lured within range by the use of berley then you will catch everything from snapper and kahawai to maomao and reef dwellers. You may also hook formidable opponents like kingfish, but without heavy duty fly tackle you have little chance of stopping them.

The serious saltwater fly fisherman will have a 12-weight Composite Developments rod with double grips and plenty of butt strength, coupled with an all-aluminium American reel designed to handle the searing runs of big fish and the creeping corrosion of seawater. His leaders will be tapered with a heavy shock tippet next to a section of test weight line for records.

But you can also use your trout rod to test this style of fishing, and when you hook a speedster like a kahawai you will wonder why you waited so long to try it. A Japanese friend and expert trout angler once remarked that "compared to trout, sea fish have no delicacy." He is right. But compared to all saltwater species, trout of similar size have little strength. The trout offers a completely different challenge, but sea fish are spectacular when hooked on a fly rod. There is no subtlety at all — voracious strikes and bruising runs. Cheap trout reels are not designed to handle the heat and pressure created by the blistering runs of ocean speedsters

> When catching fish which are to be returned unharmed, grasping the fish with a wet towel holds them firmly and also is less damaging to the fish. If held upside down, the fish will not usually struggle.

> One tough, attractive bait which is used on kite-fishing longlines is also useful where small 'pickers' are a problem. Cut mullet into strips, and soak in a mixture made by mashing a can of sardines and a can of asparagus in an ice-cream container. Canned asparagus was used in sailing ships' emergency kits for attracting fish, and contains a chemical which fish seem to like. Such bait will keep for weeks in a fridge.

and you may well ruin a reel if you hook into a tuna or kingfish. But that is a challenge you can aim at, and you can start modestly on smaller, common species like kahawai. In fact kahawai could have been invented solely for saltwater fly fishing. They can be found close to the surface and at river mouths, and will eagerly take a fly. They jump like a trout, but pull twice as strongly.

Look after your tackle after a day at sea, carefully washing everything including your line, and treating metal parts with Tackle Guard.

Speed of presentation is important when casting a fly to fast-moving species on the surface like kahawai, trevally or small tuna, and a shooting head which can be pitched with only one false cast is better suited than a full tapered fly line. A sinking line will penetrate the waves quicker, and a short, strong trace is easier to use than a long one.

Flies should imitate the prey — a Grey Ghost is a favourite for kahawai, cast out and stripped quickly; while a pink nymph will do the trick when fish are feeding on krill. When drifting flies down a berley trail, a blob of white and pink marabou which simulates a piece of berley may produce better than a fish imitation. Vary the size of fly before worrying about any other factor.

Special saltwater flies can be purchased. These are magnificent coloured streamers with stainless steel hooks (which need regular sharpening), and will hook most pelagics if the correct size is used. I have found a cheap smelt fly like a Grey Ghost in size 6 or 4 to be just as effective, and we throw them away at the end of the day after they have been chewed and well salted. If targeting big fish like kingfish, a piper or sprat imitation is certainly an advantage.

A clear area of deck where shooting line can be spread prior to casting will make your fishing more enjoyable, and some boats have canvas windbreaks around the bow for this purpose. The skills of the boat driver in reading the movement of school fish feeding on the surface and his ability to place the angler within casting range are also important.

Tips for big fish bait

When people are targeting big snapper, the question is often raised — what is the best bait to use? The most common baits are bonito, or more correctly skipjack tuna, and pilchards because they are so readily available. They work, too, but are soft in texture because they have been frozen out of necessity.

There are many tricks to overcoming the problem of soft baits being stripped by small fish. Some people salt the bait to preserve and toughen it, and this certainly helps. Give the bait a good coating of sea salt or rock salt. Tuna should be filleted, and the fillets opened down the centre and salt rubbed in. The liquid which is drawn off must be drained regularly. Pilchards or strips of bonito can also be secured with cotton wound along the length of the bait, or even fuse wire or rubber bands wrapped around it to keep it on the hook.

But the best solution is to obtain fresh bait. Big snapper love to eat fish

> Crabs can be a nuisance, stripping the bait. One solution is to add a small piece of cork or polystyrene to the trace above the bait. This will float it up off the bottom, away from the crabs.

which are found in the area where they live, but they probably have few opportunities to catch healthy bait fish. So the enterprising angler can solve the snapper's problem, and his own, by catching fresh bait and offering it with a hook or two hidden in the body. It may be a piper, a mackerel or a sprat. These all work well, and many would argue that a freshly killed slimy mackerel is the most effective bait of all. It is much better than the common jack mackerel, or yellowtail. Piper is also good and can be presented either whole, or cut into sections. If the beak is snapped off, the piper will not revolve in the water when moved gently in the current, and the head can be secured to the trace with a short section of soft wire like fuse wire.

Sprats, or yellow-eyed mullet as they are known to scientists, are another good bait, and one which will keep well even when frozen. Large specimens should be used, and they are so tough that the little 'pickers' will not spoil the bait. These can be rigged like any whole fish, either with a single hook through the head, or the more common double-hook rig with one at each end of the fish. The popular rig will have a hook protruding from each side, or the hooks can be simply pushed through the body with the shanks lying alongside the flanks. The bait will be more attractive if the stomach is well punctured, either with a knife or with the hooks, so that the body juices can leak out and send a signal to the roving snapper.

This type of bait is well suited for fishing from the rocks where there is a rocky, weed-covered bottom. The bait has enough weight to cast without an additional sinker. When boat fishing, a line baited with a sprat can be left out while smaller fish are caught with a second outfit using pilchards or bonito, and this activity will help attract the occasional big one. Large quantities of berley will attract fish of all sizes, which will make the big snapper more likely to approach the area.

Bill Penney is happy with the 7.3 kg Hauraki Gulf snapper which took a lightly weighted whole pilchard.

Sail Rock rises straight up out of 30 metres of water, a steep pinnacle that must resemble a sail to some sailors when seen from a distance. But for anglers, it is a beacon that promises fish — big kingfish, snapper and occasionally unwanted species like barracouta. The rock is only a few kilometres from the Hen and Chickens Islands, about 30 minutes' travelling in a runabout from the beach at Waipu. The whole area is rich in fish, and is well known for the schools of snapper which congregate there, either to feed or to spawn.

When we arrived at Sail Rock, Rodney Carter deftly threaded a pilchard onto two hooks and slowly let it down to the bottom 40 metres away. A successful charter skipper, Rodney launches his boat from the beach at Lang Cove, near Waipu, and fishes around the islands on most days. He has developed two techniques which produce large numbers of snapper — he drifts over the reefs and keeps moving around until he finds fish, and he fishes whole pilchards which are also kept moving up and down.

Like all successful fishing, local knowledge and knowing where to locate fish are the key ingredients. Rodney moves from one small patch of foul bottom to another, fishing around Sail Rock and the main Hen Island.

He ties a loop on the end of his trace, which is just shorter than the body length of a pilchard. One hook slides freely above the knot and the other is looped on the end — a very simple rig. The top hook goes through the head of the pilchard, from under the jaw and out through the skull, and this one takes the weight of the baitfish. It can swing on this hook, and also swims straight through the water when retrieved, which is very important with the style of presentation used. The bottom hook is reversed through the flesh below the tail, and a small ball sinker resting above the pilchard completes the rig.

"I use a small sinker so that the bait sinks slowly as it is fed out. This is important, because the snapper may be in mid-water, or 7 metres above the bottom. When it hits the bottom I let it drag for a bit then wind it up slowly. This way you are fishing all the way down and all the way up again. The person who does the most work like this will get the most fish," explained Rodney.

He does not wait for snapper to chew on the bait, but strikes as soon as he feels the fish, and it is usually a strong take. "They don't mess around when they take it."

Our first strike was a long, silver barracouta — not popular with most anglers. But Rodney was not concerned. "We often get snapper with them, so you have to put up with catching them," he said. The next fish took the pilchard with a strong run, and Rodney picked it as a snapper. The flashing silver and pink shape soon appeared and the gleaming fish was lifted over the side.

He can afford to be particular about which fish he takes home, and prefers to release the larger snapper, keeping the smaller ones for the pan. "They are much sweeter, dipped in flour and cooked quickly on each side."

The minimum legal limit is 27 cm long, but many anglers feel that 30 cm would be acceptable. The fillets off a 27 cm fish are small, and some flesh is wasted in the process of removing the fillets. Perhaps they would be better cooked as whole fish, after being scaled and cleaned.

But at the Hen and Chicken Islands it is not a problem which often arises. Most of the snapper landed are chunky fish of 3 kg or more, occasionally reaching the 10 kg mark — which for many anglers is only a dream.

CHAPTER SIX
GAMEFISHING

The strike is the essence of all fishing — and when that strike is an electric blue marlin crashing a lure it is the ultimate moment in sportfishing.

More and more New Zealand anglers are experiencing the heart-stopping thrill of a marlin strike from their own boats as they venture out onto the blue water in search of the great fish. Gamefishing from trailer boats is becoming more popular every summer, as people realise they can safely fish 20 or 30 kilometres from shore with as much chance of hooking a marlin as the big charter boats. In fact, in many ways small boats are more efficient for this type of fishing through their quicker speed and manoeuvrability. People also have better access to information and techniques as well as improved tackle.

The biggest single handicap is the lack of experience among the anglers and skippers. It is typical of the traditional Kiwi approach that most will just go out and do it, learning as they go from their own mistakes.

Another problem with gamefishing is that the opportunities to improve techniques are limited, simply because of the nature of the game — we do not get many strikes in the course of a day's fishing!

For many years, fishing for gamefish was the domain of the charter launches based at the traditional ports of Mayor Island, the Bay of Islands

> The tip ring on your favourite rod can be damaged by winding the swivel hard against it, as so often happens when not watching while winding in. A tap washer on the line above the swivel will protect the tip ring.

The majestic sight of a 364 kg blue marlin, the reward for patient hours spent trolling. Photo courtesy John Batterton.

Trolling for marlin and tuna off the west coast. Small boats venturing out to sea should carry full safety equipment and travel with other boats.

Boating sharks in small boats can be dangerous. It is better to get a rope around the head or tail and tow them.

and Whangaroa. It was regarded as a sport for the wealthy, and groups of keen fishermen would save to share a charter once a year.

But several factors have brought gamefishing within reach of anyone with access to a 5 m runabout. They include the development of stand-up fishing tackle, a huge upsurge in the popularity of lure fishing, and advances in marine navigational and safety electronics and equipment, with EPIRBs, GPS, temperature indicators and depth sounders available at reasonable prices

Other factors are improved design and reliability in trailer boats in the 5 to 8 m range, increasing numbers of gamefish in our waters, and the discovery of new fishing grounds off the west coast.

In the days of Zane Grey, in the late 1920s, catches of 100 gamefish in a season by one boat were legendary. After decades of declining catches, the mid-90s saw increasing numbers of fish, particularly marlin, returning to our waters, for a number of reasons. Firstly, the proliferation of tropical visitors like mahimahi and spearfish, which were unheard of a generation ago, is an indication of rising water temperatures. Every summer the fish follow the warm currents which carry the food down from the north via the East Auckland Current. Secondly, the steady increase in the practice

The development of short-stroke, stand-up rods has brought gamefishing within the reach of anglers in trailer boats.

Left: The sharkcat is well suited to offshore gamefishing — roomy and stable, it has two motors with separate electrical systems for safety.

> A fisherman won a tournament by tagging seven striped marlin out of eight strikes, by doing things a little differently. Chris Hawthorne used the following system:
> - Light 3.3 m leaders of 113 kg (250 lb) mono on lumo sprockets and purple beer barrels.
> - Needle-point sharpened stainless 11/0 hooks with cut down barbs, with two hooks set in line with each other.
> - No taglines and very light release clips on the outriggers.
> - Drag set at 6 kg with no change throughout the fight.
> - Trolling speed of 8.5 knots.
> - Once baitfish were found he stayed in the area.

of tagging and releasing gamefish must also have a beneficial effect. In an average season three-quarters of all gamefish caught are tagged and released.

Thirdly, in 1994 no licences were issued to foreign longliners in the 200-mile zone. Since the moratorium on commercial marlin fishing, which was mainly by foreign longliners, was introduced in 1987, licences have been issued only outside the closed period of 1 November to 1 July. These are for tuna longline fishing, but the larger marlin are probably attracted by the hooked tuna and are then caught as a bycatch in large numbers. The fact that there were no longline vessels working our northern waters was a clear indication that the marlin could migrate unhindered.

In the 1995 and 1996 seasons marlin appeared early, before Christmas, and were still being caught in June at the Three Kings, the last area where they are found every season. As well as larger numbers of fish, there were more big marlin visiting our coast. The 1997 season started slowly but ended strongly.

The greatest marlin fishing season ever recorded in New Zealand waters was the 1995 season when 2,500 marlin were caught in Northland waters in the 12 months from 1 July 1994 to 30 June 1995, with the majority being hooked during mid-summer. In that season Bill Hall's famous boat *Te Ariki Nui* landed 75 marlin, tagging and releasing all but two which had died.

The previous season saw the Bay of Islands Swordfish Club record its best season since records were started in 1924 — a total of 1,081 gamefish, including 472 marlin.

For the season ended 30 June 1995, the club recorded more than 1,600 gamefish, of which more than 640 were marlin. This was a spectacular increase, for in the comparable period in 1991, there were only 571 gamefish recorded, including 241 marlin. Other species caught include broadbill swordfish, mako, hammerhead, blue and thresher sharks, yellowfin tuna, mahimahi, kingfish, and short-billed spearfish.

Other clubs, like the Whangarei Deepsea Anglers' Club, based at Tutukaka, and the Whangaroa club have also had record seasons. A bonanza was also recorded further south in the Bay of Plenty, where traditionally more tuna and fewer marlin are caught. This also reflects the higher number of small boats fishing compared to large launches, and fishing methods are geared more towards tuna, with marlin often a welcome bycatch.

The Mercury Bay Ocean Sports Club recorded 458 gamefish including 97 marlin, 7 spearfish, 116 yellowfin tuna, 89 sharks and 27 kingfish. The Tauranga Game Fishing Club also experienced one of its best seasons for many years, with 105 marlin, 119 yellowfin tuna, 60 sharks, 128 kingfish (84 tagged), 4 mahimahi and 16 short-billed spearfish.

At Whakatane, anglers also experienced a good season, though not a record one for the Whakatane Big Game Fishing Club. However, the number of yellowfin caught was well up. The club used to record over 1,000 tuna in a season, but since 1989 when 900 tuna were caught the numbers have been disappointing. The 1995 season saw 38 marlin and 703 tuna

A striped marlin with the line wrapped round its tail drowns as it is drawn backward to the boat.

landed, including 152 caught by members in the last three hours of fishing on the last day of the annual national gamefishing contest at the end of February.

Charter captain Rick Pollock's boat landed 60 tuna in one day, and the club's season total of 688 gamefish tagged and released included 550 kingfish caught by anglers fishing on Pollock's boat.

That is why Whakatane is called 'the yellowtail capital of the world'.

The increasing popularity of small-boat gamefishing has seen fish like large mako sharks, marlin and tuna now being caught off the Hawkes Bay and Wairarapa coasts, and the potential for bluefin tuna, big sharks and even broadbill swordfish off the west coast of the South Island is exciting.

Tuna are caught commercially all along the west coast, and sport fishermen have been catching big tuna, albacore and sharks out of Milford Sound for many years. The southernmost gamefishing club, the Tautuku Club at Dunedin, records mainly sharks with some tuna every season.

The fast-growing west coast game fishery is restricted to trailer-boats because of the limited access, and conditions determine when anglers can

Knots are the biggest cause of breakoffs. Peter Pakula says you only need two knots — a uni knot and a plait.

THE COMPLETE NEW ZEALAND FISHERMAN

Right: Giant bluefin tuna like this 245 kg monster are one of the rarest trophies in New Zealand waters. Photo courtesy John Batterton.

Far right: Auckland fisherman 'Sock' O'Connell is happy with his 56 kg yellowfin tuna hooked off the Manukau Harbour in mid-summer. The west coast fishery is proving a rich resource for small boat anglers.

Mike Nola of Dargaville is a successful small-boat angler, catching many marlin off the Kaipara each summer. His recipe includes towing two witch doctors to attract fish (more important in a runabout with an outboard motor than a large launch), replacing the entire leader after each fish is caught, and he also re-rigs the hooks on the lure. He figures the next fish hooked could be the fish of a lifetime, so why take any risks?

get out to sea. It started at Raglan about 20 years ago during a local fishing contest. It was a beautiful day, and the sea was so calm that a couple of fishermen in a tinny decided to head out to sea, thinking it would raise a few eyebrows if they could come back with something really big. They put out a lure and headed off, returning in the afternoon with the first marlin to be landed there.

This got people excited, and keen fishermen like local farmer John Donald started exploring the offshore waters in 6 m aluminium boats designed to handle the conditions on the bar. They hooked and battled big sharks and marlin, learning by their mistakes. It was real pioneering stuff, and established the west coast as a fishery of enormous potential.

Fishermen started cautiously heading out to sea from other ports like New Plymouth and Kawhia, and crossed the notorious bars at the entrance to the Manukau and Kaipara Harbours. Others launched their trailer-boats in the surf at Muriwai and Piha, and Ninety Mile Beach.

The biggest concentration of marlin is found off the Kaipara Harbour, where the rich water spilling out of the country's largest harbour every six hours, and a deepwater offshore trench, attract the fish. An exciting new fishery was born, and it relied solely on small boats.

Using ocean currents to find gamefish

The movement of the gamefish is determined by currents and water temperatures carried by the major current flowing across the Tasman Sea at about 30 degrees latitude — the Tasman Front. When this current reaches New Zealand it splits, with a portion turning north and the rest attaching itself to the continental shelf and flowing south-east as the East Auckland Current. Little is known about west coast currents, but many fishermen believe that this current splits at the top of the North Island, with some water travelling down each coast.

They say that often one coast receives the larger proportion of the current — and the fish — as it fluctuates, perhaps moved by strong winds. But it certainly does vary from season to season.

In general terms the El Nino summers of 1990-95 had predominantly westerly air flows, with resulting good fishing on the east coast. Prolonged westerly conditions also made fishing the west coast impractical.

But the summers of 1996 and '97 saw the arrival of La Nina — the name given by world meteorologists to the opposite phenomenon, with an easterly flow across the southern Pacific Ocean. The moist northerly and easterly conditions resulted in boom seasons on the west coast, with large numbers of fish and favourable sea conditions. Conversely, game fishing was average on the east coast in '96, and poor in '97.

The East Auckland Current is always there but is stronger in spring and summer, bringing warm, almost tropical temperatures — the blue water currents which game fishermen seek. Research by NIWA shows that the current moves at speeds up to one knot, can be 65 kilometres wide and 2,000 metres deep. It may be in sight of land one week and 150 kilometres out to sea the next.

In late summer the current seems to spill over the continental shelf and move closer to the coast. NIWA has identified three permanent high pressure eddies — the North Cape Eddy, the East Cape Eddy and the Wairarapa Eddy (Fig. 40).

What is of interest to game fishermen is a sharp offshore turn which the current takes north-east of Great Barrier Island. The current then moves south through the Bay of Plenty, and the main flow turns north near East Cape while the remainder spills around the cape and flows south as the East Cape Current.

> Drag settings are all based on the speed of pulling down the scales against the drag. You can pull it too quickly. Solution — do it at two different speeds to check your drag setting.

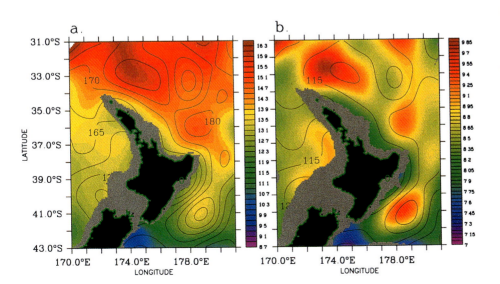

Fig. 40

The path of the edge of the East Auckland Current is shown on graph (a) as it flows down the east coast to East Cape. Temperatures up to 16.3 degrees were recorded at 200 metres under the surface. Graph (b) clearly shows the three major eddies which show up as hot spots at a depth of 600 metres where temperatures reach 9.85 degrees. Graphs courtesy of Phil Sutton, NIWA.

When spooling gamefishing reels, the line must be packed on tightly. If your tackle shop can't do it on a line-winding machine with the correct tension, it is a two-man job — one person in a game chair to wind the line on, and the other with gloves to put tension on the line. A gaff handle or similar spindle will provide a smooth tension and if gloved hands can not apply sufficient pressure, jam the edge of the spool against something. Braided dacron under mono line will provide a cushion to absorb pressure exerted by mono line reverting to its original shape after stretching, and will protect the spool. If the line is all dacron, it should be loaded wet so there is no air, and it will dry as hard as a rock and not bury into itself. This can be done by streaming the line out behind a slow-moving boat, and reeling it back on. No weight at the end is needed as water pressure provides enough tension. Whether loading dacron or mono line, the key is to wind it on evenly, one row at a time. Don't angle it across the face of the spool or it will jump around on the strike and could be damaged by sawing against the angled coils.

The well-known gamefishing grounds in Northland and the Bay of Plenty are on the edge of the East Auckland Current, which occasionally sweeps close to land all along the east coast from North Cape to Tutukaka. Regular hot spots where marlin congregate can be found over underwater canyons like the massive drop-offs 12 miles north of North Cape.

Prime fishing water is found along the edge of the continental shelf, and where islands intersect the currents, like the Cavallis and Poor Knights groups.

In the Bay of Plenty the current can be well offshore, but Mayor Island is perfectly placed to act as a base. At the eastern end of the bay the current runs between White Island and Whakatane, moving closer inshore towards Cape Runaway before swinging north off East Cape and out over the Ranfurly Banks — a rich fishing ground swept by powerful and turbulent currents.

The west coast has few features on the sea floor, which shelves gradually away from the coastline so anglers have to roam wide areas to find favourable currents and temperatures. There are some features like the Mokau Trench, 52 miles from Raglan, and the Kaipara Trench, which are favourite fishing areas.

Gamefishing is like hunting, and successful fishermen are continually watching for clues — changes in water colour and temperature, activity on the surface, birds circling or diving. Water of a deep indigo colour and high temperatures are the prime signals, as gamefish will be found from about 17 to over 23 degrees. Marlin and yellowfin tuna prefer warmer water, and are rarely encountered below 16 degrees. Albacore, bluefin tuna, and most sharks will tolerate cooler water, down to 13 degrees.

Current lines are one of the main indicators to look for. These are the 'highways' along which schools of pelagic fish travel, and are usually different temperatures and colours from the surrounding water. Currents will be marked by a line of foam or flotsam on the surface, a winding, narrow slick, or ruffled water where the wind is blowing against the current flow. A difference of even half a degree can act as a barrier to fish, and predators will herd baitfish against such barriers.

Surface activity such as school fish feeding and birds diving are obvious signs that school fish like tuna are likely to be found.

Some successful marlin fishermen prefer to follow solitary birds like petrels, or 'mutton ducks', and the tiny terns referred to as 'Jesus birds' because they appear to be walking on the water as they dip delicately to pick up minute organisms.

Tuna also accompany dolphins, as they share the same diet of pilchards, sauries and anchovies. The tuna spend more time at great depths, regularly rising to the surface in the early morning and late afternoon, but can be found at any time of day or night. Tuna fishermen will follow a pod of dolphins for hours hoping for tuna to rise.

Reefs, pinnacles rising from great depths, and offshore islands are all prime fishing areas; charts are useful for locating offshore canyons and

This kingfish took a plastic lure trolled on the surface at the Hen and Chicken Islands. The kingfish could be seen taking squid on the surface at the time so a lure was the obvious choice.

seamounts, where upwelling currents carry nutrients and plankton to the surface, attracting baitfish and predators.

Fishing a figure-eight pattern in a favourable area is far more effective than simply trolling aimlessly for miles across an apparently empty ocean.

Lure fishing

The lures

Fishing lures is not so much a question of the right or wrong way of doing things, but more a question of what works for you — there are differing opinions and personal preferences. By all means experiment a little, and talk to successful fishermen. Nothing gives confidence more than experience and time on the water. Other forms of trolling, such as towing bibbed lures for kingfish, or harling smelt flies for trout, involve slow speeds and long lines so the lures are working in the zone where fish resume normal behaviour after the boat has passed. Blue water trolling is the opposite; the boat and the water it disturbs are part of the system.

Today's lures employ modern resins and plastics, rubber and occasionally metal, and the head shape determines the way a lure moves through the water.

While lures may bring more strikes than baits, the hookup rate is much less. But fish are hooked in or near the mouth and can be released with less injury.

Skirted lures vary in materials, size, colour, design and optimum speeds; but the most important aspect is to have confidence in your lures and always use proven performers, perhaps combined with others being tested.

There is a big difference between fishing lures effectively and just towing them around the ocean. The variables include the lures used, how they are rigged, where the lures are set behind the boat, and the boat speed.

There is such an array of types, sizes and colours available that the choice of lure can be confusing. Ideally the lures should match the size and colour of baitfish in the area, but unless a fish is cut open you may not know what the preferred food is. The marlin or tuna may be feeding on 10 cm needlefish or sauries, or 15 cm koheru, squid, small pufferfish, or 30 cm mullet.

Terrified baitfish leaping out of the water as they are chased can provide a clue. The answer is to use a variety of sizes and colours — but use the same type of lure.

Many newcomers believe you must have big lures to catch big fish like marlin. Not at all; in fact more and more charter skippers are successfully using small lures which may appear to be tuna lures, not those for marlin.

Peter Pakula maintains that straight-running lures are preferable to lures which duck and dive. "Marlin are messy feeders, and when they open their mouths to strike they lose sight of the lure so you don't want one which moves sideways at the critical time. You want to make it easy for the fish to eat it," he says. Makes sense.

The lures we use evolved from lures which originated in Hawaii —

The heavier and longer the leader used, the more you restrict the action of all trolling lures.

Using too large a hook impairs the action, while too small a hook results in fewer hookups.

hence the popular term konahead. The first lures were primitive affairs, with wooden heads and feather skirts. Today's lures employ modern resins and plastics, rubber and occasionally metal. Basically, a marlin or tuna lure has a hard resin or soft rubber head, and several layers of skirts made from brightly coloured rubber or PVA. That is where the variety starts.

The head shape determines the way a lure moves through the water, and it can be long or short, tapered or straight, with a face that is either flat, angled, concave or convex. The different styles are designed to perform best at different speeds, which is why they should not be mixed up too much.

Some have pointed metal heads for fast trolling, others may have holes to create a jet effect as bubbles stream through — but the best lures will have action.

Rigging lures

There are three methods of rigging lures — with knots, crimps or shackles, or a combination of these (Fig. 41).

Wire leaders are not recommended for lures unless you are being plagued by mako sharks — the only species of shark to regularly take lures — or intend fishing the tropics where some of the fish, like wahoo, have very sharp teeth. One option is to have a short length of wire, say 50 cm, which can be rigged through the lure and attached to the end of your leader. It's a lot of messing around, and the wire could put off a more desirable fish.

Use one of the brands of tough monofilament made specifically for leader material, e.g. High Seas. One rule of thumb is to use 180 to 200 kg test for marlin lures and 50 to100 kg test for tuna lures. If in doubt use heavier mono, as marlin will often hit the smaller tuna lures, but it must be able to fit through the hole in the lure head!

Hooks are either stainless steel or galvanised. Stainless hooks obviously are more resistant to saltwater, but are not actually true stainless steel and will rust if left immersed. Whichever hook is used, it should be straight, not offset, and forged for strength, with flattened sides. The southern tuna style, Mustad 7691S, in sizes 7/0 to 12/0 is popular. Hook size is balanced to the size of lure, with the lure head able to pass through the bend in the hook. If using one hook, go to one size larger — the bigger

> The optimum speed for lures varies from boat to boat.
>
> While lures may look great running on top or at the back of pressure waves, they catch more fish when run on the lower third of the front of a pressure wave.
>
> For best results, do not mix types of lures, rather mix sizes and colours.
>
> When running large and small lures together, run the larger more aggressive lures closer to the boat.

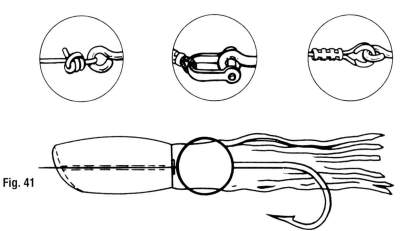

Fig. 41

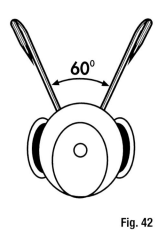

Fig. 42

hook rides free of the lure's skirt, and holds better.

Theories abound on how hooks should be sharpened. A few minutes with a vice and file can radically alter the point of a hook. Some professionals like to accentuate the cutting edge on the inside of the barb, giving it better penetration into the tough mouth lining or bill of a marlin. Another approach has the actual barb ground down, also to make penetration easier. Some Hamilton anglers who fish out of Raglan like to grind back the point on their hooks, saying that they achieve a better hook-up rate with the short points. Others maintain that the shortened points are wider in cross-section compared to the long, thin factory points, and require more force to sink them into the fish.

Then there is the argument that rounded points will hold better because they do not have the cutting edges which can enlarge the hole during a fight and increase the likelihood that the hook will drop out.

It is all a question of preference, but it is logical to have a system requiring the minimum pressure for the point to penetrate and to seat the barb.

Another subject which arouses strong debate is the single-hook versus double-hook rig. Some very successful marlin fishermen like Bill Hall prefer a single hook, which is tied to the leader rather than crimped. Yet logic would suggest that two hooks must be better than one.

With double-hook rigs the angle at which the hooks are set is also open to discussion. Pro anglers across the Tasman, like Peter Pakula and the late Malcolm Florence, contend that a 60-degree angle, with the hooks sitting upright, gives the best hookup rate. On this rig the hooks will also act as a rudder to prevent the lure from spinning. As Pakula points out, "A lure that is rigged incorrectly with two hooks is not as effective as the same one rigged with a single hook."

With two hooks, he recommends setting the hooks so that they ride in a balanced V formation, with both hook points riding upwards far enough apart to create two targets. The top of the lure is between the top of the V. This rig is particularly suited to flat-faced pushers and lures with offset leader holes (Fig. 42).

A two-hook rig attached by a metal shackle enables hooks to be switched easily, and reduces the number of hooks to be carried.

With a single hook, Pakula recommends rigging it on a loose loop so that it rides point up. A 'stiff' rig can cause the lure to spin, resulting in line twist.

To increase hookups, the hook should be placed well down the skirt, with most of it protruding out of the skirt's end. This also reduces the problem of the skirts tangling round the hook. Note the IGFA regulations relating to hook placement: part of the hook must be concealed inside the skirt.

There are many inventive anglers who are continually trying to make small improvements to their rigs. Nigel Wood in Rotorua has come up with an ingenious method of shrink-wrapping his hooks — double or single — on a heavy brass swivel so that the angles can be adjusted. The pressure of the wrapping holds the hooks in place.

Fig. 43

GAMEFISHING

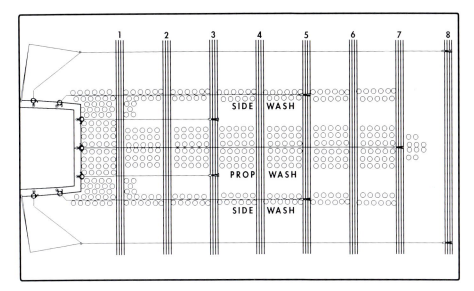

Fig. 44
Suggested lure positions in relation to the pressure waves. Lures on heavy tackle should be closest to the transom, and a short tag line on the transom will keep the line low and prevent the lures being pulled out of the water (see Fig. 45).

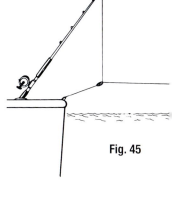

Fig. 45

Peter Pakula favours a diamond point with four razor edges formed by hard work with a file running back past the barb. He also cuts down the barb for easier penetration. I have used them all, and my favourite hook style is the one firmly fixed in the mouth of a big fish!

The other end of the leader has a crimped loop for attaching to the heavy swivel on your line, with either a flemish eye (Fig. 43) or preferably a loop protected by armour spring.

Some fishermen melt the tag end at the bottom of the crimp with a match to create a blob as an added precaution against the crimp slipping. But if the correct size of crimp is used and swaged correctly it should not slip, and a protruding tag end can catch the line.

Fishing lures

Before putting out lures, check the hooks are not tangled and the skirt hangs freely. Also check the leader, crimps and knots for any sign of abrasion or fatigue. Monofilament line which has been stressed through movement will turn a cloudy white colour. This is common at the base of a crimp, and it takes only a minute to replace any suspect links in the tackle.

There are various patterns than can be used for placement of lures, but factors to remember are as follows:

Keep the boat running straight while putting out the lures.

Set the longest lines first.

Put the drag up to the strike position and click the ratchet on before attending to the next one. Attach a safety line to each rod as it is set — a premature strike can happen. Rods have been pulled over the side with lures just dangling on the surface!

Set the lures so you can turn the boat without tangling the lines. The boat should always be turned towards the side with the shortest lines out.

Stagger the lures on the various pressure waves behind the boat (Figs. 44, 45 & 46). Don't spread them too much. If a fish rejects one lure it may go for another if it is close.

A single hook can be attached either with a uni knot or nail knot, or crimped. When tying a knot in heavy line, you will need pliers to tighten the tag end and ideally a vice to hold the hook.

Knots should be retied after each strike. It is a simple way of changing lures also, dispensing with the need for pliers and crimps. But you must be confident of your knots!

A pattern of Pakula lures which has proved successful at tournaments around the world. Extra lures can be added in the centre or in the long shotgun position, but maintain the same head shapes (Courtesy Peter Pakula).

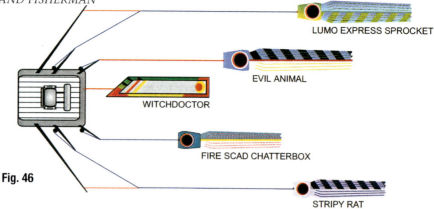

Fig. 46

Positioning is important. The lure should ride the lower part of the front of the pressure wave where it is visible, has more water to travel through, and is easily accessible.

Longer lines should be on the outside of the pattern, and shorter sets in the middle. The exception is a 'shotgun' — a long line running from a high rod in the centre of the rail on the flying-bridge or rocket launcher.

Lures can be set too far out. The longer the line, the more stretch it will have and the more difficult it will be to set the hook. The end of the prop wash is the maximum distance back to set lures. Fish will come right up to the boat.

You can run lures in the middle of the prop wash. Fish can see the silhouette from underneath.

Set the lures so they do not tangle. The number of lures is not an issue except when you want to excite tuna with as much action on the water as possible. What is more important is the number of people on board and the sea conditions — can you get the lines in quickly? One rod per angler is a good approach, but don't expect the skipper to help: he will be busy running the boat. The rougher the conditions, the fewer lures you can run safely and without tangles.

Each boat seems to have a sweet position where more strikes occur. Our favourite spot for yellowfin on my old 6 m Sharkcat was the port corner, with a large black and purple pusher run close to the boat — the swivel to the leader would not even be in the water. Such short lines need to be held low with a very short tag line.

Medium length lines can be run from the rod tip, while the longest lines are run from outriggers.

Once the lures are set they need to be tuned. When swimming correctly, a lure will wobble violently as it swims up to the surface, grab some air like a living creature, then dive again trailing a thick stream of bubbles for three or four seconds. This is called 'smoking'. If it runs under the water without a smoke trail it is said to be 'lazy'. If it comes right out of the water and skates, this is called 'blowing out'. Watch the lures and see how they are swimming. If some are blowing out, slow the boat until they stop. If they look lazy, speed up a little. The optimum speed is just slow enough to avoid blowing out, about 9 or 10 knots in calm seas, and down to 6 knots in rough conditions. If it is too rough to fish at 6 knots, it's time to go home.

The hole in the metal sleeve should match the diameter of the line as closely as possible, to reduce movement inside the sleeve. The first crimp is made slightly up from the end of the sleeve, to produce a slight flare at the end. Then the sleeve is rotated 180 degrees for the middle crimp, and rotated again for the last crimp, again leaving a small flare at the end. The rotations result in a nice straight crimp — otherwise it can bend. Either put a flemish eye around the hook eye, or preferably a protective loop with armour spring — because mono line rubbing on metal will eventually chafe under tension.

A change in the direction of the boat will also change the performance of the lures. For example, turning to run with the sea will increase boat speed and lures will start to skate and tumble across the surface. You can reduce speed, let more line out, or do both. A sudden turn can also run the outside tagline across other rod tips and create a belly in the inside tagline, which may also foul other rods.

The different items used when trolling are :

Safety line — a short length of strong line for securing rods and reels, tied to the gunwale or transom with a shark clip or similar clip on the end. The clip can be slipped into the lug on the front of big game reels which is designed for clipping the reel to the straps on a fighting harness. If using reels without these lugs, a simple way to secure the reel is to wind the safety line around the rod just in front of the reel and clip the shark clip to the safety line itself.

Outriggers — long fibreglass poles attached to the sides of the boat for holding lines out to the side, enabling lures or baits to be fished from a higher angle, with a greater spread, and further back. A tag line is usually used in conjunction with the outrigger, and more than one line can be fished along the pole.

Drop back — the loop of line between the rod tip and the clip on the outrigger or transom which falls away when a fish strikes, giving the fish some slack line before the tension comes on. Applied intentionally when fishing baits to allow fish time to move away with the bait, drop back is usually regarded as a handicap with lures.

Tagline — a length of strong line (venetian blind cord is fine) tied to the outrigger line or the transom, with a release clip to hold the fishing line.

Release clip — a clip securing the line, designed to be pulled free on the strike. It can be a roller troller mechanism from the USA with tension adjustment, or a size 62 rubber band wrapped around the line. When connecting directly to the outrigger line, i.e. not to a tagline, a clothes peg gripping a piece of paper folded tightly with the line wound around the middle several times can be used; but this is better suited to fishing baits.

Paihia professional skipper Jason Wootton always uses a rubber band, claiming a better hookup rate on strikes than with roller trollers. It is a question of personal preference.

While one crew member is scanning the horizon for signs of activity, another should always be watching the lures, alert for a fin or the flash of a fish. The gear should be checked regularly to ensure lines have not crossed, lures have not turned over and caught in the leader, or have picked up debris like weed. Also check drag levers which may have been knocked loose, and rod tips for line wraps — all recipes for disaster when a big fish hits.

Teasers

There are several different types of teasers or attractors which can be towed with your lures. They are particularly useful in boats which do not create large wakes, like small outboard-powered and multi-hulled boats,

The roller troller on a tagline holds the trolling line down, lowering the angle of pull on the lure behind the boat and preventing it skipping clear of the water.

Wet the line before setting the drag on your reels. Monofilament line behaves differently when wet, and that is how it will be during a fight.

A towel or wet sack dropped over the head of a large fish and covering the eyes will help keep it quiet while hooks are being removed.

Boone birds are curved wooden teasers that attract gamefish with their fluttering action on the surface.

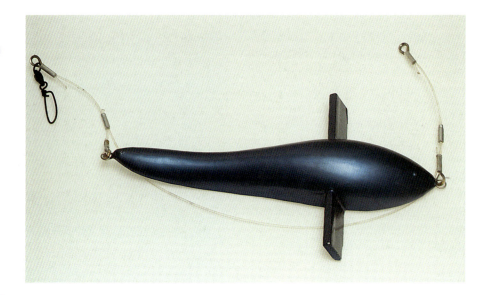

Many people do not realise that the strict laws governing record catches ban some accepted practices in this country, such as the sliding keeper hook rig. All hooks on lures or baits must be fixed if a record claim is to be made. A good two-hook rig that meets IGFA regulations and has accounted for many big snapper is simply made by tying the first hook to the bottom of a 1 m trace with the longline knot, then adding the second hook about 10 cm up the trace. The distance between hooks is determined by the size and type of bait to be used. The hooks used should be both the same size, as the fish is just as likely to be hooked on either. A 1 m trace allows easy casting of the bait — a problem if the trace is too long. No more than two hooks may be used for record catches.

and should be run in the clear-water zones alongside the prop wash. These include:

Birds — curved wooden teasers that flutter madly on the surface like a seabird that can't launch itself. They can be very effective when trolled on a separate line behind the prop wash in clear water, with a hookless lure attached two metres behind to add stability. Birds only work in calm conditions.

Daisy chain — a string of small plastic squid, lures or dead baitfish that skip and splash on the surface. Sometimes rigged with a hooked lure or a bird at the end, they simulate a school of squid or baitfish fleeing a predator and are good for attracting tuna. Half a dozen empty beer cans punctured and threaded on a piece of rope with knots to keep them separated make a useful teaser.

Drone — a bent polished stainless steel blade with reflective foil that wobbles and gyrates. Usually used with dead baits or lures that have little action, like squid or feather lures.

Cowbells — a series of shiny spoons on a length of wire that send out flashes and vibrations. Cowbells run deep and can be used alongside baits or lures, at speeds up to 5 knots. They were developed in the US for freshwater fishing but are effective on species like kahawai, kingfish and salmon.

Pakula Witchdoctors — long, weighted teasers with mirror sides that stay deep below the prop wash where they wobble violently and send out flashing arcs of light. They perform at any speed up to 20 knots, and are effective when used in conjunction with lures and baits.

All teasers should be run with lures close to them, and one lure always set directly behind.

Speed
The optimum trolling speed is determined by four factors:

The size of boat — a runabout performs differently from a large dis-

Jim Byrne had always wanted to throw an expensive gamefishing rod and reel over the side, and he got his chance when a huge blue marlin spooled him.

Jim and his boat *Tickle Pink* are legends in the fishing-mad town of Whitianga, and he has spent a lot of time trolling the blue water off Tutukaka also. He holds the record for a blue marlin weighed at Whitianga, a respectable fish of 237 kg. But when he hooked a big blue one day in March 1995, he knew he was in trouble.

"We had six 37 kg rigs out and one 6/0 with 24 kg. You know which one it took! It spooled me in 30 seconds."

Before the line could run out completely and break, Jim quickly tied the end of a 37 kg outfit to the 6/0 reel, and threw the rod and reel over the side.

He continued to play the big marlin on the 37 kg rig, but with the other rod and reel attached to the line he knew that the sheer weight in the water could easily snap the 24 kg line.

"There was huge pressure on the 24 kg line, so we backed up as fast as possible and I had the 37 kg reel in free-spool to reduce the pressure. With 750 metres of 24 kg and 400 metres of 37 kg line out, there was over 1000 metres out! We just wanted to get the rod and reel back, but the fish dived to the bottom and died," he said.

It would be almost impossible to put enough pressure on the line to lift the marlin off the bottom, without snapping the lighter line. So Jim and his mates rigged a makeshift jag, tying a 15/0 shark hook to another 37 kg line, weighting it with two dive weights, and attaching it to the main line with a loop.

The water was over 300 metres deep, and they slid the hook and loop down the line to the fish, then proceeded to try and jag the big hook into its flesh.

"That was a bit of a long shot, but it worked. It was a real fluke," said Jim.

Slowly, by moving the boat forward and hauling on the jag line, they managed to get the dead weight moving off the bottom.

Then, two and a half hours after throwing the rod and reel over they appeared under the boat and Jim grabbed the rod. The line had run all the way out, with just one turn left on the spool and the weight of the fish had been hanging on the knot securing the line to the drum.

"We got the marlin two thirds of the way up, when the shark hook pulled out! So I finished the fight on the 24 kg line. It was not a problem once we got it off the bottom."

The *Tickle Pink* returned to Whitianga where the marlin was weighed at 306 kg. It was disqualified as an official catch because of the different lines used and people involved in landing it.

"I had always wanted to throw an expensive rod and reel over the side. It was my own one, too!" said Jim.

placement hull. All boats seem to have a level of performance at which fish are attracted. It may be vibration or turbulence; some call it the harmonics; there may be electromagnetic factors; but the revolutions of the engine and propeller undoubtedly influence the response of gamefish. The boat and its propeller are the largest fish attractor of all. But if we have a boat which is hot when it comes to attracting fish, we do not question why; we are too busy trying to catch them!

The sea conditions — you will troll faster in calm conditions and slower in rough conditions. If it is too rough to fish at 6 knots, it is too rough to fish.

The design of the lures employed — some are designed for fast speeds, other require slow speeds.

The cost of running your boat — a runabout must be off the plane, but an extra knot may cost a lot in fuel consumption if the hull is being pushed through the water at half plane. Experience tends to suggest that 8-10 knots is the most effective speed for most boats. But do not be limited by that approach. Sometimes a change in speed and engine revolutions will result in a strike.

Drag setting

This is a hot issue, and opinion is divided on how heavy drags should be set while trolling.

With the lever in the strike position the drag should be pre-set at between one third and one quarter of the line weight, i.e. 6 to 8 kg of drag. Most professionals I talk to prefer to err on the heavier side, with 8 kg of drag for 24 kg line and 12 kg for 37 kg line.

When the lever is pushed past the button right up to full drag you will have 70% or 80% of the breaking strain applied to the line, but this will be rarely used.

Drag is set by attaching a set of scales to the snapclip on your line and pulling down quickly from the rod tip at 90 degrees until line slips off the reel. The type of scales which registers the weight with an indicator is easier to use than where you have to peer closely and try and read the gauge while pulling on the line. It is not a perfect system, but apart from lifting a weight until line slips off the reel, there is no other way.

Before adjusting the tension knob on the side of the reel always pull the drag lever right back to neutral, then slide it back up to strike to test it.

For trolling lures the drag has traditionally been set on strike, to force the hook or hooks into the tough bone of a marlin's mouth. With other species like mahimahi and tuna the hard strike works fine, but marlin do not always attack the lure voraciously. Sometimes they just mouth it or tap it with their bill, and the hook does not hold.

A new trend among many successful marlin fishermen has the drag backed off to 2 or 3 kg, allowing a marlin to easily take line, then smoothly tightening up to the strike position when the fish is about 100 m out. Some claim a higher hookup rate with this technique.

Both systems have their advocates. It is over to you. There will be days when the marlin just won't stick and in frustration you start playing around with factors like drag and boat strikes. On other occasions everything goes smoothly and you think you have all the answers. The wild card is the fickle behaviour of the fish, which of course makes the game so interesting.

The strike

It is said that gamefishing is 95% boredom and 5% total panic. Some may challenge the breakdown. But the sight of a marlin 'in the gear', lit up a vivid electric blue as it crosses from lure to lure, is guaranteed to pump a surge of adrenalin through the veins of the most hardened fisherman.

Tips for trolling blue water

One crew member should always keep a lookout from a high point, watching the horizon for signs of birds, splashes, or current lines. Also keep an eye on the temperature indicator, and watch for changes.

When planning a course, head for underwater canyons and reefs if there is no surface activity. Workups and feeding birds will often be found where there is a deep pinnacle or reef.

Log all strikes on the GPS. Eventually a pattern will emerge. Return to the point where a fish was hooked. Predators are pack animals and a couple of hours spent in the same area is a good investment of time.

A zig-zag course will cover more variation in bottom contour and currents than a straight line. Gamefish travel with the swells, so a course that crosses the swells will be more productive.

GAMEFISHING

At other times the first indication of a strike is a crashing wrench on a rod as the reel sings its tearing wail, or a line is torn from an outrigger. Then the big question is: what is it? It could be a tuna, marlin or shark. But if a fin suddenly appears behind a lure it will be a marlin, and often it will follow a lure, perhaps swinging over to check out another one, while the anxious fisherman on strike is willing it to devour the lure.

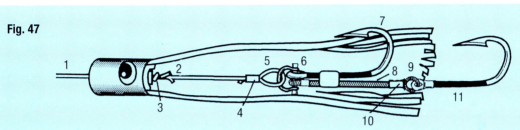

Fig. 47

Double-hook rigs can be put together in various combinations of fixed or loose hooks. A proven consistent rig is the shackle rig, with the hooks lying point upward at an angle of 60 degrees apart. The illustration (Fig. 47) shows:

1. The leader
2. Rubber band wrapped round the leader. This is used to position the hooks within the lure, and as a shock absorber if no rubber button is used.
3. Rubber button (an 11 mm plumbing washer) to protect the leader from abrasion resulting from the back of the lure working against the line and crimp. It can break at this point without protection.
4. Crimp of correct make and size for the leader used.

In this single hook rig, the distance is set by adding a rubber band inside the lure. This acts as a cushion to protect the crimp against the back of the lure head when pulled up tight, and also allows the line to pull through if a fish grabs the lure by the head, hopefully hooking it in the mouth.

5. Stainless steel thimble, part of High Seas leader system. These have a gap when purchased, which must be closed with pliers prior to inserting in loop. When using thimbles, always pull leader tight around thimble and snug against crimp before crimping to secure — this reduces possible movement, thereby reducing the chance of fatigue.
6. Stainless steel yachting shackle with extended pin. The strongest link, they can be tightened with a twist of pliers. Use a small shackle which will pass through the thimble.
7. Stainless steel, southern tuna style hooks are most commonly used for gamefishing (Mustad model 7691S). Both hooks are the same size for balance.
8. Connecting wire is semi-rigid 7x7, minimum 275 kg test. The crimps are chrome-plated brass, swaged with the appropriate bench press (not with hand-held crimping pliers). Wire should be checked for fatigue and corrosion. The 60-degree set is implanted when the wire is crimped. After crimping, the wire may be twisted to align the hook angles in relation to the lure. Toothpicks can also be jammed into the back of the lure head to hold the hook rig in position.
9. The loops at each end of the wire should be snug, but loose enough to give free movement on both the shackle pin and the hook eye. This movement of the hooks allows the lure to work at its best. A tight loop would cause fatigue in the wire as the lure's action worked the hook against the wire. Fixed hooks can also act as a keel and alter the lure's action.
10. The shrink wrap on the wire loop covers the crimp, leaving the crimp end clear for inspection, and also leaving the hook free to swing but preventing the hook from flicking around and hanging up on the wire.
11. Shrink wrap on the hook shank adds colour (bright yellow or red electrical tape which shrinks in heat from a cigarette lighter) and also acts as an indicator of how the lure was taken by recording bill or teeth marks as scratches. For example, if there are no marks after a strike, the fish was just tangled in the leader.
12. A loose collar over the hook shank and wire prevents the wire hooking over the leading hook. It can be unheated shrink tubing, a small ring, or a section of plastic tubing. This rig allows the lure to work to its maximum with the hooks centrally aligned with its back, and with no line twist.

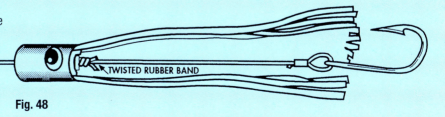

Fig. 48

When using shackle hook rigs, you need only a couple of spare rigs for a lot of lures, and can change damaged hooks quickly. It can be used on all lures, varying the size to fit the lure.

You can try increasing the speed, or simply pulling on the line if you know which lure it is following. The change in the action of the lure may be sufficient to provoke a strike. Or, flick the reel into free spool for a couple of seconds to drop the lure back into the marlin's face. The same effect is gained by lifting the rod and dropping the tip suddenly.

Some skippers carry a pre-rigged live bait which can be quickly attached to a line and fed to the fish in this situation.

At the strike, some fishermen like to gun the boat to drive the hook home. This actually makes no difference if the fish is running away from the boat as the reel drag is applying a constant pressure. What it does do is wake up any crew members who may be catching up on lost sleep, and generally raise the excitement level a few notches. Nothing wrong with that, provided all on board are expecting the sudden surge and are hanging on tightly, not half-way across the cockpit to grab a rod. It will also clear the other lines away from the fish, which is useful in avoiding possible tangles.

But if a fish reacts by leaping or dashing directly towards the boat, then the 'boat strike', as it is called, is essential to take up slack line. Under no circumstances should the boat be slowed or stopped.

Provided there is plenty of tension on the fish, the rod can be left in the holder while the other gear is pulled in quickly and calmly — unless it is a huge blue marlin that is stripping line at an alarming rate; then you have a problem and have to move faster.

With the gear safely stowed and no loose hooks left lying exposed, the fish is probably 100 metres away and the angler can take the rod while the boat is slowed. The lateral pressure on the rod can make it hard lifting it out of the holder, and it seems natural to grab the rod with two hands above the reel and lift in the direction of the pull, which is towards the fish. But this can also take pressure off the fish, and it may be lost at this point.

What the angler should do is take a firm grip with one hand above the reel and one below. The lower hand pushes against the rod butt while the other hauls back on the foregrip. As the rod clears the holder this push/pull grip maintains pressure until the rod is firmly locked into the gimbal.

After the strike, the boat continues away from the fish — top position — then turns downwind to come onto a course parallel to the fish — bottom position.

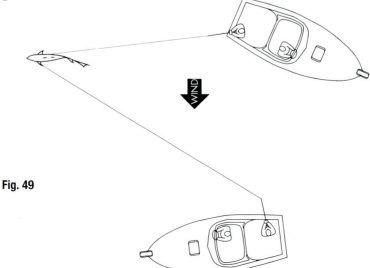

Fig. 49

An advance discussion on roles to be adopted when a fish strikes is useful, and one person is designated to give the orders — usually the boat's captain.

Fighting the fish

Once the fight is well and truly engaged, the fish usually tears across the ocean in a blistering first run with an effortless power that never fails to impress. The trick is to maintain steady pressure and get the boat in the best position to control the fish. It doesn't matter if he takes half of your line in a 500 m burst. You can recover it.

Positioning of the boat is the key factor in the fight. A good skipper can compensate for an inexperienced or clumsy angler by using the boat to keep the line tight, but even a top angler cannot compensate for a bad skipper (Figs. 49, 50 & 51).

Some pointers which will increase your chances of success are:

Don't try to do too much with a big fish on its first run. Concentrate on making sure the boat and crew are organised.

> When using rubber bands as release clips, you should know the breaking strain involved and match the line and rubber band. If you use too strong bands with light tackle, you can break the line on the strike. Size 62 bands are commonly used with 24-37 kg line.

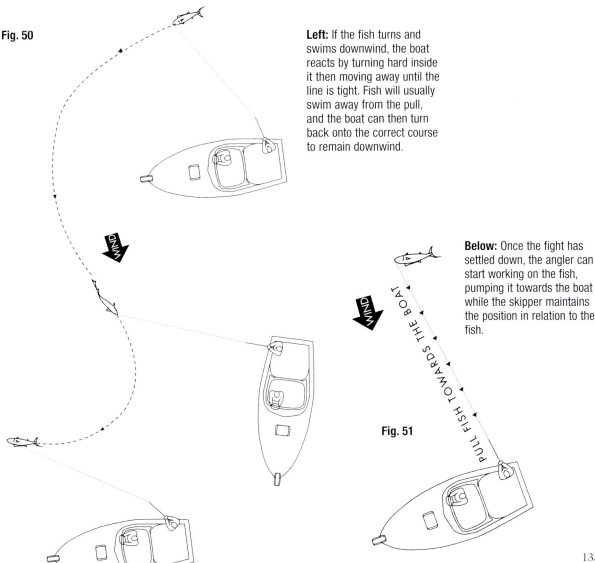

Fig. 50

Left: If the fish turns and swims downwind, the boat reacts by turning hard inside it then moving away until the line is tight. Fish will usually swim away from the pull, and the boat can then turn back onto the correct course to remain downwind.

Below: Once the fight has settled down, the angler can start working on the fish, pumping it towards the boat while the skipper maintains the position in relation to the fish.

Fig. 51

Water floods the cockpit, adding to the drama as the launch backs up on a big marlin. Photo courtesy John Batterton.

Keep the boat moving forward at all times. The skipper must know where the fish is and what angle the line is at. If he can't see it, tell him.

Get downwind of the fish so the boat doesn't drift over the line.

Try to keep the fish out to one side and move parallel with it, and try and fight it from the side throughout. This will tire the fish faster. Also, a change in the direction of pull can pivot the hooks and they could come out.

Don't let the fish swim at its normal pace. It will gain more from a rest than the angler will.

If you are not used to manoeuvring the boat, keep the fish on the windward stern quarter.

Always keep the line tightly stretched. The slightest amount of slack can lose the fish. If the fish swims toward the boat or jumps, gun the boat away from it while the angler winds quickly until line comes off the reel again.

If the fish sounds, never fight it straight up and down. Drive away from it even while it's diving, and try and keep the line at 45 degrees. This will continually plane the fish to the surface. Fighting straight up and down puts little pressure on a big fish but a lot of strain on the angler. A fish under the boat can also move the line to the other side of the boat or dangerously close to the propeller.

Make sure line comes onto the reel level and tightly. Tight coils can dig into loose underwraps, creating a costly jam.

Make sure you can release drag quickly when needed. Thumb pressure on the line or the sides of the spool adds tension which can be released instantly.

An inexperienced crew can fight the fish with the clicker on the reel, which allows the skipper to hear what the fish is doing.

When several people are hooked up at the same time, you must walk around the boat to follow your fish. This involves passing other anglers, and if you bring the two rod tips together the crossed lines will be clearly shown and you can figure out which rod goes under which.

Stand-up technique

When fighting a fish with a rod the key is to use the rod, not the reel, to put pressure on the fish and regain line. The reel is simply to hold line and release it at a predetermined level of tension. Rod technique can win, lose or unnecessarily prolong the fight. This applies to all fishing.

You can simulate and practise the stand-up action by rigging a small pulley to a rafter or strong branch and running the line through and down to a bucket of water. The weight depends on the tackle used: half-full is fine for 24 kg line. Put on your rod belt and harness, connect the rod and stand back about 15 metres to flatten the angle.

Increase drag and pump the bucket up off the ground. The correct technique is to raise the rod to 45 degrees then lower it quickly while winding in the line gained. But the rod must remain loaded while line is recovered. This retains pressure on the fish, and keeps it swimming towards you. The slightest slack on the downstroke will allow the fish to turn its head and you will have lost the advantage.

This is simulated very effectively with the bucket — the trick is to lift the bucket gradually, but never allowing it to go down. Keep going until the bucket hits the pulley, then back off the drag and let it down slowly without over-running line — another useful discipline to practise. Repeat the exercise until it feels comfortable, then try and do it a little faster. What happens? The bucket drops between strokes!

With the bucket on the ground increase the drag until you can just lift the bucket without it slipping. At this setting, raise the bucket slowly then lower the rod and try to wind in without dropping the bucket. You can't!

Now try lowering the rod slowly and winding. You will find the slower you lift, the less drag you need. That's the key; it's a combination of stroke speed and drag. The smoother you are, the faster you can do it; and the quicker you can raise the bucket to the pulley without it dropping between strokes, the more chance you will have on a fish. But also see what happens if you jerk the rod: the bucket slides back to the ground.

It's harder than it appears, and is an excellent exercise for honing your technique, or starting a novice. There is no better preparation than understanding how the combination of smooth rod action both up and down and drag setting can work together — if you had to rely on the real experience to learn, it could take a long time!

The other key factor is to keep the advantage. When the fight is dead-locked, short quick pumps of the rod with perhaps only half a turn of the reel handle each time, will keep the fish pointed towards you. You are forcing it to swim the way you want. You are in control.

In the hands of a skilled fisherman this technique can be deadly, bringing a powerful fish quickly to the boat.

It is a comfortable, efficient system: a full back harness is used to spread the weight evenly. With the rod settled in a gimbal resting against the thighs, you can apply leverage against the fish simply by leaning back. You don't have to be super-fit to endure a long fight, and you determine the speed of the strokes. If you need to rest, simply lean back away from

---

The modern rod buckets which rest on the thighs have made life much easier for the angler, but in the battle with a big fish a lot of weight is exerted on the fulcrum where the rod butt rests in the gimbal. The angler's stance can make a big difference to the comfort and effectiveness of the system. The legs can be widely spread to give a stable base on a platform which may be rolling on the sea. But the rod bucket can easily slip off one leg, and the whole system collapses. This is avoided by simply turning each foot slightly inward in a pigeon-toe effect, and the rod bucket will be rock solid.

the rod, which is clipped to the harness.

One hand should remain on the spool throughout, to spread the line as it comes in and to add extra pressure by clamping down on it. This extra drag can be released instantly when needed.

Extra weight can also be applied by gripping the rod high up the foregrip at shoulder level and hauling back.

As we have learned, the action should always be smooth and steady, for the line will not break on a straight pull — it takes a sudden surge of the fish to snap it.

Everybody must be ready to react quickly — the skipper may have to jump the boat forward or spin it round, while the angler has to continually monitor the pressure on the line, back off drag or wind furiously to compensate for surges by the fish.

But in the excitement and the heat of the moment even the most experienced fishermen can 'lose it'.

The whole fight should be like a dance, with the boat and fish moving back and forward in unison, connected by the line as it goes in and out under a finely tuned tension kept constant by the delicate application of the motor, the rod and reel, and the angler's hands as they respond to the fish.

Game chair technique

Large boats will be equipped with fighting chairs, and the basic method is to brace the feet on the footrest or the side of the boat and lean back to pump the fish. The angler will be connected to the rod by a kidney or back harness, and the rod rests in a gimbal at the front of the seat. Some fishermen like to remove the back of the chair to allow greater movement, and a crew member usually stands behind to swivel the chair to face the fish.

When fighting giant fish on heavy tackle — 37 or 60 kg — another technique is used where the angler has a harness around the buttocks and pushes with the legs, sliding across the seat like a rower. At the height of the power stroke the angler is lifted off the seat by the weight of the fish, leans back and settles down on the seat before sliding forward again. The seat can be soaped to add lubrication.

At the boat

As the swivel comes within reach, one member of the crew will be ready with gloves to grab the leader. The angler steps back, allowing the wireman, as he or she is called, to take the weight of the fish. The skipper keeps the boat idling forward, and as soon as the weight goes off the line the angler backs off the drag in case the fish breaks away. This is the most risky part of the exercise, because a short line does not have the stretch of a long line, and any weaknesses in the gear will be exposed. The line may have rubbed on a fin or bill, or touched the propeller. A weak knot can give under the tremendous tension applied by a fish thrashing at the gunwale. As the leader is pulled in there should be no loose coils which could whip around an arm if the fish gets away.

The deckhand hangs on against the awesome power of a 450 kg blue marlin while the tagman stands ready. The leader should be wrapped only once around each hand so it can be released in an instant by pointing the hands at the fish if it cannot be held. Photo courtesy John Batterton.

You need to find the marlin, and one approach is to troll lures until you strike fish, then put out live baits; or look for schools of bait on the depth sounder which may be as deep as 30 metres — and fish there.

A 230 kg blue marlin shows why it is regarded as one of the toughest and most spectacular of the great billfish. Photo courtesy John Batterton.

> When rigging lures, some dental floss wrapped tightly halfway down the leader will snag the lure as it slides up the leader, keeping it away from a hooked fish. This prevents the lure acting as a counter weight against the hook when the fish jumps, and may also save your lure if the fish breaks off.

All actions should be smooth, and as the fish comes within range the gaffman moves in from behind the wireman, leaning over to place the gaff carefully behind the line. A wild lunge can be disastrous, knocking out the hook or snapping the line.

Gaffs must be sharp and of the correct size. A large gaff is hard to sink into a small fish, and a gaff designed for snapper is useless on a marlin.

An experienced gaffman can slip the hook behind the lips of the lower jaw on a hapuku, kingfish or tuna. The fish will then use its energy to help boat it, 'swimming' up and over the side as it reacts to the gaff. If not confident of a lip shot, go for the throat or shoulder (Fig. 52). Avoid the centre of the body or tail or you will have to pull a powerful fish sideways or backwards.

On marlin, the meaty shoulder is the favoured target, with the gaff coming over the fish and pulling into it. A flying gaff with a detachable head attached to a rope is usually used, and a second gaff or tail rope will secure it.

Marlin can be dispatched with a heavy club, but tuna should be spiked. We use a sharpened Phillips screwdriver on yellowfin, hitting the soft spot on the top of the head between the eyes and angling the spike back at 45 degrees. When it hits the brain the fish shudders, the fins extend and it dies instantly. Tuna are better table fish if bled, and a knife inserted at right angles into the lateral line one handspan behind the pectoral fin will sever an artery. Push the knife in until it hits the backbone.

Sharks can provide real trouble, and a 'big shark/small boat' combination can be extremely dangerous. Their tough skin is hard to penetrate, requiring super-sharp gaffs with cutting edges, and the jaws are the best

Right: Gaffing a powerful fish like the mako shark can be a recipe for trouble if the fish is not fully played out.

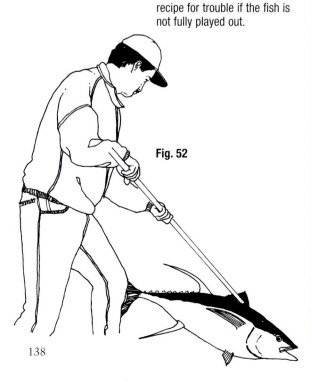

Fig. 52

Take care when removing hooks from 'dead' fish. A second, trailing hook can be flicked into a hand or arm in an instant.

target. Sharks have a propensity for rolling when gaffed, and hand-held gaffs are ineffective. Many fishermen prefer to use a wire or cable noose which can be fastened over the line with a clip and slid down over the head of the shark, securing it either in front or behind the pectorals. Another around the tail will complete the job. Large makos will be dragged behind the boat, or lashed to a duckboard; but not brought aboard. Sharks can be hard to kill with a club, but a sharp knife inserted behind the head to sever the cartilaginous backbone is effective.

If a shark is to be eaten (and small makos are excellent as steaks or smoked), cut off the tail and hang it over the side, allowing the ammonia-rich juices in the backbone to drain.

Safety

People can be badly injured when strong fish are brought to the boat, and if the fish is still 'green' (not played out), the accident-potential scale rises. The combination of a rolling boat providing unsteady footing, strong line, gaff points, powerful fish and sharp hooks is a dangerous one.

Experience and cool heads are not always involved. Ensure there are no loose hooks or gaffs lying around. Gaffs should be carried with the point covered until it is time to use them, when they can be hooked over the back of a seat with the point facing down. A knife should be kept handy to cut line in an emergency. Wear non-slip shoes. When a fish hooked on a double-hook rig is brought into the boat, watch for the second hook, which may be swinging freely. A 'dead' yellowfin once gave a dying head-shake while the hook was being removed from its jaw and the second hook was impaled through a hand in an instant.

Big sharks on a line secured to a cleat have been known to pull cleats free, leap into the cockpit, and pull the stern under in the face of a following sea — a dangerous scenario.

Exercise common sense and care, and avoid panic when handling big fish. Don't take risks in a small boat. Big sharks should be cut free.

A small lure set a few metres back in the middle of the wash can catch skipjack and albacore tuna throughout the day. While these speedsters are fun on a light rod, we use a heavy rod when trolling so you don't have to stop the boat or pull in the other lines when the small one goes off. Our favourite lure is a red and white feather lure about 12 cm long. Green and yellow or purple are also good skippie colours. We use these small tuna for bait, but they also make fine eating if bled and put straight on ice.

A few gannets started turning up, and . . . birds could be seen squabbling over what turned out to be small meatballs.

Eugene grabbed his landing net and leaned out to scoop up a netfull of wriggling anchovies.

We have all heard about meatballs of bait fish, the phenomenon which occurs when predators like tuna or sharks rip into a school of anchovies, pilchards or needlefish. But I had never seen one outside the Bay of Plenty, where they are common, until looking for marlin on the first day of the Westcoaster tournament, based at Huia on the Manukau Harbour. As a member of one of the Composite Sports teams, I was fishing on Eugene de Bruyn's boat, *Sea Genie*, with Marty Johanson and his rep for the South Island, Richard Jessep. Actually, the video camera held more appeal for me, as we were gathering material for our television show, *The Outdoor Journal*.

The marlin were scarce, and in fact had been all that summer off the Manukau, but catching albacore was no problem. Richard wanted to catch one, having never seen tuna caught before, so Eugene rigged a green hexhead squid on 15 kg tackle and dropped it into the wake. The pakulas on 24 kg and 37 kg Fin-nors were popping nicely out the back, but it was the little hexhead that attracted attention.

Richard landed his first albacore, a glistening, fat fish of about 7 kg; and then he and Marty got out the jig rods loaded with 10 kg and had a lot of fun hooking up from the bow of Eugene's walk-around fishing machine.

You can catch albies all day when you find them in the mood, but we wanted something bigger to put the tournament firmly on the fishing map in its inaugural year.

As it transpired, Marty got a fresh report from Mike Nola in Dargaville that the marlin were hot off the Kaipara and they burned a lot of petrol travelling up there the following day, where Marty landed a nice stripey to bring back to Huia.

In the afternoon the wind dropped away and the sea flattened until it looked like the middle of Lake Taupo on a hot day. A few gannets started turning up, and then small puddles of the majestic

The albacore circled the stern of the boat, wheeling and diving, with their long, curved pectorals extended — like jet planes performing at an air show.

All that remained was a mass of sparkling scales slowly settling in the clear water, stark but beautiful testimony to the savagery of life in the ocean.

birds could be seen squabbling over what turned out to be small meatballs.

The albies were churning the anchovies into tighter and tighter balls. The terrified baitfish were using their only defence — to swim in a dense mass, presenting a shimmering wall of movement designed to confuse the predators. The albies didn't seem very confused because the meatballs disappeared in a minute or two, as fish after fish slashed through them. Eugene grabbed his landing net and leaned out to scoop up a netfull of wriggling anchovies as a small school of bait immediately dived under the stern of the boat to escape the slashing albies. The video camera was taking it all in, and when the albacore started attacking the anchovies hiding under the outboard motor Eugene decided he would catch one in the net. Netting a free-swimming tuna!

Marty threw anchovies in front of the net but the albacore were like bullets. Eugene reversed the net and suddenly scooped up an albacore. Then he got another one, but they jumped out of the net just as fast as they swam into it. The frenzy continued as Eugene dangled an anchovy on the surface. Suddenly it disappeared and he yelped as the albie's tiny teeth ripped his finger.

As the number of anchovies dwindled, the albacore circled the stern of the boat, wheeling and diving, with their long, curved pectorals extended — like jet planes performing at an air show.

The water was unusually calm and clear and all of the action was captured on video. It was a rare opportunity to study tuna feeding, and when there were no anchovies left we started the motor and put out the lures — but as we idled away a sole survivor which had been hiding under the boat wriggled frantically in our wake, trying to catch up with the boat. There was a flash of silver and blue, and it was gone.

All that remained was a mass of sparkling scales slowly settling in the clear water, stark but beautiful testimony to the savagery of life in the ocean.

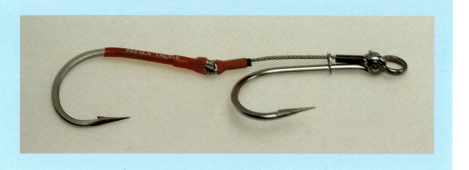

To ensure the swimming action of lures is not impaired, use free-swinging shackle rigs with two hooks set at 60 degrees and in line, or a swinging single hook.

Using baits

There is nothing more appealing to predators than a live bait. So why do we not use bait all the time? Simply because it's just not practical to have a supply of live bait handy at all times. So we use lures, occasionally a dead bait, and when the opportunity presents itself we put out a 'livie'.

A live bait sends out a signal that the big fish home in on. There may be thousands of small fish swimming alongside, but a marlin or kingfish will single out the wounded individual. Like the great predators of the African plains, the gamefish will take an easy meal in preference to a fast-swimming healthy fish which requires energy to track down. It is this response to prey in distress that fishermen take advantage of when they use live baits. That is why dead baits are less effective, but we use them when we have no option.

Generally speaking, the bigger the bait you use, the bigger fish you are likely to hook. Baits are fished in the same type of water where lures are used, but at much slower speeds. However, live baits are more commonly used when fishing over reefs surrounded by deep water and ocean currents — known fish-producing spots. It makes more sense than just wandering over the ocean at two or three knots hoping to cross the trail of a prowling fish. Black marlin are often found near reefs and headlands, and are more likely to be attracted to a live kahawai than a skirted lure. Broadbill swordfish are caught only on baits, usually at night, and striped marlin are regularly hooked on livies set for kingfish.

The other advantage of baits is the variety of depths which can be covered. Lure fishing is like scratching the surface of the sea, while baits can be deployed at depths up to 100 metres. All that prevents you dropping a bait into an abyss is the difficulty of hooking a fish with such a huge amount of line out, and its associated stretch. I guess you could try a boat strike, driving away from the fish to set the hook, but it is not a technique we have spent time investigating.

Finding baits

Fresh is best, and baits are usually caught on the way to the fishing grounds. Kahawai are commonly used — not so much because they are a favourite food of big fish, but because they are easily found and caught, saving valuable fishing time. Mackerel can be caught on jig flies at night under a powerful light which attracts them to the boat, and flyingfish can

When fishing for yellowfin tuna and you find a meatball — stay with it once you have it under the boat. You might be catching only skippies and albacore, but the yellowfin often turn up after several hours.

be scooped up in dip nets. Baitfish will also be found in dense schools over reefs and around isolated rocks, and can usually be caught on trolled or jigged lures. These could be trevally or maomao. One of the best baits for marlin is skipjack tuna, and an abundance of 'skippies' is a good sign that marlin may be in the area. It makes sense to offer your quarry what is prevalent at the time.

Keeping baits

Large baits like skippies or albacore will not survive in a bait tank but can be kept alive wrapped in a wet towel with a hose delivering a continuous supply of seawater into the mouth. Special tubes to hold the tuna in a similar way are used in the US.

Smaller baits will stay alive in a bait tank. The tank should be round or oval so the fish swim in a circle, with a good turnover of water, and surface area is more important than depth. Dead or sick baits should be removed from the tank, and when choosing a bait the liveliest specimen will be best. A muslin aquarium net is useful for catching a lively fish in the tank.

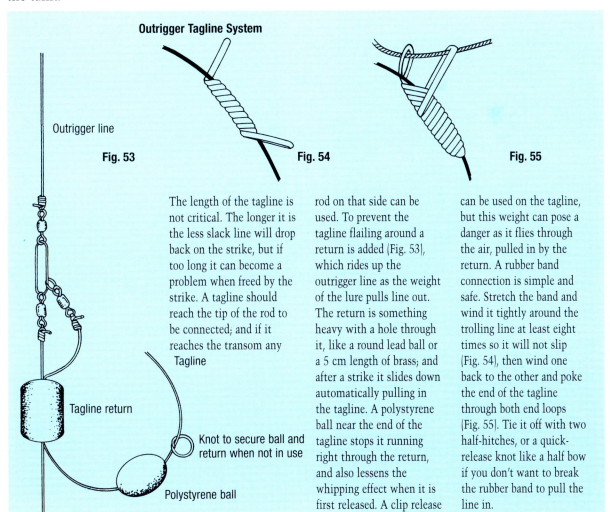

The length of the tagline is not critical. The longer it is the less slack line will drop back on the strike, but if too long it can become a problem when freed by the strike. A tagline should reach the tip of the rod to be connected; and if it reaches the transom any rod on that side can be used. To prevent the tagline flailing around a return is added (Fig. 53), which rides up the outrigger line as the weight of the lure pulls line out. The return is something heavy with a hole through it, like a round lead ball or a 5 cm length of brass; and after a strike it slides down automatically pulling in the tagline. A polystyrene ball near the end of the tagline stops it running right through the return, and also lessens the whipping effect when it is first released. A clip release can be used on the tagline, but this weight can pose a danger as it flies through the air, pulled in by the return. A rubber band connection is simple and safe. Stretch the band and wind it tightly around the trolling line at least eight times so it will not slip (Fig. 54), then wind one back to the other and poke the end of the tagline through both end loops (Fig. 55). Tie it off with two half-hitches, or a quick-release knot like a half bow if you don't want to break the rubber band to pull the line in.

A line run directly off an outrigger will have a lot of slack line on a strike and the fish may spit the lure. Fig. 56 shows a line trolled on a flat line (off the rod tip) 45.5 m behind the boat. There is no slack line on the strike. Fig. 57 shows the lure in the same position, but because it goes through the outrigger it takes 56.6 m of line. When a fish pulls the line free there is 11 m of slack line. The solution is the tagline, as shown in Fig. 58. The lure is again 45.5 m out, but needs only 46.8 m of line, giving only 1.3 m of slack line.

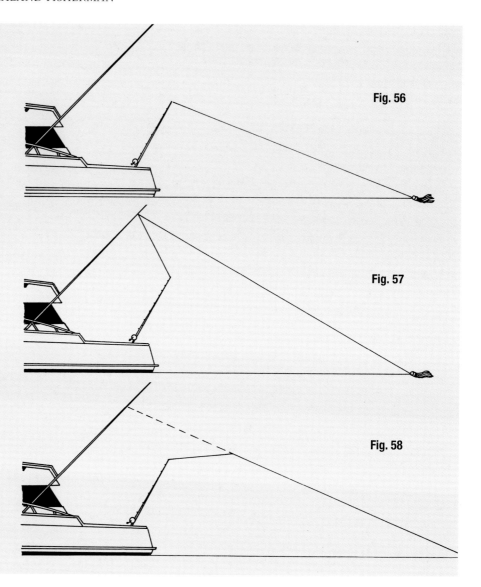

Fig. 56

Fig. 57

Fig. 58

Rigging baits

There are many ways of rigging baits, depending on whether they are to be set from an anchored boat, trolled or drifted. Traditional methods used large game hooks or special livebait hooks with straight shanks and points. But unless a marlin or broadbill is the target, smaller hooks will allow your bait to move more freely; and octopus beak hooks can be used as well as the specialised livebait style. Heavy leaders will also inhibit the bait, creating drag which can drown it. Some big fish have been taken with the hook tied directly to the main line when fishing for sensitive fish in clear water. While the leader guards against abrasion, it should be in proportion to the stress you can apply through the main line. As a guide, use 30 to 150 kg leader with 6 to 8 kg line; 50 to 200 kg for 10 to 25 kg tackle; and 50 to 300 kg for 37 kg tackle. If sharks are expected, a wire leader will be used. For rigging baits you will need a bait needle, rubber bands and some light line like Dacron or unwaxed dental floss.

Fishing baits

Whether skipping a dead bait on the surface or trolling a livie, the speed should be no more than three knots. For many years skip-baits were the main method of marlin fishing in this country, but are no longer popular. They were trolled from outriggers on each side of the boat, often with a 'swimmer' (a live kahawai, or a dead one with the backbone removed to give flexibility and movement) in the centre. A weight ahead of the bait or tied under its chin was used to keep the bait under the surface. Most live baits are presented from a drifting boat, and set at different levels. A weight can be added to the leader; a live bait can be presented under a balloon or simply allowed to swim away from the boat. The hook can also be placed to encourage the bait to swim in a particular direction, or to upset the natural swimming action so it sends out stronger vibrations and flashes of light off the flanks — an invitation to predators to come and get it (Fig. 59).

Fig. 59

Tackle

Reels with a large spool give a faster retrieve — important when you need to recover line quickly. So a 50/80 reel loaded with 24 kg line is easier to wind under load than a 50-wide reel, simply because it's bigger. The smaller the spool and the higher the gear ratio, the harder it is to wind the handle. Reels should have smooth drags which are easily altered: this is why lever-drag reels are more popular than ones with a star-drag. With their strike buttons and markings, lever-drags allow you to set a known drag and increase or decrease it in relation to the original setting.

Most good reels have two speeds, which offers a real advantage to the angler. Changing to low gear does not alter the drag, but it gives you the ability to put extra pressure on a fish by keeping the rod high and using short, slow strokes; to winch up a deep fish; or to rest during a long fight while winding slowly and maintaining pressure on the fish.

Rods are generally over-rated by manufacturers. A rod rated for 24 to 37 kg line will be best suited to 24 kg gear at the most. One simple test is to rig your line to a weight about one-third of the line class and try to lift it off the floor. If the rod bends all the way to the butt it is too soft for the work at hand. Rods should fold away in the top third when under load, leaving you plenty of power to add extra weight to the fish. As a rule of thumb the lighter the line the longer the rod will be. Short-stroke rods are popular but have to be fully loaded to work and can be a handicap for the inexperienced angler. A longer, stiffer rod makes it easier to maintain a tight line; you gain more line with each stroke; and it's easier keeping the line away from the side of the boat or the propeller.

For heavy work a stand-up rod should be 2 or 2.3 m long, and a chair rod slightly longer.

Use a good quality old-style gamefishing line which has a uniform density and no extra coatings or weak cores. It's all you have between you and the fish. Dacron is difficult to handle; is not suitable for trolling lures, and is used mainly by charter operators. The stretch in monofilament line

> Baitfish can sometimes be hard to find and are usually on the surface only in the early morning. The crew of *Predator* discovered after throwing dinner scraps over the side one morning that cooked rice with curry sauce turned the mackerel into a feeding frenzy, and they can be caught on 1/0 hooks baited with chunks of skipjack tuna.

> Outriggers should be stiff, to ensure a hard strike and drive the hook home. Older riggers are sometimes too soft and will not have a good hookup. Solution — add a stay between the tip of the rigger and the front of the boat.

acts as a shock-absorber, provided you keep the line tight. Some people spool 24 kg reels with 37 kg line to give them some extra insurance. It reduces the amount of line you have to work with, but if a fish takes nearly all your line you have serious problems anyway — and the heavier line will certainly help!

The most important accessory is the stand-up rod belt and harness, which allow heavy tackle to be used away from the game chair. With the old belt-mounted gimbal it sometimes felt as though the rod butt was grinding directly into the navel. A good rod belt should rest comfortably on the thighs, and the harness should distribute the weight evenly across the lower back. Test the gear with a heavy rod tied to something, and if it suits you personally you should be able to fight a fish for hours without any strain on your back. If using a chair, also test your outfit for comfort before you find yourself tied to a big fish.

Tips for tagging gamefish

More and more fishermen are tagging their gamefish, particularly marlin. Since the moratorium on commercial billfish fishing was put in place in 1987, sporting anglers realised they must also play their part in conserving fish stocks. The percentage of marlin tagged has steadily grown to more than 60%. There are a few pointers which will help the fish survive.

- Use lures not baits, and fish the heavier 24 or 37 kg tackle to get the fish to the boat as soon as possible.
- Once the leader man has the fish under control at the boat, insert the tag as high as possible in the shoulder, directly under the dorsal fin. The fish is counted as tagged as soon as the tag is inserted — even if it escapes immediately.
- The best way to control the marlin is to grab its bill using gloves.

The tag is in and the catch is official. This Northland striped marlin is ready to be released from the launch *Harlequin*. Photo courtesy John Batterton.

Marlin like this Northland stripey can be held by the bill while the hook is removed and a tag inserted in the shoulder, then towed behind the boat to fully revive them.

- Under no circumstances should the marlin be pulled into the boat.
- To help revive it tow it by the bill slowly until it swims freely. This could take some time.
- Marlin under 90 kg cannot be officially weighed. If in doubt as to the weight estimate, a rule of thumb is a marlin that is 2.3 m from the tip of the lower jaw to the point of the tail is about 87 kg. A 2.4 m length of ribbon can be attached to the line with a safety pin and allowed to drop down the fish to indicate its length.
- If in any doubt — let it go!

Gamefishing with a downrigger system

The downrigger system is an effective method of presenting baits or lures at depth (Fig. 60). On freshwater lakes it can be used, where legal, to troll lures; and at sea it is not used as much as it should be. The advantage is that the lure or bait can be fished at a precise depth, and when used in conjunction with a depth sounder to show where the bottom or the baitfish are, it is a real advantage. The disadvantages are the time spent rigging and setting the downrigger, the problems arising if the weight jams on the bottom, and the slow speed at which it is fished. In our waters sharks are often hooked on baits fished deep, and if lures are used they should be designed to operate at slow speeds.

Your boat speed is limited to one or two knots when trolling with a downrigger, otherwise the weight will rise up at an angle. A rod with a strong butt which will bend when rigged is important, as a full bend ensures an upward jerk which helps set the hook on a strike. The downrigger has a winch to store line, preferably with a meter indicating the amount of line out; a boom to keep the line away from the boat; a mounting base to attach it to the boat; a line of braided stainless steel for strength and minimum water resistance; a heavy cannonball weight; and a release mechanism to connect the fishing line to the weight. The release may be a plastic pressure clip, or a simple rubber band rigged as on an outrigger tagline.

The bait or lure and the weight are lowered together with the fishing reel in free-spool with the clicker on to prevent an over-run. At sea the bait can be set 10 metres behind the spool, but when trout fishing the lure should be run further back — perhaps as much as 30 metres.

As well as putting your lure at the exact depth required, the system allows you to fish up to 40 metres deep on lakes, and play trout on light line once the line has separated from the heavy weight.

In the United States downriggers are used extensively for salmon fishing off the coast and in the Great Lakes, with several lines run from the same downrigger cable at varying depths.

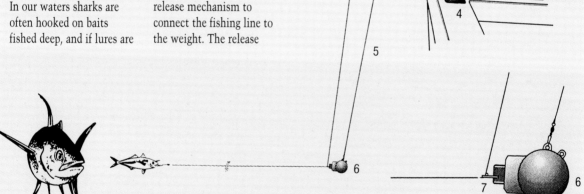

Fig. 60

Live baiting — you can put 16/0 tuna circle hooks in a vice and tweak them to offset them. Some fishermen believe it adds to the hookup rate.

Gamefishing safety at sea

The boom in small boat blue-water gamefishing off the rugged west coast promises new fishing challenges and excitement, but also raises concerns among Coastguard organisations around the country.

It usually involves crossing a bar to reach the open sea, or launching from a surf beach which involves different hazards. The Manukau Volunteer Coastguard offers the following advice:

■ Carry the recommended safety equipment — lifejackets (it is now mandatory to carry one for each person on board), marine VHF radio, EPIRB, spare motor, flares and spare fuel.

- Contact a club and go out with boaties with local knowledge.
- Check the monitoring frequency of the local Coastguard (VHF or SSB).
- Check the weather and check bar conditions in advance.
- Anticipate the effect of tide changes on bar conditions. Slack tide is usually best.
- Wear lifejackets at all times, and warm up motors first. Ensure loose gear is secured.
- Never turn back in front of a breaking wave if it is closing fast. Head into it and accelerate as you hit it to force the bow up and over it. You can approach unbroken swells at a slight angle for more comfort.
- If a wave breaks over the boat dumping large volumes of water in it, don't turn back for shore as the boat will lose speed and manoeuvrability. Turn on the bilge pump, or bail it out when clear of the breakers.
- When coming in through surf, wait and pick a swell to follow in, staying one boat length behind it.
- When going out or coming in, always take time to read the swells and pick your time before proceeding. Once committed it is dangerous to change your mind.
- Some problems and their solutions:
  - Cavitation — a loss of steerage, usually in rough, aerated water. Return to neutral and gradually increase power again.
  - Boat overturns — turn off motor and jump clear; but stay with the boat at all times.
  - Engine fails — keep bow pointed at waves by dropping the anchor or a sea anchor, and let out rope slowly. Or, if shallow, crew stand in water and hold bow line while you paddle to shore for assistance.

Trolling live baits for marlin — Bruce Smith trolls his live baits for marlin with the reel set on hard strike. Bruce Martin and Bill Hall let fish run with line for 100 metres, then gradually tighten on it, moving the drag lever slowly up to the strike mark. Bruce Martin: "They don't know they are hooked when the boat is well away. They are invariably hooked in the corner of the mouth with these hooks. We use 37 kg tackle because they fight much harder without using energy jumping like marlin hooked on lures. Fight the fish with the drag set hard up on 'sunset', and back up the boat to get them in quickly and release them. When the marlin come in they are all lit up and in good condition. Cut the leader at the eye of the hook, and they often just fall out when the pressure comes off."

More tropical visitors like the short-billed spearfish are turning up in our waters. Is this a sign of global warming, or a shift in ocean currents? Photo courtesy John Batterton.

A return to old fashioned bait fishing techniques helped well known Bay of Islands charter boat skipper Bruce Smith beat all records for catching marlin — with 131 landed on his boat, *Striker*, from only 165 strikes in the 1997 season. The 100th marlin for the season was a milestone never before achieved in New Zealand waters, and Bruce's charter party insisted he had the honour of catching that fish himself.

The dream trip started with the first morning's fishing on April 25 at the Middlesex Bank near the Three Kings Islands when a striped marlin was boated by 7.30. "That was number 99 for the boat for the season," said Auckland fisherman Murray Hansen, "we said to Smithy, 'The next one is going to take all of the line, unless you get down here and stop it. It's your fish'." So the captain took the chair normally reserved for his paying guests, and quickly boated the fish.

Murray and his companions Robert Famularo, Tony Hopkins and Bren Dorman were on their third marlin fishing expedition for the season.

Murray: "I had actually never caught one before. I had my own boat for four years, and took a couple of charters at Tutukaka. Last year we chartered *Striker* and got a couple over three trips — but I had not caught a marlin until last week. Now I am up to 16!"

Bruce Smith, his crew and anglers smashed all records after boating the 100th marlin. The previous record for a season's catch in recent times was the 75 marlin caught on Bill Hall's *Te Ariki Nui*. Early records are vague, but it is believed that the most ever caught on a single boat was in 1948 when Les Blomfield landed either 91 or 94 marlin. The Tauranga fisherman Fred Wilkins recorded 106 gamefish in a season, but these are thought to have included other species like sharks and kingfish. The official season runs from July 1 to June 30.

But no boat had recorded more than ten marlin in a day's fishing — until that Anzac Day. Bill Hall had caught ten marlin twice, Bob Ash was the first with a party on his boat, *Anita Rose*, and Smithy had done it only three weeks earlier.

"The afternoon bite was unbelievable. We had three hours of non-stop playing fish, and finished with fourteen for the day," said Murray. The next day was even better, with fifteen marlin landed.

The key was the use of live baits. Bruce towed lures until he found the marlin, which attacked the lures in packs of nine or ten fish at the peak of the action. "Then we put out livies. We used tuna circle hooks, with a dacron bridle rig through the eyes of the bait — koheru, trevally, pink maomao, jack mackerel — whatever we could get," he said.

He threaded the dacron once through the eye sockets with a needle, and tied it to the bend of the hook with a short loose loop in between. With one bait 10-15 m and another 20-25 m behind the boat he trolled at 2-3 knots until a marlin struck, which was usually immediately. "We had the angler holding the line with only a short drop-back (loose line) so the marlin were hooked in the mouth. The angler can feel the fish take the bait, then he grabs the rod out of the holder. This is the way the Americans do it. It really involves the angler, and it's good exciting stuff.

"We started out using downriggers, but the marlin were hitting the baits on the surface so we didn't bother with deep baits," said Bruce.

With heavy tackle and 37 kg line the marlin were brought to the boat quickly so they could be tagged and released in good condition. The galvanised hooks were cut off and left to rot out in the saltwater, enabling the marlin to be released quickly.

Murray said live baits were hard to obtain on the third day, but marlin were still taking dead baits. "We had so many that we decided to catch one on light line, so we put out a livie on 8 kg gear. Two marlin came in, and the smaller one took it. We played it for three hours, and tagged it but it swam into the propeller and injured its tail so we had to kill it."

The party on *Striker* caught 33 marlin in three days, and all but two were released. They achieved a remarkable hookup rate, with 33 marlin landed from 39 strikes. Eight had been taken on lures, two on dead baits and the rest on live baits.

The baitfish should be rigged quickly and returned to the water as soon as possible. Traces can be pre-rigged ready for use, with the bridle loop already on the hook. Fish held upside down with a wet towel will not struggle.

Top left: This bait requires an open-eyed livebait needle and a size 16 recurve hook with a loop of 37 kg dacron line hitched onto the hook.

The loop is pulled through the eye sockets in front of the eyes.

The loop is slipped over the hook.

The hook must be aligned in the centre of the bait's head so it will tow straight. The amount of slack in the rig is a matter of choice, but the hook can be spun around, twisting and shortening the bridle if desired. The hook point should then be passed under the twisted line to prevent it untwisting.

Other boats also joined the bonanza. "Rick Pollock had a quadruple strike on Friday and tagged them all. Later in the day he had another quadruple— two bronze whalers and two marlin — and tagged those too. That is quite an achievement," said Bruce.

After a slow start to the marlin fishing that summer, the North Cape and Three Kings areas produced magnificent fishing. One theory was that a large proportion of the marlin travelled down the west coast instead of the east coast, and the fishing on the traditional grounds off the Bay of Islands was poor, but when they congregated at the Three Kings fishing grounds on their annual migration north, the long-range boats were waiting.

Murray Hansen could not praise the *Striker* crew enough. "In terms of service and professionalism, New Zealand gamefishing has really come of age. The crew of Smithy and his deckhands, Brian King and Dean Nicholls, are the most dedicated and professional we have ever seen. On the day we caught fourteen the closest boat caught nine, and when we caught fifteen the next boat had five. There was a short bite time, and you had to be ready. When a fish came in you had to get the gear back in the water straight away," he said. The crew always had new leaders lined up ready to be clipped to the line, with dacron tied to the hooks ready to be hooked up to a fresh bait.

Bruce Smith was proud of his crew's performance. "It's good for New Zealand gamefishing," he said. His boat finished the season with an incredible 160 marlin to its credit.

The switch from lure fishing to the more traditional live bait fishing for marlin not only contributed to the huge increase in numbers caught at the prolific Three Kings grounds, but also made light tackle feasible. While it can be difficult setting the hook on lures with super light line, a live bait increases the chances of a successful hookup.

Three world records were set in early June 1997. One went to a young Auckland woman fishing on *Striker*, Mia Griffiths. Her striped marlin of 161.4 kg caught on 15 kg line was a pin fish for the Bay of Islands Swordfish Club, and beat Robyn Hall's record of 153 kg set in 1987.

Veteran captain Bill Hall on *Te Ariki Nui* started the season on January 1 with a world record catch for a junior angler, and ended with the 85th marlin also a world record claim. He was slower to adopt live bait, as he wanted to be sure that the fish could be released and if they were deeply hooked would not survive. The use of recurved hooks seemed to solve that problem. But Bill still caught more marlin on lures than any other boat.

Bill's long gamefishing career is sprinkled with record catches and innovation. He is credited with discovering the Three Kings grounds in the early 1980s. The last marlin of the 1997 season was another landmark catch — the first marlin ever caught in New Zealand waters on 4 kg line, and also the heaviest weight fish to line ratio (29-1).

The stripey of 116.2 kg was caught by Auckland angler Campbell Fraser, and Bill said: "After 35 minutes we had a shot at it. I backed up and the deckie (Jim Troup) grabbed the leader. He had on huge welder's gloves which went halfway up his arm, and said, 'If I get that leader, it's not going anywhere. Get ready to grab my feet.'

"The leader was wrapped around his gloves so tightly that we had to cut it off him. We had a bigger one on 4 kg tackle the previous day. It went under the boat from one side to the other, and after three hours we had it right by the boat. The angler got excited and put his thumb on the reel and the line popped. That marlin was a good 140 kg. We had his thumb in splints the next time!"

The previous world record for a striped marlin caught on 4 kg line was a fish of 74.16 kg, caught in Costa Rica in 1989.

Bill had also lodged a world record claim for a marlin of 125.4 kg caught by Fraser's brother, Geoff, on 8 kg line about 10 days earlier.

A 93 kg marlin which Bill's wife, Robyn, caught two months earlier was the first caught by a woman angler on 6 kg tackle in New Zealand.

Bruce Smith's landmark catch — the 100th marlin of the season which his guests insisted he have the honour of catching. Photo courtesy Murray Hansen.

Below: Jubilant skipper Bill Hall (right) with deckhand Jim Troup and angler Campbell Fraser (left) with the first marlin ever caught in New Zealand waters on 4 kg line. Photo courtesy Bill Hall.

Another top Bay of Islands boat, *Predator*, finished the season with 104 marlin, including a world record which replaced Robyn Hall's 6 kg catch. Skipper Bruce Martin said that when he passed the 100 mark he decided to use light tackle. "We had no charter, so it was my wife Ann's turn," said Bruce Martin. She boated a marlin of 142 kg after a 20 minute fight, which also qualified for the exclusive '20-1 club'.

"We had another two on 6 kg — one for one hour and one for four hours, before losing them, but Ann's catch was a good finish to the season."

The end result — chunks of juicy yellowfin tuna freshly smoked over manuka chips.

When a speedster like a hooked marlin or tuna swims in a large circle the line is torn through the water, slicing it and leaving a long shimmering bubble trail. Then suddenly the line snaps and it is all over, leaving the angler breathless and shaking with adrenalin and disappointment.

Two factors contribute to this common problem — the tension applied to the line by water resistance and the increasing drag from the reducing diameter of the reel spool as line is pulled from it.

Tests in the United States show that the extra drag put on the line and knots increases with the speed of the fish and the amount of line in the water. With 500 metres of 24 kg line out and a marlin swimming away at 15 knots, there is 12.7 kg of force being applied to your line. If the marlin is swimming at 19 knots the force increases to a massive 22 kg.

But with only 200 metres of line out the extra force on the line drops to 5.5 kg with a fish going 15 knots, and 9 kg at 19 knots.

The tests also show that with half of the line out (500 metres on an average 24 kg reel), the smaller diameter of the spool required double the force to pull line off at the same speed.

So if the drag on the reel is set at strike with half the line ripped off the spool and the fish has turned and put a belly in the line, you are in trouble. The initial 8 kg of drag is now 16 kg, and the pressure of the line being pulled through the water adds anywhere from about 12 to 22 kg of extra drag — a total of between 28 and 38 kg of drag on line which will break at 24 kg or under. No wonder the knots break so easily!

If the next marlin heads for the horizon, then decides to turn to the right or left, forget about backing the boat up. The solution is to back off the drag instantly, even into free-spool. Then turn the boat and follow the line where it enters the water, not the fish, and recover line to eliminate the belly as quickly as possible.

The albacore tuna is a prolific speedster which readily takes lures. It is highly prized as a table fish, but makes poor cut bait as the flesh is soft and lacks the oil found in its cousin, the skipjack tuna.

Land-based gamefishing

In many parts of the North Island large kingfish patrol rocky coastlines in constant search of prey. These magnificent gamefish inspired a small group of dedicated anglers to form the NZ Land-based Gamefishing Club, a club specifically for anglers who love to catch big fish from the rocks. They specialise in targeting kingfish and sharks from the shore, and the ultimate aim of each member is to one day land a marlin. At the end of the 1997 summer this was yet to happen — although several had been hooked and lost.

The rods used for land-based gamefishing are basically an adaptation of a conventional stand-up gamefishing rod. About 2.2 m long, they have a very fast action that sees the tip fold away under load. This reduces the leverage advantage to the fish, while retaining the length to keep the line clear of rocks as the fish is brought in. Reels are conventional game reels with either lever or star-drag systems, capable of holding about 1,000 m of 15 or 24 kg mono.

Terminal tackle includes a wide selection of hooks, from size 10 or 12 for catching baitfish, up to 4/0 to 9/0 offset hooks for casting large unweighted baits for snapper, and 8/0 to 10/0 offset gamefishing hooks for presenting live kahawai and trevally as kingfish baits. For livebaiting, a 3 to 4 m trace of 50 to 80 kg mono is attached to a good-quality ball-bearing swivel, which is connected to the main line. A balloon tied to the top of the swivel with dental floss completes the rig (Fig. 37).

A berley trail is set up, with bags of minced berley tied to the rocks and chunks of pilchards thrown in by hand. The baitfish have to be caught before serious fishing can commence. This is usually not a problem, because they will be attracted to the berley first, and if there are no baitfish around there will be no kings either. Kahawai are the most popular baits, but mackerel and even maomao or small snapper have been known to hook kingfish. Spare live baits can be safely kept in cool rock pools, and unused baits should be returned to the water at the end of the day.

If a dead bait is used, it must be kept moving, however slowly. A whole piper can be rigged for casting and skipping across the surface by snapping off the beak and hooking it through the head from under the jaw. The point of the hook should pass through the bony part in the centre of the skull, ensuring it stays on the hook. The piper is cast out and slowly retrieved across the surface, leaving a V-shaped wake.

If the bait is to be fished deep, a small ball sinker above the hook will take it down, and the retrieve is more gentle and slower.

Lures and surface poppers can also be used effectively from the rocks, particularly for catching kahawai.

Big kingfish must be gaffed, and the shot should be in the head so that the reaction of the fish actually helps drive it on to the rocks. It is a tough battle trying to pull a threshing, powerful kingfish sideways onto the rocks if it has been hooked in the flank. If the fish is to be released, and many are, it should be lip-gaffed through the skin just behind the lower jaw.

CHAPTER SEVEN
FLOUNDER FISHING AND NETTING

Many people regard flounder, commonly referred to as flatfish, as one of the sweetest eating of all fish — and they are easily caught. Of the nine species of flatfish found in our waters, the sand flounder and yellow-belly are the most common, with soles also found in cooler areas.

The traditional methods of catching flounder are spearing at night, and with set or drag nets; but they do offer fine sport when hooked on light line. A handy spear can be made by welding a short section of 6 mm steel

These fishermen are dragging a net in the surf at Baylys Beach near Dargaville — one of the places where flounder, sole and mullet can be regularly caught in the surf all year round.

into the end of a galvanised pipe and sharpening the tip, or attaching a spear point to a broom handle and wrapping some sheet lead around the shaft for weight. A heavy spear requires little pressure to impale your fish. A single point is preferable to a prong, and a barb is not needed.

You will find flounder in knee-deep water at night around the edges of harbours, estuaries and river mouths throughout the country. Choose a calm night, and if it is cold a wet suit will be welcome, and walk slowly through the shallows, taking care not to stir up the silt and mud and obscure the bottom. The flounder move onto the flats to feed on worms and small crustaceans like crabs, and will remain motionless, covered by a fine layer of sand. Any shape which looks at all like the diamond outline of a hiding fish should be checked.

A spotlight with the battery in a backpack or towed in a small punt or an inner tube raft will illuminate the bottom in front of you; and underwater lights are also available which cut out the surface glare, improving the visibility. Keep the spear point under the surface as you wade along, so a quick jab is all that is needed to impale your quarry. The surface splash of a plunging spear may be enough to frighten the flounder, and they move surprisingly quickly when spooked. The spear should be pushed right to the shaft, and the fish lifted with a forward scoop to keep it on the spear.

If you do not have a small craft on a tow rope, an onion bag secured to your waist will be handy to carry your catch.

The incoming tide produces better than a falling tide, and it is easy to become disorientated at night and lose sight of the shore. On wide flats like the Manukau Harbour the tide moves swiftly and could trap unwary fishermen. If there are no shore lights to serve as beacons, you can leave a lamp burning at your starting point as a precaution.

Flounder on hooks

Flatfish are strong swimmers, and when hooked will put up an impressive struggle. Light line not only makes the fishing more enjoyable and sporting, but you will catch far more fish than if using strong line. A spinning outfit with 2 kg line is ideal, and will cast well with a tiny ball sinker above a swivel, or a couple of split shot near the hook. Use small hooks, like size 10 trout hooks, baited with red garden worms, scraps of mussel or pipi, or kernels of sweetcorn or green peas. The movement of a worm hooked through the centre, or rigged on two hooks, will attract the flounder. Or, you can use a double hook rig with a worm on one hook and a different bait on the other.

You can fish from the shore on a rising ride, or from a small boat on the edge of the channels which the flounder travel through to reach the flats.

One technique used successfully at the Taieri River mouth near Dunedin is to troll slowly with a silver spoon which kicks up the sand, attracting the flounder to a baited hook directly behind the spoon.

Flounder move into harbours during the warm summer months, but can be caught drag netting in the surf during winter.

Big flatfish like this 45 cm turbot, which is the largest member of the flounder family, can be caught netting in the surf on west coast beaches, or speared at night while wading the shallows.

Netting

A wide variety of fish can be taken in set nets, particularly species like parore, red moki, butterfish and porae which rarely take baited hooks.

Nets should be set parallel to the shore, preferably off a rocky coastline as close to the rocks as is safe, leaving sufficient clearance for the movement of waves and tide. Leave the net for at least one cycle of the tide, and if left overnight you will certainly catch fish which are coming in to feed among the rocks in the security of darkness.

Another technique to target flounder is to set the net at full tide when the fish are in the shallows by rowing a dinghy across a small inlet on a harbour and returning at low tide. Many years ago this was a favourite outing on an inlet of the Manukau. We splashed across the mud flats, untangling flounder and kahawai caught in the mesh, then plunged into the shallow channel in the centre where most of the fish had retreated and chased them with hands and feet. It was a muddy, wet exercise but a productive one that had special appeal to young boys.

When setting a net from a boat it pays to lay it out on shore, and fold it onto a sack across the stern so it will slide off smoothly.

A separate anchor rope securing each end of your net will help absorb the pressure from waves and currents, and reduce damage to the net. The rope is attached to a sturdy float bearing your name and phone number as required by regulation, with an anchor and a short length of chain at the other end. Attach the net to loops on the rope, leaving a gap of about 10 metres between the anchor and the bottom loop. The loops should be half a metre closer than the distance between the top and bottom of the net when extended.

Flounder can also be caught on an incoming tide over shallow harbour flats. Run the net out parallel to the beach at low tide in about half a metre of water. Fish will often be felt hitting the net as you are setting it. Then pull the net in at high tide. If it is left after the tide turns, the outgoing current will push the belly in the net out in the opposite direction, washing out some of the fish you have caught. If there is a lot of weed and debris in the water, leave the net set for a short period only — maybe an hour — so the weight of the material intercepted does not shift it.

The other method of netting is to drag your net off a beach. One person remains on shore anchoring the rope while another rows a dinghy or walks out in a wide arc, paying out the net before returning to shore where both ends are slowly pulled in.

This can be exciting work, particularly when the final belly of net reaches the shallows and fish can be seen splashing frantically. Ensure the bottom of the net is held on the sand so fish cannot escape under it. It is a popular method of catching flounder on west coast beaches through much of the year.

When targeting mullet, look for tiny ripples on the surface of the waves which indicate a shoal, or try fishing where a brown stain marks a concentration of plankton being washed ashore. Flounder can be located by checking for worm beds at low tide and returning when the tide is nearly full. These beds will be revealed to experienced eyes by the masses of tiny holes in the sand concentrated over an area the size of a bedroom.

In the surf, a net can be dragged along by walking slowly and 'trawling' for mullet, but flounder are best fished with a different technique. Two anglers walk out together into the surf then separate, paying out the net until it is fully extended, and dragging it back to the shore.

CHAPTER EIGHT
KITE FISHING AND LONGLINES

Shore-based Kiwi fishermen have come up with many ingenious methods of sending a longline out to sea from a beach. The kontiki raft, which sails out under wind power, is probably the best known. The original version uses a time-release device with a barley sugar which, when dissolved, makes the sail drop and releases a weight which slides down the line. This anchors the whole contraption and ensures the hooks are on the bottom. Later the raft and fish are hauled back to shore.

Another machine has been used for pulling a line out to sea with wave power. Called a Galloping Gertie, it involves a swinging shield which catches a receding wave, pulling the apparatus along the bottom. Then the shield swings back, allowing the next incoming wave to roll over it, and popping up again to catch the next wave out. I have never seen or used this machine, but some old-timers have recounted their adventures with the Gertie which they maintain certainly did the job — if a little ungainly and slow.

A battery-powered submarine has also been developed to tow a fishing line out from a beach, and no doubt does it effectively, if expensively. Pipe guns firing gunpowder, and spud guns firing a chunk of potato have all been employed with varying results — including firing the sinker and hooks over the horizon after snapping the line which had been carefully laid out on the sand! Other fishermen attach their lines to huge balloons, but like a kontiki this system relies on the wind blowing directly offshore.

> For the terminal rigs, always use line which is lighter than the main line, so only the end section will be lost if it becomes snagged. A difference of 10 kg in breaking strain of the lines is all that is needed.

Kite fishing

About ten years ago an Auckland commercial fisherman, Paul Barnes, started playing around with kites, adapting a principle used successfully for hundreds of years by Pacific Island fishermen. He soon developed efficient kite systems which have revolutionised shore-based fishing. Today, people using his kite-powered techniques can do virtually anything a boat fisherman can do.

Paul has developed many different kites and rigs for fishing different situations and conditions around the coast, and serious kite fishermen catch a lot of fish. On some west coast beaches, like Kariotahi Beach between Port Waikato and the Manukau Harbour entrance, huge snapper up to 14 kg are caught regularly.

There are three basic types of rigs — a longline, a dropper rig, and a casting kite.

> Kites can be tacked across the wind by tying a screwed-up plastic bag to the end of the cross-spar on the side you want it to veer towards. The extra weight is enough to tip the kite over, causing it to slide across the wind in the desired direction.

The appendages on these longline hooks have been developed by kite fishing entrepreneur Paul Barnes, and comprehensively tested over two years. They are the most environmentally friendly fish hooks in the world. The wire appendage prevents snapper and other fish from swallowing the bait and becoming gut-hooked, reducing the mortality among young fish caught by both commercial and recreational fishermen. After catching more than 2,000 snapper in the Hauraki Gulf, Paul has concluded that using this hook will result in:
- a reduction in the incidence of gut-hooked fish from 30–40% to less than 2% of the catch;
- limit bags weighing more, as it targets larger fish (small fish reject it);
- 30% fewer snapper killed for the same weight of landed fish;
- reduced bait costs;
- undersized snapper catch cut by 50%;
- an increase in catch of 30 cm-plus snapper;
- reduced losses of gear and fish to sharks as they are not attracted by the dying gut-hooked fish on your longline;
- reduction in fish eaten by lice, as lip-hooked snapper are more lively.

Where the bottom is clean, a longline (Fig. 61) is dragged out by the kite attached to the end.

These lines are up to a kilometre long, with a main line of 65 kg monofilament on a large reel mounted on a beach spike. The traces (up to 25) are clipped on and slide between stoppers two metres apart. With the Japanese recurved longline hooks Paul always uses, the fish swim away with the bait until the trace reaches a stopper, then the hook turns, hooking the fish cleanly in the corner of the mouth almost every time. Different lures like soft-head jigs representing a small baitfish or squid can be added, perhaps with a tail of a strip of squid, for targeting mid-water species like kahawai and kingfish as the rig trolls out and is wound in again — a total of two kilometres of trolling, from the beach!

A plastic milk bottle partially filled with sand anchors the kite to the surface, preventing the wind power from lifting the whole line up off the bottom. Unlike other methods, the kite anchors the line once it has reached the required distance offshore, preventing it from being swept down the beach by currents or rips.

But if you want to fish on the outside of a reef, or over a reef, a dropper rig (Fig. 62) where the main line is suspended in the air and the fishing section hangs under a float is the ideal setup.

The line can be a kilometre-long line carrying up to 25 hooks, or you can use a small casting kite to carry out the line on your fishing reel. This kite can be as small or as powerful as you like, depending on the weight

KITE FISHING AND LONGLINES

of line used. The distance fished is determined by the amount of line on the reel. With a regular surfcasting outfit, a casting kite produces the longest cast you will ever make. If really serious, you can use a short, heavy boat rod and a large reel like a 9/0 spooled with 1500 metres of 24 kg gamefishing line, carrying four or five hooks at the end. These rigs can be fished with the kite left flying, or it can be separated and retrieved on a second line, allowing you to play your fish without the pull of the kite adding to the weight on the end.

Kite fishing is all about balance: ensuring the tackle fits the wind strength and line weight, and the amount of lead used and the amount of sand in the float are all in balance so the baits are presented on the bottom where the fish are, or where you want them to be. You can also troll live or dead baits or lures on the surface with a kite, even tacking it across the wind if it is not blowing directly offshore.

Paul produces a range of kites designed for wind strengths from as little as five knots, up to howling 60-knot blasts.

Fig. 61

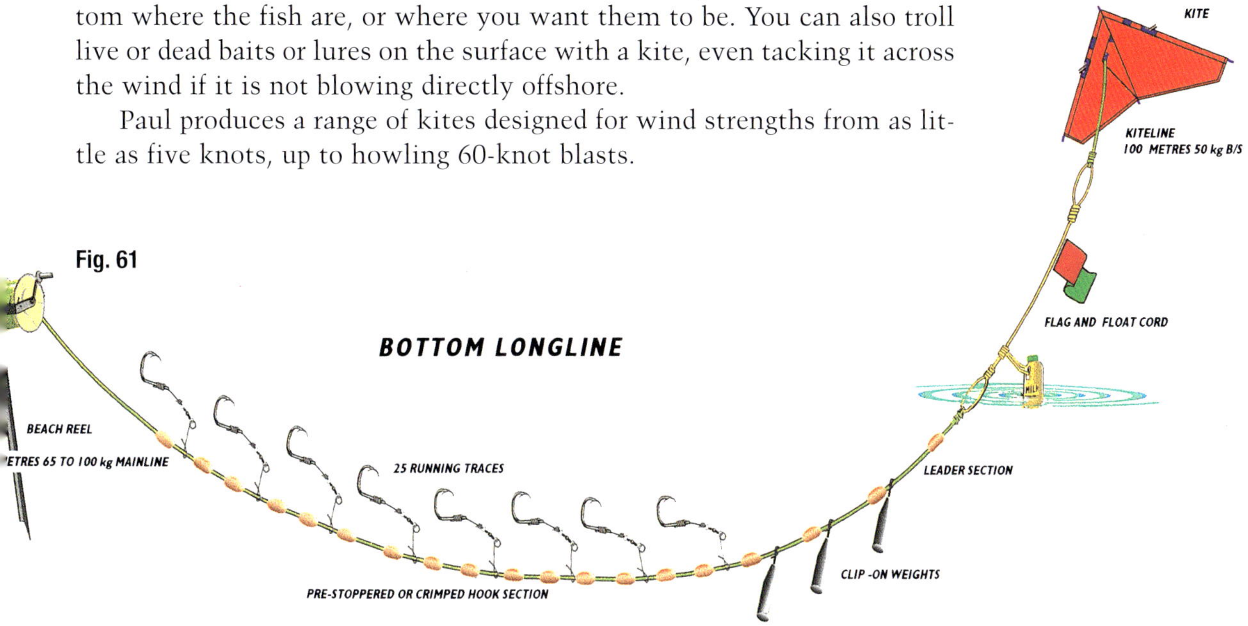

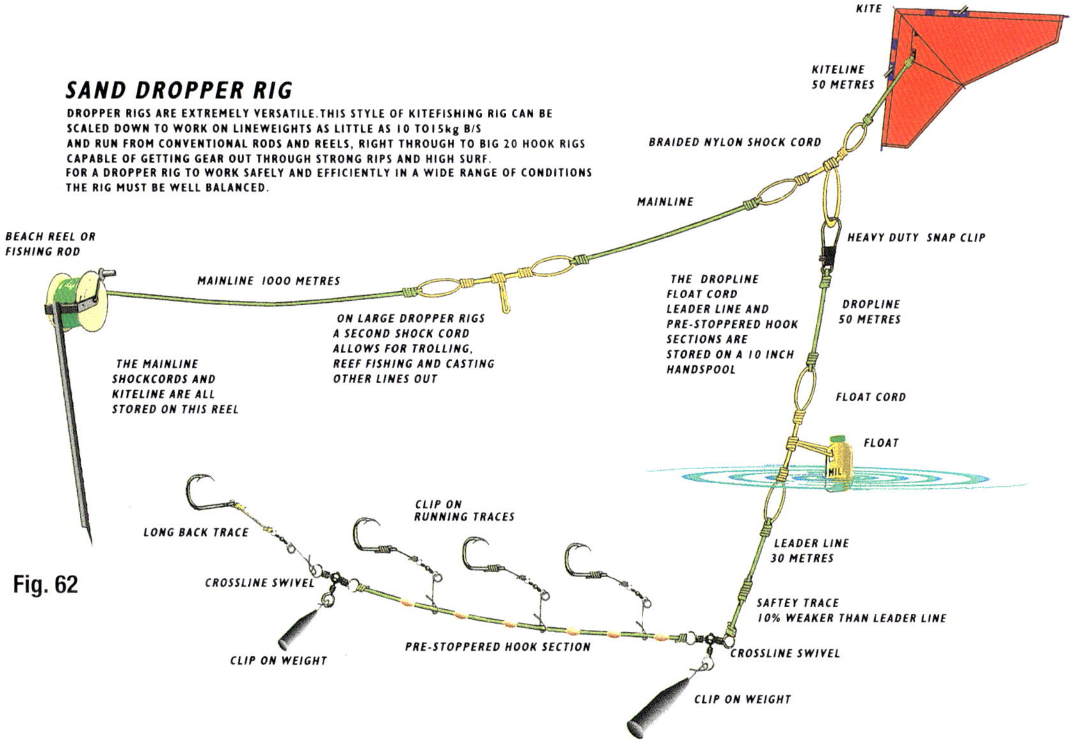

BOTTOM LONGLINE

KITE
KITELINE 100 METRES 50 kg B/S
FLAG AND FLOAT CORD
BEACH REEL
ETRES 65 TO 100 kg MAINLINE
25 RUNNING TRACES
LEADER SECTION
PRE-STOPPERED OR CRIMPED HOOK SECTION
CLIP-ON WEIGHTS

SAND DROPPER RIG

DROPPER RIGS ARE EXTREMELY VERSATILE. THIS STYLE OF KITEFISHING RIG CAN BE SCALED DOWN TO WORK ON LINEWEIGHTS AS LITTLE AS 10 TO 15kg B/S AND RUN FROM CONVENTIONAL RODS AND REELS, RIGHT THROUGH TO BIG 20 HOOK RIGS CAPABLE OF GETTING GEAR OUT THROUGH STRONG RIPS AND HIGH SURF. FOR A DROPPER RIG TO WORK SAFELY AND EFFICIENTLY IN A WIDE RANGE OF CONDITIONS THE RIG MUST BE WELL BALANCED.

KITE
KITELINE 50 METRES
BRAIDED NYLON SHOCK CORD
MAINLINE
HEAVY DUTY SNAP CLIP
BEACH REEL OR FISHING ROD
MAINLINE 1000 METRES
ON LARGE DROPPER RIGS A SECOND SHOCK CORD ALLOWS FOR TROLLING, REEF FISHING AND CASTING OTHER LINES OUT
THE DROPLINE FLOAT CORD LEADER LINE AND PRE-STOPPERED HOOK SECTIONS ARE STORED ON A 10 INCH HANDSPOOL
DROPLINE 50 METRES
THE MAINLINE SHOCKCORDS AND KITELINE ARE ALL STORED ON THIS REEL
FLOAT CORD
FLOAT
LONG BACK TRACE
CLIP ON RUNNING TRACES
LEADER LINE 30 METRES
Fig. 62
CROSSLINE SWIVEL
SAFTEY TRACE 10% WEAKER THAN LEADER LINE
CLIP ON WEIGHT
PRE-STOPPERED HOOK SECTION
CROSSLINE SWIVEL
CLIP ON WEIGHT

163

The wind was howling, and to find a fish meant finding a spot out of the wind. Not an easy option. But with some lateral thinking, the wind can also be turned to advantage. I put the question "Any ideas where we might find some fish in these conditions?" to kite fishing supremo Paul Barnes. "Meet you at Te Ari Point," was the response.

"It's forecast to go to 60 knots in the afternoon, so we will use a flexiwing kite," Paul explained as the gear was being set up on the clean sand of Pakiri Beach. This kite is a technological marvel. It is designed to fly safely in winds of 15 to more than 60 knots. The secret is a rubber band on each side of the kite, connecting the fabric to the end of the spar. When the wind gusts heavily the bands stretch and the face of the kite reduces in size, cushioning the extra force and maintaining a steady amount of drag. Conversely when the gusts drop away, the face of the kite expands.

At ground level, the wind was whipping off the beach in turbulent swirls, the effect of a belt of pine trees adjacent to the dunes. But 50 metres up the wind was pure and strong, and the red kite soared easily, flexing its wings as it adjusted to the force which carried it higher and higher and out over the breakers. When the kite neared 150 metres, Paul attached the line to a plastic milk bottle half filled with wet sand, and tied the end of his fishing line to the handle also. Ten short traces with square, wickedly curved longline hooks baited with strips of squid were then added by clipping the traces at intervals to the main line. Crimped metal stops spaced along the line ensured the traces could slide only a short distance and not tangle. The movement allowed a snapper to swim away with the bait, until the clip reached a stop and the hook was forced through the corner of its mouth.

It is an efficient method of fishing, based on commercial longline systems, and Paul maintains that the squid strip is the best bait for snapper — particularly if the dangling end is split several times to release more odour and also add movement.

"Remember these baits will be trolled out for a kilometre, and back again if they don't have a fish on," he added.

As the kite steadily pulled the two lines out to sea, the spool on his heavy-duty game reel revolved smoothly.

"There's a thousand metres of 20 kg line on that," explained Paul. "If you can get past 500 metres, you will catch fish. The paddle crabs out to 300 metres will strip the bait if you fish in that zone."

These small kites can be used on regular surfcasting rods, either attached permanently to the line, or connected with a lolly which dissolves in about five minutes, releasing the fishing line. The kite then has to be brought in on a second line, and more rods can be set. The problem with surfcasting outfits is the lack of line capacity: the reels will hold up to 300 metres, which may not be far enough to ensure results.

When his reel finally ran out of line the kite was out of sight, then, like all fishing it was just a question of waiting.

"The snapper are moving down the coast in huge schools, getting ready to spawn, so we won't leave it long," said Paul.

A passing vehicle stopped and the driver leaned out for a yarn. He had stayed out all night, also kite fishing, and had his limit of snapper in the back. "I had a good sleep in the sand, down out of the wind," he said.

After only 15 minutes, Paul started reeling in the heavy line. With the combined weight of fish and

Longlines in boats

Traditional set lines are either droppers or longlines. Droppers are mainly used in deep water for species like hapuku and bluenose, and use a heavy main line with 2-5 short traces at the business end, recurve hooks baited with a tough strip bait like squid, kahawai or barracouta, and a heavy weight like a sash weight for an anchor. A small float at the surface, with a larger float on 10 m or more of rope, completes the outfit. The second

Kite fishing experts Paul and Peggy Barnes with the john dory that was too greedy, and two of the snapper from the one set of the kite-powered longline which yielded six snapper, a kahawai, two gurnard and the john dory on 15 hooks at Pakiri Beach, north of Auckland.

the kite pulling against the wind, it was a long, steady process. He was able to wind comfortably while sitting on the butt of the short, stubby rod, with the reel resting on the top of a chilly bin. "You don't need harnesses for this sort of fishing."

With about 300 metres left, he pulled the line in by hand to prevent the pressure exploding the spool. A line of fish appeared in the water, then marched steadily up the beach. Two snapper, followed by a bright red gurnard, then a dogfish, a kahawai and more snapper — a total of eight fish on ten hooks. "Not bad for the first cast," said Paul with a grin.

The second cast produced more gurnard and snapper, then, on the last hook a fin broke the surface in the shallows and a dark body flapped on the sand. It was a huge john dory that had swallowed a small kahawai which had taken a bait, and refused to let it go while it was dragged in for a kilometre. Finally the dory expelled the kahawai when it reached the edge of the sand — too late to escape.

float is insurance against rising tide or waves lifting the rig and bouncing it along until the current carries it away. Such lines are often lost when the fisherman underestimates the power of the current and waves. This can be an efficient method of catching deepwater fish, and you can go line fishing or trolling while the dropper works for you.

The 50-hook longline is a popular method of catching a limit bag while enjoying the beach, water-skiing or sailing. Check the regulations

Fresh bait is always best. Popular baits are fresh kahawai, mullet or trevally, squid and octopus tentacles. Mullet and trevally are excellent baits, and kahawai can usually be caught on the first set by using pilchard chunks on some of the hooks, but these do come off easily. This freshly caught kahawai is tough, and catches fish; fresh kahawai which has been scaled and filleted is good for big snapper. Mussels, pipis or small crabs will hook trevally and dogfish.

If you want to preserve bait, cut mullet, kahawai or trevally into strips about 15 mm wide and 50-65 mm long. Place the strips skin-side down in a flat container and cover with plain table salt. Repeat the layers of baits and salt, adding some fish oil or other attractant if you wish. Refrigerate for 24-48 hours, drain off excess fluid to prevent the bait turning mushy, then freeze it. Bait treated this way will last for months when frozen, and up to two weeks refrigerated.

because in some parts of the country there are restrictions on the number of hooks per line, number of lines per boat, or even a total ban on lines that are left unattended.

You should use tough baits which are not quickly stripped by paddle crabs or small 'pickers' — like chunks of squid, or fresh mullet or kahawai. Baits placed on recurved longline hooks should be hooked through just once, or they tend to corkscrew as they are pulled through the water.

Setting and retrieving longlines can be hazardous if the wind is blowing. The basic technique is to drop the main anchor and drift first, then motor up against the current or wind so that if you have a tangle, or a hook becomes stuck in the gunwale or a finger, you can quickly ease off the pressure. If the wind is blowing you away from the line, you can get into real trouble quickly and a sharp knife should be kept handy for emergencies. Some inexperienced people have been nearly pulled overboard when a hook has caught in an arm or jersey and the boat is out of control in a strong breeze or current.

A new concept in longlines makes them user-friendly. It is a shorter (60 m) main line on a hand spool, with traces stored separately. You just clip a 1 kg weight to the end and drop it over the side, then motor upwind or upcurrent, feeding out the line and clipping the traces on until you reach a three-way loop. To this you clip the grapnel anchor. A float is clipped to the end of the line. When you want to retrieve it, you pick up the float and pull it in, at the same time lifting the line off the bottom and bouncing the weight at the other end across the bottom. The boat can be left to drift while you pull in your line. It makes more sense to use two lines with 12 and 13 hooks, rather than one long one, allowing you to fish different areas and find the fish. By the time the second line is set, you can pull in the first one.

CHAPTER NINE
CRAYFISH, SHELLFISH AND SQUID

Crayfish

There are two species of crayfish in our waters — the common red crayfish, also called the spiny lobster or rock lobster, which is found throughout the country, and the packhorse crayfish, also called the smooth-tailed lobster or green crayfish, found mainly in Northland.

Many myths used to surround the life history of the crayfish, and while indeed the whole story is still not known, it is much better understood today. After mating, the female lobster lays her eggs, fertilising them from her store of sperm just before attaching them under her tail. She then migrates when they are about to hatch, taking up position on deep rocky reefs where there is plenty of current, and shakes the hatching larvae off by flapping her tail. Then they're on their own in the plankton for a couple of years. At first, crayfish larvae look like squashed spiders, and live in open waters. After moulting and growing, they eventually turn into a final larval stage which looks like a translucent miniature crayfish, with one small difference: it can swim both forwards and backwards. It then settles on the sea bed and begins to look and behave like a small adult. Crayfish live for tens of years.

A large crayfish is a prize that few fishermen see unless they are proficient divers, and its capture is most welcome.

The management of our crayfish has been turbulent, like all sea fisheries, involving controversy and huge amounts of money. But the stocks are healthy and it is one area where the fisheries managers seem to have got it right. Credit must be given where it is due. Restrictions on the commercial harvest coincided with rising prices through the advent of live export to Japan and other markets, and the return to commercial fishermen is among the highest in the industry — and the easiest to earn, as many crayfishermen can fill their quota in a few weeks. Not a bad return on the capital invested in a boat and several hundred pots, with earnings of several hundred thousand dollars a year.

The result is a happy situation for crayfish stocks and recreational fishermen, where the authorities have so far resisted calls from the commercial sector for increased quotas following rising populations.

Divers and droppers of pots can now expect a good feed of fresh crayfish, and crayfish are even returning to some areas near cities like Auckland where they have not been seen for many years, though remote coastal regions still usually offer the best catches.

Crayfish are found throughout the country, and experienced divers can often find them while diving from the shore, but boats will provide greater opportunities.

Diving

Spears and hooks are prohibited. They give an unfair advantage to the diver and also damage undersized fish. But grabbing a crayfish by hand is a technique which comes with experience. Most people wear gloves, and the object is to quickly grab for the body. As the crayfish darts backwards into its rocky shelter under a ledge or in a hole the hand will connect with the feelers, compensating for the backward movement. A good grasp on the spiny base of the feelers will trap the creature. But if you grab above the base, the feelers will just snap off.

Crays will be found living in shallow water at certain times of the year and can be caught while snorkelling. However they are most easily caught using scuba gear, and will be found on reefs, in caves and among kelp.

Sometimes a single rock surrounded by sand will hold a good stock of crays, and if the rock appears on the depth sounder screen with fish above it, there are more likely to be crayfish at the base.

The main season is from September to February, and females may not be taken when they are carrying eggs under their tails, usually from April to June, when they are said be 'in berry'. Crayfish also shed their shells at least once a year, and may not be taken when the new shell is still soft.

Setting pots

The anticipation when hauling up a craypot that has been freshly baited the previous day is one of the great joys of fishing. When the pot rises through the water and a cluster of red bodies can be seen in one corner the fisherman hauls with renewed vigour.

The big question then is: are they legal sized? In some areas the crays are so heavily fished they are caught almost as soon as they reach legal size, and other places seem to be a nursery, like Waihau Bay in the eastern Bay of Plenty, with a large proportion of small crays.

Several years spent at Waihau Bay saw crayfish on the table every day. Three or four pots set in 7-8 metres of water out in front of the house would yield 30 or more crays every morning, with half a dozen kept for eating. The common beehive-type of pot sold in most shops was not favoured. Locals maintained the shiny wire repelled the crayfish when they climbed over it, and would paint the wire with tar or black paint.

The most successful pots had large frames of reinforcing steel welded together, with a flat rectangular bottom and rounded upper section. This was covered with black plastic mesh, with the top half of a bucket situated in the middle at the top for the crays to enter. They never seemed to be able to find their way back out.

Some home-made pots featured a mesh purse to hold the bait, but our baits suspended by string from the roof seemed to do the job adequately.

There is much argument as to what is the best bait, and the crayfish do seem to develop a dislike of certain baits. As with much fishing, fresh bait is best. Fish which prey on crayfish, like rays and snapper, are definitely not recommended. Their odour has the opposite effect to the desired one.

Pieces of a kingfish frame, with the fins and tail, work very well, and the head is the best part — maybe it has the most flesh on it.

Strange baits like a wild duck, pukeko or possum which has been singed in a fire are rumoured to be used successfully further round the east coast; but a little experimentation is a good investment.

But if a pot yields nothing, then it should be moved to a different location; even a few metres can make a difference.

Crayfish are nocturnal, so pots should be left overnight, and the owner's name and address must be on the float.

Crayfish on the line

With increasing numbers of crayfish, reports of them being hooked on baits lowered for reef fish are becoming more common. Fishermen report a few tugs and a weight coming on their line, which when pulled in is found to have a large crayfish on the hook.

The crayfish has obviously been attracted to the bait, which was probably dropped in front of its lair, and while pulling the bait towards its tiny mouth has alerted the fisherman whose strike is sufficient to jab the hook point into the joint of a leg or under the carapace.

Such catches are fortuitous and should be regarded as a bonus. A lot of time could be wasted if crayfish were targeted in this manner, but an old stocking could be packed with bait scraps and offal and suspended from the anchor chain on a rocky bottom. If a crayfish gets trapped in the fine mesh and comes up with the anchor, a long-handled net will be useful to ensure it comes aboard.

Shellfish

Gathering shellfish is a strong tradition which is popular throughout the country. While the succulent toheroa is still off-limits, smaller delicacies like tuatuas are easily found on most ocean beaches, while pipis and cockles are more common on shallow banks in inlets and harbours.

Beds of shellfish can be located by looking for holes in the sand at low tide, or feeling with toes while wading the shallows on a falling tide. Scallops and horse mussels, which taste like scallops, are often thrown up during storms; beachcombing immediately after a blow can be rewarding.

Scallops can also be picked up on very low tides in some areas, and close to Auckland the shallows off Cornwallis and Clarks Beach on the Manukau Harbour attract hundreds of people during the season.

But the most common method of gathering scallops is dragging a scallop dredge over the beds. Scallops seem to react to fishing pressure and will move long distances, so the local knowledge on where they can be found is invaluable — as it is with all fishing. When towing your dredge, extra rope should be kept in the boat, with a float like a milk bottle attached ready to throw over the side if the dredge becomes stuck on the bottom. It is easy to swamp your boat when the dredge strikes a rock and

Young mussels clinging to rocks at Ninety Mile Beach are uncovered by the receding tide.

drags the stern down in a following sea.

Two pieces of tape stuck to the transom make a quick measure to check the size of your catch as you clear the dredge.

Apart from isolated sections of coastline, mussels will rarely be found within wading distance of shore and a snorkel and pair of flippers are needed to harvest wild mussels.

Pauas have also suffered from fishing pressure and remote areas will provide the best fishing. They prefer rocky areas which are open to ocean swells, and good paua spots can often be located by the smooth pink rocks they like to cling to.

Regulations governing the gathering of shellfish are strictly enforced and always ensure you are familiar with the rules covering seasons, limits, minimum sizes and restricted areas.

Squid

The giant squid occasionally dragged from the depths on trawl nets are among the most mysterious creatures in the ocean. In contrast the two common squid species are important links in the marine food chain, and among the most abundant.

The huge squid caught in early 1996 by the research vessel *Tangaroa* in deep water at the Chatham Rise is the largest recorded, but little is known about these giants. That specimen was eight metres long, weighed

Squid are among the most prolific creatures in the sea and an important food source for many fish. This voracious squid has caught a hapless flyingfish near White Island.

about a tonne, and was estimated to be three years old. It must have consumed vast amounts of food to grow so rapidly, and one can only speculate on the fierce struggles which occur between these immensely strong creatures and the sperm whales which prey on them.

These battles take place in the dark, silent depths a thousand metres or more below the bright surface. The suckers on the long tentacles of the giant squid have two circular rows of rasping teeth, which must be used for grasping prey, and also to grip the whales which often carry the scars from such encounters. The parrot-like beak at the centre of the nest of writhing tentacles would be no match for the tooth-lined jaws of an adult sperm whale.

Writers of fiction have fuelled the myths surrounding giant squid, attributing fearsome attacks on sailing ships to these deepwater denizens, which have actually never been seen alive. Scientists discount such legends, but are seeking to learn more about these fascinating creatures.

There are two kinds of common squid in our waters: broad squid and arrow squid. They are popular sources of food for a variety of sea life, from dolphins, tuna, marlin and broadbill swordfish, to kingfish, snapper, hapuku and many other fish. Everything in the sea seems to like eating squid, which is why they are so prolific and fast-growing.

But what do the squid eat? They must be able to catch some small fish, for they will eagerly attack a bait like a whole pilchard, and a lure like a jig. We know they rise to the surface at night, for that is when the foreign fleets catch huge quantities off our coast, luring the squid to the boats with powerful lights. The squid are hooked on metal jigs armed with rows of needle-sharp jagged points which are rotated on endless circulating belts, flipping the hapless squid into the belly of the floating factory.

Squid are, of course, popular as fish bait; and also in salads and as crumbed squid rings, which is how most people encounter them. When small snapper are prolific, squid is a sensible bait to use as it resists the nibbles of the small 'pickers' better than the soft fish baits. It works well when cut into strips, after the tough, thin, speckled skin has been removed to reveal the bright, white flesh.

It is ironic that, with so many squid landed in our waters, some of the best bait is whole baby squid imported from California. These 15 cm specimens make excellent baits when used whole, and some anglers add extra appeal by squirting thick fish oil into the body cavity, or even poking a whole pilchard inside it.

But next time the crumbed squid rings are served steaming on the plate, spare a thought for the mysterious giant squid and the squid rings it would produce.

CHAPTER TEN
HISTORY OF TROUT AND SALMON

The trout and salmon we fish for in New Zealand have their origins in the dawn of time, 100 million years ago, when the seas held fish which people would later call the Salmoniformes. This ancient family of fishes gradually split as different members followed different paths down the slow process of evolution. Over millions of years, which saw cataclysmic geological and climatic changes that moulded the various species, there began to emerge a group of graceful, brightly coloured fish known as the Salmonidae — or salmonids.

While the common ancestor of all the modern salmonid fishes has long gone, one line evolved into a subfamily of toothless fish known as

Rivers like the North Umpqua River in Oregon are home to the steelhead from which our rainbow trout are descended. This river was a favourite of the famous angler Zane Grey, who built a cabin on its banks.

whitefish, and includes Rocky Mountain whitefish found in western North American rivers, the huge sheefish of the frigid Arctic water, and the ciscoes. A further split in that line led to another subfamily whose survivors include the delicate grayling of Europe and North America.

None were native to the southern hemisphere, but a native grayling was found in New Zealand. However it did not survive long after the arrival of Europeans, though the reason for its demise is unclear. How a member of the Salmonidae developed in apparent isolation in such southern latitudes is another of the mysteries of nature.

Another separate line of fish developed into the complex subfamily Salmoninae, and it is this group with which we are most concerned. It has branches in Russia (the lenok); Europe (the huchen); and also includes the chars (brook trout, Dolly Varden and Arctic char); the Pacific salmons (quinnat or chinook, coho, chum and pink); and of course the trout family.

For many years both brown and rainbow trout were classified with Atlantic salmon (*Salmo salar*) — *Salmo trutta*, the European brown trout; and *Salmo gairdneri*, the rainbow trout. But recently ichthyologists have reclassified rainbow trout as *Oncorhynchus mykiss*, and regarded them as more closely related to Pacific salmon than Atlantic salmon. All of these fish are anadromous, which means they spawn in freshwater rivers, and either live in freshwater or return to their natal river after years of roaming the sea. Why some go to sea remains unclear, but it does allow families to develop from individual river systems in numbers which a river would be unable to sustain if all of the fish lived there permanently. The fertility of the oceans allows the fish to grow quickly compared to river-dwelling fish. Perhaps it is also nature's way of ensuring the species survives if a disaster like massive flooding or volcanic destruction overtakes a particular river, for there will always be several year-classes at sea which will return. Or some fish may be forced to enter rivers foreign to them, which is probably how the family of salmon and trout colonised new regions and evolved into different subspecies.

This propensity for migration developed early in the evolution of our favourite family of freshwater fish and appears to have been at a time when there were waters of intermediate salinity in thousands of estuaries throughout the northern hemisphere. This allowed the ancestors of our trout and salmon to easily travel from the rivers to oceans. Over time this migratory instinct became deeply rooted and is one of the qualities which appeals so much to modern man. Migratory behaviour is present to some degree in all salmonids, even though some modern subfamilies are landlocked. These fish, usually trout rather than salmon, are exercising their inherent instincts when they ascend tributary streams and rivers to spawn then return to the main body of the lake to recover. Their offspring descend to the lake where they grow and mature, returning to their natal stream to repeat the process.

The powerful urge to migrate reaches its peak in the Pacific salmon and steelhead, and it is the chinook or quinnat salmon (*Oncorynchus tschawytscha*) and the steelhead which are of main interest to New Zealand anglers.

The Hunter River at Makarora yields its rainbow trout grudgingly.

Behavioural characteristics imprinted into fish over many generations are important elements in the management of our fisheries. One example is the 'big fish' programme in Rotorua which involved many years of research before the key factors which control fish behaviour were identified and utilised. The steelhead is a rainbow which runs out to sea like a salmon, but unlike the salmon it does not die after spawning. American anglers, and in particular fly fishermen, revere the steelhead as the ultimate gamefish. The five species of Pacific salmon do not command the same respect as either steelhead or Atlantic salmon. Both are members of the trout family and keenly sought by anglers. All of the salmonids require cold, aerated water in which to spawn, and cold ocean water to roam and feed in. They obviously could not pass through the warm equatorial oceans or spawn in warm tropical rivers, which is why none occurred naturally below the equator.

The Romans gave salmon its name, Latin for leaping fish; and the modern classification *Salmo salar* and its connotation is one which anglers have long appreciated. Many British terms derive from early Saxon names for salmon — parr, pearl, smolt, grilse, kipper and bagget. Kipper once meant a spawned-out salmon, which we know as a kelt or slab. A corruption of the term is kype, which refers to the severe hooking of a male salmonid's lower jaw, indicating sexual maturity.

The British formalised angling for salmon and we owe much to this heritage. But there are some elements which were not transplanted in the new colonies. In the Old Country land was privately owned and the fish became the exclusive property of the aristocracy. Poaching by a commoner was a serious offence punishable by laws having more in common with the rack than confiscation of one's gaff. As angling became a sport the salmon took its place alongside the grouse, pheasant, stag and equestrian expertise, representing an inviolate way of life manifested by peerage, manor houses, idle grace, and hereditary wealth and position. The term salmon came to represent an exclusiveness which was not supported by corresponding qualities as a gamefish.

But in this country we have adopted the equality of opportunity inherent in American angling, rather than the traditional British approach. While the British salmon, and to a lesser degree trout, were becoming the exclusive domain of the aristocracy, the great runs of salmon and steelhead trout in the American Northwest were being destroyed by logging, commercial fishing, and the construction of dams. Hatcheries were built with little attention to the origin of the stock used, and fish released into rivers and never seen again. Today, the American steelhead fishery relies on hatchery fish.

Scientists have learned much about the genetics and the instincts which drive these magnificent fish, and in New Zealand we have benefited from the mistakes of the early managers.

The first attempts to introduce trout and salmon to New Zealand failed, but the pioneering sportsmen who formed acclimatisation societies to introduce and establish populations of fish, game birds and animals to the virgin waters and forests were determined. Finally, in 1867 a consignment of brown trout ova survived the trip from Tasmania, and the first freshwater gamefish had arrived in the new country. The Tasmanian trout had come from England, and over the next 20 years more shipments of ova came from Tasmania, Italy, Germany and England. Hatcheries were built throughout the country to raise fish for liberation and some of the first stocks were hatched at the ponds in the Auckland Domain, and transported to a hatchery at Okoroire Springs near Matamata.

Several shipments of rainbow trout ova were sent from California, but it was not until 1883 that some of the delicate eggs, which were packed in ice and charcoal, were hatched in Auckland. Millions of trout fry were liberated in streams around Auckland, but the delicate fish were not easy to transport around the country.

The former Conservator of Wildlife in Rotorua, the late Pat Burstall, had a special interest in the history of the Rotorua lakes fishery and related a delightful story which illustrates the unscientific nature of some of the early trout liberations: "The fish were transported in cream cans with holes punched in the lids to provide aeration. You can imagine the cans rocking about on the horse-drawn carts, and one day a shipment was being transported from Okoroire to Reporoa when the drivers stopped at the old Lake Tavern on the edge of Rotorua for a drink. They stayed a bit too long in the pub, and when they came out to resume their journey they found some of the young trout belly-up in the cans. So they tipped them into the nearest stream, which was the Utuhina Stream — and that's how trout became established in Lake Rotorua!"

Other species were imported, including American brook trout and the Loch Leven strain of brown trout from Scotland which are said to survive today in the Motu River in the Bay of Plenty.

A hatchery at Masterton supplied ova to other hatcheries in Taranaki, Marlborough, Nelson and Westland; and in 1887 the hatchery was reported as having "1700 Loch Leven trout, 250 brown trout, 30 black burn trout, 80 Carpione trout, 12 rainbow trout, 48 Atlantic salmon, and 85,000 ova." There must have been some strange fish introduced and raised at hatcheries in those early days; but fortunately the only species which flourished were rainbow and brown trout and quinnat salmon. Isolated pockets of brook trout, lake trout and land-locked Atlantic salmon have also survived in some parts of the country.

It was not until the early 1900s that Pacific salmon arrived in New Zealand, and like the trout they found an environment that matched their native one in terms of latitude, habitat and water temperatures. An abundance of food, combined with a lack of competition and predators, contributed to the success of the magnificent northern hemisphere gamefish in our lakes and rivers. The salmon which have become an obsession with some Canterbury fishermen are called chinook in Northwest America — an Eskimo name for a warm wind. They were originally found in vast numbers from northern California up the coast to Alaska, but are now rare in California. The best fishing is found in remote parts of the British Columbia coast and in the great rivers of Alaska. Local fishermen there have different names for the fish at various stages of its life: black-mouth when small, then spring salmon up to 35 pounds (15.9 kg) above which they are called tyee or king salmon. The name which has persisted in New Zealand, quinnat, is an Indian name now rarely heard in the salmon's original domain.

Our stock came from the Sacramento River in California between 1901 and 1907, and the young fish were raised at the hatchery on the

It was not until 1883 that some of the delicate rainbow trout eggs which were packed in ice and charcoal were hatched in Auckland.

A steelhead fisherman on the North Umpqua casts across and downstream with a floating line and large dry fly.

It was thought a separate steelhead existed in some lakes . . . but it is now accepted that all of our rainbows are descended from the original stock.

Hakataramea River and liberated into that river and the Waitaki. By 1915 the salmon had colonised the Rangitata, Rakaia and Waimakariri Rivers, and ova taken from returning adults was hatched and the fry liberated in other rivers. Today, salmon runs occur in most east coast rivers between the Wairau and Clutha. Runs in the four main rivers vary between 2,000 and 20,000 fish in a season.

Other fisheries have been established either through liberations or natural colonisation, and salmon can now be caught on southern west coast rivers like the Taramakau and in harbours at Dunedin, Christchurch and Wellington. Stray individuals have been recorded in some North Island rivers including the Hutt, Wanganui and Rangitikei Rivers.

The story of these fisheries has been one of extremes, with the wild fishery facing extinction in the mid-1980s while salmon farming flourished. However, the recovery was dramatic, with metre-long fish weighing 15 kg or more challenging anglers in the 1996 and 1997 seasons.

Various factors are blamed for the demise and subsequent rejuvenation of the fishery — restrictions on commercial harvesting at sea, the decline of commercial hatcheries and releases of millions of fry as they proved unprofitable have all coincided with the turnaround in the wild fishery, and the reduction in kahawai stocks may mean less predation on baby salmon. Changes in the environment, both in the river systems and at sea, also affect the survival and growth of salmon. These could be natural influences like flooding at critical times, variations in rich ocean currents, or artificial stresses like reducing flows by taking water for irrigation.

Our fisheries are the only established salmon fisheries in the southern hemisphere, and offer the most exciting and rewarding fishing for these great sport fish outside the US and Canada.

Fisheries managers have tried unsuccessfully to establish steelhead fisheries, releasing young rainbows into estuaries and river mouths; but for some reason the trout have either gone to sea and lost the ability to return, or migrated upriver to become residents. However brown trout do leave the rivers and, like salmon, head out to sea to take advantage of the plentiful food available there. Sea-run brown trout fisheries are found

Rainbow trout develop unique characteristics in terms of colouring and shape in different environments.

A sea-run steelhead from the North Umpqua — the name implies strength and vigour, and personifies the spirit of wild fish in a wild environment.

mainly in the South Island rivers, and the fish which return as large silver trout are highly prized by anglers

For many years anglers argued that there were several different strains of rainbow trout in New Zealand. It is true that fish will develop unique characteristics in terms of colouring and shape in different environments.

It was thought a separate steelhead, *Salmo irideus*, existed in some lakes because these fish exhibited the steel-blue back and silver flanks of the American sea-run rainbows. The trout in Lake Rotomahana are said to be the purest strain in the country, undiluted by liberations of stock from other fisheries, and indeed the Rotomahana trout do have lovely, rich colouring. But it is now accepted that all of our rainbows are descended from the original stock, with different environments producing fish of differing appearances.

The name steelhead tells us much. It implies strength and vigour and personifies the spirit of wild fish in a wild environment. After about twenty generations, it is the same blood which flows in many of our trout today.

CHAPTER ELEVEN
TROLLING AND HARLING

When we were youngsters we caught all our trout by trolling zed spoons and eye spoons along the edge of the drop-off where the shallow shelf fell away into deep, blue water. This 'blue line' as we called it was quite distinctive and easily followed. The lines on our old English fly reels were fast-sinking fly lines, and the rods were all types and lengths — old fly rods and short, stubby spinning rods.

In those days on Lake Tarawera there was no such thing as lead-core or wire lines, and the only extra depth to be gained came from adding a tapered lead weight with coiled wire at each end, which was wound onto the line just ahead of the trace. Life was carefree and simple and the fish eagerly grabbed our flashing spoons, often tearing free with a head-shaking jump after the first wild rush, leaving a small boy shaking and trembling. On arriving at the lake after the seemingly endless drive from Auckland, a phone call was always made to 'Uncle Joy', better known to Rotorua trout fishermen and duckshooters as J.F. Thomas. His advice was always the same: "Put on a yellow-bodied fly and harl it slowly up the left side of the bay." We knew what he was going to say, yet the advice of such a wise, seasoned angler always instilled fresh hope and anticipation in our young hearts.

Another tradition was to load the old Seagull outboard into the boot and drive into Rotorua where Uncle Joy lived at Kawaha Point and kept a sturdy clinker boat moored by the house. The trips along the foreshore off Fairy Springs always yielded trout, and the fishing always seemed much easier here. A really adventurous trip would take us across the lake to troll in the lee of Mokoia Island, or across the lake to the Awahou Stream mouth where multiple strikes were assured in mid-summer. Here we used copper and red penny spoons, and sometimes tied on a Tamati — an old pattern like a Split Partridge, with a red-and-yellow body made from a dark turkey wing.

Although we did not realise at the time, we were using bright lures in clear, bright water and dark-coloured lures in the darker waters of Lake Rotorua. This remains one of the basic premises of trolling or harling.

Trolling a lure or harling a fly on a shallow line can be looked at in the same context. They are probably the most productive methods of catching trout on lakes, and can also be very rewarding and enjoyable. As the quality of lake fishing has diminished, so the technology and tackle available to anglers has become more sophisticated. Electronic depth sounders give an instant reading of the contours of the lake bed. But even with this help available, there is no substitute for local knowledge and experience. As with all fishing, the thinking fisherman will mentally note some of the

Jenny (left), Katie and Paul carry on the Thomas tradition at 'the secret spot'.

variables at the time he catches fish. Occasionally trout may be caught by accident, but usually a pattern develops. There are a number of variables involved: season, time of day, weather, water conditions, depth fished, speed of the boat, type of lure used and contour of the bottom.

Some waters remain open to fishing all year and fish can be caught near the surface throughout the year, but the best seasons for harling are undoubtedly spring and autumn, with some good fishing also to be found during the hot months.

Lakes in New Zealand can be separated into three distinct types: the cold lakes, including some of the hydro lakes among the mountains of the South Island; shallow lakes created by hydro development; and the natural trout lakes including those of the Rotorua-Taupo district. Generally speaking, the first two groups of lakes contain small forage fish which trout feed on, but insects are also a very important factor in the diet and this determines the way we fish for them: either fly fishing, spinning or deep trolling.

We are left with the central North Island lakes as our main area for fishing with shallow water trolling techniques, which can also apply to the hydro lakes on the Waikato River system, and other small lakes.

Because smelt are such an important part of the trout's diet, the migration of smelt into shallow water to spawn in early spring and again in autumn contributes to the most productive fishing. Depending on the

Prolific shoals of smelt are the prime source of food for trout in the Rotorua and Taupo lakes. They were introduced into Lakes Rotorua and Rotoiti from sea-going smelt trapped in the lower Waikato River between 1906 and 1909. Smelt were not established in other lakes, including Taupo, until the 1930s.

timing of warm spring conditions, the smelt usually start moving to the shallows in October, with the runs peaking in November and December. An unusual phenomenon occurs when swarms of smelt move through the Ohau Channel from Lake Rotoiti to spawn on the shallow, sandy shelves along the eastern shore of Lake Rotorua. Trout follow the migrating smelt and some excellent fishing can be found by trolling silver lures in the shallows, and fly fishing at the Rotorua end of the channel before the season fully opens on 1 October. The fishing in early October can be frantic, with anglers lined up along the banks of the channel all casting into the same stretch of water.

As with most fishing, dawn and dusk are without question the best times, but some memorable days will be encountered when the fish are feeding actively throughout and seem bent on suicide. In contrast, unproductive days soon fade in the memory. It does balance out and we always have to 'pay our dues' for those wonderful occasions by enduring hours on seemingly fishless water. It is a quirk of human nature that the successful fishing trips, like backing winners at the race track, are the ones we cannot resist recounting to other, less fortunate souls.

When fishing near the surface, the weather is more important than when deep trolling. Ideal conditions are when the surface is ruffled by a breeze but it is not uncomfortable. We have had great fishing when it has been quite rough, with the trout seeming to gain energy from the oxygen-enriched surface water and slashing at our smelt flies. The worst conditions are on a hot, calm day. Trout can be more easily seen splashing and rising in such conditions, but in calm water the fish can also see the line clearly, and it's time to bring out the deep tackle. When the smelting season is at its peak trout can be caught all day, particularly if it is overcast, windy, or dull with rain.

Apart from the lure used, the depth which is fished is probably the most important factor. Of course this is determined by the line used. In some places a monofilament line will work, but I do not like trolling with a full mono line as it has a lot of stretch, making it harder to set the hook on a strike. The fish will be found along the edge of a weed bed or a shelf. Good fishing will always be found along a drop-off, and this can be followed accurately with a depth sounder, or by sight. You can also fish across the top of a shelf, and one technique is to zig-zag from one drop-off to the other side.

We like to use old fly lines that are starting to crack and have outlived their usefulness for casting. But a line which produces well on one lake may not work on another, so we have several harling outfits for different uses — one suitable for Tarawera and another for Taupo. It is important to have plenty of line, to get the lure well behind the boat, so the old fly reels used are filled with backing of 15 kg dacron or monofilament. A full spool diameter also gives a faster retrieve when winding in.

On the Rotorua lakes a slow sinking line is the best all-round one, particularly when fishing at dawn or dusk when the fish are near the surface. As the light strengthens it may be necessary to change to a faster sinking line, and if a heavier-density fly line is not available a few metres of lead-core line tied to the end of the main line will do the trick.

When using several lines, one line will invariably catch most of the fish because it is at the correct depth for the fish on the day. The best depth is 3 to 5 m on most lakes, going down to 5 to 7 m on Taupo. Some Taupo charter operators who do a lot of harling make up their own harling rigs with 5 m of lead-core line tied directly to either heavy monofilament or dacron backing, with a small swivel a further 50 m along the line as a marker. A knot or a change to a different line can also be used as a marker. When it is let out through the rod the skipper knows that his guests have the right length of line out every time.

Another vital element is the length of trace used. The rod-length traces we used as youngsters would today be considered too short. But everything was simpler in those days. Whether fish are now smarter or increased boat traffic disturbs them, traces cannot be too long. Up to 20 m of light mono is used with small flies in clear water, and heavier line when trolling lures. Some successful Taupo fishermen use 2.5 kg breaking strain traces, while most use 3 or 4 kg line.

The speed at which the boat moves is more important with lures than with flies. About 2 knots is fine for harling, but speed also affects the depth the lines will reach, and the wind is another factor. How often have you found that a run in one direction across a favourite shelf produces fish, while going back the other way you get nothing? There is probably a strong headwind slowing the boat and pushing it off the correct heading. In this case, it pays to wind in at the end of a run and zip back at speed to start again — but don't drive across the fishing water: take a wide detour.

Trolling speed affects the action of wobbling lures like cobras or tobys, and this can be critical. Most lures are designed to wobble or flick from side to side rather than revolve, and one check is to watch the lures beside

> When fishing two or more trolling rods, a strong pull on the middle rod will indicate whether the lines are tangled. If they are, another rod will bend as you move the rod.

> A small auxiliary motor is usually used for trolling or harling to avoid the problem of spark plugs in the main motor becoming fouled with oil.

One of the most durable trout lures — the family of tobys, with a mother-of-pearl lure on the left. Above is the hook rigged on a split ring with a red plastic tag which can be used to replace the manufacturer's hooks which are usually too small.

the boat at different speeds to determine the best action. As different lures work best at slightly different speeds, some fishermen use only one type of lure on all lines. This is starting to get rather technical and the object is to relax and enjoy fishing rather than make work out of it. One solution is to operate the boat in an elongated S-pattern, which often provokes a strike. This also applies to deep trolling. The lines on the inside of the curve will slow down and sink while the outer lines speed up. This varies the lure speed and action, and also the depths covered. Some fishermen also slow or even stop the boat, allowing the lines to sink, then start again. It all gets back to being adaptable, and thinking about what you are doing.

Thirty-five years ago we had little choice in lures, and apart from a Parsons' Glory we used spoons like the old zeddy, eye spoon or penny. I remember when a fantastic new lure arrived from the States. Somebody caught a limit bag on it and we all wanted one. It was a plastic frog called Peter Pope's Hotshot, and this was shortened to hotshot. It was strange looking thing, with a short beak on top and a bulbous body painted green and yellow, and it wobbled furiously. The trout went crazy over it, too, and one Christmas holiday my younger brother, Graham, landed more than 50 fish in one week by trolling the smallest size of hotshot along the edge of a shelf. The hotshot was followed by the flatfish, a similar lure which works on a wide variety of fish throughout the world — including our trout. After the flatfish came the cobra, then the Tasmanian devil and king cobra. These would all go through periods of being fashionable and I think the trout do build up some kind of resistance to a particular lure which they are bombarded with continuously. Throughout the years the toby remained constant, and still does today. It is one of the best all-round lures for trolling or spinning.

So which lure do you use? The choice is wider than ever. But there are some well-tested favourites for different water, and there are some factors which influence our choice. The prevailing light and water conditions affect the colour of the lure. For example, on a bright day try a cobra in bright silver or gold, or a green or silver toby. Conversely, in dull conditions, use a dark lure like a black or purple cobra or toby, changing as the light changes. The most popular lake lures are the tobys, cobras, devils and flatfish. Another variable is the size, and the small 2.5 cm cobra can be deadly when fished on a harling line. Our favourite is white with a black herring-bone pattern on the back, and a yellow belly. One successful Tarawera fisherman scrapes the paint off the belly of his green-and-yellow cobras. This exposes a dull grey colour, actually inside the plastic, and it catches a lot of fish.

We do not seem to have much faith in the abilities of lure manufacturers. Some people dip their cobras into hot water to soften them, and then bend them to increase the action. Another trick is to rig these types of lures backwards. Other people try and improve their lures by painting them with nail polish. We are always looking for that extra angle!

Everyone has their favourite lures, usually well worn and beaten up. This applies to harling and fly fishing flies as well. Some even seem to perform better as they get more chewed by the trout, and I have two old tobys which I treasure. They are such good fish-catchers that I am reluctant to use them in case I lose them, and will only do so with trace material of at least 7 kg breaking strain. They are both the old quarter-ounce models, one green and the other black although they have lost all of the original paint, and actually look more like silver tobys with a few scraps of paint stuck on. Such lures were invaluable to a fishing guide, and I always polished them with sandpaper before using them. This continual polishing has worn down the metal so they are lighter than new ones, and must have a slightly different action. They were so successful that I tried to create replacements by soaking new tobys in water till they rusted, then polishing them on both sides. So far this approach has been notably unsuccessful.

A fly which has been torn up by the sharp teeth of hungry trout is far superior to a flashy new fly. I often tie harling flies with lightly dressed winds and a wool body which is teased out with a needle, to emulate one which the trout have partially destroyed. Again, it is never as effective as a genuine performer.

Smelt patterns should represent the smelt found in the particular lake fished. The Lake Rotorua smelt are dark in colour to match their environment, and are quite large. So a dark fly like a Ginger Mick or Parsons tied with dark wing feathers will work well, in size 4 or even 2. Conversely, on Taupo, where the water is clear and the smelt much smaller, use lightly dressed flies in lighter colours and sizes 6 or 8. In bright conditions a Grey Ghost, Yellow Lady or lightly dressed Silver Rabbit are typical patterns, changing to darker flies in the evening.

As well as size the body colour can be varied. Some professional guides put out four Parsons' Glorys, each with different bodies — say a yellow, red, orange and lime green — all in size 8. When a fish strikes one fly the others are changed, perhaps leaving out one variation. Lime green is an excellent colour for smelt fly bodies, particularly in the fluorescent version, and is also popular on the Rotorua lakes. On Tarawera, where the smelt are larger than those in Taupo, I use long-tailed flies with no hackle, on a size 6 hook.

Most commercial patterns are over-dressed and can be modified by pulling out some of the hackles, but it is better to tie the fly correctly in the first place. Just compare a wet smelt fly with the real thing and see how it matches in general shape and size.

Another excellent harling pattern on many lakes is the Red Setter, and again some versions are better than others. I fish Tarawera a lot, and here I like a light orange body — an old faded specimen is great — and light brown hackles which lie back along the body. Red Setters with the hackles sticking out at right angles are better suited for fishing deep, retrieved in short jerks to simulate a koura. When fishing near weedy areas smelt flies should be dark, like a Green Orbit, to match the dark smelt in the area. The western end of Kawakawa Bay at Taupo is one spot where this pattern works well, as there is a lot of weed around the reef, and rather than change to a yellow or silver-bodied fly for covering the adjacent sandy areas a combination is the logical approach.

But there are some special situations where, for some reason, the commonly used flies and lures just do not produce the expected results. One example is Lake Okataina, where koura feature prominently in the trout's diet, along with bullies and smelt. Here, a tandem rig with two large rabbit patterns with either orange, green, red or yellow bodies works well.

Another good combination is two Green Orbits, with a size 2 at the end and a size 4 a metre up the trace, particularly in mid-summer when the green dragonfly larvae are active. In May and June when the mature trout are starting to think about spawning, a big Marabou fly with a bright orange tail and body is worth trying on all of the lakes, particularly Okataina.

These double-fly rigs are simple: the first fly is threaded on the end of the trace and a small swivel attached so the fly slides down and rests against the swivel, covering it with its body. The trailing fly is added by tying a 1 m piece of trace to the swivel, with the fly at the end. This rig seems to be more effective than the alternative method often used by fly fishermen, where the end section of trace is tied directly to the bend in the hook of the first fly. Perhaps the leading fly has a little more movement when sliding free on the trace rather than when fixed between two lengths of trace.

Lake Rotoiti is another lake which can be frustrating to anglers; and one problem is the restriction on using lead-core or wire lines. But the modern super-heavy fly lines available and the LED fast-sinking line allow the angler to get a lure down 20 metres. The popular line is a combination of a 10 m shooting head, called an SD850, and a full-length LED line. The 850 refers to the line's weight in grams, and it is designed to sink like a stone. The combination is, in order from the backing end: 100 m of

Harling flies should match the size of smelt found in the area.

LED, one SD850, another 50 m of LED, a second SD850, then 25 m of trace. At dawn, just the first two sections may be needed, with more line let out as the morning becomes lighter and the fish move deeper. You can also let out all of the line plus some backing, then stop the boat and let the line sink. This is another technique for use during high summer on deep lakes where true deep-trolling lines cannot be used. It is an expensive outfit, but it catches fish. A tandem rig of Parsons' Glory flies in size 6 is a good one on Rotoiti, and the addition of jungle cock 'eyes' to the flies is worth the extra expense.

Lures like cobras and Tasmanian devils come with a wire running through the middle, and the first thing to do is pull it out and throw it away, including the hook, which is usually too small. The wire is light, and often breaks during use, for example midway through the fight with a large trout! The lure is then rigged by running the trace through the middle and tying it to a small swivel. If the trace will not poke through the lure, try twisting the trace where it enters the head. The swivel is pre-rigged on a split ring with the hook and an optional red tag, and should be small enough to fit inside the end of the lure so that it sits snugly on the split ring. I prefer plated rather than stainless steel hooks, as they are sharper, with a large eye for fitting onto the split ring, and a long shank. Some different versions can be used, like exchanging a smelt fly for the bare hook. Another advantage of this rig is that the lure slides down the trace when a hooked fish jumps and it is less likely to throw the hook — a common problem when shallow trolling with lures. As the trout shakes its head, the weight of the lure swinging against the hook dislodges it, and many fish are lost at this point.

A second small swivel is sometimes added a few metres up the trace to prevent line twist. Be careful not to wind through the end eye when the fish is close to the boat, as it will jam if the fish makes another run. The fish should also be within reach of the net, so on a small boat where the

Cobras and Tasmanian devils are favourite trolling lures and come in a huge variety of colour combinations.

fisherman cannot move far from the gunwale, about 2 m up from the lure is the right distance. But another swivel can become tangled in weed and it adds more knots in the system which are extra weak points. It is a matter of personal choice.

The business end can be a single fly, single lure, a combination of two different flies, or a fly with a lure behind it (not the other way round — the lure must be free to wobble). But no more than two lures may be used.

Tackle used for harling and shallow trolling consists of a rod 2-2.3 m long, with a soft tip action and a long butt for sitting in a rod holder. The reel should be a large-capacity single-action fly reel, but the plastic reels

Today's fly box for lake fishing carries old fashioned patterns on the left, with new flies incorporating silicon and polystyrene like boobies, silicon smelt and Globugs, on the right.

popular for deep trolling can also be used. Free-spool reels used for saltwater fishing are fine for deep trolling, with their rapid retrieve, but the drag systems are not sensitive enough for the lighter tackle used near the surface.

Popular lures on all lakes are cobras and Tasmanian devils in traffic light, fluoro green and yellow, fluoro pink, green and yellow, white and yellow, spotted gold, green and black, purple, clown, and skeleton (black and white). Tobys in green, black, or toby flash; flamingo in rainbow or blue; and flatfish in silver, green and yellow, or orange, are also very good.

Good flies include smelt patterns such as Parsons' Glory, Dorothy, Grey Ghost, and slim Rabbits in various body colours, Silicon Smelt, Mallard Smelt, Yellow Lady and Green Orbit. Then there are the classic lures such as Red Setter, Mrs Simpson and Hamill's Killer

There are always lures and flies which are local favourites, and a few dollars invested at the nearest tackle store can make all the difference. Like all fishing, having confidence in your tackle and knowing where to fish are just as important as what is tied on the end.

Deep trolling

I can recall when the first lead-core lines became available. It was during our regular Lake Tarawera Christmas holiday in the late 1950s, and a friend of my father, Jim Liggins, an accomplished and experienced trout fisherman, had what was referred to in awed tones as a 'magic line'. It was one of the first deep-sinking lines we had seen, and Jim would head across the lake to Humphrey's Bay every afternoon and catch a limit bag of eight trout on his 'magic line' and a mother-of-pearl spoon. His unfailing success was the subject of much discussion among the lakeside fraternity, and the cause of much envy and anxiety in a boy who spent every day trolling up and down waiting for the longed-for strike of a trout.

Looking back I guess what happened is that the rainbows in the lake moved down to a level of about 15 m during the day and would never have seen a lure at this depth before. They hit the mother-of-pearl spoon eagerly. It is one which has all but vanished, probably because of the cost of the raw material from which it was made. No doubt a cobra, flatfish or toby would have been equally effective. It was more a question of fishing virgin water.

Since then many trout have crossed the back of my boat, and lead or wire trolling lines have accounted for a lot of them. Deep trolling is the least attractive method of catching trout, but one of the most productive. Fly fishermen often scorn the troller, accusing him of being a 'meat fisherman' who does not give the trout a chance. This is not the case at all. While trout may be caught by simply heading out across the lake with a couple of lead lines over the back, there is a lot of skill and local knowledge in locating and hooking the fish. However, the actual playing of the fish is not as demanding as when they are hooked on light harling tackle.

On many lakes deep trolling is not permitted, and it has no application on shallow lakes. But it is important on Tarawera, Rotoiti, Okataina and Rotoma in the Rotorua district; at Lake Taupo; and on many of the South Island lakes like Dunstan, Hawea and Wakatipu. Because the lures employed are attractor lures which trigger a response from the trout through their colour and action, as distinct from lures which represent an item of food like smelt flies, a wider variety of lures will catch fish. Some American anglers I have discussed this with maintain that trout fishing is 80% presentation and 20% lure choice. While they are talking about fly fishing, many of the principles remain the same and apply equally to deep trolling.

The memories of an afternoon spent trolling on Lake Wakatipu with Queenstown fishing guide Geoff McDonald remain clear. It is a spectacular setting, with the deep blue water dancing with reflections of the jagged mountains which frame the sky on all sides. The air on a crisp autumn day is unbelievably fresh and the old excitement of fishing new water bubbles up. We travelled for 20 minutes down the lake to put the lead lines out on the deep side of a ledge not far from shore. Geoff explained that he had been catching plenty of fish here. The lures were cobras and tobys, and the fish a mixture of sleek, silver rainbows, hard-bodied yellow browns and slim salmon. These land-locked Atlantic salmon don't grow very large, as they are mainly plankton feeders, but they are beautiful to eat.

South Island lakes see little fishing pressure compared to the central North Island lakes, and they have healthy populations of wild trout; trolling along the edge of a drop-off will produce fish. Sometimes it is not necessary to put out all of the 100 m of lead-core line. These lines are colour coded, with 10 m of each colour, and at normal trolling speed of 2 knots will sink 1.6 m for each colour used. A full line should get down 15-16 metres.

The cold southern lakes are not as productive as the northern lakes, and the fish do not usually grow as quickly or as large. The reason is the constant water temperatures which barely change during the seasons: only the top metre or so will warm up. Combined with a lack of shallow shelves, this severely restricts the growth of weed and its associated production of trout food.

The art of deep trolling is to place the lure in front of the fish, so an understanding of what happens in lakes is useful. Variations in water temperatures exert a strong influence on trout movement within the body of a lake, and for deep trolling we are discussing deep lakes. The deeper the lake, the less temperature variation there is in the depths, while surface temperatures vary widely with the seasons. Our deep lakes are lakes which stratify. This means the body of water within the lake is divided into three layers — an upper layer where there is very little variation in temperature; a second layer, or thermocline, where the greatest rate of temperature change occurs; and a third, bottom layer with virtually no change in temperature as the depth increases. It is the thermocline that is of the greatest interest to trout anglers, for its movement up and down within the lake determines where the fish will be found at different seasons. What this basically means is that we have to fish at different depths.

TROLLING AND HARLING

The stratified zones are not static, but move according to climate, wind, and the area and depth of each lake. When surface and bottom temperatures are close, the stratification breaks down and the lake becomes mixed throughout the water column. In shallow lakes there is little difference between surface and bottom temperatures, but in Lake Wakatipu the bottom temperature remains constant at about 9 degrees C (there is a lot of heat stored in the bulk of the lake) while the surface temperature fluctuates between 9 degrees in August and 17 degrees in February.

Lake Taupo is constant at 11 degrees in the depths, rising to 19 degrees at the surface in midsummer. Lake Tarawera is a lake of medium depth, and the bottom temperature will vary between 11 and 12 degrees, while the surface rises to 21 degrees. In all deep lakes the surface and bottom temperatures are the same for a short time in midwinter.

Wind is an important factor in determining when the water becomes mixed, and varies from year to year. So the weather, as always, has a strong influence on our fishing success.

While research has not been done on all lakes, we do have an indication of where the thermocline is in some lakes throughout the year, as shown in Fig. 63.

The position of the thermocline is more important to fishermen during summer, as the difference in temperature between shallow and deep layers is far greater and the trout are more likely to be found at the thermocline during the day. In winter the thermocline is much deeper, but is not relevant as there is little difference between temperatures at top and bottom. The thermocline usually forms in early summer, the strong winds we experience in spring keeping the water mixed. This is why we tend to concentrate on harling in spring, moving to deep lines as summer progresses and the fish move down with the thermocline. They can still be caught on the surface in the early morning and evening, but the 'heavy artillery' comes out after the sun rises, particularly if it is a hot, calm day.

The most popular deep trolling line is the lead-core line — a fabric outer over a soft lead wire core — and comes in two weights or breaking

Fig. 63

	Manapouri	Moke	Ngapouri	Pupuke	Rotoiti (NI)	Tarawera	Taupo	Waikaremoana	Whakatipu
Lake depth (m)	444	44	25	55	93.5	87.5	164.5	248	380
November			7-11	2-7		12-15			
December			5-10		10-15	10-13	25-28		
January			4-8		16-20	16-20	32-36		
February	25-32	12-14	6-10		18-21	16-20	33-35		54-57
March	40-60		10-13		18-22	20-25	32-35	22-32	
April			11-14	14-16	23-26	23-27	38-40		
May			18-20	17-19	30-32	33-40	42-46		
June		60-80		26-27½		39-42	50-55		96-100 (north) 150-160 (south)

From *New Zealand Lakes* (Auckland University Press, 1975; ed V.H. Jolly and J.M.A. Brown)

strains. This line deteriorates with age, and the outer covering can rot, so the lines should be dried after use if being stored for long periods, and replaced every few years. I use sections of old lead lines to make up harling outfits, splicing a few metres on to an old fly line or to monofilament line. Lead-core lines are usually 100 m long, but longer lines can be made up.

Wire lines are also used for reaching even greater depths than lead-core lines. There are two types: stainless steel wire, manufactured and sold specifically as trolling line; and copper wire, which is actually made for use in electric motors but also makes an effective fishing line. This can be bought from some electric-motor repair shops, and is sold by weight. A popular rig is 150 m of copper wire on a single-action reel, attached to backing. With so much wire the join with the backing is rarely put out, as there is sufficient line on the reel for a fish to pull some out when hooked. They do not run far when dragging so much weight through the water. But the join does rattle down the rod, and is prone to catching in the guides. Wire is difficult to handle, and to join with other lines. A loop is easily made and the tag end twisted around the main line, and trace or backing can be tied to the loop. But these joins should be replaced regularly because they create weak points and can break after prolonged use. For the same reason kinks must be avoided, and if a kink does form the line must be untwisted carefully, reversing the angle which formed the kink.

Copper wire is softer than stainless wire, and is easier to work with. It can also be marked by rubbing with sandpaper, leaving a shiny section which is easily seen, so you can measure how much line is being used. Stainless wire is thinner and has less resistance in the water, so it sinks deeper. However, extreme care is needed when letting out both types of wire to ensure the line does not over-run. Wire tends to spring off the spool, and when putting out the line the boat should be idling slowly until the first few turns of wire are fed through the rod guides. Once the wire is in the water and the reel is running smoothly with no drag (it can be controlled by holding the rod upside down and thumbing the spool) the speed can be increased to 15 or more kilometres an hour. This gets the line out quickly; but do not turn the boat until all lines are fully out or they may tangle.

Unfortunately tangles do occur and you may troll for an hour or two without knowing that your lines have tangled and the lures are not working — you are wasting your time. It can take a long time to wind in a deep line, and a rough method of checking for this problem is to take up the slack on one rod, then lift the rod as high and as fast as possible. If another line is hooked up, the tip of its rod will dip. This test can be repeated several times for confirmation that you have a problem.

When fishing in very deep water in midsummer it may be necessary to get down to 30 m or more, so a super long line of 200 m of wire is sometimes used. This creates a heavy weight, and should be resorted to only if there is no alternative. A combination of wire and lead-core line can also be very effective — 50 m of lead-core line attached to the end of 100 m of wire. This line performs better than an extra-long wire line. It may be the way the lead core moves through the water, or perhaps the wire sends out different vibrations; I don't know — you would have to ask the fish.

What is common to all deep trolling rigs is a very long trace at the business end. A swivel small enough to pass easily through the rod guides connecting the line and trace, with a second swivel about 1.5 m up from the lure, will avoid line twist, and a fly can be added so that it lies above the second swivel. The trace is usually about 25 m long, of 4.5 kg monofilament, sometimes lighter in bright conditions and where the lake bottom is clean.

Sunken trees and snags are good for the lure business. I have heard stories of scuba divers finding dozens of good lures stuck to some trees in popular trolling areas. Unfortunately you have to get close to the edge to catch fish, and will get hung up occasionally. The best way to retrieve a snagged lure is to back up the boat, following the angle of the line in the water until you are directly above or even behind the snag. Persistent tugging will often pull it free, but if the line is also caught up in the branches of a snag — and you can feel it rasping when this happens — you will lose gear. Don't use the rod to break it off, but pull directly on the line, after first wrapping it round a cloth wrapped round your hand.

The development of inexpensive reliable electronic depth sounders has made deep trolling far more efficient. The trout are found close to where the bottom falls away steeply, and popular trolling spots are along the edge of a shelf, around a reef, and where deep water cuts in close to the shore, creating a deep hole. With 100 m of lead-core line out the boat should follow the contour between 15 and 20 m deep, and with wire lines of 100 m about 5 m should be added to the depth fished.

A common technique is to approach a hole from an angle of 45 degrees out in the lake, letting out the lines as the boat starts its approach run and timing it so that the boat slows to trolling speed as it hits the hot spot. After fishing through the hole you can wind in the lines and repeat the run, as we call it, or continue along the edge of the lake. When a fish is struck it makes sense to go around and over the spot again, and you often catch several from the same hole. Many good runs involve following the edge of a shelf, trolling just outside the drop-off, which angles in to a corner of a bay where a beach ends and steep rock walls drop away into deep blue water. This will require a sharp turn as the boat comes to the corner, but it will be a few minutes before the lures reach that point and some fishermen increase the speed as the lures come in from deep water towards the shallows. The action of a lure changing speed often attracts fish.

Trout can also be caught in the middle of a lake, fishing over very deep water. Schools of smelt will show on the depth sounder as blobs in midwater and trout will often be found there also.

The general pattern is to fish shallower depths at the start of the season in October, using only about five colours of lead-core line; going deeper through summer and autumn; then returning to short lines in winter. Many of the points relating to harling also apply to deep trolling. The main difference is that we use lures rather than flies. That is not to say a fly won't catch fish if presented on a deep line. We have caught fish on large, dark flies on wire lines, but the action of a lure is important in attracting fish in the low light of deep water. Most popular lures are the tobys in small and large sizes, cobras in medium and large sizes, Tasmanian devils, and flatfish. All of the colours used from shallow trolling work well, and every year some new colours are added to the range available. My favourites are spotted gold (barley sugar), yellow and white (zebra), green and yellow, orange, traffic light and fluorescent pink cobras or devils; black or green toby; and silver flatfish (particularly on Taupo).

You can vary the size and colour of lures used, but always stick with at least one proven lure and if the fishing is hard try different depths rather than change lures. After all, we tend to experiment with different lures when the fishing is hard, which is not fair to the new ones we are testing. It's the old story — where the lure is and what it is doing are equally important as the type of lure.

A point worth remembering when using flatfish lures: keep the lines well apart or use only one deep line. These lures wobble furiously but they also move from side to side, and when lines become tangled with flatfish on the end it calls for a sharp knife and a bundle of wasted line.

While the advent of lead-core lines was a major development in a fishery that sees few radical changes, there is one more new method in limited use. It is the downrigger, a system developed in the United States for fishing at precise depths with light mono line instead of the heavy wire or lead-core lines (see Fig. 60 for a discussion of the downrigger system). The downrigger has a short arm which suspends a thin wire cable that has a heavy iron ball on the end. The depth fished can be accurately controlled, and some models have electric winches and gauges to monitor the depth. The balls are available in various weights, and the fishing line is attached to a short wire line with a spring-loaded release clip.

The advantages are obvious. The depth can be controlled precisely, and when a trout is hooked the line pulls free and the fish is fought on a light rod and line. Opponents argue that the system can be too effective, and that small trout brought to the surface quickly from great depths will suffer from the changes in pressure and temperature and cannot be released. Downriggers were permitted on Lake Taupo only after the Department of Conservation conducted surveys of the survival rates of fish caught by different methods. Trout were captured on downrigger lines, wire and lead-core lines and surface trolled lines, and kept in huge nets. There was little difference in the survival of trout caught on downriggers at the greatest depth (35-45 m), of which 15% died, and those hooked on wire lines (20-30 m deep) of which 12% died. The least mortality occurred among fish caught at more shallow depths by lead-core lines (8-15 m; 8% mortality) and by harling (3-5 m; 2.2% mortality). The tests involved 50 trout caught by each method.

Where the limit bag is only three fish per day as on Taupo, being able to safely return unwanted or undersized fish to the water is important. It appears that downriggers may also be legalised for a test period on some

Releasing trout will help preserve our fisheries, particularly on rivers and streams. When releasing a fish, avoid touching it if possible; keep it in the net or grasp it with a wet towel. Never touch the gills. Ideally, twist the hook out with needle-nosed pliers or a similar instrument while the fish is in the water.

When releasing trout, hold the fish gently and wait until it swims away.

Rotorua lakes.

Length is not as important as action with rods used for deep trolling. 'Soft' rods such as those favoured for harling are not suitable as they bend too much when the full weight of a deep line is applied. Trolling rods are usually 2 m long with a stiff action for the lower two thirds, and sufficient bend at the tip to allow fish to be played near the boat.

Two types of reels are used for this type of fishing. The most popular is a single-action reel with a large spool. It has a drag knob in the centre of the spool, and a button for engaging the clicker. There is a lot of cranking involved when a long line is used, but isn't that what you are there for? An advantage is the ability to apply delicate pressure to the rim of the spool with the palm of the winding hand. This is important as the drag systems are not sensitive; one of the biggest problems encountered is applying too much drag and the fish breaks the trace or tears the hook out. You can fish with very little drag — just enough to stop the line running out while trolling, with the clicker on to indicate a strike. I switch off the clicker when playing a fish so I don't have to wind against its pressure, and also to dispense with the awful scratchy sound.

The other type of reel used is a free-spool saltwater reel, fixed to the top of the rod. This has the advantage of the geared winding system giving a faster retrieve, and often a level wind which ensures the line is evenly spread across the face of the reel. Otherwise you must remember to spread the line as it comes in, and apply pressure so it goes onto the spool tightly. A loosely-wound line can easily jam when pulled out by a fish.

The downside is the drag system, which is not designed to provide the subtle pressure needed for trout fishing. This is not a problem when the line is a long way out, with plenty of stretch to cushion the trout's lunges.

But the drag should be eased off when the fish is near the boat on a short line. These reels usually have a star drag and a wide spool, but more expensive models may have a lever drag.

With the rod in a holder the fish will hook itself when it strikes, but when playing a fish it is important to let it run if it wants to and the heavy tackle can be deceptive. Often a hooked trout will jump after an initial run, looking like a herring in the distance, but any trout which can swim to the surface dragging 150 m of heavy line through the water will be a good one. It should be handled carefully.

When the first of the trace is wound onto the reel extra care is needed. As the line shortens there is less stretch, and the rod, not the reel, is used to bring the fish to the boat. Just cranking the reel risks breaking off the fish, and you never know how well it is hooked until you have it in the net. Often the hook falls out at that stage and you realise how lucky, or skilful, you have been. Lead the fish to the net smoothly with the rod, winding line slowly. Don't rush it. You may have spent half the day waiting for a strike. Get the most out of it and enjoy it. When the fish is beside the boat the person on the net should wait until it is lying on the surface, not swimming upright, and scoop the net from underneath the fish, always taking it head first. The fisherman on the rod must be ready to drop the rod tip instantly if the fish makes a sudden lunge, and the drag should also be backed off a little if the fish gets away. A lot of trout are lost unnecessarily at the boat. Above all, don't panic — unless the boat is drifting onto a snag at the same time!

CHAPTER TWELVE
SPINFISHING AND JIGGING

Fishing for trout should be relaxing, and it should be enjoyable. When you start making hard work out of it, the fun ceases. It's hard to think of anything more peaceful than wandering up a river, flicking a lure into likely looking runs and pools, perhaps sitting on a sun-bleached rock and watching a large rainbow cruising its elliptical orbit in a pool where the water is so clear the fish appears to be suspended in mid-air. The challenge is figuring out how to cast a lure into the pool so it won't spook the trout, but will intercept its beat as you carefully wind it in. All fishing is a series of challenges: some small, some large, some overpowering. In learning to overcome these challenges we add to our store of fishing skills, which always seems to be just a touch inadequate.

One of my favourite trips involves flying deep into the Kaimanawa Ranges, south-east of Taupo, where the Cessna lands on a plateau high above the headwaters of the Mohaka River. Here, it is joined by the Repia

If undisturbed, rainbows will be found at the tail of a pool, cruising an elliptical orbit.

and together they create a respectable piece of water with enough flow to carry our four-man inflatable raft. This is loaded with camping gear and food packed in large plastic drums, plus rifles and fishing rods. While the upper Mohaka is prime fly water we prefer to carry two-piece spinning rods. They take up less room, and spinfishing is a more efficient method of fishing the wide pools during the heat of the day when the deer are resting. There are always plenty of fat brown trout, their sleek golden flanks splattered with red-tinged black spots, eager to chase the spoons and wobblers we offer them. When split and hung over a smoky manuka fire while the river murmurs a few metres away these Mohaka browns pay a fine compliment to whatever we have brought along to keep the cold out. I have eaten a lot of fish in restaurants, but seldom any that tasted better.

In the hands of an expert a spinning rod is the most deadly piece of equipment, short of a hand grenade, for separating trout from their environment. It is also a practical method of introducing newcomers to the fun and frustrations of trout fishing. Basically, it involves casting or flicking a lure which pulls the line behind it, into the water and then winding it back in again. The lure sends out vibrations which trigger a reaction from trout. Perhaps it signals a struggling insect or wounded baitfish. Or maybe the trout are simply curious. It is not so important why they follow lures and often strike them; that they do is sufficient. What is important is to have an understanding of what tackle to use, where to find trout, and how to present the lure.

A good spinning rod will be 2 m long and light with a firm action and a springy tip for casting. This is one area where graphite is a definite advantage: the light, strong rods are ideal for casting lures all day while wandering up a river. Taking a cheap option will prove costly in problems on the water. Spinning reels can be found in some department stores at ridiculously cheap prices, and they will perform accordingly. The bail arm will be made from bent wire and will soon fall off, the gears will be lovely and soft and won't last much longer, and the drag will jam. Stick to reputable brands and you will be well served. A quality reel will have a stainless steel or aluminium spool, the bail arm will be stainless or plated brass with solid end fittings, and the side plate protecting the gears will have three screws for easy access. The drag should be smooth, with delicate pressure adjustments from a big knob on the front of the spool which can be easily turned by cold, wet fingers. The whole mechanism will run like a sewing machine and will be finely balanced. Many reels come with spare spools, often with one having greater capacity for carrying heavier line, which may be a blessing when the river you have been following all day suddenly seems to sprout a crop of snags in a pool full of big fish and you are two hours' walk from the car.

If your reel is loaded with line that is too light, you will throw the lure for great distances, occasionally without the line following it; and you may also find yourself checking trees for fish on the other side of the stream. But if the line is too heavy, you will have trouble casting any distance, and the lure will not swim well. When discussing line weights, it is tempting to bury the metric terminology with the fish guts and talk in pounds, which seem so much more appropriate. For better or worse, officialdom has decreed that the fish we seek now grow in kilos, so we should catch them on line which is rated accordingly. On streams and most rivers line of 2.5 to 3.5 kg breaking strain is fine, increasing to 4 to 4.5 kg line for big, fast rivers.

Throwing small lures around the edge of a lake calls for line of about 3.5 kg, but if dropping a lure into the depths a stronger line will have less stretch and will be more effective.

If the reel is not fully loaded with line, casting distance will be reduced by the friction created as the line flows up and over the lip of the spool. If too much line is put on the reel it will overflow and spring out in loose loops. Some manufacturers put a mark on the spool to indicate the correct loading.

Setting the drag tension is important, and if in doubt tighten it a little more. If the rod is used correctly, keeping it fully bent, you should not break off a hooked fish. But you will find it hard to land a fish with the drag set too loosely. As with saltwater fishing, set the drag at about a third of the line's breaking strain.

Check the last few metres of line regularly, and discard it if damaged. If the line becomes badly twisted by the action of a revolving lure, floating the line down the current with nothing on the end will help straighten it. Line that is badly twisted should be replaced.

Spinfishing is a gentle business. The cast is more of a flick of the wrist than a heave, and when playing a fish a steady, smooth pressure from the rod will overcome it more efficiently than hauling frantically and winding as fast as you can turn the handle. If a stubborn trout tries to swim under a bank or is determined to reach a sunken tree, apply side pressure by holding the rod sideways and keeping it fully bent. A smooth, light touch is called for, with no sharp, jerky movements. When a fish swims towards you, hold the rod high and wind as quickly and smoothly as you can, even taking a few steps backwards if necessary to keep the line tight.

In deep, slow pools the lure can be worked through the pool from the side and even fished downstream. It should be allowed to sink to the bottom, and fish will often be hooked as the lure turns and swings across the current below the angler. On most streams, however, the lure is cast upstream and fished back towards the angler. It should be moving slightly faster than the current to ensure the correct action is achieved. The trout are facing upstream and their food, and the lure, are presented to them by the current. Cast the lure upstream, wait for it to settle, then wind in at a steady speed. Trout will often follow it, and a faster retrieve as the lure moves into shallow water will often provoke a strike from a following fish. Sometimes you can see a shadow following your lure, or just a flash of silver deep in the water as a fish turns on it. Most lures will swim better if retrieved at an angle slightly across the current. Of course, this angle changes as you cover all of the water.

The two main types of spinning lures are wobblers or spoons, and true spinners. Popular spoons include small glimmies, zeddies, flamingoes, eye spoons and the larger tobys — all in a variety of colours. They all catch

> When playing a trout, be gentle but firm. The hook can easily be torn from its mouth. The harder you pull, the harder the fish will pull. If it runs, let it go, unless it is obviously heading for weeds or snags. Use the rod, not the reel, to tire the fish. Keeping the rod parallel to the water and to one side will tire the fish more quickly. Don't give it slack line, but maintain a steady tension. Try and play the fish on the shortest line possible, and it may be necessary to run along the bank to keep up with your quarry.

fish, but generally small lures are used in small water, and larger ones on big rivers and lakes. This is really a question of practicality as longer casts are needed and the lure has to sink deeper on the big water.

Spinners have a blade which revolves around a central shaft. The most popular are the Mepps family of lures from France, and the Veltic spinners and insects from Scandinavia. Mepps lures are available in small sizes which require little movement to make them work, and are ideal for small streams.

As well as these favourites there is a whole range of different lures. Many years ago when guiding, I once spent a frustrating morning trying to lure some rainbows we could see clearly cruising in the Waikato River near the Aratiatia Rapids. They refused our tobys, flamingoes and Mepps. My tackle box contained a selection of trolling lures like cobras and Tasmanian devils, but they were too light to cast any distance. So I rigged a small ball sinker above a swivel and tied a baby cobra about 45 cm below it. The visiting fisherman lobbed this rig upstream and it quickly sank. He started a slow retrieve that had the cobra wriggling nicely — and the trout suddenly woke and took notice of us. It was a nice feeling.

You can enjoy good sport in midsummer where tributary streams enter a big river like the Waikato, and the trout stack up like sardines in the cold water. A good rig here is a fly fished below a ball sinker, rather than a wobbler. A Hamill's Killer or Red Setter can produce a limit bag when dragged slowly along the edge of the bank right at the angler's feet. Cast the fly well out into the river and let it sink and swing around downstream. Knowing just how much slack line to let out to get down to where the fish are lying, without hooking the clumps of weed trailing in the current, is a matter of trial and error.

The giant trout found below the spillways of many hydro dams are among the most difficult to tempt because they are so well fed by the endless stream of assorted delights delivered by the spinning turbines. They are not impressed by our offerings. The logistics of getting a fly or spoon down to the fish in the powerful, deep currents is an added challenge. A big spoon or rabbit fly below a weight is among the best lures for these monsters. If local regulations allow bait fishing, a live bully or a worm will produce even better results.

We have found that the brown trout in the many fine rivers in the Nelson district love Mepps spinners, while a black toby cast out near a stream mouth on the edge of Lake Wanaka, allowed to sink into the blue depths and retrieved slowly up and over the edge, often produces a succession of kilo-sized rainbows.

While spinners are designed for stream fishing, wobblers are ideally suited for spinning, or threadlining as it is often called, in lakes. You can cast from the shore, or from a drifting boat. It is a question of working the parts of the lake likely to hold fish. This will be in the channels in weedy lakes, or along the edge of a shelf in a deep lake. During the heat of summer when fish move into deep water a spinning outfit can give an angler access to fish which could otherwise be reached only by deep trolling. On some lakes this is not permitted, and the technique of deep ledgering or

Spinning lures include those with blades, and small spoons and wobblers.

threadlining has developed. It is really just spinning in deep water, and instead of retrieving the lure across a stretch of water it is retrieved vertically. The hole in the corner of Waihaha Bay on Lake Taupo, and the northern shoreline of Lake Rotoiti from Hinehopu to Honeymoon Bay, are popular deep spinning areas.

I well recall stories about Foster Hamlett, the Wildlife Service ranger on Lake Tarawera, sitting on a rock in the corner of Humphrey's Bay and taking a limit bag of big trout with a threadline and zed spoon in the days before leadlining was introduced. But the technique is more popular on Lake Rotoiti, specifically because lead-core and wire lines are not permitted, and many a pleasant summer afternoon is spent tied to the pohutukawa branches overhanging deep water. Popular trees are easily identified by the ropes permanently hanging there. Patience is needed here. Cast out your lure and wait for it to sink all the way to the bottom. There is not much point in casting a long way, for the lure always finishes up directly under your boat. I guess human nature demands an impressive cast being made, rather than simply dropping the lure over the side. Depending on the weight of your lure it may take a third of a can of soft drink, or something else, before it is wound back up to the surface. Tobys used to be a favourite here, but some fishermen also like to use an orange Tasmanian devil, bringing it up as fast as possible. There are no fixed rules. Vary the retrieve, sometimes jigging the lure up and down before retrieving it. Different combinations can be used also — a large Red Setter below a lead weight, or rigged on a dropper loop above a lure, often works well. The fly can be given plenty of movement by wiggling the rod tip, and varying the speed. Trout will often follow a lure right to the boat, but most seem to be near the bottom and this zone can be fished more efficiently by bringing the lure up about a third of the way then dropping it back again. By experimenting with different lures and different actions, the right combination will be found.

Early one morning we were having difficulty enticing the big Rotoiti rainbows which were rising all around us in the calm water. We had tried cobras, tobys, smelt flies and bully imitations as well as the Red Setter, which usually does the trick. I found a packet of Mr Twister rubber lures with curved tails. There was a variety of sizes and colours, used with a

Trout jigs are miniature versions of saltwater jigs.

hook which had a painted, round head made of lead. The hook is inserted through the length of the body, leaving a tail which wiggles furiously with the slightest movement. I had hooked trout while harling with a small white one of about 2.5 cm on Tarawera, so I tried that one first. No good.

The next one given an opportunity to prove itself was 5 cm long, with a shiny, dark grey tail. A small sinker above a swivel helped it reach the bottom, and when retrieved slowly it did something to those finicky trout. We didn't murder them, but the two we did catch made two more than we had before.

Jigging for trout

With the boom in saltwater jig fishing over the last few years it was inevitable that some enterprising fishermen would test it on trout. The good news is — it works! The bad news is, it's not as easy as jigging on the sea.

In a lake, jigging differs from spinning in that you are actually doing the fishing while the jig is on the bottom. When it is being retrieved you are only winding it in to get it back to the bottom again because the boat has drifted and your lure is no longer directly underneath your rod tip.

The lures used are also different from spinning lures. Jigs are designed to sink quickly, and have extra weight at the hook end to prevent the lure flipping over and the hook tangling the line. Most saltwater jigs are too heavy for trout, both in practical terms and because there is a maximum legal weight limit of 40 g in many areas. The small versions of snapper jigs weighing 18 or 25 g are ideal for trout, particularly when painted silver-grey, green-yellow or blue-white.

A pioneer of trout jigging, Terry Beckett, specialises in fishing Lake Tarawera; and the technique he has developed applies equally to other lakes. "We always catch fish on the bottom, between 15 and 20 m. You can catch them throughout the season, but during summer the trout are concentrated at this level and we catch more," explained Terry as we headed across the lake to fish a wide shelf near Twin Creeks. The first lesson was to forget the stroke we use for snapper, where the jig is lifted sharply as the rod moves through an arc of half a metre or more. Through trial and error Terry has discovered that trout seem to prefer a jig which is barely moving on the bottom, just lifting off and fluttering back. Terry coined the term 'jiggling' to describe his action. It is just a small flick of the wrist and, like snapper jigging, the lure must be moved continuously. Weed does not grow below about 10 m so the lake bottom is clean apart from empty shells, mussels, sticks and leaves. Jigging also combines an element of hunting, using an electronic fish finder to locate groups of trout. A pattern soon emerges and landmarks can be used to identify good spots.

The boat drifts with the breeze across the shelf or hole being fished, and when a weed bed or change in depth is encountered, the boat motors back to the starting point to repeat the drift. Drop the jig until it hits the bottom, then jerk it up. It should never be allowed to remain still. As the boat drifts it moves away from the line, which is then wound in and the jig dropped again. If the wind is too strong and the boat drifts quickly, find a sheltered spot. Terry once caught seven rainbows in seven drops while fishing like this.

A fish may be hooked at any stage of the drop or retrieve, but most hit the lure on the bottom. The take may be soft, so get into the habit of striking at any change in the behaviour of your lure.

A spinning outfit is not suitable for jig fishing, as the rod is too soft and the reel does not give the precise line control needed. A good jig rod is 2-2.3 m, with a firm tip action so that the rod will lift the jig quickly, rather than bend with its weight. It must also be light and sensitive. A small, quality free-spool reel is essential for successful trout jigging. A pistol-grip style of rod allows the rod and reel to be operated with one hand. The reel should have a release button which can be depressed with the thumb, and the thumb can then feather the spool as the jig sinks. As soon it stops, clamp down on the spool with your thumb and start 'jiggling'. Keep the reel in free spool so that as the boat moves you can let some line slip out, to keep the jig on the bottom. When a fish is hooked, you can strike it by lifting the rod sharply and put the reel into gear with your other hand.

The line should be 3.5 to 4.5 kg breaking strain; any lighter and it will have too much stretch, making it hard to set the hook. Jigs are tied directly to the end of the line, with no swivel or trace added. Sometimes a small fly is used instead of the hook, or a large fly offered on a side loop about a metre above the jig. A dark green rabbit pattern with an olive body is a good one to use in conjunction with a jig.

This method of fishing requires continuous concentration and is far removed from sitting back with the rods in holders while the boat driver finds the fish.

When it comes to trout fishing there is not much that can really be called new — just new ways of doing something old. Jigging for trout is new to most people. Give it a try in your area; you might be surprised at the results.

CHAPTER THIRTEEN
FLY FISHING

Trout and the angler

The trout is a marvel of nature. It is an enigma, a fleeting shadow which draws anglers back to the water time after time. The trout is not impressed by power or wealth, but responds only to the ability of the fisherman. A graceful, delicate fish, he is at one with his environment and is found only in the best of nature — cold, clear water. His shining flanks contain the power to both thrill and frustrate the angler. To be a successful fly fisherman, some understanding of the biology and behaviour of the trout and his food organisms is necessary.

The trout's world has a mirrored ceiling, except for the round skylight or window directly overhead. Where the water is discoloured or deep this has little effect. But in clear, shallow water the stones and weeds on the river bed are clearly visible, reflected on the underside of the surface.

Trout have good night vision, and this affects feeding behaviour. During a hatch when large numbers of insects are on the water, the trout 'locks on' to the shape and colour of a particular insect. This selectivity has nothing to do with being smart, but it does cause the trout to ignore all other objects, requiring the angler to match the food item — or 'match the hatch'. Because of the way in which rays of light entering the water are bent or refracted when striking the surface at an angle, the trout's vision is like a cone. For the fish it is like looking upward through a 'fish-eye' lens, with objects in the centre clearly identified and those at the edges compressed or blurred. A fisherman approaching a trout should keep low and use any cover to break up his outline. A hands-and-knees approach is often necessary if the trout is in open water. The angler's floating fly should be placed upstream and on the near-side of the fish so that it drifts into its field of view. This also prevents the line from crossing the trout's window. A fish lying deep is watching for food near the bottom, and a sunken fly or nymph should be presented well ahead and to one side so that it will drift into its field of vision.

Vibrations are transmitted through the water five times faster than sound in air, so extreme care is needed when wading or walking along the edge of the water. The sense of smell is not a major factor in the trout's search for food, but it can detect some smells like insect repellent, and hands should be washed before handling lures or flies.

Reading the water

With all trout fishing, the ability to 'read' the water is paramount. Local knowledge is important, but the accomplished angler can look at new

The trout's world has a mirrored ceiling, except for the round skylight or window directly overhead . . . in clear, shallow water the stones and weeds on the river bed are clearly visible, reflected on the underside of the surface.

Opposite:
Approach each pool carefully and slowly from downstream. Trout can be spotted in the clear water of wilderness rivers, and just as quickly spooked.

water for the first time and figure out where to find trout and how to approach them. There is more variation in rivers and streams than in lakes, and a look at where to find trout in flowing water may be helpful.

The trout is very efficient biologically, and obtains food with a minimal expenditure of effort. It is not clever in the sense that people may be, but is driven by the need for three things: food, comfort and shelter from danger. A position favoured by trout is called a lie, and the classic lie is immediately downstream from an obstruction which interferes with the river's flow.

There are three types of lies which hold trout. The ideal situation is one that offers protection and food. Another lie will provide plenty of food but no protection, and trout in such spots will be very alert. The third offers shelter from strong currents and predators, but no food. Prime lies will be found behind obstructions, which may be obvious ones like logs or rocks or may be stones that the angler does not notice. They may protrude from a bank or may be in midstream. Trout often hold in the cushion of water in front of a boulder and, if it is a large one, they will be found on the edge between the fast water and the slow eddy downstream. But the prime position is where the V is formed.

In big rivers with powerful currents most of the trout will be found within a few metres of the banks, behind boulders or gravel bars, and along the edge of the main current where it joins the slow water created by the drag of the bank.

Spring creeks flowing through limestone country are prime trout water, not only for their ability to remain clear and fishable after heavy rain, but because of the mineral-rich water which fosters prolific insect and trout growth. Here, the lies are different again and trout will be found under and along the edges of beds of watercress and islands of flowing weed. The quiet eddies along the banks will yield trout and any overhanging grass or bush should be carefully checked. Trout will often fall for an imitation of a terrestrial insect like a grasshopper or cicada in such situations. The endless swirls on the surface will wash hatching insects out of the fast water in midstream and into the slower water near the bank, and the wind can also blow food to one side of a stream.

Meadow streams in flat country will meander, gouging out first one bank then the other, leaving deep corner pools with undercut banks and relatively shallow runs between pools. The deep undercut banks provide trout with excellent security, and the current delivers food, so they should be fished carefully and thoroughly.

Most of our streams are freestone streams where the water bounces and dances through a riffle or a set of rapids then spreads lazily into a pool. This sequence of riffles and pools is repeated endlessly, and trout will be found in both types of water except during droughts when the riffles become too shallow. In the riffles the larger boulders form lies, and if the current is not too strong the entire riffle can be considered prime trout country if it holds at least half a metre of water. The broken surface gives the fish a sense of security, and the bottom will be rich in food. But the biggest trout will be found in any deep runs or pockets.

A different approach — the author fishes from horseback on the Whakatane River near Ruatahuna, where the local Tuhoe people use their horses both for transport and for fishing!

Pools offer different types of lies. In the depths the trout are safe from birds, and there is less current near the bottom. Food organisms will also be found there, making the deep pools prime trout lies. The trout spend more time in the pools during winter, something the early season angler should be aware of.

Where the current flows into a pool, trout will lie in deep water below the lip where the water spills over, bringing food to the waiting fish. There is usually a reverse current on one side at the head of the pool, and the eddy will trap food which attracts trout. These reverse currents can be difficult to fish and your line often ends up going in two different directions. Where the current flows through the centre of a pool, the trout will lie along the edges if it is strong, and in the current as it weakens.

As a pool tails out it usually widens into a fan and becomes shallower. The current here is much slower and, if undisturbed, trout will feed here,

Prime trout country, with aerated water flowing into the head of a pool and large boulders providing shelter from the current.

The mayfly is the basis of modern fly fishing and embodies all that is graceful about the art. This colourful adult hatched from the swimming nymph at twilight.

Fig. 64
Adult caddis or sedge.

Fig. 65
Horny-cased caddis pupa.

cruising in regular orbits if they are rainbows and lying motionless if they are browns. Such water must be approached with extreme caution, and there always seems to be one brown which surprises the wary angler as he creeps forward, rocketing away like an arrow into the depths.

The confluence of a side stream or tributary with the main river always creates good trout situations, like the V below a boulder but on a larger scale.

Trout food

The successful fly fisherman needs some knowledge of the natural world he is entering, for he has to emulate nature as faithfully as possible. But he does not need a degree in entomology. If somebody wants to make a lifelong study of it, that's fine, but I have yet to meet a trout that is concerned about the Latin name for its dinner. A basic understanding of what that dinner is likely to be and where it is found is all we have ever found to be necessary.

Trout will eat mice and small birds on occasions, but a mouse or fantail imitation will gather cobwebs in most fly boxes. One place where I have heard of a deerhair mouse fly used successfully is on the wide, slow reaches of the lower Tongariro River at night when the big brown trout leave the shelter of overhanging willows and forage in the shallows. It may also work well on some of the fine southern rivers like the Mataura. Trout will also eat birds' eggs if given the opportunity, and they love their own eggs. But these are of neither practical nor legal use to the fisherman. Trout will also eat small fish, crayfish and other creatures like water-boatmen, snails, tadpoles and freshwater shrimps. These last few are of interest to the angler fishing backwaters, which brown trout love to frequent.

Studies in New Zealand and Australia reveal that 95% of trout food is bottom fauna, with the remaining 5% taken from the surface. These ratios vary during the year, as most surface feeding takes place during summer. Small fish are not taken until trout reach two years of age, and even then are not significant in numbers, but can make up 20% in volume. The exception is sea-run trout which rely heavily on fish for their diet while at sea.

The variety of insects which comprise the staple diet is quite small. No data will apply to every situation, but the general picture does help the angler who is considering what type of fly to use. The most common aquatic insects eaten are varieties of caddis (about 60%), followed by mayflies (14%), stoneflies (5%), midges (8%), other aquatic insects (5%), and terrestrials (8%). The last group includes cicadas, wetas, grasshoppers, ants and beetles. Stoneflies may be more significant in some mountain rivers, and mayflies will not be found in rivers that have significant pollution.

When you consider that the mayfly, caddis and stonefly larvae live on the riverbed for up to two years, yet spend only a few days as an adult, it is no surprise that the aquatic stages are so important to the trout. In the adults, mayflies have upright wings while the many caddisflies, also called sedges, have wings that slope down, covering the body (Fig. 64). They are easily distinguished.

Some nymphs and larvae hide under stones for protection, while others carry their own protection in the form of hard shells or a coat made from sand particles glued together. Caddis larvae are indeed nature's stonemasons (Fig. 65 and Fig. 66 — top half).

Many feed on microscopic plant matter, while larger varieties are carnivorous and quite voracious. The dragonfly larva lives up to its name, consuming a wide variety of creatures, including small fish. Some mayfly nymphs are free-swimming, and consequently are of particular interest because they are frequently exposed to the trout (Fig. 66 — bottom half).

A look at the life cycle of the mayfly group gives an indication of the various stages which are relevant to the trout and the angler. Even though caddisflies are more numerous and are taken by trout in far greater quantities, it is the mayfly which forms the basis of modern dry-fly fishing, embodying all that is graceful about the art. Adult mayflies range in length from 4 to 35 mm, and may be bright yellow, black, olive, brown, grey or cream. All but a few days of their lifespan is spent underwater as a nymph, feeding on algae and plant debris. There are four different types. Crawling nymphs live under stones and pebbles and are cylindrical in shape; burrowers have soft bodies and live in silt and fine sand; clingers are flat in the body and are found in fast water; and swimmers use their torpedo-shaped bodies to wriggle around the rocks like small minnows (Fig. 67).

All carry a pair of wing pads on the back, which become darker as the animal develops into an adult. When mature, the nymph swims or drifts to the surface, where its skin splits down the back and the adult emerges. This first stage as an adult insect is called a dun.

Caddisflies follow a similar pattern, and the larvae swim to the surface where they hatch, while stoneflies and dragonflies crawl out of the water on to a stick or stone where the adult hatches.

The nymphs and larvae are vulnerable when they leave the safety of the riverbed and make their way to the surface, and while struggling in the surface film are also easy prey for trout. The dun sits on the surface for a few seconds while its wings harden, and will also be taken at that stage. But more nymphs, emergers and flies trapped in their husks and unable to complete the process are taken than duns.

The angler must pay close attention, for trout that are locked into feeding on emergers will ignore a high-floating dun imitation even though they may appear to be feeding on adult insects on the surface during a hatch. Trout taking emergers will leave a ring on the surface, but if taking duns they will often suck in air with the insect and leave a bubble.

Most duns are dull with grey wings, hence the popular Blue Dun fly. Emergers are imitated by a small wet fly, or a nymph tied with scraps of foam rubber to simulate air bubbles trapped in the surface film.

Mayflies will hatch at approximately the same time each year, depending on the weather, and the time of day is usually quite predictable — early afternoon in spring, morning and evening in summer, and early

Fig. 66
Sandy-cased caddis pupa.

Carnivorous swimming mayfly nymph.

The 2.5 cm free-swimming nymph is one of the largest mayflies, and husks left on streamside rocks provide clues for the observant fisherman.

Fig. 67
Clinging mayfly nymph — small and dark, about 15mm long.

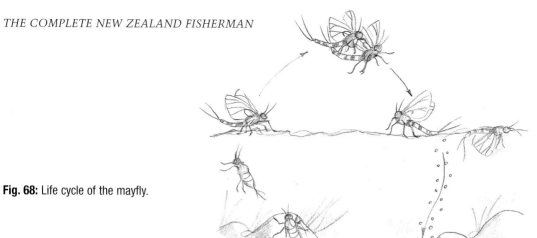

Fig. 68: Life cycle of the mayfly.

afternoon again in autumn. The famous evening rise is a period of intense activity when a major hatch of mayflies or caddisflies occurs, often lasting well into the night. The newly hatched adult will rest on bushes by the river. It cannot feed, for its feeding organs have degenerated. One or two days later it again moults and the sexually mature adult, called a spinner, emerges.

Rising on transparent wings, the colourful spinners swarm in a mating frenzy near the water. This nuptial dance rises and falls as the males and females seek each other out and mate before dropping exhausted on to the water. The females have one last act to complete before dying. Their slender bodies convulse as a stream of eggs is deposited, sinking slowly to the stream bed to begin the whole cycle again, while the bodies of the dead parents float quietly away in the characteristic cross-shaped silhouette of the spent spinner (Fig. 68).

When feeding on a spinner fall, the trout perform the classic head-and-tail rise, sipping the dead flies and ignoring all other food. The ring of the rise will be small, but will leave a tell-tale bubble.

Some mayflies live for only one day as an adult. I once saw a cartoon in an American fishing magazine that featured a typical fly fisherman wearing waders and hat, carrying a rod, with a vest festooned with the myriad accessories available to the budding fly angler. Our angler was standing on a cloud, obviously in Heaven, and a voice declared loudly: "Congratulations, you are going to be reincarnated. You are going back as a mayfly. Have a nice day."

Many caddisflies are also found in lakes as well as streams and rivers, and they are very prolific. Of the six main types, five find protection in some form of mobile home: the stick caddis, spiral-cased caddis, net-building caddis, sandy-cased caddis and horny-cased caddis. The trout swallow them, home and all. The sixth variety is a green free-living larva with centipede-like legs.

Other flies whose larvae are important to the angler are the stoneflies, dobsonflies (creeper or toe-biter), midges (chironomids, bloodworms), dragonflies and damselflies. Because their life cycle revolves so completely around water, it is easy to understand why the various species of flies are so important to trout and to fishermen.

Fishing streams and rivers

Unlike most lake fishing, you don't have to be an early riser to fish rivers. The best fishing is usually when the sun is on the water. Trout can be spotted more easily, and are more likely to rise to a dry fly on a hot, sunny day. Windy days are more suitable for nymphing, but on most water the nymph fisherman will outfish the dry fly exponent every time. The logical approach is to be prepared to use either, switching as the conditions demand.

Presentation of the fly is critical to successful fishing. The artificial must appear lifelike. If the natural flies are drifting freely with the current, either on the surface or near the bottom, the artificial must do the same. If the natural fly being emulated swims in short bursts, the artificial should behave accordingly and the line stripped in jerks. The angler's fly should enter the trout's circle of vision like a natural. At no stage should the line or leader fall over the trout. The influence of the current must be taken into account when judging where to place the cast and how long to make it. It is mainly a question of common sense and, if in doubt, you should always ask yourself how it would appear from the trout's point of view.

With both nymph and dry-fly, the control of the line on the water is a crucial element in achieving correct presentation. On a long upstream cast the line is stripped in to maintain contact with the fly and to remove any slack line, but without increasing the speed of the fly's drift. It is a question of timing and experience. Mending the line by flicking a loop upstream may be necessary several times during a drift where the current in the centre is faster than that where your fly is drifting.

Fishing the nymph

There are several accepted techniques for fishing nymphs. The most common approach is to fish upstream, casting a line which is no longer than necessary. There are no prizes for distance casting outside of a casting competition, and the fisherman has more chance of placing his fly exactly where he wants it with a shorter rather than a longer cast. Also, the chances of hooking a fish increase greatly with a shorter cast. The majority of casts will be 5 to 12 m It is better to spend extra time getting into position to make a good cast which can be controlled, than trying to reach a trout from afar.

Whether casting to a fish which has been located, or fishing blind to cover promising water, the cast should be made from below the fish and to one side, casting up and across at an angle of about 45 degrees so that the fly, and not the line or leader, drifts down to the fish. The objective is to place the fly upstream and to your side of the trout. If the luxury of a companion or guide spotting the fish is available, then an accurate report can be provided on the effectiveness of each cast. In most cases the first cast will offer the best chance of hooking a fish, so it should be made carefully.

The amount of drift required will depend on the depth of water and speed of current. If the trout is lying in deep water, sufficient drift must be allowed for your nymph to sink to that level before it reaches the fish.

When fishing fast pocket water, a series of short casts will be made, covering all of the best water. But the drifts will be short and fast, as will the rate of casting. Conversely, a deep pool or long slow run will take much longer for each cast to drift through it. A stretch of riffle water can be covered with a series of casts, lengthening the line with each cast to cover the water in a fan-like pattern. The angler will then move upstream to a new position and repeat the pattern.

Sometimes it is necessary to fish a nymph downstream because a trout cannot be approached from below. It can be difficult judging when the fly has reached the trout, but if it swings across the current in front of him he may take it. A caddis pupa fished across and downstream on a sinking line can be very effective. Trout will chase the fly as it swings across the current as if it was trying to escape.

Another technique developed in the United States involves simulating a nymph rising from the bottom as if preparing to emerge. Called the Liesenring lift, it involves casting up and across the current, allowing the nymph to sink nearly to the bottom as it drifts downstream. As the line comes down the rod tip is lifted to maintain tension and then lowered as it passes the angler. Just before the line straightens in the current the angler lifts the rod smoothly extending the arms up above his head. This lift raises the fly off the bottom and swings it to the surface.

Except in shallow riffles and very shallow water, the nymphs used will be weighted with copper or lead wire wrapped around the hook under the body. The amount of weight used is determined by the depth, and in areas where more than one fly may be used, two weighted nymphs will enable deep water to be probed. Or one large weighted nymph may be used like a sinker to deliver a small unweighted fly to the fish.

Where trout are feeding on emergers a technique called greased-line nymphing is employed. A floatant is applied to the leader, leaving the tippet and fly to sink. This is fished almost like a dry fly, with the nymph floating just under the surface, and can be a deadly way of taking trout. The strike will be felt, or the floating portion of the leader can be seen jerking under as a trout takes your fly.

All of these methods involve a floating line, and in some cases the strike will be felt. If the trout is visible you may see it turn toward your fly and the flash of white as the mouth gapes will be the signal to strike. Coloured indicators which wrap around the end of your fly line can be used, but with or without an indicator the end of your line should always be carefully watched. Any hesitation or change in movement could signal a take. Where the water is not too deep, a dry fly can be attached above the nymph by tying a length of tippet from the bend of the dry fly to the eye in the nymph. It will serve both as an indicator and as an extra offering for the trout. A pattern like the Royal Wulff, with its distinctive tuft of white calf hair, can be easily seen on most water.

In some situations a sinking line or sink-tip line is called for. In very deep pools a long leader on a floating line just will not sink far enough,

The Royal Wulff is a popular dry fly, and the tuft of white calf hair makes it easy to see.

Master fly fisherman and world authority Ernest Schwiebert tied this size 12 olive nymph in his fingers on the banks of the Rangitikei River to simulate the swimming mayfly.

and a line where the tip section sinks can be useful. It is particularly effective on wilderness rivers where the current pours into a deep pool. By casting across the current where it enters the pool, then stripping off more line and roll casting, the line and fly are swept into the body of the pool by the current. The head takes the weighted nymph down quickly, and it probably appears to the waiting trout like a natural washed down from the rapids above. A size 10 black Stonefly nymph usually takes the big rainbows that inhabit these pools, and a Hare and Copper is another favourite. The sink-tip line can also be fished up and across slow pools and handled like a floater, allowing the fly to dead-drift through the pool. In all situations, line control is crucial. Take up slack line to keep in touch with your fly without interfering with its drift, and let out more line as it drifts downstream, continuing the drift for as long as possible. Once the line starts to drag the fly, it's time to pull it in and cast again.

On a mountain river I once watched one of the world's great fly fishermen, American writer Ernest Schwiebert, hook several trout while using a full sinking line and casting across the river and slightly upstream. He retrieved the slow-sinking line with slow pulls, making his olive mayfly imitation swim like one of the swimming mayfly nymphs we had earlier disturbed while walking upriver.

All fishermen have their favourite patterns, and having confidence in what you are using is half the battle. If in doubt, ask at the nearest tackle shop. Many popular patterns do not resemble any particular natural nymph, but are representative of a group of naturals. The Hare and Copper is such a pattern, and is probably the most widely used fly in the country. Size and colour are the two most important variables. In fast water the trout barely has time to evaluate the fly, and provided it is roughly the right size and colour it will be accepted. If the trout are proving uncooperative, try a different size of a proven pattern before using any other fly.

The depth at which you fish can also be varied by using the same pattern of nymph with less or no weight. Just because the trout took a weighted fly yesterday does not necessarily mean it will today. Such vagaries are part of the mystery and appeal of fly fishing.

Fishing wet flies

To most New Zealand fishermen the term wet fly refers to the large flies used to catch Taupo trout. Such flies are also often called lures. Those who study fly fishing in more traditional terms, for it is indeed a practice steeped in tradition, will tell you that a wet fly is a tiny thing that is fished just under the surface of a river with a floating line.

I must confess a true wet fly is not a fly I have tied to my own tippet very often, though it proved its worth on one occasion when fishing the Ruakituri River in the hills between Gisborne and Wairoa. This river can be frustrating for the tyro, and supremely rewarding for the skilled angler. Like much fine fly water, the Ruakituri is restricted to fly fishing only and holds both brown and rainbow trout. It is a typical rapids/pool, rapids/pool freestone river, with some deep holes against undercut cliffs.

Late on a warm summer evening the trout will usually start rising in the long, oily pools and if the correct size and colour of dry fly is selected the fishing can be marvellous. Some friends and I were fishing a large pool close to our camp one evening, but the trout were proving maddeningly difficult to hook. They ignored various dries which drifted alongside the hatching caddis, and the surface was dimpled with rising fish. Suddenly a rod arched, a reel sang and a large trout splashed in the gathering dusk. "What are you using?" I shouted to Hughie, who replied with a wide grin, "Why, wee wets of course. They're taking emergers." Hugh McDowell, of Rotorua, is noted for his skills as a tier of flies as well as a fisher of flies, and it was pretty obvious to Hughie what was going on. But then he grew up fishing strings of wet flies on the streams and lakes of Ireland, and is one of the few fly fishermen I know who regularly uses them on our waters. That evening Hughie was fishing a single wet fly from a position at the head of the pool where the current surged into it. He was casting across the current, letting it take his line down to where the flow widened and slowed and trout were feeding in the roiling current lines. The wet fly drifted under the surface film like a caddisfly trapped in its nymphal husk, then swung across as the line straightened. The trout took with a vicious pull, and the game was on.

A wet fly resembles either an emerging fly or a drowned adult. This is why it must usually be presented close to the surface. Traditionally, wet flies are fished in a string of two or three flies. They should be attached to droppers rather than tied along the leader. A dropper can be formed by joining two pieces of tippet using a blood knot. The tag end on the upper section is left deliberately long so a fly can be tied to the end. Secured in this fashion, the flies will drift freely. The advantage of using two or three flies at once is that a variety of patterns can be offered. Popular wet flies mirror well-known dry-fly patterns, so each has its wet version: Kakahi Queen, March Brown, Greenwells Glory, Black Gnat, Coch-y-Bondhu and so on.

The accepted method of fishing wets is across and downstream, and they are also effective when fished down through riffles. In some instances they can also be presented to trout lying below the surface, fished on a sink-tip or slow-sinking line. If you are having trouble matching the hatch one evening, don't forget Hughie's 'wee wets'.

Another trip to the Ruakituri taught us how to take trout from deep in the slow pools during a hot, dry period when the river had dropped and the rapids were streaked with algae. Without the foaming, oxygenated water tumbling down the rocky staircases between pools, the trout had retired to the cool depths and become quite lethargic. A fresh approach was needed. As so often happens, it took a visitor to come up with a technique we might not have thought of. He was a competent, experienced fly fisherman and after our heavily weighted Hare and Copper and black Stonefly nymphs failed to secure a strike after repeated drifts through the pools, Howard took out his fly box.

I had long since given up the practice of scoffing at some of the unusual and weird concoctions which are used successfully in other countries. I had been wrong too often. Never say, "That won't catch a fish!" because it probably will. Howard figured the trout were not feeding in the oppressive heat, and needed something to get them going, maybe make them aggressive. He wasn't concerned why they might eat something — he just wanted a response. He selected a great monster of a thing about 7.5 cm long with a black chenille body, wisp of black tail, and black hackle at the head. The body was bent, as if tied on a wide-gap snapper hook, and it was heavily weighted. "That," announced Howard, "is a Hellgrammite, and trout love them!" Hellgrammite is an American term for a grandaddy creeper, and it's a popular pattern on big western trout rivers. The secret to this one was that it carried so much weight it was sure to bounce along the bottom of the pool where the trout had taken up residence. It made casting difficult, and Howard sort of lobbed his evil-looking black lure (it seems sacrilege to call it a fly) into the head of a long pool with a line which had the fastest sinking head available. The whole end section disappeared into the green depths. Howard then walked slowly downstream, keeping pace with his line, and moved the lure with short jerks. A trout jerked back, and we all politely asked Howard if we could borrow a Hellgrammite.

Another pattern that will do the trick in similar circumstances is a leech imitation, another American fly which has emigrated. It has a long marabou tail, a body of black or olive chenille on a long-shanked hook, and black hackle wound palmer-style along the body. This pattern has tremendous movement when retrieved, and is also an effective taker of trout on lakes.

The only other occasion when I have used a Hellgrammite was while fishing for steelhead on the North Umpqua River in Oregon. After two fishless days, not unusual when steelhead fishing, my companion suggested I try one. It was equally as big, black and heavy as the Ruakituri model; and it worked there, too. My first ocean-run steelhead rainbow trout was a lovely 5 kg jack, which was carefully returned to the river.

There is one other method of presenting flies to trout which deserves mention. I have never tried it, but only because the opportunity has not arisen. It is fishing flies with a spinning rod, which can be deadly. The whole object is to place an artificial fly in front of a trout, hoping he will

The romance of the fish

A trout is a fish. But it is not that simple — for surely a fish cannot drive people to drink or destroy friendships and marriages yet elevate a person to the greatest heights of satisfaction and achievement. A trout can, and often does.

A trout is like a spirit which taunts and lures, something out in the darkness or deep in a pool, something which demands its pound of flesh before offering itself. For every angler must pay his dues, and the scales always balance the investment of time and effort with the rewards.

For every red-letter day there is a fishless one. Perhaps we don't realise it because we tend to recall only the best days. That is human nature. That great fish, the marlin, impresses with its brilliant electric colour at the moment of striking a lure, and shocks with its violent power. The shark frightens and awes with its savagery. But these creatures are fighting not just an angler but a heavy boat and a rod that can hold an ox. In death the colour fades to dull grey meat.

The hunter is at one with his quarry at the moment of killing, the supreme ecstasy which climaxes the hunt when the trigger is pulled. But then the link is severed. The trout offers a continuing romance, the angler extending himself through the light rod and sensitive line to connect with the fish. It is a one-on-one situation, particularly for the fly fisher. When dead the supple grace and shining colours of the trout endure. What other creature continues to increase in allure after death?

Game fishermen and trout anglers share a common regard for the fish they seek. Unless a specimen is wanted for its value as a trophy, to be preserved, or for official weighing as a potential record, it will be released. To others, a good fish for the table is just as worthy. While the intangible value of a fish cannot be measured or compared, each is equally important. The fly-only, no-kill philosophy does not impress the youngster who catches his first trout on a worm or a spinner. But hopefully he will grow to accept some of that philosophy.

It is a sad state when angling and environmental pressures reduce great fisheries to artifical put-and-take situations. In some waters all fish caught must be returned to the water.

This is the case in many countries. Fortunately New Zealand still has the resources, awareness and time to prevent it happening.

Most anglers go through a stage where it is important to build up a score and kill as many trout as possible. As most proponents of the catch and release philosophy went through the same stage, any criticism should be delivered with care.

But more and more trout anglers are aware that rivers cannot take excessive pressure, and that a good percentage of fish caught should be released. They are also aware of the threats from proposed electricity generation schemes and development of catchment areas where pine trees replace native bush.

With youngsters also aware of the values of conservation and management based on that principle, prospects are good. But it has been costly. The golden days have gone, along with the code of ethics and unwritten laws which determined how gentlemen behaved on the river.

Just as tackle and techniques have changed, so have many of the values associated with sport fishing — some for the better. But provided we learn from the past, the losses will not have been in vain. The need to release fish of all species is a constant reminder that the care and future of our fisheries are in our hands.

eat it. Unless a person has a strong preference for using a fly rod (and many do), there is no reason why a spinning outfit cannot be used as effectively. In some situations, e.g. where there is no room for a back cast, it is more practical than a fly rod and you can cast the lure out with an underhand flick.

The system is uncomplicated. A nymph can be tied to the end of the

The need to release fish is a constant reminder that the care and future of our fisheries are in our hands.

In certain places it is desirable to harvest the trout to ensure a healthy fishery, particularly lakes where stocking is necessary to maintain the population, or there is excessive natural regeneration. But this does not lessen the value of each fish. The trout remain the same, and if we do not treat them with respect and appreciate their value, we will be the ones to suffer.

It is difficult for people to understand the passion a big game hunter or angler feels towards his quarry. The American outdoor writer Robert Ruark had spent months chasing kudu, the holy grail of African safari hunters, and said he would rather own the kudus he did not shoot than collect a record trophy by a main road, or have it wander into camp looking for instant taxidermy.

"None of it is any good unless you have to work for it, and if the work is hard enough you do not really have to possess the trophy to own it.

"The value of a trophy is computed directly in terms of personal investment in its acquisition," said Ruark.

There is another quote which sums things up well: "It's not the fish you catch that keeps you going, but the fish you hope to catch."

line, which should be no more than about 2 kg breaking strain, and one or two split shot pinched on the line about 25 cm above the fly. On this rig, a nymph can be fished at a dead drift, or retrieved in short jerks. The reel is also an effective mechanism for paying out line to allow the fly to continue drifting with the current. The same water that is covered by a fisherman with a fly rod can thus be fished over with a spinning outfit. The amount of weight can be adjusted to suit the depth; and of course the fly can also be weighted.

Another variation is to use a plastic bubble to provide weight for casting, either empty or filled with water. This can be used in combination with a nymph, wet fly, dry fly, or streamer fly, and the bubble should be far enough from the fly so as not to detract from it.

Fishing Taupo rivers

In terms of our angling history, nymphing for lake-run spawning trout is no longer new, but it is certainly a recent development. When upstream nymph fishermen meet downstream wet fly exponents on a pool on the Tongariro River, some heated discussion can occur. The traditional method of casting across and downstream with a fast-sinking line or a shooting head requires the fisherman to move steadily down the pool he is fishing, while the nymph fisherman moves upstream.

The anglers are fishing for trout which, like their steelhead forebears, are moving upstream to spawn, and while in the river or stream do not feed actively. They will respond to a fly or nymph, and both methods will catch fish; but for time spent on the water nymphing is more productive except perhaps when the water is discoloured.

Smaller Taupo tributaries like the Waitahanui, Waimarino, Hinemaia and Tauranga-Taupo are ideal nymph water; and in Rotorua the Utuhina, Ngongotaha and Waiteti Streams, which are the only tributaries open to fishing, are all suited to upstream nymph fishing.

The choice of nymph is less important than the amount of weight that can be added. In Rotorua and Taupo, flies larger than size 10 may not be weighted, and no split shot or any other type of weight may be added to the line. However, you can use two nymphs and a common practice is to use one 'bomb' which is heavily weighted, and about 15 cm above it an unweighted nymph which will swim better. In fast or deep water, two 'bombs' are used to get down to the fish.

Globugs in various colours and sizes are the most popular pattern, with the obvious resemblance to trout eggs making pink or orange the most commonly used colours. These are often fished in conjunction with a regular pattern like a White Caddis, Hare and Copper or Halfback. Nymphing has opened up water on the Tongariro which was previously ignored by anglers heading for the big, famous pools. These small runs and backwaters hold surprising numbers of trout, and there is always a good population of juvenile fish which, while small, are active. On the bigger pools the tail-out section and the edge of the fast current at the head provide good nymph water. Basically, a nymph can be fished anywhere the flow is not too strong.

As the trout are not feeding actively like resident river fish, the nymph or nymphs must be presented literally on their noses. They will rarely move any distance to take it. The key factor is to get the nymph down to the level of the trout, which are usually right on the bottom; and in fast water like much of the Tongariro and Waitahanui a long drift is needed.

The line is cast as far as possible upstream and slightly across, and all of the water covered from one position before taking a couple of steps upstream.

When using floating lines, line control is important. Slack line should be recovered without pulling the nymph, and regular mending of the line on the water will increase the length of the drift, as will flicking extra line onto the water after it has floated past. Downstream drift is limited only by the amount of line which can be laid on the water in loose zig-zags. When a fish strikes, cover the same water again for there will probably be more in the same position.

Identifying strikes can be a problem, as often the line or indicator simply stops. If the end of your line has sunk, it is even harder to detect. A variety of strike indicators have been developed, including some since banned, like polystyrene bobs which are regarded more as floats than indicators. Some effective indicators are made from bunches of yarn in different bright colours, which are tied to the end of the line. Some can be moved up and down the butt section of your leader, varying the depth fished. When dipped in fly floatant, these wool or yarn indicators work very well, and also help keep your line on top of the water. The authoritative Taupo angler Keith Draper suggests using black yarn, which is more visible than fluorescent colours in some light conditions.

As with all nymph fishing, your fly should drift down with the current, unencumbered by any drag from the line. The length of leader used will determine the depth fished, and the ability to handle an extra long leader is a real advantage on deep runs. Many Taupo anglers do not bother with a tapered leader, but use a long section of 3 to 4 kg mono with a tippet of 2 kg line. The way in which the leader lands on the water is not as important as when dry-fly fishing, because you are not actually fishing until your nymph has sunk and drifted several metres downstream — not the water where your cast lands.

You will lose a lot of flies on sticks and rocks, but if you don't get caught up on the bottom occasionally, then you are not fishing where the fish are.

There is a delightful story told about a couple of fellows fishing the Reed Pool on the Tongariro. They were becoming frustrated, as every time their lines swung round towards the tail of the pool where the trout were lying, their flies hooked a deep snag. After losing several flies they moved to the head of the pool and watched as another fisherman walked into the lower section and started to cast. The pair smiled as his line stopped, obviously hooked on the snag. Placing his rod on the bank the fisherman waded out into the river, running the line through his hand. Reaching down, he grasped something and struggled backwards. Slowly a large waterlogged branch appeared, and when he reached the shallows the man started to pick flies off it.

"What a useful chap," one of the anglers commented to his mate, but they stopped smiling when the enterprising fisherman proceeded to drag the branch back out into deep water and deposit it once more in the river.

Wet-fly fishing for spawning trout also involves putting a fly in front of the fish repeatedly, and again like steelhead the trout prefer a fly which swings across rather than moves steadily up the current. Either a high-density weight-forward sinking line or a shooting head will achieve this presentation when cast across the river at a downstream angle. When your cast lands, immediately mend a loop of line upstream then hold your rod high with both hands to keep line out of the water. This way you are in direct contact with the sunken section or head, and can follow the line around as it sinks and swings across the current. If a belly is allowed to develop in the current in front of you, the fly will be pulled downstream and you will lose control. By lengthening each cast you can cover all of the available water from one position at the head of a pool, then take a couple of steps downstream and start again. In this fashion you will cover the pool in a series of arcs. When a fish takes, the line just stops, so any hesitation or bump should be struck hard. All of the kinks and loops have to be straightened before the hook is driven home.

The leader can be quite short, perhaps only half a metre so the fly does not swing up in the current, and about 3 to 4 kg breaking strain. A Globug or nymph on a dropper above your fly can be added as an extra option, but casting long distances while standing waist-deep in the river can be difficult enough without having two flies which may tangle.

Dry-fly fishing

One of the greatest pleasures for a fisherman is spending a day casting dry flies onto pocket water and riffles on a small stream, carefully working upstream, covering all of the water.

There are three distinct types of dry-fly fishing. The first is the classic 'matching the hatch', where the fisherman must match what the trout are taking, in both size and colour. It may be a hatch of size 14 cream caddis, or a fall of size 12 dark brown mayfly spinners. The naturals are easily identified, but it gets tricky if there is a variety of insects on the water, or if the trout are taking emergers. On large rivers like the Mataura and Clutha the trout can be very selective, and in most cases inexperienced anglers will use flies that are too large.

The second technique is when casting to a trout which can be seen and is proving uncooperative. Provided it has not been spooked by a dragging fly or section of line, the trout can be offered a range of flies until it accepts one, or you switch to a nymph. This is delicate fishing as each cast must be precise in direction and length from the angler's position downstream, and low down the fly may appear to be drifting over the trout when in fact it is falling short. It is a fine balance between risking putting the leader over the fish, and casting short. More accuracy will be achieved by stalking closer and reducing the length of cast needed. Sometimes only one or two casts can be made before the fish moves away.

Perhaps the most challenging trout are those found in spring creeks where the water is gin-clear and the fish are easily spooked. The angler must crouch low and place his cast precisely in the right spot so that only the fly drifts within the trout's circle of vision. In these circumstances an

extra long leader with a 1 kg tippet may be needed, with a size 18 or 20 dry fly.

Trout are also located when they rise, and a few minutes observing the water before fishing is often time well spent. The cast is made with more confidence and care when covering a spot where a trout has just risen.

The third type of approach is fishing blind up a stream or along the edge of a river using an attractor type of fly — one which does not represent anything in particular, but attracts the trout. Flies like the Royal Wulff are popular for this type of fishing as they are easily seen. Another midsummer favourite is a grasshopper or cicada imitation. Trout will be found along current lines which are usually well defined, and a line of foam marking the edge of a strong current immediately below a willow branch drooping into the water cries 'Fish!' to the observant angler.

As with nymphing, reading the water is important, and the discussion covering where trout are found is equally relevant to dry-fly fishing. The approach is the same, with a diagonal cast upstream covering the water. But the dry-fly fisherman also concentrates on the fast water: riffles, pocket water and the inflow at the head of a pool are all likely spots. Slow pools are ignored unless a rise occurs. Fishing will also be harder when a river is either high or very low.

When casting across the current you have to mend line upstream by lifting the rod, pulling extra line off the reel, then flicking the loop upstream. You can also fish downstream with the parachute cast, where you lift the rod sharply just before the fly lands on the surface. This pulls the whole cast upstream before it touches the water. After the cast settles, lower your rod tip slowly as your line drifts down with the current. Extra line can be laid on the water in zig-zag loops by flicking the rod tip from side to side, giving a longer drift.

Keep a low profile when stalking brown trout in shallow water. In these conditions the odds are stacked in favour of the trout.

The hackles on a speckled brown mayfly imitation ensure it will sit upright in the surface film.

When fishing in bright conditions the leader floating on the surface film casts a shadow which can spook the trout. A formula which will make the leader sink, leaving only your fly floating, is a mixture of Fuller's earth (available from chemists) and detergent.

Dry flies should always be coated with a floatant before casting, and there are several commercial preparations which will do the job well. After catching a trout your fly will be smeared with fish slime, which is designed to help the trout move smoothly through the water. Your fly should not move smoothly through the water, but float on the surface. You can wash the fly and dry it with a paper towel or handkerchief before recharging it with floatant or, better still, tie on a new one. The reverse applies to nymphs, which can be rubbed in the slime on a trout's body to make them sink faster.

A hat with a good brim and a pair of Polaroid sunglasses will prove invaluable when spotting trout or looking for promising lies.

Remember: approach the river with care, cover the water thoroughly, concentrate and fish out each cast positively.

Fly fishing on lakes

Rotorua lakes

In the days when I was a 12-year-old boy, the big Tarawera trout averaged 4 kg in winter, but they grew so quickly that the same fish were about 3 kg in spring when the season opened. Today, fish of these proportions are still caught in autumn and winter as they prepare for the spawning runs. It is the highlight of the fly fisherman's season on the big lakes at Rotorua — like a fever for some dedicated fishermen who get out of bed at 3.30 in the morning to be first in line for the 5 o'clock start.

The first big fish appear off the stream mouths at the beginning of April. Heavy rain followed by a cold snap will get the fish moving; but the main runs start in late April, with May and June the prime months. Tarawera, Rotoiti and Okataina have similar characteristics. They are deep, rich in trout food and carry low populations of trout. With little natural spawning occurring, the population is managed to produce big trout through the numbers liberated.

The fish congregate off the stream mouths and beaches where they were released as fingerlings and are never easy to catch because they cease feeding actively, but will snap at a fly. Success comes with perseverance, and some fly fishermen will average 10 hours of fishing for each fish caught. At night the trout overcome their fear of shallow water and move in to lie in the current, or cruise the beaches. A floating or intermediate-density line will present the fly in front of the trout, making it easy for it to suck in. The line is cast out into the darkness and retrieved slowly over and over again. But it never becomes boring. There are always plenty of comments floating around, punctuated by fish splashes and other nocturnal sounds. Someone might get a tug, another has a good pull, or it may just be a touch or a message. Sometimes it will be a strike.

Angling pressure at a stream mouth can push the trout out beyond casting range, but if the spot is rested for an hour they usually move in again. This is not so important on a beach, where the fish are cruising up and down, or schooling off the beach. The flies used don't vary much. The basic rule is 'the darker the night, the darker the fly'. Moonlight makes fishing harder, and a breeze ruffling the surface or clouds covering the moon will help. Small flies work better than larger ones, and size 6 and 8 are popular.

Flies which have a luminous body are much in vogue on dark nights. The fly is 'charged' with a torch beam and fished for several casts until the glow has faded. The effectiveness of these 'lumo flies' diminishes as the light increases; in moonlight it is a good idea to use a regular fly in tandem. A small group of fishermen in Rotorua and Taupo has been using these special flies for more than 20 years, trying to keep it secret in the belief that if everybody used them they would not be so effective. The secret is out now and the flies are widely used. Their effectiveness probably has diminished, but they do have their place.

While cold, dark nights with an offshore breeze are favoured, local fishermen also wait for a strong wind to blow into the beaches where the trout gather. The wave action and freshly oxygenated water stimulates the fish, which move into the shallows and can be caught on orange-bodied flies or Globugs during the day. An easterly storm during winter is a signal for anglers to head for The Landing at Tarawera.

Another technique is to use a sinking line with a smelt or bully imitation and leave the fly lying on the bottom until the trout can be seen cruising towards it; then twitch the fly, moving it very slowly.

The main beaches for this type of fishing are the Tarawera Landing, the beach adjacent to the road at Okataina, Ruato and Hinehopu beaches on Rotoiti, and alongside the main highway at the northern end of Rotoma.

Another prime time to fish is at dawn, and on a frosty morning the trout become active for a short time. They will take Kilwells, a Red Setter or a Mrs Simpson; and smelt patterns as the light brightens. The killer patterns and Red Setter should be tied to represent small bullies, with smooth, flowing hackles and feathers — red bodies in winter and yellow in spring and summer.

A new method of fly fishing is becoming popular on all of the lakes — the 'heave-and-leave' technique, using a Globug. A ball of orange, red or green chenille in various combinations, it can scarcely be called a fly. These lures are used successfully on trout which are feeding on salmon eggs in Alaskan rivers, and they work just as well in our lakes at all times of the year. The Globug is cast out over the drop-off into deep water, either from shore or from an anchored boat, with a shooting head or fast-sinking line. A special floating variety which incorporates polystyrene will float up above the weed and remains suspended in the water, waiting for a passing trout to swallow it. And they do. It can be a very productive technique, and some movement may be imparted by jiggling the rod tip or retrieving slowly. As an alternative to fly fishing, Globugs can also be fished on a spinning rod, with a sinker adding weight for casting, rigged above a swivel

---

Carry a small whetstone and touch up the point of your hook before using it. Also check the point after catching a fish, for a tooth can easily turn the sharp tip. Flies will also be damaged by striking stones on the back cast.

Changes to the administration of our freshwater fisheries have created two licence areas.
Fish and Game Council licences can be purchased in each district and are valid throughout the country. A separate licence, issued by the Department of Conservation, is required for the Taupo district and is valid only in that district.
A new tourist licence for overseas visitors may also be introduced. If in doubt about licences or regulations, which do vary from district to district, check with a local tackle shop or Fish and Game office.

This Rangitaiki River brown trout fell to the popular Hare and Copper nymph after refusing a variety of dry flies.

about half a metre above the bug.

Spring and summer bring a change to the style of fly fishing on the Rotorua lakes. The fishing starts slowly in October, improving as the water temperature rises and smelt move into the shallows to spawn, and insect activity also increases. More emphasis is placed on smelt patterns, which should be thin-bodied with long tails. On deep lakes a sinking line will get the fly down, and even though it is always tempting to cast to rising fish the best approach seems to be a slow, deep retrieve. The trout you can see are hard to catch. In November the dragonfly larvae start hatching and a Hamill's Killer or other dragonfly imitation will take trout when fished near weed beds. Lake Rerewhakaaitu is one lake which offers fine wading for fly fishermen, and as well as dragonfly patterns a Kilwell works well.

When the trout are chasing smelt, you can experience some fast and exciting fishing by wading along the shallow shelves and casting out over the edge, or fishing from a small boat. On a wide, shallow shelf like the one off Kariri Point on Tarawera, or at Mission Bay on Rotorua, fishing from a drifting boat can be a lot of fun.

Long, thin smelt flies with bodies of yellow wool or lime green chenille will take fish. Another pattern to use on a bright day is a simple silicon body with a wisp of white tail.

If trout are not actively smelting, they can be caught by fishing into deep holes from an anchored boat, with a Red Setter or smelt flies. This technique is best at dawn and dusk, but will produce the occasional fish at any time of the day.

During a hot, calm summer Lake Rotorua can become unhealthy for the trout, which move into cold-water stream mouths in large numbers. These conditions are usually accompanied by a bloom of algae and extra weed growth, bringing accusations of pollution in the lake. It is a natural condition, but is no doubt exacerbated by the inflow of nutrients from farmland and habitation. You cannot expect to have 50,000 people living around the lake without some effect. It is a bonanza for fly fishermen, who line up at the mouths of the Hamurana, Awahou and Waiteti Streams. At night, you can feel the cold current against the back of your waders, indicating you are in the right position; the stream water is often blown to one side of the rip and you must be in the current to catch fish. A slow retrieve with a floating line or slow-sinking line will yield fish, and there are good numbers of large brown trout which move into the shallows as well as rainbows. When these mouths are 'on' there will always be a line of anglers spread across the mouth, day and night, with others fishing from small dinghies anchored in front of them. Smelt patterns used here are darker, like a Ginger Mick or Green Orbit, to match the dark-coloured water. Killer patterns are also used and a caddis nymph fished on a floating line will also take fish.

The lake created by a hydro dam on the Rangitaiki River near Murupara, Lake Aniwhenua, has developed a reputation as a producer of huge trout. In recent years the number of trophies coming out of Aniwhenua has reduced considerably, but it is still a fine fishery — and most of the fish are caught by fly fishermen. Unlike the Rotorua lakes, the diet of the trout is insect-based, and both brown and rainbow trout can be caught by wading the margins and fishing for sighted trout with Swannundaze or damselfly nymphs. Most people fish from drifting or anchored boats, working nymphs along the edges of the many banks of weed with a floating line and long leader. A leech pattern on a sink-tip line, fished into a hole, will also take trout.

Fly fishing Lake Taupo

Taupo is one of the world's great fisheries. It is a self-sustaining, wild trout fishery that is complete in all respects, offering every type of trout fishing except bait fishing. Kilo for kilo a Taupo rainbow is one of the toughest customers to have on the end of a fly rod. He is not carrying the extra body fat of a Rotoiti hog, and to my mind is the finest eating trout in the country. You will catch him while fishing a Hairy Dog or Red Setter off a rocky point in deep water. You can stalk him on a shallow beach as he chases smelt almost onto the sand on a bright spring day. Or you may prefer to fish one of the many stream mouths around the lake, where the trout line up on one side of the rip and the anglers line up on the other side.

The techniques used on the Rotorua lakes apply on Taupo also. Night fishing at small stream mouths calls for a quiet approach, a floating line and similar flies. One difference is that many Taupo fishermen prefer large flies, tied on size 2 hooks. The Fuzzy Wuzzy, Marabou and Hairy Dog are some that are popular in the larger models. The rips fish best in autumn and into winter, when the trout prepare to spawn.

Larger stream mouths like those at Hatepe, Waitahanui, Whanganui, Waihaha and Waihora all fish well during summer also, peaking in late March and April. Here, slow-sinking or intermediate-density lines are

> When striking a trout, raise the rod firmly — don't jerk it violently. Many fish are broken off by over-enthusiastic strikes. The longer the line the firmer the strike should be.

The production of trout in Lake Taupo varies tremendously, depending on the recruitment from spawning, survival and growth of young fish, and harvest by anglers, both in the lake and the tributaries. Keeping the right balance is a difficult job, and fisheries managers became very concerned at the decline in fish numbers in the late 1980s. Trout production in 1988 was estimated at 540 tonnes, and in 1989, 340 tonnes. A survey of the number of fish caught in the 1990-91 season estimated a total harvest of 175 tonnes (113,000 trout). But the level of harvest was very high when compared to the total trout population, and drastic measures were needed. The response by the authorities was to cut the limit bag, from eight to three trout per day, in December 1990. The Department of Conservation fisheries experts monitor the population closely, and every year in November they survey the lake with sophisticated sonar equipment to assess trout numbers. By the 1994-95 season the population in the lake at that point in time was estimated at 210,000 fish — nearly double the estimated population of 1990-91.

DOC surveys of anglers on the water show that in the 1990-91 season 75,767 licences of all types were sold, with a total angling effort of 665,000 hours for 113,000 trout killed. Comparable figures in 1995-96 were 66,844 licences, 643,000 hours and 129,600 trout harvested. Of these trout 79,700 were estimated to have been caught in the lake, and 49,900 taken from tributaries.

The surveys of anglers also illustrate the effectiveness of different fishing methods. During the summer of 1996/97 the best results came from harling in spring and early summer, but by late summer the fish had moved into deep water where only wire lines and downriggers could reach them.

Wild trout populations fluctuate through cycles of troughs and peaks, and the 1994-95 levels represented a peak which has since declined. The number of trout measured each November is not the total number of fish available through the whole year. The population is like a sink full of water, with the plug out and the tap on. The level remains relatively constant but there are always new fish reaching legal size and other fish dying or moving into the spawning tributaries. Juvenile trout grow fastest, increasing in length by 1 mm a day through spring and summer.

Overall, the total trout population and the numbers caught by anglers are similar. So there is not a lot of margin for error.

(Source: *Target Taupo*, Issue 24, Department of Conservation)

used; and at the Waitahanui rip local fishermen go to great lengths to get their flies further out in the lake. They use custom-made rods up to 4.3 m long capable of throwing an entire line, and then float a second line attached to the first one down the rip, letting the current take it out to the waiting trout. A whole range of flies are used, from Split Partridge and Rabbits, to Hamill's Killer, Mrs Simpson, Parsons' Glory and Red Setter.

At night these spots can be quite competitive, and fishing positions are jealously guarded. One experienced Taupo fisherman went to great lengths to disguise the fact he was catching fish. He removed the pawl from inside his fly reel so there was no clicking sound. When a trout was hooked he continued to hold the rod parallel to the water, playing the fish in and out on the silent reel; and when it was close enough he held the rod behind him and reached along it to the tip, grabbed the line and reached underwater, gently pulling in the trout. Gripping it through the gills he broke its neck and tied it to a string round his waist under the water, then resumed fishing. He claimed another fisherman a metre away would not know that he had just caught a fish.

Some fishermen have been known to cast across and hook the end of a successful angler's line, pull it in, and cut off his fly — to see what he was using!

I am sure such tactics are not needed today, but the rips at the delta of the Tongariro can also be rather competitive. Here, it is vital that the boat is positioned in the centre of the current on the edge of the sandy lip where it drops away into deep water. When the lake is low, the rip is well defined and easy to locate. But if the lake level is high, there will be little indication at the surface and you have to look for leaves rolling along the bottom to locate the current. A high-density line or shooting head will get down deep, and this spot is one of my favourite fishing holes, for when you hook trout in deep water they put up a great fight. It is one of the few spots where you will consistently catch the big, well-conditioned deep-water trout that are usually caught only at night, or by deep trolling.

The four mouths of the delta face in different directions, so a sheltered mouth can always be found whichever way the wind is blowing. A tandem rig with two different flies is commonly used here, often combining a smelt pattern like a Doll Fly with a Red Setter or Globug. Add a Mrs Simpson and Fuzzy Wuzzy and you just about have it covered.

If the fish are not biting, it is more likely that the boat is not sitting in the right spot in the current than a question of using the wrong fly. If you are hooking sticks and leaves on every cast the boat will be sitting too close in, so let out some anchor rope. If you are not hitting the bottom no matter how long you wait for the line to sink, you are positioned too far out over the drop and need to move the boat in. By first dropping the anchor in shallow water you can determine the distance by adjusting the amount of rope used, and a second anchor thrown off the windward side will keep the stern stable — which is important. Ideally, the stern will be sitting where the bottom drops away.

If the line is being pulled to one side by the current, you need to move the boat to that side, by relocating the anchor, until the line is running straight over the back. Sometimes it is necessary to move several times before the best position is found. But it is worth the trouble, for you will catch more fish.

The flies must be allowed to sink to the bottom and retrieved either in short jerks or a slow, steady retrieve. When fishing over the back of a boat, hold the rod low, pointing to where the line disappears into the water. It can then be easily lifted when a trout hits.

It is a relaxing way to fish, sitting back in a comfortable boat, dropping the line on the floor as it comes in and then standing on it while trying to cast. There is plenty of time to look at the lake, which changes moods in different light conditions and weather, to swap stories with your companion, or watch other people catch fish while waiting for your line to sink.

The strike is the highlight of all fishing, and when a strong fish takes your fly with a heavy pull it is the sort of strike you remember for a long time.

This spot also fishes very well at night. It pays to arrive in daylight to ensure you are in the correct position, and if there is a moon the fishing

When netting a trout, lead it to the boat or shore with your rod. Shorten the line and wait until the fish is lying on its side at the surface, then dip the net under it head first. A fish still swimming is almost impossible to net.

A Taupo trout is nearly ready for the net. Wait until it is lying on its side before slipping the net under its head.

will come on as soon as the moon rises. Unlike shallow-water stream mouths where moonlight is a disadvantage, deepwater rips like the Tongariro and the Tauranga-Taupo mouth fish better in moonlight. The only other spot I know that performs like this is the Log Pool on Lake Okataina, but boats may not be anchored within 100 m of the small stream mouth.

Use flies with plenty of hackle to provide movement when night fishing at the Tongariro delta. There are a lot of koura, or crayfish, on the bottom, and they often attack your fly, becoming hooked in the legs as you react to the delicate tugging. Often when groping down your line in the dark to check your fly your hand will slip over a large, spiny koura; and it certainly wakes you up.

On the Taupo fly fishing calendar the smelting season is a phenomenon that fishermen look forward to with great anticipation. When weather and water temperatures combine, usually some time in November, the smelt move into the shallows in huge schools — and the trout follow, losing their fear of shallow water. They will often chase smelt almost onto the beach. But during the day the trout found in shallow water are usually poorly conditioned kelts recovering from spawning. Better-quality fish will be caught at dawn, dusk and at night, particularly at stream mouths. The fisherman who comes across this activity when the wind is stirring up the water, which disguises his presence, will enjoy some grand fly fishing.

A slow-sinking line is less intrusive than a floater, and a sparsely dressed smelt pattern retrieved quickly by stripping in the line will provoke a strike. I prefer small flies, matching the size of smelt, which are about a size 8, with a Grey Ghost, Dorothy, Parsons' Glory, Jack Spratt, Yellow Lady or Taupo Tiger — all useful patterns in various body colours. Doll flies and Silicon Smelt also work well, but you should use silver-bodied flies in bright conditions, and duller colours when it is overcast.

Once, while resting in the warm spring sun on the beach at Waihaha, I was splashed by a trout which had chased some smelt into a few centimetres of water. The rainbow almost swam up onto the sand in its eagerness to get the frantic smelt. Reaching over, I grasped my rod without getting up, as I did not want to spook the trout, and flicked a fly into the shallows. It only travelled the length of the leader; the trout grabbed it and I caught it while still lying down. It was a spawned-out slab which did not fight well, and was soon returned to the lake.

Fly fishing other lakes

While the lake fisheries at Rotorua and Taupo are based predominantly on a diet of forage fish and crayfish, there are many lakes throughout the country which call for a totally different style of fishing, and they can produce some huge trout. These lakes are often small man-made lakes for electricity generation or irrigation, and they yield their trout grudgingly. They are fisheries where the trout feed mainly on insect life rather than baitfish. Many of the fly patterns used here are the same as those employed on rivers and streams, but the techniques for fishing are different.

High-country Canterbury lakes like Coleridge are affected by low tem-

The bottom-dwelling freshwater crayfish or koura is a rich source of food for trout big enough to take them. Such trout have deep orange flesh and are prized table fish.

Road kills

A hawk fluttering up in front of the car was always a signal to slow down and check what was squashed on the tarmac. If the feathers or fur were light brown, it called for a closer inspection.

As a result, the spare room at home was continually cluttered with plastic bags leaking smelly clumps of fur and loose feathers. The road kills were always a prime source of materials for making trout flies, and many a trout has been hooked on a fly containing strands of possum fur, mottled brown feathers from the breast of a mallard duck, shiny blue-black feathers from the flank of a pukeko, or long brown and white feathers from the thighs of a hawk. The highways provide an endless smorgasbord of materials for the enterprising fly-tier.

But much of the tradition of fly-tying has gone the way of split cane rods and streamside manners. Older anglers mourn their passing.

When I opened a fly box while sitting in a boat near Turangi, it was sad to see it packed with clean, slick 'flies' with none of the lingering odour of squashed feathers or fur.

"Don't you use red setters any more?" I asked Mike, head guide at Tongariro Lodge. "Only on Rotoaira; it's the fly to use there," he replied.

We were anchored on the lip where the bottom plunged down into the hole, off Tokaanu, and I hadn't taken much notice of the fly tied on the end of the short trace when I cast the shooting head line out. Pulling it in to cast again, I could see it was an ugly brown thing, with two large white bulbs on each side of the head.

"What on earth is that?" I asked.

"It's a koura imitation, and the boobies make it float up off the weed. The trout are feeding on crayfish at the moment," explained Mike.

This fly had a couple of polystyrene bulbs attached to make it float. I had seen nymphs tied with similar tiny bulbs, but not large wet flies for lake fishing. We had always used a Red Setter or Fuzzy Wuzzy to simulate the jerky crayfish on the bottom of the lake.

Opening Mike's fly box I was faced with an array of white, brown, bright orange, and transparent lures. There were Globugs with polystyrene beads, smelt imitations made from soft rubber, and others incorporating strands of silver flash and synthetic fibres. Not one traditional trout fly could be seen. Mike is a successful professional fishing guide, who helps people catch large numbers of trout, and he knows what fly to use.

He suddenly jerked his rod up, and it bowed under the pressure of a strong fish. "You catch this one," he said, handing the rod to five-year-old Paul, who struggled with the long fly rod. "Let him pull the line out," said Mike as the reel spun and line was ripped from the spool. Carefully he coached the youngster on how to hold the cork handle and wind with the other hand. He quickly mastered the rhythm, pulling heartily to keep a bend in the rod and winding slowly when the trout allowed him to. Slowly it came to the boat, and Paul shouted "There it is!" as the gleaming silver belly broke the surface.

Mike slipped the net under the fish and it lay gasping on the floor. "Do you want it?" he asked. The trout had a deep belly, but tapered quickly towards the tail. Its stomach would collapse if cut open, and it would not offer the bright pink, firm flesh we enjoyed when cut into pieces, dipped in egg and bread crumbs, and lightly fried. Paul and I agreed it should go back to recover, and Mike gently lifted the long trout by the tail and slipped it into the dark water.

"What fly had it taken?" I asked, and Mike held out a pure white thing sporting twin white bulbs at the head, with a soft rubber tail, and a fluffy white wing made from synthetic fibres.

"Smelt fly," he said. "We murdered the fish with it last summer in the shallow water around the delta (where the Tongariro River splits and flows into the lake). The smelting was fantastic."

He was not even retrieving his fly when he hooked the trout. It was just sitting up off the bottom waiting for a fish to swim by and eat it.

Fishing the paddocks

The water level in Paddock Bay fluctuates a lot. After heavy rain, Lake Wanaka rises and the grass on the low-lying pasture is inundated. The trout love it, particularly brown trout, which are not afraid of shallow water. The freshly flooded paddocks provide rich grazing for the trout, and the worms and grubs forced from the ground are easy pickings.

There was a strong wind blowing offshore when we arrived at the bay, about 20 minutes drive from Wanaka. Gerald Telford is an expert at this type of fishing, which can be deceptively difficult. He takes people fishing for a living, and knows full well that the success of a day is determined by the inexperience of most of his visitors. "You can spot the trout if the surface is not too ruffled. The browns may be one metre from the edge, or six metres. Rainbows will be further out," he explained.

The grass on the lake bottom was coated with a fine fuzz of algae, and it dropped away to clear sand along a jagged lip that roughly followed the shoreline. Gerald picked a small black nymph from a row of similar flies in his fly box. "Try this," he said, offering the size 16 nymph. It had a wisp of hackle and a green sheen to the black body. "Black and peacock — an old favourite here."

"There's one!" said Gerald, pointing to a dim, dark shadow lying motionless on the clear lake bed and about 10 metres out. "They're almost impossible to catch when they lie still," he added, stripping line and carefully casting the light, tapered fly line. The shadow slipped away when the line split the shining surface of the lake, spreading V-shaped ripples.

A slow stalk along the shallows revealed nothing. "Try fishing blind. Cast out, let the nymph sink, and bring it in very slowly," he advised.

The wind blew stronger and it became impossible to see into the clear water. Then a faint pull on the line resulted in a firm swing of the rod, but there was no resistance.

"You have to pause, then strike. These browns move slowly," said Gerald.

The North Island lake tactics obviously needed some revision.

When the breeze strengthened even more, it was time to shift. "We'll try Hawea. I like fishing for cruisers there. They are easier to catch, and you get bigger fish." Good reasons to try it.

On a clear day the fluffy, white clouds clinging to the mountain tops look as if only a stamp is needed to complete the postcard. The road winds above the lake, and cruising fish can be spotted from the side of the road. But the same wind blows here, and a narrow arm of the lake promised enough shelter to make the fishing enjoyable.

Hawea appeared less prone to fluctuating levels, and the shore was firm sand with a little mud. The shallow lake bed was clean, with no weed.

"Try in that deep gut," offered Gerald, then he wandered along the beach to a quiet corner. The gut was quiet, too, but a shout signalled action and his arcing rod confirmed it.

"That was quick," we said. He just smiled. "I saw a flash as I lifted the fly to cast. Must have followed it in." The rod thumped, and soon a yellow trout with red and black spots lay in the shallows. Gerald gently picked up the 1 kg brown and slipped the hook out before easing it back into the water. With a flick, the trout was gone.

"See the light colour? It blends in with the clean bottom. I have seen them change in a couple of hours to match the bottom. Nature's camouflage ensures that when living over a dark, weedy bottom the trout will develop dark colours, with the reverse when their environment is one of clear water and a light-coloured lake bed."

A trickle of water ran down the sand at the edge of the beach behind Gerald. "That's why you fished here?"

"They sometimes hang around a current, even a small one. We were getting desperate for a fish!" You can't beat local knowledge.

Gerald gave up a farming career for the tourist business. Based in Wanaka, he caters for fly fishers and some hunters, offering chamois and deer hunting in the mountains. His spare time is spent searching for new water to fish, so when he is not working he is fishing.

"What better way to feed a passion?" he asked.

Bright conditions call for a delicate approach and an extra long leader when casting dry flies on South Island lakes like Wanaka.

peratures for much of the year, and even in midsummer the temperature will drop radically at night. This often restricts insect activity to the middle of the day, and a rise may occur at any time. A hatch of manuka beetles in November or December can trigger a feeding spree, and much of the fishing will be to cruising brown trout. A large dry fly like a Humpy or Royal Wulff is cast out and left until a trout is spotted, then the fly is tweaked as the trout approaches. Blustery conditions are common in the high country, and sometimes it is necessary to fish along the waves with a small lure like a Hamill's Killer or Kilwell on a floating or slow-sinking line.

Classic still-water techniques have been influenced by British methods, developed for fishing on reservoirs. Long casts with floating lines, extra-long leaders and tiny nymphs fished over weed beds can produce some excellent brown trout on small lakes like Rutherford's Dam, Blakely's Dam, Poolburn and Manorburn Lakes in central Otago. When cicadas are hatching, a large dry fly drifted on the surface offers exciting fishing. The same techniques can be used on large lakes like Wanaka, Hawea and Wakatipu, particularly over shallow, weedy areas.

Fly fishing guide Gerald Telford searches the margins of Wanaka's Paddock Bay for cruising trout. What better way to feed a passion?

The fisherman waded out into the lake until the water level was just below his waist. There was a loud scratching noise as he stripped line from his protesting reel, then a soft swish-swish as he cast out into the darkness.

Similar swishing sounds floated up and down the line of dark figures standing waist deep parallel to the beach.

A cigarette briefly glowed a dull red, then died away. The angler cast again, waited for his line to sink below the calm surface, then started to slowly knit the cold, wet line into small loops that fitted snugly into the palm of his left hand. Suddenly he stiffened and his body tensed as he felt the gentle tug on the line. Lifting the rod smoothly and strongly with his right arm, the fisherman grasped the fly line tightly in his left hand. A heavy splash echoed across the still water and the rod jumped and throbbed as a large trout flopped and surged, shaking its head from side to side.

The fisherman held his rod high in the air, stumbling backwards and winding frantically to take up the loose line. His reel screeched as the big rainbow surged away, diving deeply into the black water.

Slowly the arcing pressure of the long, thin rod stopped the fish, it turned and allowed itself to be drawn towards the beach. As it neared the shelving sand the trout panicked and again tore line from the fisherman's reel. Again it gave in to the unyielding pressure transmitted down the line to the hook of the small fly lodged in the corner of its mouth.

The fisherman stepped back from the water, gently easing the trout onto the sand at the edge of the lake. Its tail flapped feebly as the fisherman slipped a black rubber boot under its flank and flipped the long, thick body up the beach. Heart pounding, he knelt and fumbled in the pocket of his bulky parka. Gripping a short, squat piece of thick wood he rapped the trout on the head, above the eyes. Then, slipping two fingers into the gills he carried the trout to his car and dropped it into a plastic box in the boot, before wading back out into the lake. He was quietly excited and could not wait for daylight when he would weigh the trout. It was a huge one, easily the biggest he had ever caught, and looked as if it could pull the scales down to 5 kg or even more.

Fish started rising, forming spreading rings on the shining surface of the lake as the first pale light washed the rim of the mountain and the black line of hills on the other side of the lake.

Lights flashed briefly as the anglers lined up along the beach searched fly boxes for lighter-coloured flies. Slim brown flies replaced the short black patterns and were cast out with new energy towards the splashes and rings which marked the feeding trout.

This was the magic hour. On cold, frosty mornings when the first light of dawn replaced the solid darkness which seemed to intensify as if trying to resist the coming daylight, the trout became restless. After cruising slowly all night they greeted the growing light with renewed vigour.

The sight of big trout rising in the bay gave the anglers fresh hope after casting and retrieving their long lines for two hours since fishing was permitted to start at 5 am.

Occasionally a trout was hooked, and the calm water was broken by the leaps and frantic splashes as the big fish struggled to escape.

Finally, after half an hour of intense activity the trout stopped rising. The fishermen wound in their lines and stopped to chat and exchange experiences over a thermos of hot coffee.

Those who had caught trout proudly laid them on the sand. Fish were hung from scales while others were slit open and gutted.

The fisherman who had landed the big trout was happy. It was 5.5 kg and he basked in the praise from fellow anglers. The satisfaction of catching such a perfect specimen would be dulled if there were no others to exclaim over its short, deep body; the small mouth and thick shoulders; the perfect fins and unblemished pink and silver gleaming flanks. Envy is a common trait among anglers. But it can be excused when the sun is warming hands numbed by the frost and the successful anglers gladly answer questions like "What fly were you using?" by offering their fly boxes and pointing to the still-wet flies. They tell the truth for a change.

The word spreads quickly. "Tarawera is on! They are getting them at The Landing and at Te Wairoa!"

Careful handling ensures a trout will survive when released.

It also happens at Ruato, the popular stream mouth on the edge of Lake Rotoiti where the road up to Lake Okataina leaves the main highway. This fishing continues through until August, but the best runs are the first ones when the trout are still fresh from the lake, strong and brightly coloured. After a month of hanging around the stream mouths the trout change. The silver flanks darken, and the flush of pink turns deep crimson. They become lethargic and refuse the anglers' offerings, frustrating those who get out of bed at 3 o'clock in the morning to be sure of pole position by the stream mouth for the first cast at 5 o'clock.

Other anglers will head for the main beach at Lake Okataina, wading off the stony point at the end of the beach. As with all fishing, a handful of the anglers catch most of the fish. They catch big trout. For the fish come from the best stock: big, wild adults which had their eggs and milt gently squeezed from their bodies three years earlier. The eggs were hatched in trays at the Ngongataha Hatchery and the baby fry carefully raised until as yearlings they were put into the lakes to grow and repeat the cycle. Over two and a half years these trout have grown rapidly, reaching the splendid proportions which make them unique in the country. There will be hundreds of 'double figure' trout caught in the three lakes over the winter season. Many will be carefully put back into the water, while others will be taken home to be cooked or split and smoked. A few fish will be taken to a taxidermist for preserving and mounting.

The spawning runs have started.

A South Island rainbow throws itself from the river in an effort to dislodge the tiny hook in its jaw.

The trout in irrigation dams are invariably browns, which are better suited to this type of water where they feed on midges, snails, water-boatmen, damselflies and sedges. When the surface is rippled by a breeze it is hard spotting fish, and a nymph or dry fly is fished blind. On calm days large trout can be seen cruising the weed beds, and accurate and careful casting is needed. When the trout are lying motionless on the lake bed they are difficult to tempt. During a sedge hatch in the evening a sedge pattern skated across the surface can provoke some crashing strikes.

The small lakes are fertile and trout grow quickly. It is not unusual to take a bag of brown trout averaging 2.5 kg or more, and fish up to 9 kg have been reported. Both rainbows and browns can be spotted cruising the shallow ledges on the big southern lakes, and they can be hooked on a dry fly which is cast ahead of the trout's path and twitched slightly as it draws near. A Royal Wulff, Adams, Blue Dun or Elkhair Caddis can be used, but watch for naturals on the water to provide a clue as to the size and colour to adopt.

Where streams and rivers run into lakes, fish will be found feeding on food carried down the current. It may be a variety of nymphs, or try a Grey Ghost or Mrs Simpson as the trout could be chasing baitfish.

Still-water techniques work well on certain North Island lakes where insects comprise the bulk of the trout's diet. One such lake which can be alternatively maddeningly frustrating and supremely rewarding is Lake Otamangakau — called the Big O by locals — near Turangi. On some days it seems to be devoid of fish life, and on others fish can be seen rising all over the surface. The cicada population fluctuates in cycles, and every few years there is a prolific hatch of the noisy, locust-like insects. The ever-present wind blows thousands of cicadas onto the lake where they struggle furiously, setting off a feeding frenzy as trout smash into them with violent splashes. An imitation can be a simple grasshopper fly or Muddler Minnow fished dry, or a hand-crafted creation with a balsa wood body and shiny wings that looks as if it will fly off if given a chance. Cast the fly out on a floating line, give it a twitch occasionally, and wait for the action. The Otamangakau trout are fit and strong, as a result of the cold water, and do not give up when hooked.

One fisherman who specialises in fishing the Big O is Taupo guide Ron Bergin. He fishes from a small boat painted dark brown, because he maintains that big white boats will put off the trout. As the average depth of the lake is only 2 m, that makes sense. Ron uses a 6-weight outfit with a weight-forward floating line and a 6 m leader of 2.5 kg monofilament — no tapered leader or tippet, just a long length of light mono. At one time he faithfully used imitations of various insects, but has now condensed these down to one standard pattern. It is a dark olive nymph tied on a number 10 hook, that looks like a combination of a snail, damselfly and caddis. When wet, this fly is almost black. If the fishing gets hard, Ron will try something different — perhaps a peacock herl pattern, or a bloodworm. This tiny red 'worm' lives in the sediment on the lake bed, and is actually the larva of a small black midge. It is sometimes imitated with a simple red fly hook with no dressing at all.

A cased caddis larva was torn from its lair among the stones by a sudden surge in the current. Its soft body was protected by a shiny, chestnut brown, curved tube about 10 mm long. Tumbling in the swirling current the tiny creature was swept down towards a large round rock protruding above the surface of the river.

About a metre downstream from the rock a brown trout lay, finning gently and enjoying the cold caress of the water on its spotted, golden flanks. From above, the trout was almost invisible, its green/brown back merging with the mottled colour of the stones on the river bed. The rays of sunlight touching the surface were broken by the dancing wavelets, sending a kaleidoscope of shadows filtering down through the water. The trout's body lay in the calm water behind the rock, but its broad, spade-shaped tail was washed by the currents spilling around the rock, exactly where the two flows met in the tail of a V before rushing on down the river.

The caddis was pushed into the bulge of water, which roiled up where the force of the river met the immovable rock, then slid around to one side and fell into a miniature eddy on the edge of the calm pocket. Frantically the tiny creature's legs scrabbled at a pebble, trying to escape the remorseless grip of the current. But the current suddenly shifted again and sucked the insect from its sanctuary, spinning it round a few centimetres above the safety of the small stones.

The trout's black eye, rimmed with gold, focused on the brown caddis as it approached on the same level, and the dark tail bent out in the direction of the morsel. The large body drifted like a shadow across the current. There was a white flash as the mouth gaped and the caddis disappeared, joining a mass of fellow larvae in the trout's stomach while the water was ejected through its gills. The rudder bent the other way and the trout slid back to its position.

A shiny green beetle launched itself from a manuka bush by the river's edge and suddenly a gust of wind snatched at it, sending it tumbling onto the water with wings buzzing frantically. Trapped in the clinging surface film, the beetle scrabbled in vain, sending out rings of tiny wavelets as the current swept it downstream in small circles towards the rock. Ever the opportunist, the brown trout watched the round skylight above as well as the hazy patterns to each side. When the beetle first appeared on the edge of the trout's vision it was a blurred shape. The nerve ends in the line along the trout's flank sensed the vibrations emanating from the struggling insect and both eyes tilted upward, locking onto the beetle, recognising the silhouette of tiny wings and round body bulging the smooth surface. This time only the lower half of the broad tail bent to the right, and the pressure of the flowing water pushed the trout outward and up. Like a jet plane cleaving the air the trout slid gracefully up till its snout broke the surface and the jaws parted, inhaled the beetle and closed gently. The long body drifted back and down, and a final flick of the tail propelled it forward to resume its position.

The boy kneeling in front of the manuka bush had been patiently watching the river downstream from the rock for five minutes. He had not seen the flash of white as the 1.5 kg brown trout took the caddis larva. He had never heard of Mr G E M Skues, the Englishman who invented nymph fishing towards the end of the last century, creating a furore among those who abhorred anything other than a floating fly. He had not read what Skues wrote:

I can only advise
You make use of your eyes
And watch for that wink under water.

Not only does the wink or flash of white indicate a feeding trout, but it also signals a strike before it is felt.

Like Skues, the boy did not have the benefit of Polaroid glasses and so had not seen the trout lying on the sun-dappled riverbed. But he did see the rise as the trout took the green beetle, and felt gratified that his suspicions were confirmed and a trout was indeed lying in what appeared to be such an obvious station.

The boy's trembling fingers fumbled as he opened the small plastic box, holding his meagre selection of dry flies. He desperately wanted to show the Old Man that he could bring home a trout, on his own. "What shall I use?" he thought. The Old Man had told him to watch and observe; to look for insects flying; to resist the temptation to cast into every piece of likely-looking water without first sitting and watching. The five minutes he had spent watching had seemed an eternity, but he had been rewarded and now it was up to him to catch the trout.

Something tickled the back of his neck and his skin crawled. Quickly brushing his neck with a flick of his fingers the boy saw a green beetle crawling indignantly across his shoulder. With relief he thought, "That's it. The Old Man always said that if there wasn't a hatch on the water try a nymph, or try the sort of imitation which the trout might see at any time. That trout just rose to something. I'll try a beetle."

His first cast was a sloppy one, and the line hit with a small splash on one side of the trout's rock. The boy's heart raced. "I hope I haven't spooked him," he muttered. His next cast was better, but the current pulled on the line between the rock and the riverbank, bulging it downstream and the fly skated across the surface.

"Take it easy," the boy said to himself, recalling the Old Man's advice: "Everyone panics a bit inside when he sees a stag that looks as if he's wearing a tree on his head."

On the third cast the line shot out smoothly, and the fly settled gently beside the smooth path below the rock, about a metre above where the trout had taken the beetle. With a quick flick the boy sent a loop darting up the line, and as the fly drifted easily towards the trout he jerked the rod tip, sending a shiver down the line and causing the artificial beetle to quiver. Tiny ripples danced around the fly, a gleaming brown snout appeared as if in slow motion and the fly disappeared. The boy's heart pounded as his left hand tightened on the loose line and his right arm lifted the rod. Exhilaration flooded his body as he felt the weight of the trout and the rod bucked as the fish flopped and splashed, before tearing line from the boy's hand as it turned and raced down the river. Holding the rod high, the boy ran after the trout, leaping from the grass onto the stones that marked the water's edge. The trout stopped in the deep pool below the run where it had taken the fly, and the rod thumped as the fish shook its head from side to side. Carefully the boy eased back on the rod, forcing the trout to turn towards him, and he slowly wound the handle of his reel as his quarry surrendered line.

The trout was tiring and its next run was shorter. The boy let it go, then again turned it with side pressure from the rod. He paused for a moment, then as the trout slid towards him the boy stepped back as he gained more line on his reel, slipping the line through the fingers of his left hand as it gripped the rod. Finally the exhausted trout lay in the shallows, its head beating weakly against the stones. Kneeling, the boy grasped it behind the head, forcing his fingers into the gills as the Old Man had taught him. If he was going to release the trout he would not have touched it, but would have prised the hook from the tough skin on top of the jaw and pushed it back into the water.

The boy rapped the fat brown trout on the nose with a smooth grey river stone, then clutching his prize he started to run back to the farmhouse to show the Old Man. He would return tomorrow, for he knew that another good trout would move into the lie.

Nature's camouflage . . . the brown trout's light colour blends in with the clean lake bottom.

The trout are found in the channels between the weed beds, which are abundant in this lake. With the boat anchored on top of a clump of weed, you cast out a long line and give the lightly weighted nymph time to sink before starting a very slow retrieve. A quick jerk at the start helps remove any kinks from the line lying on the surface, and may also attract the attention of a watching trout. Another reason for straightening the line is that the trout usually take gently, and you will miss strikes if not in direct contact with your fly. Secure the stern of the boat with a second anchor, or a paint tin filled with concrete, which does not pull up half the weed bed with it and can be lifted quickly when a fish is hooked to avoid tangling the anchor line. Try different spots around the lake, rather than sticking with one spot hoping fish will come along.

The big trout which come out of Otamangakau are legendary. Every summer Ron Bergin catches more than 20 double-figure (4.5 kg plus) trout with clients, and his personal best catches are two rainbows weighing 6.6 and 8.4 kg.

Neighbouring Lake Rotoaira is another interesting fishery. It is a natural lake which is more prolific than Otamangakau, and provides some wonderful fly fishing for trout feeding on damselfly larvae among weed beds in the shallows. The hydro scheme which created Otamangakau, the Tongariro Project, has affected Rotoaira. It is a catchment lake for water diverted from the upper Tongariro River and from Otamangakau, and the influx of cold water has reduced the productivity. But there are still good numbers of fit though small rainbows, and one successful technique is to drift across the shallows casting small Hamill's Killer or Red Setter flies on sink-tip lines, and stripping them in quickly.

Another lake which fishes well to a damselfly or dragonfly larva imitation is Waikaremoana. This lovely lake holds a good population of both rainbow and brown trout, and in spring the browns can be spotted cruising the shallows, where they are easily seen against the white sandy bottom. A green nymph or small Hamill's Killer presented on a sinking line will attract their attention. Let the fly lie on the bottom until a trout approaches, then give it a jerk. The browns will venture right into the shallows after the hatching dragonflies, and it is a recipe for some exciting fishing.

The various techniques discussed can be used throughout the country. It is a question of determining what the trout are feeding on and where they are likely to be at different times of the year. One example is the Kai Iwi Lakes, in the sand dunes near Dargaville, and Lake Ototoa, a small lake north of Auckland. These all hold small rainbow trout which can be caught by still-water techniques in summer and by fishing small black flies on fast-sinking lines during winter when the trout are feeding on koura. But trolling with cobras on sinking lines will also produce fish.

A few years ago I was fishing the Poutu Canal where it runs into Lake Rotoaira with a Japanese friend, Hamano, an accomplished fly fisherman who has fished throughout the world. There were a few fish rising, but the fishing was slow and Hamano was studying the water when he remarked on the number of small bullies he could see lying among the rocks at his

> Rubbing slime from a trout onto your fly or nymph when lake fishing will make the feathers lie smoothly and will help it sink.

feet. He took out a packet of flies he had purchased in Turangi, and selected a small Mrs Simpson and put it on, after first changing to a sinking line. Hamano fished the Mrs Simpson with slow, deliberate pulls, pausing between them. He soon had a strike and landed and released a rainbow of about 1.5 kg. Two more fish quickly followed.

The bullies Hamano saw had been swimming slowly in short bursts, stopping to hang motionless above the rocky bottom before moving again. By simulating not only the bully but also its action, Hamano had found the key to the particular situation

A successful fisherman will think about the fishing and the variables involved and, above all, will be adaptable.

A fly or not a fly?

When is a fly not a fly? Or, when is fly fishing not fly fishing?

These are dilemmas which arise regularly to haunt some trout anglers, while others smile. The questions also create problems for the managers of the trout fisheries, particularly in Rotorua and Taupo.

Fly fishing for trout is an evolving method of angling, with new materials and techniques continually being developed and, in some cases, widely adopted. But it is also steeped in tradition, more so than any other form of fishing. When upstream nymphing became popular on the Taupo spawning tributaries, many anglers were shocked at this departure from the traditional downstream, wet fly approach. It also led to conflicts on the river, when anglers fishing upstream literally met those casting downstream halfway through a pool. The question of who had the right of way was often loudly debated.

A nymph traditionally represents the larval form of an insect, and to be effective on fast deep rivers like the Tongariro the artificial flies must be weighted with lead or copper wire so they will sink quickly to the bottom where the trout lie. But it is illegal to add weight to larger flies, so a definition was required: what constitutes a nymph? The management authorities resolved the problem by declaring in the regulations that only those flies tied on a hook smaller than what is commonly called a size 10 could be weighted. The term nymph does not apply in the regulations; it is determined by the dimensions. To be weighted, the hook must be smaller than 17 mm in total length, and no more than 5.5 mm across the gap between the point and the underside of the shank.

The next development created a furore that continues. The more old-fashioned anglers throw their hands up in horror when the subject of Globugs is brought up. "It isn't fly fishing," they maintain.

It is also true that there is a certain amount of snobbery attached to the art of fly fishing, particularly dry-fly fishing, but that should not affect the rule-makers. It is difficult to legislate to make anglers behave according to a certain code of ethics, and the opponents of Globugs accuse the proponents of adopting a total lack of ethics.

A Globug is commonly described as an imitation of trout ova, also called roe or eggs. The lure originated in the United States where it is effectively used in various forms to catch trout and salmon. The propensity for trout to eat their own eggs is well known to poachers, who may drift a dollop of real trout eggs down the river attached to a hook.

There are many variations of the flies which may be called Globugs, or muppets, which have metal bead eyes attached. But when drifted down the current in conjunction with the upstream nymphing technique, these flies can be deadly on trout which are making their way upstream to perform the annual spawning ritual. Every winter hundreds of fly fishermen will cast Globugs in the Tongariro and other streams, hoping to hook a fresh-run rainbow trout.

The definition of a Globug raises more questions. The old fashioned Red Setter pattern of wet fly or lure has been probably the single most popular pattern on the Tongariro for the past 40 years. But

Bullies swim slowly in short bursts, stopping to hang motionless. Flies which simulate these popular forage fish should be fished with in short jerks.

when sparsely dressed, with two bright orange blobs of chenille for the body, this pattern could be likened to a double Globug.

The controversy continues to rage, but the authorities distance themselves from the ethical arguments. They do not like having rules which are hard to enforce, and prefer to restrict the harvest by regulating methods, seasons or limit bags. The general acceptance of Globugs in the Tongariro fishery is clearly indicated by the incidence each winter of trout recorded through the trap on the Whitikau Stream — the main spawning tributary in the Tongariro system. More than half of the 100 or so trout which have flies stuck in their mouths after encounters with anglers are carrying a variation of the Globug pattern.

Then there is the form of Globugging practised on the lakes. At least the upstream nymphers have to cast their Globugs, and actually fish them down the current like any other fly. But on the lakes, some anglers just sit and wait for a fish to come along and eat their Globug. This really upsets some anglers, who claim it is more like snapper fishing than trout fishing. But the reply may be that it is more sporting than dredging trout up from the depths with 100 m or more of wire or lead-core line, which is legal and is popular in mid-summer.

In lake fishing, a different form of Globug is used. It is usually larger than the version for the rivers, and has a small polystyrene ball tied into the body to make the fly float. This is then cast out at a river mouth, or off a drop-off, with a short leader attached to a fast-sinking line or shooting head. The line sinks to the bottom, and the fly floats up about 25 cm and moves gently in any current — or just sits there. Eventually a trout comes along and, for some reason known only to the trout, swallows it. Sometimes this form of angling can be extremely effective, and the swallowing aspect creates another dilemma. If the angler wants to release the fish, which is often the case, it may be hooked deep in the throat or near the gills inside the mouth. Trout eating such flies are usually hooked deeply, and can be fatally injured by removal of the hook. It is better to cut off the fly and let the trout take its chances with it still attached. Hooks rarely remain embedded for long in any fish after it has escaped or is released.

This Globugging in the lakes is now popular in the Rotorua lakes, and is also common in deepwater fly-fishing spots like the Tokaanua hole and the mouths of the Tongariro and Tauranga-Taupo Rivers.

The managers in Rotorua and Taupo do not see themselves as arbiters of fishing ethics. They want anglers to catch fish. Only if a particular method becomes too deadly and the populations are threatened, or it is abused, will they consider banning it.

Why a big, healthy, well-fed rainbow trout will eat something that looks like a large, fluffy pink and white marshmallow, is a mystery. But they do. They also eat clumps of weed, perhaps to capture small organisms living among the growth; and objects like sticks, pieces of pumice, leaves, cigarette butts and stones are often found inside the stomachs of trout.

Which raises the obvious question — if they are so unconcerned about their diet, why are trout so darned difficult to catch?

Fly fishing tackle

We often hear the question: "I want to get a good, all-round rod that I can use on small streams with a dry fly, and also fish the big South Island rivers. What is best?"

When using one rod for all rivers and streams there is an element of compromise involved; but a 2.76 m (9 ft), 7-weight graphite rod would be the most suitable to cover the greatest number of situations. For delicate dry-fly fishing on small streams a 5-weight rod, 2.6 m (8ft 6in) long is ideal. The shorter rod is easier to handle in a confined area and most streams have healthy borders of shrubs, long grass or trees. A shorter rod is less tiring when casting all day, and the average cast on a stream is no more than 6 or 7 m.

We also have a lot of wind, particularly among the mountains where much of the finest water is found. A longer rod will give more control in windy conditions, is an advantage when long casts are called for, and also gives greater control of line on the water.

Rods are available in all combinations. You can get a 2.76 m (9 ft) rod for a 5-weight line, but generally the longest rods take the heaviest lines. Graphite fly rods will handle two line weights and are usually rated accordingly. For distance work, the heavier line should be used as this will load the rod better, making casting easier. If delicate casting is needed, go for the lighter line. It is not necessary to get too technical.

The ideal combination for fly fishing in New Zealand is two outfits — a 2.6 m rod for a 5-weight line, and a 2.76 m rod for an 8 or 9-weight line. Which lines you select are a matter of personal preference. Double-taper lines give a more controlled delivery and are better suited to the light rod, while forward-taper lines are designed for distance casting. If fishing big lakes is going to feature in your itinerary, then a weight-forward line will go on the bigger rod.

The serious fly fisherman will accumulate a collection of rods, reels and lines. A lightweight, double-taper floater is fine for close work, but a heavier weight-forward floater is needed for those long casts on the Mataura or Tongariro, or Lake Otamangakau on a windy day. My favourite Lake Tarawera rod has a weight-forward fast-sinking line on it, with a Deepwater Express shooting head on a spare spool.

We could go on and on discussing tackle, but if you are reading this in bed you will probably fall asleep shortly, or if the sun is shining outside you are no doubt just about ready to hop in the car and go fishing. If you are sitting in an aeroplane, keep reading.

We have touched on the subject of leaders, and there is not much else to say about these. The main thing is to use a tapered leader where presentation is important. I have seen graphs listing the length and diameter of each section of a hand-made tapered leader, but it seems an awful lot of knot tying, and every knot you tie is a potential weak point. Tapered leaders of excellent quality are available in tackle shops. The monofilament used varies a bit, but if in doubt use one which is stiff in the middle section. Forget about the end bit: you break that off and tie on a tippet. If you need an extra-long leader, say 6 m, for a fish in super-clear, shallow water, you may have to add two tippets of reducing weight.

Most dry fly and nymph leaders will be about 4 m long. Shorter leaders can be used for small streams. When fishing streamer flies in a deep lake a tapered leader is fine, but not necessary. I like a piece of mono of 3 to 4 kg, roughly the length of the rod. This is not because the trout require that length, but it's easier to put the fly away in the end of the cork or the keeper without having to pull the join through the tip ring.

Your leader will be tied to a loop at the end of the fly line which has been put there by your friendly tackle dealer. Or, you can attach a short piece of heavy mono leader material with a nail knot, and then either tie on each new leader or put a loop in the end of the butt section. This makes it easy to change leaders which can be tied to the loop, or a loop on the end of your leader makes it easy to slip one loop through the other.

Fly patterns

There are as many fly patterns as there are things for trout to eat. The best advice is to ignore most of them or you will go crazy worrying about missing out on something. As mentioned earlier, many nymphs are representative of a range of insects and it is not necessary to try and match each individual larva exactly. I doubt whether a feeding trout counts the number of tail filaments or gills on a nymph before deciding to swallow it. Provided your artificial roughly matches the size and colour of what the trout are taking, it will work for you. Even if it doesn't match, it may still work. Of equal importance is the way your fly is presented.

Nymphs which will prove useful in sizes 10-16 are Hare and Copper, Gold-Ribbed Hare's Ear, Pheasant Tail, Possum Fur nymph, Green Stonefly, Damselfly, Midge Pupa (in small sizes), Speckled Brown or Nelson Brown; Black and Peacock, caddis imitations in brown, green, grey and cream; Latex Caddis, Halfback, Black Creeper, Black Stonefly; and (for spawning trout) Globug variations. Some should be weighted and some unweighted.

Popular dry flypatterns include Blue Dun, Sulphur Dun, Twilight Beauty, Kakahi Queen, Black Gnat, Green Beetle, Dad's Favourite, Pye's Sedge, Greenwell's Glory, Red-Tipped Governor, Adams, Royal Wulff, Henryville Special, Elkhair Caddis, Humpy, Muddler Minnow, Joe's Hopper and other cicada and grasshopper imitations.

On Taupo tributaries flies used are the same as those used on the lake, with the rule of 'dark conditions, dark fly' also relevant. In bright conditions a smelt fly like a Parsons' Glory or Grey Ghost may be used, but generally the bully imitations like a Mrs Simpson work better. The Red Setter is the most popular pattern on the Taupo rivers, but others like rabbits in green or orange, and Fuzzy Wuzzy are worth trying.

Popular patterns for lake fishing include Red Setter, Kilwell, Mrs Simpson, Marabou in various colours, Leech, Rabbit in different colours, Silicon Smelt, Parsons' Glory, Dorothy, Green Orbit, GT Smelt, and Visa Smelt.

A Kilwell or Mrs Simpson is a good bully imitation, and should be tied so it tapers smoothly. Many commercial patterns are over-dressed.

Above right: The Red Setter is a favourite for lake and river, and is one of the most enduring and successful trout fly patterns. The hackles should flow back at an angle, with longer hackles at the head.

For night fishing, try a Black Phantom, Lumo, Scotch Poacher, Craig's Night Time, or Marabou.

Catching a trophy trout

Visit a taxidermist and you will be surprised at the number of huge trout he has in his freezers, waiting to be mounted. They come from all over the country: short, deep rainbows from the lakes and great long browns with protruding jaws. Trophy trout — that is fish over 10 pounds or 4.5 kg — can be targeted, and there are many places where they are found.

The lower reaches of the Tongariro River hold a large population of brown trout, many of them close to the magic mark. These fish can be caught at night, slowly fishing black flies on the bottom at one of the river's mouths where it plunges over the shelf and into the lake. When the cicadas are hatching on a hot summer day, large browns can be stalked along the river bank and will respond to a carefully presented cicada imitation which is twitched as it drifts lazily with the slow current. Big sea-run browns are caught regularly in the Selwyn and other streams entering Lake Ellesmere, particularly when live bullies are used.

Some rivers like the Hollyford in south Westland and the Taieri host good populations of sea-run fish; and many huge brown trout are taken from the Waikato River every year.

Brown trout are less discerning in their dining habits than rainbows, and will also tolerate more uncomfortable water conditions. A newspaper once reported a Hamilton fisherman catching two giant brown trout on a large toby while fishing below the effluent outfall of the dairy factory at Te Rapa. One fish weighed 10 kg gutted.

The fishing methods used can increase the chances of catching big trout, which are more likely to be found in the deep, slow water in rivers. The use of bait, where permitted, will also increase the odds.

Big trout are cannibalistic, and a lure which simulates a small trout will often do the trick. A large fly or spoon, or even a wobbling type of plug like a small Rapala with most of the hooks removed, may also provoke a strike. But the fisherman has to figure out how to get his lure down to the fish. Weight can be added to the line, although restrictions on the amount which may be used usually apply. The cast can be made well

This old brown trout resting out of the current in the headwaters of the Rangitikei River is nearing the end of its life. The fish is carrying a yellow spaghetti tag placed there by scientists to monitor its movements.

upstream, allowing the lure to sink and drift down to where the trout are lying.

There are four types of water which regularly hold very large trout and offer the best opportunities for catching a trophy. These are the headwaters of remote wilderness rivers where access is difficult; below the spillways on hydro dams; on lakes Okataina, Rotoiti and Tarawera where the Rotorua big fish programme works so well; and in man-made lakes like Aniwhenua and Otamangakau.

Professional trout guides encounter more big trout than most fishermen simply because they spend more time fishing the headwaters of wilderness rivers with clients prepared to pay for the privilege. A helicopter puts such water within easy reach, but the cost is prohibitive for most New Zealand anglers. The visitors who catch these monsters invariably return them to the water, for such fisheries cannot withstand much pressure. The guides would not take them if they wanted to kill fish. Such waters are always a closely guarded secret. Dick Fraser, who operates his own helicopter out of his Cedar Lodge at Makaroroa, tells of huge brown trout weighing 6 kg and 7.3 kg taken by clients "somewhere in the mountains".

Hanmer Springs guide John Gemmell has one river which he rarely visits, keeping it for special clients. One such client is Graham Mead, an Englishman who fell in love with New Zealand, bought a house near Nelson, and spends several months fishing here every year. Graham loves catching huge brown trout and John takes him to his special river every summer. All he will say is that it is "not near Hanmer Springs". But he does concede that it is somewhere in the South Island. They do not always fish the same water, often taking a helicopter and searching for new places.

John also tells of a high country tarn which holds some giant browns which are impossible to catch. A dead trout found there by a helicopter pilot and taken home to be mounted weighed close to 14 kg. A couple of fishermen once took a small boat in and trolled for two days, catching only one small trout. John and Graham have sat for hours watching for cruising trout and not seen a fin. "I don't know what they feed on, but they can't go anywhere and they can't spawn. They just get bigger," said John. Perhaps the plagues of mice which occur in the back country every few years, sparked by a surplus of beech seeds, provide good nourishment for the brown trout.

Some Nelson and Westland rivers have similar populations of big brown trout in their headwaters; and in the North Island the prime rivers are the Rangitikei, Ngaruroro and Ruakituri. All these rivers have good fishing in the lower reaches and unimpeded access to the sea. There are no hydro dams to prevent mature whitebait and smelt from reaching the headwaters, where they undoubtedly are welcomed by the trout. Terrestrials like wetas and cicadas add to the diet, but the food base is the rich aquatic insect life — nymphs and larvae of mayflies, stoneflies, caddis and others. Mature trout migrate upriver to the headwater, and it is unusual to find small trout in the upper pools.

The catchments of such rivers are undeveloped wilderness. There is no influence from topdressing, logging or other human activities. The trout are not exposed to raging floods, and when the rivers do flood there is ample shelter in the deep pools with steep rock ledges.

Such fisheries are fragile and illustrate the importance of protecting them, both in terms of introducing 'no-kill' policies and ensuring the catchments remain unspoiled. Fortunately, most of these rivers are in national parks or reserves and their future is assured.

Big trout are never easily caught. In the South Island rivers they must be spotted, and there may be only one fish per kilometre of river. Such fishing is challenging. The runs and pools are often shallow, and much care and skill are needed to have any chance of hooking the wary fish. The cast must be precise. Occasionally the trout will rise to a dry fly, but a carefully placed nymph offers the best chance. The extremely light terminal tackle which must be used stacks the odds in favour of the fish. But the rewards are great.

The North Island wilderness fisheries contain mainly rainbow trout. These are impressive fish: heavily spotted, with green backs and flanks flushed with lilac. In the clear pools of the Ngaruroro at Golden Hills the trout can be clearly seen. Those that are seen are the hardest to catch, for they are easily spooked. They will rise to a well-presented Royal Wulff, but a weighted Black Stonefly or Hare and Copper nymph drifted down a fast run and into the head of a pool will produce more strikes. The bigger water on the Rangitikei is legendary for its huge rainbows. They will take a swimming mayfly nymph stripped across a pool in short jerks, or a heavily weighted black nymph tumbled down with the white water entering a deep pool. A sink-tip line works well here, taking your nymph into the dark depths of the long pools; and occasionally an Olive Matuka or Rabbit pattern will do the trick.

The Ruakituri, above the Waitangi Falls, runs through some real tiger country. Just getting down to the water where it runs through steep gorges and the dense Urewera bush is a test. But a weighted black nymph or spoon will hook fish there. Landing them is another question, but I once saw a 6.4 kg rainbow which had been caught on a spinning outfit.

Ernest Schwiebert travelled from New York to fish the clear headwaters of the Rangitikei River deep in the Kaimanawa Ranges. He took this rainbow on a swimming mayfly nymph imitation.

Left: Some of our finest trout fishing is found in rivers where the catchment remains untouched by the influence of man.

The Ruakituri River offers fine fly fishing where it flows out of the native bush on the edge of the Urewera National Park.

The rainbows and browns which lurk in the tailrace below the spillway on some of the hydro dams around the country live in the perfect trout world. They have fast, deep water which provides sanctuary; and all they have to do is lie with their mouths open when the turbines are running and all manner of food is washed to them. They are literally force-fed. Not only is food washed through the turbines, but the bullies and smelt which also thrive in the rich water are caught up in the powerful torrents which roar down the spillway, and are easy prey. With little energy required to obtain their food these trout grow fat fast. But being so well fed, they are hard to tempt. The nature of the water adds further complications. Because the trout are more active when the turbines are running, that is the time to fish. But the currents make it hard getting a lure down in deep water. A spinning rod with as much weight as is permitted is one option, or a super-express shooting-head line will also sink quickly. Lures should resemble the baitfish: big Rabbit patterns in a size 2 or 4, Mrs Simpson, Parsons' Glory, or Matuka Muddler can be used. Or, it may be a Tokoroa Chicken, that bunch of feathers tied to a lead head, which is fished on a spinning outfit. Night fishing can also be productive in this situation.

Whether fishing at Benmore, Arapuni or the small power station at Tuai near Waikaremoana, the big trout are there. All you have to do is catch them.

One of the success stories of fisheries management in New Zealand is the selective breeding programme developed by Dr Peter Mylchreest at Rotorua, to save the big rainbows in Lake Tarawera. We have discussed how to catch such fish when considering fly fishing in Lakes Tarawera, Okataina and Rotoiti — and big fish are more likely to be caught by fly fishing than trolling. But the story of one man's crusade to not only save the unique strain of big trout that existed in Tarawera but to develop a breeding programme that has brought back the large trout in other lakes is a fascinating one.

Peter is a fisheries scientist who has worked on fisheries research in British Columbia, and is also a qualified medical doctor. His first love is working with trout, and for 20 years he worked for the Wildlife Service of the Department of Internal Affairs. Through Government 'rationalisation', this became part of the Department of Conservation, and has finally evolved into the Eastern Region Fish and Game Council. The politics are not relevant in this context, but the contribution made by Peter Mylchreest to fisheries management in this country is immense. He has since returned to British Columbia, leaving as his legacy the huge rainbows of the Rotorua lakes.

The concept of selectively breeding big trout was first raised in the mid-1970s when the decline in the quality and numbers of big trout in Tarawera was causing real concern. The Outlet had always been famous for its large trout, but fishing pressure was limited by lack of access. A boat trip across the lake was the only access. The decline in the fishery closely followed the opening of a forestry road from Kawerau to the Outlet.

Trout growth slows dramatically once they spawn for the first time, as the act of spawning takes so much out of them. Some Tarawera rainbows would spawn at two years old, others at three years and occasionally four years of age. These four-year-old maiden fish were the real trophies. The extra time spent maturing in the lake caused them to grow up to 7 kg. These were the trout Tarawera was renowned for, but there might be only one that size in a thousand fish. The Outlet fish were like a separate family within the lake.

Studies in Canada had indicated that a lake outlet spawning situation favoured big fish. The spawning facilities were restricted and big fish chased smaller ones away. Perhaps nature compensated by causing the trout to mature later than other fish, allowing them to reach large proportions so they could effectively dominate the spawning beds.

A parallel was found at Kootenay Lake in British Columbia where a famous strain of huge rainbow trout occurred at a place called Gerrard. It was only a small family of a few hundred trout, but they spawned at six or seven years of age, and grew up to 13.5 kg.

"What we were interested in was whether this age of maturity was inherited and, if it was, could we control it genetically. In other words, could we breed for it?" explained Peter.

The existence of the Gerrard trout suggested that genetics was an important factor. "The first step was to see how heritable the age of maturity was. We set up the fish trap at the Te Wairoa Stream and took ova and milt from two-year-old mature fish, three-year-old fish and four-year-old fish when we could get them."

This trout has been hooked before. The corner of its jaw is malformed where an old wound has healed.

If you catch a trophy trout, that perfect specimen that you want to have mounted to display on the wall, it is important that you handle it correctly. The taxidermist can only work with what he is given, and the biggest problems occur when the colour of the fish is 'setting', immediately after it is killed with a sharp rap on the head above the eyes. If possible, take a close-up colour photograph of your fish and then keep the fish out of the sun. Select its best side, which will be the show side. This side will have the least damage, such as scars or missing scales.

> It is a common fallacy that the fish should be protected by wrapping in cheesecloth or something similar. This is a mistake, as it will cause staining of the colours where the cloth touches the scales. Air circulating over the fish helps the colours to set naturally. If you can not get it to a taxidermist quickly, place it on a board with the show side up and freeze it, ensuring nothing touches the fish or fins. When completely frozen, the trout can be placed in a plastic bag, but take care with the fins as they are fragile and are easily damaged. Make sure nothing is thrown on top of your fish while it is in the freezer.

That was in 1984. The first four-year-old trout was a large jack which had been caught by a Tarawera identity, Con Campbell, and named Connebar in deference to his Scottish ancestry. The eggs were hatched and the young trout raised separately at the Ngongotaha Hatchery. They were tagged with two different codes — X tags for the progeny of the smaller parents, and R tag for the others. This R tag was to become the label for the strain of big trout which was discovered and nurtured.

The breeding trials proved that not only was the age of maturity inherited, but the older Tarawera trout also displayed another important characteristic. They grew quickly. "So we had two characteristics for producing big fish: fast immature growth combined with delayed maturity. We got quite excited, because normally in nature you have the opposite combination; fast immature growth is linked to early maturity," said Peter Mylchreest.

Some of the regular Tarawera fly fishermen appreciated the quality of these fish, and donated large specimens they had caught to the breeding programme. "To a large extent, the use of angler-caught trout stemmed from the initiative of the anglers," said Peter, and this became a vital factor in the success of the project.

It was different from other selective breeding schemes, such as those for domestic animals, in that it was based on wild stock that had done particularly well in the wild, and the progeny were returned to the wild. There was no attempt to domesticate the fish. Similar programmes overseas have failed because they were based on hatchery stock, and eventually the wild characteristics are bred out of the fish. Even in the Rotorua programme the first year of life in the wild, when most of the natural selection takes place and most of the mortality occurs, is being bypassed.

The Tarawera trout have developed other tendencies which make them different from trout in other lakes. The baby trout hatched in the few spawning streams migrate to the lake while still very young. In a Taupo tributary the juveniles might take a year to reach the lake, and are a reasonable size when they enter the competitive world which exists there.

There is intense competition among baby Tarawera trout hatched in the streams, and with limited nursery habitat available they are launched into the big wide world of the lake at an early stage. Here they feed on postlarval bullies and smelt, and grow quickly.

This strain of rainbow trout displays two tendencies which give the young fish a better chance of surviving: they spawn early in the season, and they grow fast. The eggs deposited by a hen fish in June will hatch in early spring, maybe in August, and the first fry will enter the lake in November, with others making the transition through the summer.

According to Peter Mylchreest, the unique Tarawera strain of big fish was nearly lost forever. "We started the programme in 1984, and by 1987 the four-year-old maturing fish had disappeared. We had got our hands on the last of the wild fish."

It would be a mistake to breed from just a few parent fish. Sufficient eggs could be obtained, but the genetic spread would be too limited. The first trials started with very few mature parents, but the programme is now based on at least 40 pairs of wild fish contributing every season. These fish are trapped, stripped, then released straight back into the stream, at various stages throughout the spawning runs. This ensures that their progeny will return in a series of groups over an extended period, giving anglers more access to the big trout. Because the fingerlings return as adults two and a half years after release, the liberations are carefully planned. "We try to make sure the progeny of all the parent fish we have used are well mixed in each liberation, particularly into Tarawera, to maximise the genetic base," explained Peter.

The fingerlings are liberated at points where the anglers will have ready access to the big fish when they return to the same point. So they are put into Rotoiti at various popular fishing spots like Ruato and Hinehopu. On Okataina the fish are released at the main beach where the road ends; and at Tarawera they go in at The Landing and at Rangiuru Bay. A total of 100,000 trout are raised each year to stock water in the district. Tarawera and Rotoiti receive 12,500 fingerlings each, and Okataina 3,000.

Peter stressed that the breeding programme was not designed solely to provide big trout for fishermen to catch, but more importantly to rebuild wild stocks. "The main priority is to get the fish breeding back in the wild. We are trying to create a wild gene bank. The long-term ecological sustainability of the programme depends on it. If you keep breeding hatchery fish you will certainly reduce the fitness of those fish to compete in the wild." This included closing the Tarawera Outlet to fishing a month earlier than the rest of the lake, to protect the spawning fish.

A vital part of the formula is the lack of natural spawning facilities on the three lakes. Another is the ability of the lakes to grow trout. The balance between trout population and available food is a fine one. That balance can be influenced by the numbers of trout that are liberated and by controlling the harvest by anglers. But it all depends on maintaining the health of the lakes.

The decline in the Tarawera fishery was causing great concern when, in 1985, the first winter algal blooms appeared. "Two years later we discovered that when you replace native forest with pine forest, you reduce the amount of nitrate going into the lake by as much as five-sixths," said Peter. When this effect was combined with the development of pasture in the lake's catchment, which contributed to high levels of phosphorus, the lake was being pushed towards what scientists call a 'nitrogen-limited state'. The lake is starved of nitrogen, which upsets the whole mineral balance and affects the food chain. Rotoiti also causes concern, for while it is producing good trout growth, this could be a sign that it is becoming too enriched. Nutrients are essential for production of plankton which smelt and bullies require, but there is a fine line between an adequate nutrient base and over-enrichment. One of the indicators of nutrient-rich water is the appearance of algal blooms and accelerated weed growth. Okataina is the only lake which still has a native forest catchment, producing nitrogen and little phosphorus. It has a different mineral balance. "That is the natural state. If you think about it, the trout are at the apex of the food triangle. If your food triangle is healthy and the lake's ecosystem is functioning, the trout are just a biological indicator of that. There are other factors, like trout densities, which also affect the performance of a lake," said Peter.

Meanwhile, as a result of Peter Mychreest's dedication and persistence, Rotorua fishermen now catch hundreds of 10-pound-plus (4.5 kg) rainbow trout every year.

It is the richness of lakes created by hydro electricity development that sparks the fast growth in trout put into these new lakes. When a dam is built or a lake created, like Dunstan, Aniwhenua and Otamangakau, a tremendous pool of food becomes available to trout on the newly flooded ground. Worms and insects provide a rich banquet, and the nutrient-rich water delivered by rivers running into the lakes bolsters the production of food for the trout. The result is large numbers of big trout available to anglers within a few years, but the continued inflow of nutrients usually turns such lakes eutrophic — that is, they become too enriched, weed flourishes and eventually they 'go over the top'. Trout growth falls away and the fishing deteriorates. The pattern is for such new lakes to peak in terms of trout production after five to seven years. Whether this level is maintained depends on the individual lake. Some lakes continue to sustain a healthy fishery — like Otamangakau where cold temperatures and windy conditions keep the lake mixed and cool, even in summer. Another producer of large numbers of big trout, Aniwhenua, has become an average fishery in recent years; but it may well boom again.

Bait fishing

Some childhood incidents remain frozen in the memory, like one piece of a jigsaw puzzle. A dead smelt washed up on a lakeside beach always reminds me of a youngster standing dangerously close to the edge of the fan of sand which extended a few metres into the lake at the mouth of a small stream. The lake fell away sharply into the dark, weed-lined depths where huge eels and other fantasy monsters lived. It took a lot of courage to stand so close to the edge of the delta, with the sand starting to slip and slide under the toes. But this boy was holding a stick about a metre long — it was a length of brown, dried fern stalk — and it had a piece of mono line tied on the end. At the business end of this short line was a small hook (this was past the bent-pin stage) on which was impaled a very dead but quite large smelt. Suddenly there was a swirl and a fierce tug on the line, which of course snapped. The rainbow trout which hung around this particular stream rip were large, and the odds had been very much with the trout from the outset. There was also the small matter of the fly-only designation of the bay, and the complete ban on any form of fish bait in the Rotorua district. But if the boy who hasn't tested the fine print of the rules at some stage of his fishing career has been invented, I should like to shake his hand.

A similar event occurred to the same boy while standing at the head of a small pool among ponga trees and ferns in the Hunua hills near

Dawn is a favourite time for anglers on lakes like Tarawera.

Auckland. This time it was a worm on the hook, it was legal, and that trout also popped the line with disdain.

There is no doubt that rainbow and brown trout will eat smelt. They do it all the time in many lakes, and sometimes they will even swallow one which is dead and is hanging suspended in a totally unnatural position in the middle of a stream mouth. Trout will actually eat a lot of different things in streams and lakes, which some people may find hard to believe after spending many fruitless hours trying to catch them. I have heard of trout eating a piece of chicken skin impaled on a hook and fed down the current at a stream mouth on a well-known lake, and even taking a bait sliced from the gut of an eel in a deep pool on a mountain river. Considering that eels spend part of their time chasing trout, there is an element of poetic justice involved there.

Fishing for trout with live or dead bait is popular in some parts of the country. But before we look at how to fish with bait, a word of caution should be introduced. Be sure to check regulations applying in the area you intend to fish. In many of our major trout fisheries the use of bait is illegal.

Some frustrated fishermen may be tempted to stick a huhu grub or a worm on a hook and toss it into a pool deep in the bush, but it is not that simple. There is quite an art to successfully fishing baits, and clear-water worm fishing is technically very demanding. The key is to present the bait like a natural worm which has fallen into the water and is being carried along with the current, and to present live bait in a manner which will attract trout. I have not done much bait fishing for trout since those boyhood days, but David Dannafaerd of Sutherland's Sportsworld in New Plymouth is very experienced, and Taranaki is a region where it is popular. Bait fishing is a great way for novices or children to get started in trout fishing, and they often progress to other methods.

It is used on streams and rivers more than lakes, and a variety of tackle can be employed. A fly rod with a 6 or 7-weight line, either floating or slow sinking, can be used with a trace of about 3 m of 2 to 3 kg mono. The technique is similar to nymphing, and line control during the drift is critical. A more delicate outfit is a light spinning rod with 2 kg mono, which will present a bait with less drag from the line. A little weight is needed to get the bait down in the current, but use no more than necessary. One or two small split shot can be attached to the line about 25 cm above the hook, which is usually a round-bend or kirbed hook. Popular baits are creeper, worms, cicadas, grasshoppers, green or brown beetles and small fish — bullies, smelt or inanga, alive or dead. Creepers are the larvae of the dobsonfly, and they are fearsome-looking creatures 2 or 3 cm long, black on the back and cream on the belly. Also called toe-biters because of the long, curved jaws on the head, creepers resemble a centipede with rows of legs along each side. Early in the season, in spring, they can be found along the edge of streams in the sand and silt, and later in summer will be found hiding under stones on the stream bed.

The popular method of collecting nymphs and larvae is to hold a fine-mesh net downstream and turn over stones or stir up the bottom with your foot. An assortment of nymphs and other creatures along with debris will be washed into the net. Creepers can be kept for some time in a plastic container with some damp sand, and will even stay alive for several weeks in a deep freeze. They are certainly tough little customers, which makes them attractive as a trout bait.

Smelt and inanga can be caught in whitebait nets in the rivers, but are not as popular as bullies and some bully fishermen catch a lot of trout, particularly at night when bigger fish are taken. Bullies are also best caught at night, as they are mesmerised by the beam of a torch and can be scooped up in a small net. One trick is to position the net behind the bully, then tap it on the nose with a small stick. If all goes according to plan, the bully will turn and swim into the net. Bullies can also be caught with a drag net of about 2 m of fine mesh with floats along the top and weights along the bottom. It is simply cast out over a weed bed, and dragged in again. The plastic baitfish traps commonly seen on wharves in the hands of youngsters catching sprats can also be used to collect a supply of bullies.

These baitfish can all be fished alive or dead, with a small hook poked through the lips from underneath, but are more effective when presented alive.

When fishing still water such as lakes and ponds, worms are a popular bait, hooked through the saddle, the toughest section of skin, and allowed to wriggle freely. A float is used to keep the bait suspended in the water, and may be a plastic bubble partly filled with water or a slim quill float as used for coarse fishing.

Worms are used effectively on rivers in Southland and Otago, and produce well when the water is discoloured. A bunch of worms drifted down the edge of the main current under a bubble float has accounted for many trout.

Large insects like cicadas and crickets are hooked through the thorax, while smaller beetles are sometimes attached to the hook with Super Glue. The glue is spread along the top of the shank, and the beetle sits on top of it. Favoured hook sizes are 8 for bullies, cicadas and crickets; 10 for creepers, worms, inanga and smelt; 12 for small creepers and grasshoppers; and 14 for small beetles.

Like a nymph, the bait is usually cast upstream at an angle of about 45 degrees, and should be bounced along the bottom through a likely-looking pool or lie. The bait should drift with the current, with as little resistance from the line as possible, but the angler must keep in touch with the line. A fly line will provide flotation, but a spinning outfit with mono line often requires a float to keep the bait at the required depth. However, if possible you should fish the bully with no weight of float on the line. When the bait has drifted past the angler, it is retrieved and cast again. Less experienced anglers can fish downstream, but this is not as effective except in deep pools with little current.

Bully fishing is popular and productive in many parts of the South Island. Brown trout are more common in these areas, particularly in Canterbury and Westland, both of which have strong sea-run brown trout fisheries.

This type of fishing is well suited to the slow-moving coastal streams running into Lake Ellesmere, which has a good population of brown trout. These streams have long stretches of deep, murky channels with undercut banks and thick fringes of willows, making other fishing methods difficult. But it is ideal water to drift a live bully in the early morning and evening, and well into the night.

Some fishermen like to use the traditional style of split-cane rods and fly lines for fishing bullies. But spinning outfits are far more popular, and as some sea-run browns may exceed 4.5 kg, the line used will be around 4 kg. Split shot can be added for weight if the current is strong, and a float added if it is needed to keep the bait out of weed.

The bullies are lip-hooked, with the hook penetrating through from under the lower jaw and out behind the top lip. Another method is to insert the hook point in the bully's mouth and out through the lower lip only. When fishing in lakes where there is no current, the bully can also be hooked through the back, under the dorsal fin.

"Cast up into that little channel, and pull it back slowly," said the old man. The boy cast awkwardly, and the line flopped into the brown water. He waited anxiously, then pulled a short length of line into the boat, dropping it on the overlapping wooden strakes of the old clinker dinghy. The line jerked and the boy hauled on the rod as a trout splashed and flopped among the weed.

"Easy, boy, easy," said the old man as he coaxed the boy gently. When the gleaming trout lay beside the boat, he deftly slipped the net under the prize and held it high in front of the boy. A grin split the young face as he grasped the net and fumbled to grab the trout.

The old man dipped the oars silently as he rowed the old, brown boat along the channel among the weeds, searching for another clear spot to cast to.

The boy admired his trout. Its head and back were a dull green colour marked with just a few black spots. A deep red washed the flanks, fading from the bright gill plates back towards the powerful tail. It was a solid fish, deep of body and thick through the shoulders; and when it was later split open and gutted the flesh would be bright pink and firm. It looked unlike any trout from nearby Lake Tarawera or Lake Taupo. For the fish which inhabit Lake Rotomahana are descended directly from the original strain of rainbows brought from California more than 100 years earlier. While the stocks in other waters have been mixed with trout from different lakes, the Rotomahana trout have remained pure — undiluted by the characteristics of trout from different environments.

The old man was my great-uncle, known simply as JF, and a great outdoorsman. A trip out fishing with JF was the highlight of a summer holiday at Tarawera. These trips usually involved trolling red and copper penny spoons along the edge of the weed beds between Ngongotaha and Kawaha Point, close to his home on the edge of Lake Rotorua. But occasionally JF would pick me up and take me out to his favourite fishing hole on Lake Rotomahana. In those days it was an expedition just reaching the lake, driving south from Rotorua before turning off towards Murupara, then cutting back around Lake Rerewhakaaitu towards the looming grey bulk of Mt Tarawera. His old clinker boat was kept moored among the rushes, and it was a short row around to the arm which narrowed to where the only small stream flowed into the lake.

Rotomahana can be a fascinating place, and it can be intimidating. It is a wildlife refuge, so the birdlife is extensive and varied; and as the site of the famous pink and white terraces it is rich in history. In fact the whole lake blew out during the fearsome eruption of nearby Mt Tarawera in 1886, and was three times larger after the volcanic upheaval which devastated the area. But like adjacent Tarawera, the lake received a massive injection of minerals and nutrients, creating the basis for a rich environment for trout in later years.

Even today, the Rotomahana rainbows do not endure much angling pressure. Trolling, casting lures and fly fishing are the favoured methods; but when I first fished there with JF about 35 years ago it was almost a virgin fishery. A few keen anglers including JF's dearest fishing mate, an old Maori gentleman,

Trout flies of yesteryear — a large Tamati on top; a Turkey and Red middle left; the original Matuka made from feathers of the bittern which are now banned; Ewe Wasp lower left; and the Lord's Killer, forerunner of the popular Kilwell and Mrs Simpson killer patterns.

would take the small boats out from Rotorua and leave them safely untended at the lake edge. Vandalism, thievery and bi-culturalism were unheard-of words or concepts in those days.

JF's favourite fly is also unheard of today. It was called a Tamati, which he used in a small size 8. The body was a blend of yellow, red and black wool, and the wing comprised short lengths of dark brown feather from the wing of a turkey, split along the centre. Another favourite was the Lord's Killer, also fashioned from brown feathers. Like many of the old patterns they have slipped into obscurity, replaced by flies with modern names made from synthetic materials.

JF and his mate, Darkie Hall, would take turns rowing and casting; casting into the small channels among the thick beds of weed which lined the arm of the lake where they always ventured. The trout grabbed the small brown flies eagerly, and fought strongly.

In later years, when invited to fish there with members of the Rotomahana Fishing Club, we also used spinning rods, casting small zed spoons into the same channels where JF used to catch trout with his split-cane fly rod and Tamati flies. His patterns had been replaced with factory-made patterns like the Mrs Simpson and Kilwell number two. Rerewhakaaitu and Rotomahana are two lakes where the dark Kilwell pattern is still used effectively, and the Hamill's Killer is another deadly pattern on these waters. Perhaps it is the shallow nature of much of these lakes combined with their dull-coloured water which makes dark flies so popular.

CHAPTER FOURTEEN
SALMON FISHING

Salmon fishing in New Zealand has traditionally been restricted to the great braided rivers flowing from the Southern Alps across the Canterbury Plains to the coast. With the development of salmon farming, particularly ocean ranching, their range has steadily expanded as wandering fish colonise new waters and establish new populations. This type of fish farming utilises the natural environment to grow the salmon. It starts with the release of millions of hatchery-raised young fish into a river, in the hope they will return in sufficient numbers as adult salmon to sustain a commercial harvest.

There are now some exciting new sports fisheries, which are sustained by releasing yearlings every season into waters like the harbour at Dunedin.

History

Salmon are native to northern hemisphere oceans and rivers, and the only successful transplanted fishery existing below the equator is the New Zealand quinnat salmon fishery. Several other species were introduced, and all failed except for pockets of Atlantic salmon found in Lake Te Anau. This species failed to establish sea-run populations in spite of extensive trials in the early part of this century, and the residual populations are not considered important sporting fish.

Quinnat is the native Indian name for the largest of the five Pacific salmon of the American Northwest (chinook, pink, sockeye, coho and chum) which is known by several names there — chinook, black mouth (young salmon), spring (up to 14 kg) and king or tyee salmon (over 14 kg). Unsuccessful attempts at introducing quinnat salmon were made as early as 1875 by the Hawkes Bay Acclimatisation Society, but it was not until 1901 that ova from California were successfully hatched at a government hatchery on the Hakataramea River, a tributary of the Waitaki River.

The first successful liberations were made in the Waitaki and fish returned to spawn in 1905. Salmon gradually spread to the Rangitata, Waimakariri and Rakaia Rivers, establishing strong populations. Now they can be found in other rivers like the Clutha, Ashburton, Hurunui and Waiau; and individual fish have been reported turning up as far away as the Hutt River near Wellington, and the Rangitikei River.

Smaller populations have become established on the west coast of the South Island from the Taramakau to the Paringa Rivers, and adults are caught as they pass through lakes in these systems.

Commercial harvest at sea and off river mouths is a hazard threatening salmon populations. Flooding and drainage for irrigation also have an

Salmon fresh from the sea are bright as a newly minted coin, like this prime specimen. Photo courtesy Malcolm Bell.

effect, and the numbers and size of fish returning each year fluctuate considerably.

It appears the migratory salmon may not travel as far offshore as once thought, and Canterbury salmon are believed to feed in the waters off Banks Peninsula.

Life cycle

In their native North American rivers, salmon will travel up to 2,000 kilometres to seek out the few metres of gravel where their lives began. How the migrating salmon identify the water of their natal river after years of roaming the ocean then return unerringly to the stream of their birth, is one of the great mysteries of nature. It may be a response to the earth's magnetic fields, or a highly developed sense of smell which allows salmon to recognise familiar rivers. In New Zealand this journey, which both ends life and begins new life, may involve only 100 kilometres.

Salmon need cold water to survive, preferring temperatures of about 12 degrees Celsius, which may be one reason why they have not adapted to North Island rivers.

They have tremendous stamina and are strong swimmers. Barriers such as low dams and waterfalls cannot stop them from reaching their spawning grounds. The runs may start in November and continue till late

April, but December, January and February are the prime months. The salmon spawn in the headwaters of small tributaries between April and June and, like trout, require beds of gravel washed by cold, clean, well-aerated water.

The eggs are laid in redds, or shallow depressions in the gravel, scooped out by the exhausted females which have existed on body fats and fluids since leaving the sea. The round, orange eggs hatch about three months later. The young fry make their way down to the sea over a year, where they grow in the rich environment, returning as mature three- or four-year-olds to their natal rivers to repeat the cycle. Unlike trout, adult salmon die after spawning, but their bodies continue to nurture the next generation by providing sustenance for tiny organisms as they decompose.

Canterbury salmon fishing

Salmon fishing has been through boom-and-bust cycles in the last decade, but fisheries authorities are optimistic about the future. In the late 1980s many anglers lost interest in the fishing after the fishery virtually collapsed. This was attributed to commercial harvesting of wild salmon at sea as a by-catch, and the proliferation of hatchery releases of smolts as ocean ranching of salmon expanded in the mid 1980s. The summer season of 1991/92 was one of the worst on record; but the exclusion of commercial trawlers from river mouths and the demise of ocean ranching through poor returns saw a dramatic turnaround in less than four years — the lifespan of only one generation of quinnat salmon.

The runs in 1993/94 were back to good numbers, and two years later salmon fever struck as Canterbury rivers recorded some of the best runs ever seen.

Surveys by the North Canterbury Fish and Game Council estimate that anglers harvest between 33% and 37% of the runs in the two main salmon rivers, the Waimakariri and Rakaia. Their research concluded that salmon numbers entering the Waimakariri increased from just under 5,000 adult fish in 1994 to about 12,000 in 1996. The runs in the Rakaia were estimated at 23,000 salmon in 1994, 14,000 in 1995 and just over 26,000 in the summer of 1996. Wild populations will always fluctuate as conditions in the rivers and at sea vary from year to year, but overall the salmon fisheries appear to be in good health.

Fishing the surf

If you enjoy company, then the river mouth is the place to head for. The closer you are to the sea, the more crowded the fishing will be but the salmon will also be in better condition and more likely to take a lure.

This type of fishing has become more popular in recent years, partly through advances in tackle technology which allow anglers to cast further with less effort. Fishing at river mouths is either all on, or all off. There is little in between. One reason is the quickly changing sea conditions. Early morning is one of the best times to fish, because there is usually little

Salmon fishermen gather at dawn to cast into the surf where the Rangitata River flows into the sea. Photo courtesy Malcolm Bell.

wind and it is a traditional feeding time.

Surf fishing also tends to be best when the river is not fishing well. This could be during a flood, when the clear seawater alongside the dirty river water offers good fishing, and the salmon congregate off the mouth while waiting for the flood to recede so they can move upriver. The surf can also fish well when the river is low and clear, and again salmon numbers will build up, waiting for a fresh. But the weather is the biggest factor: if a swell of more than a metre is running, it will probably be too dirty and unfishable.

Salmon can be caught at the actual mouth and in the surf on each side, and also in the gut where the lagoon narrows prior to entering the sea. But if there is a lot of fishing pressure, there will be fewer fish in the gut than off the mouth. The outgoing tide is the most productive tide, and when the salmon are running fishermen will be lined up shoulder to shoulder. The longest caster will catch the most salmon.

The most popular outfit is a 3.6 m surf rod with a free-spool reel mounted at the bottom loaded with 8 to 10 kg line. Spinning reels can be used, but they do reduce casting distance. While a variety of lures are used up the rivers, in the surf the ticer rules supreme, in 55 to 68 g weights. These should be as shiny as possible to make them more visible in the waves, and some anglers add a red tag, or fluorescent tape in green, red or yellow as extra attractants.

The technique of bouncing the lure slowly on the bottom of a river does not work in the surf, where a fast retrieve is more effective. But if there is a strong current running, work the lure through it more slowly. The strike can be difficult to detect because of the length of line involved, and you must react to any hesitation in the lure. If the drag on your reel is locked up, it will not slip on the strike and you will have a better chance of driving the hook home. But do back it off immediately to the fighting position of about one tenth of the line's breaking strain.

When bringing a hooked salmon in to the beach, ease off the drag and apply thumb pressure to the spool. This can be released instantly, an ability which can save a fish which makes a sudden lunge with a receding wave. Keep the rod high, and remember that as your line becomes shorter it has less stretch and is less forgiving. Use the waves to wash the salmon in, but be prepared to let it run out again. You are handling a big, strong fish which will not allow itself to be beached until it is exhausted. Grasp the salmon by the wrist of the tail and push it up the beach a safe distance before relaxing and enjoying your reward.

The most popular river mouths to fish are those of the Rakaia, Hurunui, Rangitata, Opihi, Orari and Waitaki — with the south side of most producing the best fishing.

River fishing

As the salmon prepare to ascend the rivers they cease feeding, and take lures only as an instinctive feeding response or through antagonism. All salmon fishing is based on repetition: your lure must be passed in front of the fish repeatedly. For this reason the presentation of the lure is the most important aspect. The salmon is unlikely to chase the lure, so it must be placed right on its nose. But the first cast in new water is often the best one, so be prepared.

Salmon are easy to find at a river mouth, but once they move upriver they spread out — and finding the salmon is the key to fishing any river. There is a lot of water which is barren, and being able to read the water and find the salmon comes only from experience. As salmon spend longer in the river they lose their vitality and bright silver colouring, and offer less resistance to the pull of the angler's line. For the novice fisherman, a trip with a local expert is the quickest way to learn how to find good salmon water.

The main salmon rivers are often described as braided, i.e. split into many channels as they flow across the plains. In most cases the main channel will be the one to fish, and the easiest spots to find are those where the whole river flows in one stream — such as a gorge — because all salmon must pass that stretch at some time.

Salmon are found in holding water, where they can lie in safety on the bottom where the current is slower, and rest after negotiating fast, shallow sections of the river. Such water will be deep, and will have a gut or channel leading into it.

When looking for likely fishing spots avoid fast water. Look for pools formed where two branches join, or the deep sections of large pools. Another type of holding water, which requires an experienced eye to locate, is the gut formed by a shingle bar running diagonally downstream from one side of the river to the other. The lip along the edge of this bar directs the salmon upstream, concentrating them as the deep water narrows.

The aim is to bounce the lure along the bottom, and if you are not snagging the bottom occasionally, you are not fishing deep enough. It is inevitable that some gear will be lost when fishing for salmon — if you don't hook the bottom you won't hook any salmon either. But like all fishing, the ability to 'feel' the lure working is an integral part of success.

Cast out slightly upstream of a right angle to the bank, hold the rod up to keep loose line above the current, and follow the line around with the rod tip as the lure sinks. Take up slack line until the weight can be felt, then let your spoon bounce across the bottom until it is directly downstream. It is like a subtle knocking sensation, and becomes recognisable with experience. Then wind slowly in case a salmon is following the lure for a short distance, finally speeding up the retrieve to cast again. Cover all of the water thoroughly, varying the angle of the cast to ensure the river bed is well fished. In deep water or fast flows you will need to angle your cast further upstream to give a longer drift.

If you are not reaching the bottom, then try a heavier spoon, or add a weight about a metre above the spoon.

The most productive part of each cast is when your spoon first hits the stony bottom then rattles and flashes its way down the drift and swings across the current. When it has reached your side of the current, it is more a matter of retrieving it to repeat the cast rather than fishing it all the way in. The more time your lure spends in the fish zone, the more fish you will hook.

Salmon take gently. In fact the lure usually just stops, as if it has hung up on a submerged branch, so you have to hook the fish. Hooks become blunted by the continual banging on stones and rocks, and there is always a slight belly of line to be taken up before the energy of your strike reaches the salmon's hard mouth. So the strike must be firm and positive.

Most of your 'strikes' will be rocks or snags, but when there is an answering tug the kilometres walked and the endlessly repetitive casts disappear in a flash. Many salmon are lost immediately as they roll or splash and the hooks fly free. All you can do is ensure your hooks are sharp, touching them up with a stone or replacing them regularly, and keep a tight line on the fish. A fresh-run salmon will use the power of the river's flow and surge downstream, forcing the fisherman to run after it.

Keep your rod high and try and stay opposite the fish, ready to move up or downstream quickly. A long line gives the advantage to the salmon. Use the rod, not the reel, to tire the fish, and direct it to a shallow area where you can beach it — walk around behind the fish and, when it is lying on its side, either flip it ashore with your foot or hold it by the base of the tail and push it.

The best times to fish are the first few hours of daylight and again in the evening; the condition of the river also plays a major role. Water which is clearing after a flood is ideal, and the best conditions are often

> A Fish & Game Council licence is needed to fish for sports fish, which includes trout, salmon and coarse fish. In most salmon areas the season runs from October 1 to April 30 — but check for local regulations as methods, baits and tackle allowed vary considerably between districts; and some waters close earlier to protect spawning fish.

Zed spoons in different colours are the most important lures for salmon in rivers. The heavier ticers are used in bigger water and in the sea. The silver ticer (top) has extra weight at the hook end for casting long distances in the surf.

said to be when the river is milky with your feet just visible when standing knee-deep. In low, clear conditions salmon are hard to hook and the experienced fisherman will use light line and small lures.

Tackle used on the river is lighter than that used at the river mouth, and rods will be 2-3 m long with a medium action. You can use either a free-spool or spinning reel, but the most dedicated fishermen prefer the overhead baitcasters for their smoother drag systems. A minimum of 150 m of 7 to 9 kg line and a selection of spoons completes the outfit. As in the surf, lures are tied directly to the main line; and the 22 g zed spinner is by far the most popular, followed by the Colorado spoon and in deep, fast water a ticer. Silver is the main colour, and some canny salmon fishermen use silver-plated zeddies for their extra shine, rather than chrome, with yellow paint on the inside surface, or a strip of green, red or yellow tape as alternative combinations.

Lead weights vary from 7 to 56 g and are occasionally added when needed to reach the bottom.

Another combination which is less popular is a fly rod equipped with a single-action reel loaded with monofilament line or a lead-core shooting-head fly line, a lead weight, and a large streamer fly (also called a lure). This rig is lobbed into a deep lie, usually in a gorge where the river is too narrow and fast for spinning tackle, and allowed to drift through the school of salmon. The technique has been dubbed 'scratching' by opponents, who claim it results in too many foul-hooked salmon, occasionally intentionally. But it has its adherents and its place; and one group has no more right to the fishery than any others adopting a method which is legal.

Controversy has also arisen over the use of bait like live shrimps or sprats, or dead pilchards. The technique of bait fishing grew in popularity after it was proved to be productive in slow water close to the river mouths. The bait is presented under a float, with a small hook either through the back or through the nose, but the slow drift involves conflicts

SALMON FISHING

Flies and Colorado spoons are used in conjunction with lead weights in deep holes in the salmon rivers.

with the regular lure-casting technique: lines become tangled, and tempers rise. Live-baiting for salmon has now been banned in North Canterbury waters, except in the Kaiapoi River where it is still popular immediately upstream of the junction with the Waimakariri River at McIntosh's.

If your catch is foul-hooked it must be returned unharmed to the water, but if you catch a dark fish with a huge hooked jaw consider putting it back and allowing it to complete the journey which has sapped so much of its energy. Such fish will have pale, soft flesh and when it comes to eating do not compare with a vibrant, firm, coin-bright salmon with deep orange flesh.

Harbour fisheries

In the harbour at Dunedin, trolling for salmon is a fast-growing sport. The runs of salmon are artificially sustained by annual releases of smolts, which return to the point of release three or four years later. This exciting fishery is a by-product of the commercial salmon farming industry, and provided funds can be raised to buy the young fish, it has a bright future.

The extent which salmon rove off the coast is not known, but young salmon do remain in the harbour at Port Chalmers, where they grow rapidly on a diet of krill and sprats.

The adult salmon enter the harbour during summer, and are generally caught on silver spoons like a large toby or flasher type of spoon, fished on 10 kg or 15 kg line with a heavier tippet. Some anglers like to use a short piece of stainless wire as a trace, for the salmon are often accompanied by schools of barracouta. The awesome dental equipment on these long silver 'snakes', as they are often called, can wreak havoc on regular mono line.

The tackle is usually basic single-action reels on sturdy rods, with a paravane ahead of the lure to take it down. Such a terminal rig requires

You have to be careful when looking for a fishing spot at McIntosh's. The locals guard their rocks jealously, and they don't welcome strangers. You certainly don't try and push in between them. But if you ask politely, and do not cast on their piece of water, they will soon tell you how the salmon are running. They will sympathise with you when you tell them you live in Auckland. We can't all live five minutes down the road from such a famous salmon fishing spot as many of them do. From the main street of Kaiapoi it's only a few minutes' drive to the car park at McIntosh's. It is very rural. The cows will lick the paint off any part of the car they can reach over the fence.

Two happy-looking gentlemen were carrying large salmon back to their cars as we arrived. Actually they were dragging them, because the salmon were so long their tails flopped along in the dust.

"Had a good morning?" we asked. "Not bad," they replied. It was barely 11 in the morning and they had their limit of two salmon each.

"I used to live in Auckland," said one bearded fisherman. "But I shifted to Christchurch." I could see why — 13 kilos of bright silver salmon, thick across the back and deep in the flanks. When split open for smoking, its flesh would be a rich orange colour; or it might be cut into chunks and bottled with salt, vinegar, cloves and a splash of tomato sauce.

We hurried on down the road, through a gate, and there was the river in front of us. Not a very inspiring scene: it wasn't the sparkling, sun-dappled water which is often associated with South Island high country streams — more of a sluggish, tidal, dirty-coloured, slow-moving stretch of water with large black rocks in jumbled piles along the near bank and a muddy beach on the other side. But it was the number of people fishing that was so hard to comprehend. They were lined up all the way along the bank — old people, young people, people of all shapes, but all with one purpose. They were all casting mechanically, their rods moving like the legs of a one-kilometre-long centipede. There were more anglers sitting in boats moored in mid-stream, just beyond the casting range of those along the bank. Over on the far side, more people waded in the shallows.

"Where on earth do we go?" I asked my companions. Ross Millichamp is a field officer for the North Canterbury Fish and Game Council. Fishing is his business, and salmon fishing his speciality. Malcolm Bell operates a tackle shop and sells salmon fishing gear alongside the free advice.

quite heavy line; but I suspect the deep trolling rigs used for trout would adapt well to this style of fishing. The salmon, which run up to 10 kg, would certainly perform well on a lead-core or stainless steel wire line and a light trolling rod.

The other method of fishing for salmon, which is becoming more popular every season, is to use live baits from wharves in the harbours. A live sprat offered under a float is the favourite rig, with the sprat hooked through the nose or back in traditional livebait fashion. Whole pilchard baits will occasionally catch salmon, but are not as effective as a live bait.

The salmon-farming industry in the Marlborough Sounds has had extra benefits for sport fishermen, as wandering salmon turn up in unlikely places like Wellington Harbour and Lake Ferry, on the Wairarapa coast. These are not big fish, averaging about 3.5 kg, but are welcomed by anglers. Small numbers of salmon are taken in Wellington, but at Lake Ferry the salmon appear in large numbers during March and April. Local fishermen have developed their own technique for fishing where the

"You could start in there," said Ross, pointing to a gap of about one and a half metres between two relaxed-looking fishermen. One was just sitting on his rock, waiting. He seemed quite happy when I gingerly stepped onto the adjacent rock.

There was a huge splash as a hooked salmon thrashed in the shallows a few metres away, then another rod further along the row suddenly bent. One of the boat anglers dipped a net and lifted a gleaming salmon. They were being caught all around us.

"About 80 caught here yesterday," said my neighbour.

"How have you been doing?" I asked. "No good," he replied. "Don't know what I am doing wrong, but haven't had a fish for 10 days."

Fishing here is a bit of a lottery. Ross said the quinnat salmon, which are fresh from the sea just a couple of kilometres away, like to rest in this stretch of the Waimakariri River, because the small Kaiapoi River meets it a little further upstream and some salmon will take that route to the hatchery where they were released. It is more of a general area than a fishing hole, but it has been called McIntosh's for as long as anyone can remember. I wondered who McIntosh was as I cast out, let the spinner swing around in the current and sink, before slowly winding it back in. This was repeated endlessly, occasionally varying the distance, angle and time for it to sink.

"You must be on the bottom," Ross had said. Up the river you can work a fishing hole thoroughly, but here you just have to do what everyone else does or there will be some horrendous tangles. The lines do often cross, but there is always a pair of hands willing to free your lure and toss it back.

More fish were caught, with neighbours dropping their own rods and scrambling down the rocks to slip a wide-mouthed net under the huge salmon. These are impressive fish, averaging 7-8 kg and occasionally exceeding 14 kg. Such fish would yield a dozen jars or more of delicate pink flesh. I cast and cast, while nearby Malcolm struck and subdued a salmon of about 7 kg.

As he was fiddling with a pair of pliers to free the shiny treble hook from the corner of its mouth I saw his lure — it was the same as mine but he had added a strip of fluorescent green tape to one side.

"Is that the secret?" I asked. He just smiled. Perhaps it was, when combined with the technique which comes from years and years of catching salmon in the great rivers of Canterbury.

We had our fish for the smoker; time to enjoy watching other people catch theirs.

current flows out on a falling tide. They use surfcasting tackle, with a flasher rig below a sinker. This is cast out and left like a bait, with the current providing enough movement for the white flies on the flasher rig to attract the salmon.

In Wellington Harbour another new fishery has been steadily growing more popular over the last few years: livebaiting for sea-run brown trout at river mouths. Small sprats are fished on spinning tackle, in conjunction with floats or bobby corks, for the trout which usually appear in late winter prior to the whitebait season. It's a mystery where the trout come from, but the Hutt River with its resident brown trout population is one likely source. They are good-sized fish, with large specimens reaching 6.5 kg. These are strong, silver-bodied fish when fresh from the sea, with few of the spots which characterise river trout, and are often confused with salmon. The quickest method of identifying trout or salmon is to look in the mouth: salmon have a black lining inside the mouth whereas trout are white.

Rules of salmon fishing etiquette,
courtesy of Ross Millichamp

Historically, salmon and trout fishing have involved strong ethics. But salmon fishing in particular seems to bring out the worst in people, as large numbers of anglers are confined to limited fishing areas and trying to catch a highly prized fish which is erratic and unpredictable in behaviour.

The following rules are offered as a common sense approach to salmon fishing behaviour.

1. Jet boaters should avoid driving through pools where anglers are fishing. Take another channel, or slow down and move to the other side of the pool where people are fishing. Also be very careful not to swamp deep-wading fishermen with your bow wave.
2. Jet boaters should not stop to fish in pools where others are fishing. Fishermen with a boat can reach far more water than those restricted to walking.
3. When boat fishing off a river mouth, stay well out to avoid tangling surfcasters' lines. A few inconsiderate boat anglers can spoil the fishing for hundreds of shore anglers.
4. Do not move into another fisherman's spot if he has moved out to land a fish. When fishing a crowded area like a river mouth, you can walk into the line anywhere there is a space. If someone packs up and leaves, then his space is available; but not if he is landing a fish. Take time to watch the locals and see what they do.
5. Do not move into a pool downstream of another angler. Most people fish rivers for peace and quiet, and crowding is less acceptable than at the mouths. If someone is fishing a small gut, it is better to find your own pool. People usually fish large pools from the top, moving a short distance downstream after each cast. Always enter the pool above other anglers. (But if they are not moving, it is acceptable to move in below, although it is polite to ask first.)
6. No angler has the legal right to prevent any other angler fishing any piece of public water. As in the previous rule, good manners should be exercised at all times, but if you feel someone is hogging a pool and not giving others a fair go, then you are perfectly within your rights to move in and start fishing.
7. Stop fishing when an angler near you hooks a fish. It takes a lot of fishing to hook a salmon, so give other people a chance to land their fish without tangling lines. This is particularly important if the fish is being played upstream of you, as most salmon run downstream when hooked.
8. When fishing in crowded areas, use similar terminal tackle and cast a similar distance to other anglers. If others are using a lead and spoon, do not join the line with a feathered lure. Different tackle will swing with the current at different speeds, and will tangle. Try and cast the same distance and at the same angle as others. Any variation is likely to result in tangles.

SALMON FISHING

Whether salmon or trout are the target, the jet boat is popular for reaching remote water — and a lot of fun.

CHAPTER FIFTEEN
COARSE FISHING

The term coarse fish is a traditional English one, applied to freshwater fish which are not classified as gamefish like trout, salmon and grayling. It refers to a range of fish species which were caught by commoners, while only landowners and aristocrats could fish for gamefish. In the Middle Ages monks were among those responsible for spreading coarse fish like perch and tench around Britain, stocking farm ponds and castle moats, to provide a source of food for local villages.

Today, coarse fishing is a thriving sport which has a strong following through six clubs in this country. Special tackle is imported from England, and regular competitions are held.

Few people realise that some of the coarse fish species have been in New Zealand longer than trout, and they have been stocked throughout the country, often under controversial circumstances. Owing to a perceived threat to trout fisheries, it is illegal to transfer fish of any species.

Coarse fish can survive in poor-quality water, and are found in many ponds and small lakes close to large cities; they provide good sport for youngsters starting out in fishing as well as the dedicated specialist anglers.

The different species in the country include perch, tench, koi carp, common goldfish, golden orf, rudd and catfish. While most are small fish rarely reaching 2 kg, perch are known to reach 4 kg, tench 7 kg and koi carp grow to enormous proportions, exceeding 9 kg.

Summer is the best season as the fish feed actively to build up reserves of fat to sustain them over the winter when they are less active.

Tackle

It is delicate fishing, requiring ultralight tackle for most species. A common spinning outfit used to catch sprats from a wharf is suitable; but the enthusiasts use rods over 4 m long and special monofilament between 0.5 kg and 1.5 kg breaking strain which is designed to sink just under the surface, and hooks of fine wire from size 12 down to a minute size 20. These hooks have a spade end, and a special hook tier is used to attach it with a snood knot.

If koi carp are the target, a stronger rod for line up to 10 kg breaking strain is needed for these powerful fish.

A selection of floats of various sizes and designs and split shot complete the basic tackle. It is important for the float to match the weight of line and bait, so the fish feels no resistance when it takes the bait. The float should sit upright with half of its length below the surface, and will

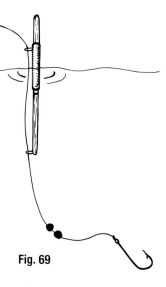
Fig. 69

easily slip under when a fish bites (Fig. 69).

Any type of reel can be used, but it is necessary to cast a short distance and fixed-spool reels are the most popular. As only a short amount of fine line is needed for fishing, a reel can be loaded with any line to fill the spool, adding about 30 m of the fishing line on the end.

Serious coarse fishermen have a whole array of equipment including rod carriers, special metal folding seats with rod supports and bait holders attached, and a tackle box under the seat. Fish are landed in a long-handled, fine-meshed net, then kept alive in a long, expanding keep net so the total catch can be weighed for competition or match fishing — and then released.

Koi carp are powerful fish which grow to more than 9 kg, but are officially classified as noxious fish and may not be transported alive.

Bait

Perch are extremely voracious and will readily take a live bait; and they will eat any live fish smaller than themselves including other perch. Live baits can be hooked through the nose or back and presented under a float as in sea fishing, or on the bottom with a small sinker added. Perch will also take small spinners fished with a spinning outfit.

Worms are popular bait for perch and also for tench. These may be brandling or tiger worms — the banded worms found in compost — or common lobworms cut in half. Other good baits include maggots, whole kernels of corn, balls of dough, bread crusts, chick peas and tiny bloodworms. Baits are hooked just once through the skin; and with a worm this is usually about halfway along its length, leaving two long sections to wriggle enticingly. Smell is important in attracting fish to your bait, and untouched baits should be refreshed regularly.

Groundbaiting with berley will attract fish to the area and encourage them to bite, and a good mixture can be made from breadcrumbs mixed with sufficient water to hold them together, and a few maggots or corn kernels added. Use the groundbait sparingly so the fish remain hungry.

The best baits for different species are:

Koi carp — worm, maggot, chickpea, corn
Perch — live bait, dead bait, worm, maggot
Tench — worm, maggot, corn, bread
Rudd — maggot, corn, bread, worm
Goldfish — worm, maggot, corn
Golden orf — maggot, corn
Catfish — worm, slugs, shelled snail, maggot, bacon

Stillwater fishing

Perch prefer open water, but other species like tench and rudd can be found among weed beds. A rake cast out on a rope is used to clear a hole among the weed, and a few handfuls of groundbait thrown in to attract fish.

Watch for bubbles rising to the surface, an indication of tench or carp feeding below. Carp produce bigger bubbles as they take in mouthfuls of silt and detritus, remove the food which is mainly bloodworms, and expel the unwanted material through their gills.

The bait must be presented close to the bottom, and the depth can be measured by attaching a small weight to your hook and testing it, adjusting the length of line below the float until the weight rests on the bottom without submerging the float.

Then it's a question of trying different baits until you start catching the fish you want. For most species the float and bait are left stationary, but when fishing worms or live baits for perch the bait is moved regularly by taking a half turn on the reel handle. Perch are found in shoals and when one is caught you should hook more in the same spot.

You can also use a technique called legering, which employs a weight instead of a float. A 3 m spinning rod and reel is ideal, with a weight through which the line can easily slide so the fish does not feel the weight about 45 cm above the hook. Some fishermen prefer a swim feeder, a plastic tube with holes along the sides which acts as a weight when filled with

Catfish

In their native North America catfish are highly prized as a sporting and table fish, but in this country are generally regarded as undesirable. Brown bullhead catfish were first released in some Auckland lakes in 1978, have spread throughout the region and are now particularly prevalent in the lower Waikato River system.

Catfish are welcomed in the diet of Asian immigrants, and 7.5 tonnes was sold in the Auckland region in one year recently. But they are also popular with children as a fun fish, because they are so easy to catch on a line. Since about 1980 catfish have spread throughout Lake Taupo, causing concern to the fisheries authorities as they were perceived as a threat to the trout population. Studies have since indicated that they may not have much impact on the trout, but DOC would still like to see them taken from the lake. Catfish grow to more than 30 cm long, and feed mainly on snails, insect larvae, small koura and plant material. It appears they may compete with juvenile trout for some food, but do not pose a threat to trout as a predator.

Catfish are found in the shallow, weedy and rocky margins where the water is warmest. They are more active during summer, feeding mainly at night, and the best fishing will be found at dusk.

Motuopa, Acacia Bay and Tokaanu are popular spots for catfish — in fact the best fishing is at places where there are a lot of people; you can fish from the wharves and breakwaters, or from an anchored boat.

Use a light spinning rod with a size 10 or 12 hook tied directly to the line, and an optional second hook on a dropper loop a short distance above it, with bread squashed onto the hook or a piece of meat or bacon rind. Usually no sinker is needed, but if the water is several metres deep one or two split shot can be added above the hooks. A float set the correct distance up the line to ensure the baits are on the bottom will help signal strikes.

Some children quickly become proficient at catching catfish, which have white meat which is said to be good eating, either smoked or fried.

A word of caution: the leading edges of the main fins carry a sharp spine which can inflict a painful wound. Use a cloth to handle the fish. If you do not want to eat your catch of catfish, dispose of them because the authorities do not want them in the lake, and it is illegal to transport them alive to any other waterway. They are extremely hardy, and can survive out of water for hours if kept moist. There are large numbers of catfish in Lake Taupo, and fisheries officers conducting surveys with fyke nets caught up to 600 fish in one night in a net set in Waihi Bay during December.

Catfish are prevalent in the lower Waikato River system and have also become established in Lake Taupo. Photo courtesy Department of Conservation, Turangi.

Serious coarse fishermen like George Western have a whole array of equipment including rod carriers, special metal folding seats with rod supports and bait holders attached, and a tackle box under the seat.

groundbait. You can fill it with bread and maggots or chopped worms, which will be dispensed in the area you are fishing. Some fishermen can hold the line and feel the sensitive bites, while others use special indicators attached to their rod tip. A simple method of detecting bites is to pinch a piece of dough to the line between the reel and the first eye on the rod. Pull off a short length of line so this hangs down, forming a V in the line. When a fish bites the dough indicator will be pulled up as the line straightens.

Fishing rivers

In moving water a different technique called trotting is employed. The terminal rig is the same, but the float is attached at the top and bottom. This is cast out and 'trotted' with the current, then pulled in and cast again.

Try and fish the slow currents in eddies and backwater. Groundbait is also used in this situation to attract fish to the section of river which you are fishing.

COARSE FISHING

The rudd is widespread and readily takes a bait of maggots or corn.

Bait for a day's fishing — worms in soil, kernels of sweetcorn, and 'gozzers' and 'pinkies' in bran.

"We call these pinkies. They are the maggots of the housefly. Big ones like this are gozzers. They come from bluebottles or blowflies," George Western said as he selected a fat red maggot from a container full of bran and wriggling maggots, then carefully impaled it on a tiny hook and cast it out into the dark water. The slim float bobbed gently near dark green waterlily pads. Cows grazed on the other side of the pond, which lies in a basin among gentle, rolling hills about an hour's drive from downtown Auckland. George watched his float intently. "See those bubbles? That means tench are feeding on the bottom," he said as he wound in the fragile 1 kg line. "We'll catch a tench now." George expertly threaded half of a worm onto his size 20 hook. "The tail section is better than the whole worm," he added, casting the 4 m rod with a practised flick. Half a minute passed, then the slim float slid under the surface. Raising his rod smoothly, the fisherman spun his reel to tighten the line then carefully led the writhing fish into the shallows, picked up a large-mouthed net on a long handle and leaned over to scoop up his prize.

"Look at that. A lovely tench," he said, cradling the dark green fish in a gnarled hand while he deftly poked a thin instrument into its mouth with a surgeon's skill and flicked out the hook. The tench was slipped into the wide maw of a fine-meshed keep net to join dozens of golden rudd and other tench which would be put back into the pond at the end of the day's sport.

George is one of hundreds of coarse fishing enthusiasts who belong to six clubs in Auckland, Lower Hutt and Christchurch. Like him, many brought with them from England their love of this delicate, specialised form of fishing. He raises maggots for bait, and even puts special dye imported from England into their food to colour them red or bronze. "Some days white maggots are best, and other days coloured ones work well — or we use a combination.

"I keep my own flies in a special cage with a lamp to keep the temperature at about 23 degrees. When they first hatch I give them sugar water for a couple of days, then put in a piece of liver. That stimulates their hormones and encourages them to breed," explained George. The liver is replaced with a fresh piece the next day, and another on the third day. "I let them blow it, and it takes two days for the eggs to hatch. I feed the maggots on ox heart, fish or boiler chickens and they grow for four days before changing into a chrysalis. We call them casters, and they are good bait on their own." It is a continuous cycle, producing fresh maggots for his weekly fishing trips.

As well as rudd and tench, he catches perch, koi carp, catfish and common goldfish. "I hold the New Zealand record for perch, 4lb 7oz — these fishermen still talk in pre-metric terms," said George, slotting a handful of breadcrumbs, maggots and golden kernels of canned corn into the pouch of a shanghai and firing it out into the pond.

"Keep giving the fish groundbait, but don't overfeed them," he cautioned.

"I was playing a three and a half pound perch the other day — we weighed it — and another huge perch came up and tried to eat it. That fish must have been 12 or 13 pounds! You have to be very carefully with perch. They have blood vessels near the skin in the throat, and if they are deeply hooked they will die. But they have white meat, and are very good to eat. Better than trout."

The float dipped again and George struck another fish. This was a rudd with red fins and gold flanks, which had taken a kernel of corn.

"When we want to drop the float in exactly the same spot every time we use this," he said proudly, pulling metre-long sections of tube from another section and fitting them together. The pole grew and grew as he extended it, slotting a slightly wider section to the end each time.

"This one is 12.5 m long, but you can use whatever length you want. See this," he said, pulling on a short length of elastic cord protruding from the tip, "it stretches, and you just tie your line to it and hold the rod up when you hook a fish. It tires it for you.

"The longest poles are 32 m, and weigh only 1 kg. They are made from liquid crystal lithium and kevlar, and cost £8,000 [roughly $19,000]. But in match fishing competitions the maximum allowed is 14.5 m."

Who said this type of fishing was coarse?

CHAPTER SIXTEEN
EEL FISHING

A favourite summer pastime as children was to set eel lines overnight on the edge of Lake Tarawera. The tackle was simple: a sturdy hemp handline with a short heavy trace and large hook baited with bacon or trout guts. This rig was tied to a snag and the business end rowed out by dinghy and dropped over the ledge where the lake bottom fell away to 15 metres. A second line was often set from the jetty on the other side of the bay.

Bursting with anticipation, the young boys raced down the beach at first light to check the lines. If there was an eel on, the line would be stretched tightly as it disappeared into the lake. When hooked, the big eels would dive into the thick oxygen weed and could not be pulled over the ledge from the beach. But when the angle was changed to a direct overhead pull from the small dinghy, the long black creature would soon come writhing up from the shadowy green depths.

These images remained firm in the mind when it came to swimming in the bay later in the heat of the day.

Big eels were quite a prize. They fought strongly and pulled hard. And they were tough to kill. Tarawera harboured some huge specimens. Many myths surrounded these grotesque, slimy fish. They often weighed nearly 40 pounds, and the heaviest we heard of was a monster of 63 pounds (28.6 kg).

A small stream ran into the bay, and when large rainbows overcame their fear of shallow water and raced up the stream to the gravel spawning beds a large eel would often follow.

On one occasion when the trout caught the previous night in the rip at the stream mouth were taken down to the stream behind the house to wash the blood and slime away after gutting, a huge black head suddenly poked out from under the bank as soon as the fish touched the water. The taste of trout was a signal the eel could not resist. A .303 rifle was quickly fetched, and the trout again slipped into the water. This time when the eel poked its head out it was met by a blast from only two metres away. When the sand and spray settled and the water cleared, the eel was in trouble. About 50 cm of it protruded upside down from under the bank, its muddy yellow belly washing in the cold clear stream water. A sheath knife with a straight blade and wicked point, the pride and joy of a young boy, could not pierce the tough skin, and the blade was slipped into the corner of the eel's broad mouth. It promptly clamped its jaws shut and was pulled out of the hole and dragged in triumph up the steep bank. The shot had missed the eel's head and merely concussed it, so it soon came to life, wriggling furiously across the lawn. Several whacks on the head slowed it

Female eels are said to travel inland and may live to great ages.

down so the fish scales could be employed, and it registered 14 kg.

An old piece of Maori lore came to mind when the severed head and the guts were deposited in the deep hole for household rubbish: "Never cut off an eel's head and throw it over the side of the canoe, or the eel will try and follow its head." That eel's headless body still wriggled, and was dropped into the rubbish hole. When flicked out onto the grass, it again slithered into the hole. Of course its primitive nervous system soon ceased to function, but the old adage remained imprinted in the mind to this day.

There are two species of eels found in New Zealand freshwater — longfinned and shortfinned eels. Longfinned eels grow larger than shortfinned eels, live further from the sea, and live to a greater age. They are fascinating creatures and their life story is well documented. The young are born far out at sea, and the tiny elvers make their way up rivers and streams in vast numbers where they grow to maturity. Eels will travel across land at night when the grass is moist, and so can be found even in waterways that aren't connected to the sea. On a full moon and high tide in autumn, large numbers of adult eels will migrate downriver to the coast where they disappear out to sea, to spawn and die.

Eels provide endless fun for young anglers who lob a baited hook into a stream or pond. Fishing at night is best. They readily take a bait of worms, fish, meat, bacon or guts, and are keenly sought by many people who eat them fresh or smoked.

Eel slime is rather distasteful, but there are several easy ways of removing it. One is to sprinkle salt over the eel after killing it. This makes it congeal so you can then scrape it off with a dull knife an hour later. A wash in hot water will also congeal the slime.

CHAPTER SEVENTEEN
WHITEBAIT

The Cascade River flows out of the mountains of South Westland, down a wide river valley. There's greenstone in the surrounding mountains, and gold in the rivers. But what really attracts people to the Cascade is the whitebait. Every spring the biggest runs of whitebait on the coast arrive in the river mouth, like liquid gold pouring in from the sea.

Whitebaiters travel to the coast from all over the country, hoping to strike the big runs of the succulent, tiny fish which can bring big dollars. The township of Haast sees its population explode from 300 to 3,000 during the season. The standard greeting on the coast is: "How's the 'bait?"

Fishing stands are licensed and jealously guarded, but no licence is needed to sell the catch. However, strict regulations control the harvest, with no fishing allowed upstream of tidal influence on all streams; some other rivers are totally closed to fishing. These sanctuaries ensure some whitebait survive to breed and maintain the resource.

Maurice Nolan runs jet boat tours on the Cascade, and he also runs cattle in the Cascade River valley. It's a remote valley, with access only by boat — a 40-minute ride down the river to the mouth where the whitebaiters are based. Before the advent of jet boats and aircraft, the whitebaiters had to travel by sea, down the coast from Haast to the Cascade River.

Every spring the biggest runs of whitebait on the coast arrive in the Cascade River mouth, like liquid gold pouring in from the sea.

It was just a shadow passing across the blurred, white line under the water. Then another thin shadow appeared, and another, and a third which widened into a mass of tiny, wriggling fish.

The old man waited patiently. He knew that a sudden move would scare the small fish. They were just under the surface, vulnerable to fluttering gulls and sleek, black shags, and wary of any movement from above.

With gnarled hands, the old man slowly grasped the long handle of his scoop net and lowered the wide mouth deeply behind the small school of fish, pushing it surely along before lifting it with both hands.

His heart pounding, he swung the dripping net onto the mud and grass and grabbed the cold, wet mesh, lifting and ruffling it to ensure none of the tiny fish stuck to the steep sides. At the bottom, the mesh narrowed to a gap of only seven centimetres; and there in the pocket was a dense greenish mass of shimmering whitebait. Though he had done it thousands of times before, the old man still felt a thrill flutter through his body when he saw the catch secure in the net.

"I'll have a heart attack one of these days," he muttered to his wife, who sat nearby on a folding camp chair, not looking up from her book.

The old man knew how a prospector must feel when he strikes gold after years of searching. To him, the whitebait which turned up every year were like liquid gold.

The days when a kerosene tin was easily filled with the delicious tiny fish were a dim memory. Every year the runs grew smaller, but occasionally he still struck it rich, half-filling his plastic bucket in just a few hours of fishing.

As 15 August approached he grew more and more restless, driving to the river bank to peer at the slow-moving water whose colour changed with the tides from green to brown and green again. During the week before the whitebait season opened the old fisherman would check his net for rips and tears. He knew that the first runs of the precious fish came with the spring tides, at the full moon. This year the opening was only a few days after the full moon — a good time. Every day he would sit patiently on his worn, wooden platform leaning out over the mud bank for the first two hours of the incoming tide. But he did not expect any whitebait to arrive at his fishing spot 500 metres from the river mouth until the incoming tide forced the rushing current back, giving the small fish an easy ride in from the sea.

Another school passed over his sighter board, a length of square plastic downpipe weighted with lead which protruded at right angles out from the bank. This time the old man was clumsy in his eager-

The Buchanan family control much of the whitebaiting on the Cascade. Fifty years ago the first Buchanans carted building materials down the river, building cabins out of the short planks which could be carried on horseback. In those days the only way of preserving the whitebait until it could be sold in the cities was by canning it. In 1953 they hacked a stretch of level ground from the bush and created a landing strip. Today, one of the family flies a Cessna to Christchurch every second day during the season, carrying 300 kg of premium grade fresh whitebait, worth on average $50 a kilo. The cabins have grown into a complex with a factory and chiller powered by a huge generator. One cabin has a pool table and bar where the 14 residents relax, and the family employs paid workers to help tend the stands. It's all part of the Cascade River Whitebait Company.

The wide-mouthed scoop nets which are so popular at North Island river mouths are rarely seen here. The Buchanans have many of the 31 licensed stands on the Cascade, sophisticated structures up to 23 m long

ness to scoop up the fish, and the seemingly poor swimmers easily darted away from his net. Only half a dozen individuals slid down the inside of the mesh, to tumble into the bucket of water when he pulled the drawstring to open the cup at the bottom of the net.

Few people understood where the mysterious little fish came from, and what they grew into. As a boy, the old fisherman had hooked the adults on worms flicked into dark, bush pools. The Maoris called them kokopu, inanga and koaro. Scientists know them as the Galaxiidae, a family of fish found in both New Zealand and Australia. Other people mistakenly referred to the smooth-skinned fish as mountain trout, mud trout or native trout. Only 10 to 15 centimetres long, the thin, brown fish always jumped out of a bucket or a pond, to wriggle away across the wet grass like an eel.

In autumn the adults migrated down to where the sea joined the river in a brackish mixture, and laid their eggs on reeds which were covered only by the highest tides. A month later another high tide covered the millions of eggs, which hatched into tiny larval fish. The combination of a falling tide and the strong current of the river easily swept the vulnerable babies out to sea where other fish decimated their numbers. The survivors learned to swim in groups, growing quickly in the plankton-rich water until they surrendered to the growing urge to leave the saline water behind and begin the long, hazardous journey back to the quiet pools deep in the bush where they would be safe.

The strong currents in the middle of the river forced the poor swimmers close to the banks, where fishermen waited with long set nets and wide-mouthed scoop nets. Darting kahawai streaked into the schools of whitebait, forcing them up to the surface where flocks of screaming gulls swooped and dived, and shags streaked through the water like deadly torpedoes.

But it was not the impact of predators which had caused the whitebait runs to diminish. Cows grazing on the riverbank consumed millions of fragile fish eggs along with their diet of long grass and reeds, and as the ancient trees were stripped from the hills the once strong banks of the dark pools were scoured and the water muddied easily.

The old man no longer caught enough whitebait for his wife to simply dust them lightly in flour and fry them quickly in hot butter. Now she mixed eggs, milk and flour to make fritters patterned with individual fish, their black eyes dotted across the yellow brown surface. He was becoming accustomed to the stronger taste of the full-bodied inanga, the more common cousin of the translucent, delicate kokopu.

But they still tasted wonderful, and he would be back on the riverbank tomorrow.

---

with scaffolding, walkways, pulleys for raising the huge box traps, and screens to direct the fish along to the mouths of the traps. There is a maximum length which is allowed, calculated on covering no more than a third of the river's width. The stands can be raised out of the water to protect them during floods, and when the season closes all stands must be removed from the river.

Stands can be sold, and may bring $8,000 on a river close to Haast, but on the Cascade huge money would be involved. Mike Buchanan has been fishing there for about 40 years, and he said they rarely change hands. "There is a very long waiting list," he says.

His own stand is upriver from the settlement, one of few on that side. No fishing is allowed between the sea and a side stream, and his stand is immediately above the tributary — the first nets the whitebait encounter on their upstream migration. It has been called "the best whitebait stand in New Zealand".

Mike Buchanan's stand on the Cascade has been called "the best whitebait stand in New Zealand".

Mike has a little cabin for resting in when the bait are not running, a powerful winch for lifting the whole structure, and rails for pulling it back from the water. The whitebait run on the incoming tide, and on a good day he is kept busy for six hours emptying the box nets which trap the fish.

While the bait fetches higher prices every year, he occasionally indulges himself, mixing "a couple of eggs with a kilo of whitebait" and frying thick patties in hot butter. There is just enough egg to hold the mass together, and it is eaten steaming hot on a thick slice of bread — sometimes with a squirt of mint sauce "for a change".

CHAPTER EIGHTEEN
TACKLE MAINTENANCE

You may have a lot of money invested in your tackle. Look after it — not just to preserve its value, but to ensure it works for when you need it.

Freshwater

Freshwater is gentle on your tackle. You will do more damage than the elements through carelessness, like laying a fly reel on the sand, or knocking a rod against a gate as you climb it. If you put any reel on the sand — and we all do it — dunk it in water without turning the handle, then shake and tap it with your hands to ensure no loose grains of sand are lurking in the action.

When we were children, the job of drying the fly lines and backing by running them out along a tennis court was an important one when we arrived home from the lake. Today's fly lines do not demand such a strict regime, but you should clean them every season with a commercial cleaner or warm soapy water. Your line will be slicker and will cast better as a result. Also think about replacing the backing every few years.

Trolling reels will perform much better if you give them a clean and lube at the start of the season. With a little attention, your freshwater gear should serve you well for years.

It is easy to subject your line to unreasonable abrasion and pressure, as when bouncing lures over the stones on the bed of a Canterbury salmon river. Either take the line off and reverse it before the next season, or replace it. Don't expect any line to last more than a few years, no matter what work it does for you.

Saltwater

The corrosive nature of saltwater is unforgiving, and a little foresight and prevention can work wonders.

Rods

All rods should be hosed down after use to remove sand and salt, and a stiff brush and a squirt of Simple Green cleans dried scraps of bait and grime from the grips. When dry, coat rods with a light oil or water-resistant spray and polish with an old towel. Also check to ensure corrosion is not building up in the bindings under the rings.

With rods of two or three pieces, the ferrules or connections should be waxed from time to time by rubbing lightly with a candle.

Check guides regularly, and replace any that are damaged. Guides on game rods have more moving parts, which demand more care. Roller guides should be washed after use and given a squirt of Tackle Guard. At the start of each season take the guides apart and wash and lubricate them. Small screws can be secured with a drop of clear nail polish.

Check for scratches or burring by pulling a piece of stocking or pantyhose inside the guides. Or run a thin bladed knife around the guide ring: any grooves or corrosion will catch the blade. A reaction between the different metals on your winch fitting and reel can cause corrosion. While this is only cosmetic, regular cleaning and a light film of grease or petroleum jelly on the reel seat and winch fitting gives extra protection.

Reels

A smooth, well-lubricated reel is one of your greatest assets on the water. You can test it by getting someone to pull line from the end of your rod. If the tip jerks or moves unevenly, then the drag on your reel needs servicing. If it is working properly, the rod tip will not move except in a smooth curve when the rod is loaded and line is pulled off. It should be smooth.

Use an oil-based lubricant with teflon, as supplied with the reel. Never use penetrating oils, which are designed to loosen corroded bits and displace moisture, leaving the action dry. The drag components should be cleaned with white spirit, allowed to dry, and if the drag is still not smooth the washers will need replacing.

If you do your own servicing, don't over-grease the gears. A thin coating is fine. Or do what we do and have your reels serviced professionally.

Gamefishing reels that are subjected to extreme pressures should be serviced every season. Gear used for bottom dunking and occasional fishing will not need such treatment. After each trip tighten the drag to seal it, then wash with fresh water. Don't use a high-pressure spray which can drive water into the action. Use a soft mist followed by a good wipe, then a squirt of Tackle Guard, which will not damage the line. Loosen the drag after washing; drag washers left under pressure can be permanently damaged.

Line

Some serious fishermen replace their line every season. But this is a big call for most people, and is not necessary. Use your common sense. If one reel has done a lot of work, check the line and either replace it, or if there

> Don't wind the swivel hard up against the tip ring on your rod and leave it there. Boat movement and vibrations will keep it bouncing around, which will weaken the line and damage the tip ring. Secure the swivel to the harness lug on your reel. A tap washer on the line above the swivel provides protection for the tip ring, and the knot.

is sufficient capacity discard the last 50 m or so. Alternatively, run it all off and reverse it so you are fishing with line which has not been used at all.

Terminal bits

All hooks and swivels should be washed in fresh water and dried. Some fishermen like to coat them with petroleum jelly or fish oil to prevent rust.

Manufacturers of skirted lures advise rubbing the heads and skirts with petroleum jelly or baby oil — not washing in fresh water.

Leaders should be checked for faults, particularly at pressure points like on either side of the lure head and at crimps and knots.

CHAPTER NINETEEN
FISH HANDLING

Releasing fish

Most people at times need to release unwanted or undersized fish. Simply tearing the hook out and throwing it over the side of the boat will reduce the chances of that fish surviving. In fact there is a lot that can be done to give fish being released the best possible chance.

Fish are designed to be supported by the water they live in, and their internal organs are easily damaged by crushing, or the impact of thrashing on hard surfaces. Also, fish have a layer of mucus covering their scales, which protects them from infection. Damage to this layer through rough handling, or even dry hands, can decrease the chance of survival.

Ideally, fish should be released without removing them from the water. Pulling a fish out of the water after a struggle is a bit like putting a plastic bag over the head of a person who has just run a marathon. If the fish is hooked in the mouth the hook can usually be removed without lifting the fish from the water. Large fish like kingfish can be gaffed through the lip and held with just the head out of water while a hook is removed. A pair of needle-nosed pliers helps by simply grasping the hook shank and twisting it. If the fish must be lifted, small fish can be lifted by using the

Kill fish quickly and put them on ice, or into seawater mixed with ice into a slurry, as is used in the commercial fishing industry.

A plastic grid on the bottom of the fish box keeps your catch clear of the blood and slime which accumulates.

line, and larger fish can be held with a wet towel or wet gloves. Hands should be wet before holding a fish, to keep them cool, as even the warmth of your hands can burn a fish's delicate skin.

Ideally the fish should be supported by placing one hand underneath, and transferring it to a wet, soft surface like a towel or piece of sponge. Fish will not struggle if held upside down. This makes hook removal easier.

If a fish is hooked deeply in the throat or gut, it will have a better chance if the line is cut as close to the mouth as possible, and the hook left there. The hook will eventually rust or be expelled by the fish. Do not use gobsticks on fish to be released.

Slip fish back into the water close to you, and head-first — don't throw them from a distance.

Don't use treble hooks, as they will tear the mouth. If you keep hooking small fish, it is definitely time to try using larger hooks.

What tires a fish during a struggle on the end of a line is the build-up of lactic acid, which is produced by its tissues as they run out of oxygen — just as black smoke is produced by a fire starved of air. Once muscles start to function normally, the lactic acid is burned up as the supply of oxygen is replenished. If a fish is totally exhausted and lies belly-up on the surface, it can recover if resuscitated. Hold the fish gently by the tail and push it through the water head-first. Game fishermen may tow a marlin

How not to release fish — damage through rough handling, or even dry hands, can decrease the chance of survival. The brown bands on the flanks of this small snapper indicate that it is stressed.

To scale fish after the skin has dried, or has been frozen, dip in boiling water first to loosen scales.

Fish can be kept fresh in a fish box or chilly bin by adding plastic milk containers, or the bladder from a wine cask, filled with water and frozen. These no-cost freezer pads are disposable, and will last all day.

held by the bill behind a boat for several minutes while it recovers. Oxygen in the water running over the gills will revive it, and once the fish starts to move it can be released to swim away.

At no stage should the gills be touched. If a fish is bleeding from gills which may have been damaged by the hook, it will have little chance of surviving. Also, keeping a fish out of water for long causes the delicate gill filaments to collapse — and the fish will die.

It is mainly common sense. Like all fishing, if the angler thinks about the situation from the point of view of the fish, the fish will have a better chance of surviving.

Game fishermen often tag fish with an internationally recognised numbered plastic tag, which can be identified if the fish is later caught again. Its growth and movements can then be analysed, and the data added to the accumulated research data which helps fisheries managers make decisions on quotas, size and bag restrictions. Such fish are best tagged while in the water — but whether a small snapper or a huge marlin, each individual fish returned to the water is one more that can breed, and may even give another angler the pleasure of catching it.

To clean fish in the kitchen, do it on a newspaper. After each fish, a couple of pages can be wrapped up with the guts and gunge. Put bundles of guts in plastic bags and freeze until ready to put the rubbish out.

Fish should be refrigerated or frozen dry — preferably unwashed. If you like to wash the scales off first, use salt water and pat the fillets dry with paper towels.

Fish fillets kept dry will last much longer than if wet. Store them in a bowl with an upended saucer in the bottom — suspended above the blood and juices which leach out and accumulate under the saucer.

One hour out of ice reduces the keeping life of fish by one day.

CHAPTER TWENTY
THE MOON AND WEATHER

The moon

There can be no doubt that the gravitational pull of the moon affects fishing because it creates the jelly-like movement of oceans on a grand scale, causing tides to ebb and flow.

Many people believe the pull of the moon also causes fish and animals to feed more actively at certain times. This has been calculated and recorded as the 'bite times' which can be predicted — a major and a minor feeding cycle lasting up to two hours within each 24-hour day. The first occurs when the moon is directly overhead, and the second when it is directly underfoot above the opposite side of the planet.

Fishermen all experience occasions when, for no apparent reason, the fish suddenly start biting. While not complaining, they may attribute this phenomenon to the state of the tide, but it may also be that the moon has arrived at a favourable position. Further evidence of the influence of the moon on animal behaviour can be noticed when driving through rural areas. Sometimes the sheep and cattle in roadside paddocks will be sitting or standing around a tree doing very little, and at others they will all have their heads down feeding happily.

Many fishermen will take the phase and position of the moon into account when planning their outings, and it is commonly accepted that the period around the full moon is poor for fishing. The reason is that the fish and other animals are not as active, or they feed at night. Conversely, the two weeks around the new moon are better. One successful Auckland snapper fisherman maintains that the fishing always improves as soon as the moon rises over the horizon. "You can almost put money on it. The fish won't bite unless the moon is visible in the sky," he says.

Of course, the moon is only one of several factors contributing to fishing success. The others are the weather, time of day, and tides when at sea.

These may all contribute, but the most important of all is to have a bait in the water!

That some theories are centuries old is confirmed by a John Worlidge, who wrote in 1698: "After a clear moon-shiny night, if the day prove cloudy, is a very good time for Angling — for it is in the nature of most Fish to be fearful to stir in bright nights."

Weather

The effect of weather on fish has been a source of argument among fishermen for centuries. Many believe that a rising barometer is best, while

> You can calculate the main bite time when the moon is directly overhead by taking the halfway point between moon rise and moon set.

others prefer a falling barometer — but there is no doubt that barometric pressure does influence fish behaviour.

Fishing generally improves with the following weather conditions:

- Light, warm rain or cloudy conditions, when light-sensitive fish will venture into shallow water.
- Moderate winds which create a broken surface, reducing light penetration.

The Ministry of Fisheries conducted a survey as part of a study of recreational snapper fishing in the top half of the North Island, which included a diary survey of 2,728 fishermen who recorded details of fishing trips over 12 months. For consistency, the analysis was restricted to trips where snapper was the only species targeted, and fishing was done by rod or line from a boat.

Of the 5,032 trips analysed, 55% took place over the period December to February. The Hauraki Gulf was the most popular area, with 49% of the angling, followed by the east coast of Northland with 24%, Bay of Plenty with 21%, and the west coast with 6%.

MAF uses a system of measuring the catch rate where the number of legal-sized snapper caught is divided by the number of hours fished. This is referred to as the 'catch per unit effort,' or CPUE. When taken on daily averages of all people fishing, the results showed strong seasonal trends.

"Snapper success was generally highest in late March and early April (1.4 fish per hour), and lowest in August (0.8 fish per hour), and rates were more variable over winter," said the survey analyst, Russell Millar, of the Department of Mathematics and Statistics at the University of Otago.

On several days the catch per hour shot up to 3 snapper for some trips, but other results on the same days brought the average down to less than 1.4 fish. "The very best trip was on April 16, with 22 snapper in 1.5 hours, but the day has an average CPUE of 2 snapper per hour because of less successful trips by other people," said Millar.

He said the main factors determining success were the experience of individual anglers, combined with their boats, tackle, bait used and local knowledge.

"The lunar cycle was found to have a significant influence on snapper success. The best time to fish is around the new moon and the first quarter, with the worst fishing around the full moon," he added.

Millar said the data showed interesting departures from the lunar pattern, including a good day three days before the full moon, and a poor day three days after the full moon — normally accepted as a good day.

"These features are seen on some fishing calendars. However, we also found that fishing was often good on days that fishing calendars predicted as very bad." The best day of the lunar cycle was seven days after the new moon, and the worst day 14 days after the new moon.

Millar said that corroboration of the data by boat-ramp interviews "leads us to believe that participants were extremely diligent about reporting successful trips, but that some unsuccessful trips were considered best forgotten and were not recorded.

"For this reason, we know that the CPUEs are a bit optimistic. We also suspect that the lunar effect could, in fact, be a bit stronger than indicated by the statistical analysis."

- Warm fronts which often encourage fish to feed.
- Immediately before and after a storm.

Bad fishing weather includes:

- Thunderstorms, which may spook fish.
- Cold fronts, which make fish sluggish.
- Glassy water and bright sunlight, particularly in shallow water.

Do koura come in cans?

Many years ago trout fishing was often combined with 'housing construction' — establishing 'villages' where koura could live. While the connection may seem tenuous, it was real, and came from a former Conservator of Wildlife in Rotorua.

The discussion arose over the question of tin cans, which some fishermen would sink into the lake by punching a couple of holes in the side. The theory was that the tin would break down and rust away, without doing any harm to the underwater environment.

Pat Burstall, the fisheries boss, pointed out that the cans actually provided excellent shelter for koura, the small crayfish which trout love to gorge on.

"But I shouldn't be publicly promoting it," he added with a grin.

On some trips a generous contribution would be made to the koura housing facilities on the bottom of certain parts of Lake Tarawera and Lake Taupo, where the fishing was always good.

But that was more than 25 years ago, and a lot has changed. Attitudes towards dropping anything other than lures into the water have changed radically, and aluminium has replaced tin for making cans. Now the poor koura have to fare on their own, and go back to hiding among the rocks and weed.

It's obviously a problem for the koura, as divers report that the bottom of the lake is barren below about 20 metres, which is the deepest that weed will grow because light does not penetrate further.

In deep water the koura have to hide in the mud, and the cans which suddenly appeared on the bottom were undoubtedly most welcome.

The cans will still be there, because a study received from overseas indicates that tin cans take 50 years to break down in sea water, which is more corrosive than freshwater.

The study reveals that aluminium cans last twice as long underwater, up to 100 years; but paper will disappear in two to four weeks. Cardboard will last up to five months, while fruit peel will drift around for as long as two years. Waxed cardboard milk cartons bob around for five years and cotton rags will last from one to five years.

But of all the material which is deposited into the sea, plastic is the real villain.

Some creatures like turtles mistake bags for jellyfish and try and eat them. The plastic ring which holds a six-pack of cans together easily becomes entangled around the bodies of diving birds or fish, causing a slow death.

This type of plastic takes more than 450 years to break down in the sea, according to the overseas study.

Squid occur in vast numbers and provide a large part of the diet of many fish and animals like whales. It is easy to imagine how a plastic bag drifting on the ocean currents can resemble a squid when located by the sonar of hunting mammals.

The plastic bags will last from 10 to 20 years in the water, and plastic cartons between 50 and 80 years.

Plastic foam, which is often found washed up on surf beaches, can float around for a thousand years before breaking down.

But plastic bottles are the worst: they last indefinitely. However glass bottles, which are made from some natural materials including silica sand, only last for a million or so years in the sea.

Many anglers have found cigarette butts in the stomachs of trout and sea fish, and they probably do little harm — but they can last from one to five years in the sea.

Not all of these pollutants are thrown into the water: many are washed down to the sea through stormwater drains. But before we throw them out of a boat or out of a car window, we should stop and think about what we are actually doing.

It is ironic that in some countries sport fisheries managers actually improve fishing by creating artificial reefs or floating devices which attract fish life. These may be old car bodies or strings of rubber tyres tied together and dumped at sea. Marine life adapts quickly, and such 'reefs' are soon covered with a host of different organisms from barnacles and shellfish to weeds and sponges. These in turn attract small fish, and so the chain begins.

The use of fish attraction devices, or FADs, has been popular in Florida and Hawaii for many years. These floating buoys may be anchored to the sea floor or just float with the currents, and act as a magnet for marine life. Sport fishing boats locate them with radio beacons, and catch large numbers of tuna and mahimahi by drifting or trolling around them. These FADs don't seem to have become fads in this country.

CHAPTER TWENTY-ONE
KNOTS

There are thousands of knots, but only a handful are really needed and it is more useful to become proficient at three or four basic knots, which can be quickly tied on a rocking boat or in the dark, than to try and learn a whole variety which require constant reference to a book. Each knot has a definite purpose and when correctly tied and worked into shape can make the difference between losing or catching a fish.

The longline knot

Our favourite knot for general bait fishing, this is a simplified version of the snood knot. It is used by commercial fishermen to attach thousands of hooks, so there is no better endorsement. The main advantages are the ease and speed of tying, and the fact that the hook lies straight at the end of the line every time. I don't like rigs where the hook is cocked to one side, which can happen with a clinch knot if the knot is not in the centre of the hook eye.

The hook or hooks must be tied to the trace before the trace is attached to the swivel. This is something you will forget several times before it becomes habit.

The knot is also easy to tie using hooks with an angled eye — push the end of your line down through the eye to start and then back up again to complete the knot.

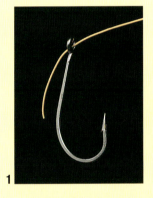

1 Pass one end of the trace down through the eye of the hook, from the hook side, and pinch about 2 cm against the shank.

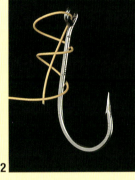

2 Wrap the line around the shank and the short piece . . .

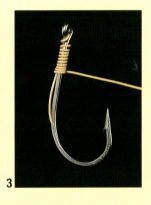

3 . . . seven times, working down the hook.

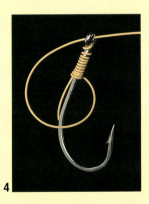

4 Thread the long end of line back up through the hook eye from the back side.

5 Pull tight.

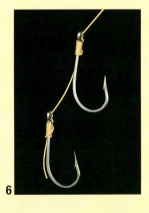

6 For a two-hook rig, thread the long end of your trace up through the hook eye from underneath, slide the hook down to the required distance above the first hook, and repeat the knot.

Quick two-hook pilchard rig

The top hook is pushed through the centre of the head of the pilchard from under the jaw, which takes the weight for casting; and the second hook goes through the pilchard near the tail. A simple and quick rig.

1. Thread a long tag end through from the front of the hook.

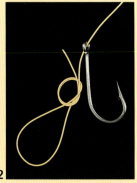

2. Make a loop with the doubled tag end.

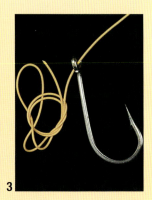

3. Tie a second overhand knot in the loop knot for extra strength.

4. Thread the loop through the eye of the second hook. The size of the loop determines the distance between hooks.

5. Pass the loop over the second hook, securing it.

6. The finished rig, with the first hook lying against the knot of the loop.

Palomar knot

This is a good knot for tying on your hook. It is quicker than a clinch knot and has slightly less bulk.
1. Pass the doubled end of your line through the hook eye.
2. Tie an overhand knot.
3. Pass the end loop over the hook and pull tight

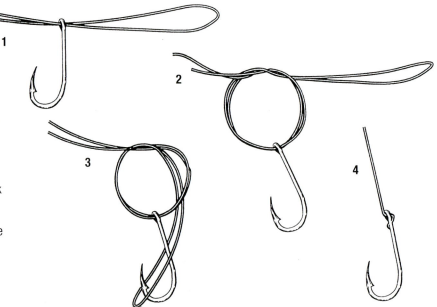

Some basic rules do apply:

Always ensure knots are pulled as tight as possible.

The number of turns taken when tying most knots seems to vary, according to which book you read. One constant theme to remember is this: the lighter the line used, the more turns needed to tie a good knot.

For example, a regular improved clinch knot requires at least six turns with 5 kg line, but only four turns with 24 kg line.

When joining lines of different diameters, you can double the thin line and treat the doubled section as one line.

To make a small dropper, for example for using two nymphs when trout fishing, add a short piece of tippet to your leader and leave an extra long tag end for the top fly.

To join a section of heavy mono to your fly line as a butt section for your trout leader, use a nail knot and tie a loop in the other end where leaders can be easily attached.

Nail or tube knot

This is a favourite of master fisherman Nigel Wood, of Rotorua, who trusts it to attach hooks to marlin lures.

If using a nail instead of a tube you have to poke the tag end back through the loops, alongside the nail.

1. Thread line through eye of hook and pass round to lie over thin metal tube.

2. Grasp both lines and tube firmly.

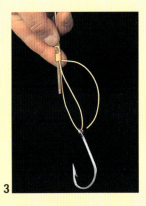

3. Wind tag end around both lines and tube at least seven times.

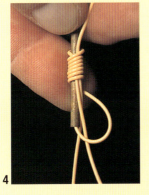

4. Pass tag end back through the tube.

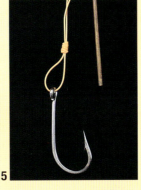

5. Pull out tube.

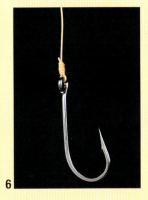

6. Tighten knot up against hook and trim tag.

THE COMPLETE NEW ZEALAND FISHERMAN

Loop knot

Many fisherman like to troll lures for trout or at sea with a knot that forms a small loop, giving the lure more freedom to move.

1. Make an overhand knot in the leader then thread the tag end through the eye of the lure and back through the overhand knot.
2. Wrap the tag end around the leader three times.
3. Pass tag end back through the overhand knot.
4. Tighten leader and tag end against the knot.

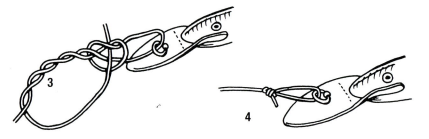

Uni knot

One of the most useful all-round knots for securing hooks, swivels, lures and joining lines. It can be tied so that a loop remains in the end, allowing a lure to move freely, and when a fish is hooked the knot tightens against the lure. For this reason it is called a "sliding loop knot" in the US, and in Australia it is known as the hangman's noose.

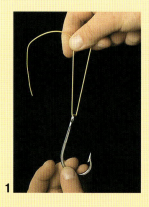

1. Pull a long tag end through hook eye.

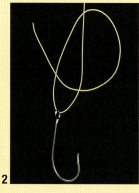

2. Bring tag round and up to pass over both lines.

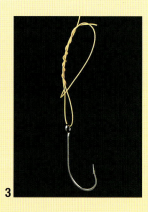

3. Wind the tag end six or seven times around the two parallel lines, passing it through the loop underneath with each wrap.

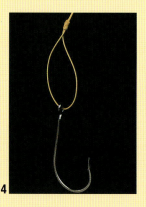

4. Pull knot tight.

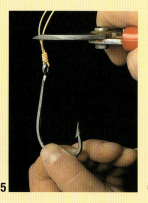

5. Clip off tag end.

6. Finished knot sits snugly against hook.

Improved clinch knot

The most popular knot in the country is easy to tie, is very strong and is adequate for most fishing situations.

1. Pass line through hook from front.

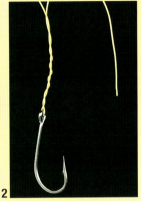

2. Make five or six wraps around the standing line.

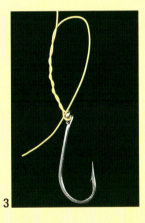

3. Pass tag end back through the small loop against the hook eye.

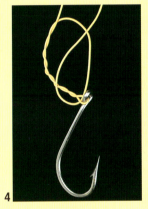

4. Pass tag end through the large loop created.

5. Finished knot should be tucked hard against the hook. I like to tighten tag end with pliers for extra security. Also leave a small tag protruding when trimming it.

A good knot for joining hard or heavy monofilament to terminal tackle.
1. Wrap three turns around standing line.
2 & 3. Wind tag end tightly back around the wraps three times.
4. Pass end through small eye against swivel.
5. Tighten.

The plait

This is a good knot for making a double line, and is favoured by serious game fishermen because it slides smoothly through the rod guides.

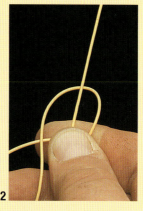

1. Make a large loop and bring tag end (held in left hand) up and over standing line.
2. Pass the tag end under the standing line and back over itself.
3. Pull tag end down through the loop and tighten. You need somebody holding the main line, or secure it from the rod with the drag tight on your reel.

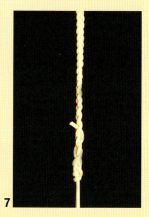

4. Plait the three lines back down towards the end loop, alternating by placing the right-hand line over the centre line then the left-hand line over it, and so on. It is important to keep all three lines tight so each plait is neat and even.
5. Push tag end through the last plait, passing it over the two lines of the loop.
6. Tighten end, then wind tag end back through the plait several times to finish. If plaits are hard and tight it may be necessary to squeeze the ends of the plait together to open gaps for the tag end.
7. Pull tight and trim end. The finished plait may be 8-10 cm long.

Double overhand loop

Loops are handy for attaching swivels, changing hooks or adding sections of line to the loop.

1. Form a loop by doubling the end of the line and tie an overhand knot with the doubled line.
2. Wrap the doubled line through the loop a second time, adding extra strength.
3. Pull the standing line and tag against the loop to close the knot.

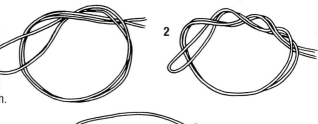

Dropper loop

This loop can be tied anywhere along the leader so multiple droppers can be added to a ledger rig.
1. Form a loop.
2. Take hold of one side of the loop and make four or more turns around the line itself. A match inserted on one side of the crossover can be rotated to insert the twists.
3. Keep open the point where the turns are made or where the match is, and pull the other side of the loop through this opening.
4. Pull gently on both ends of the line. You can hold the loop in your teeth for this.
5. Draw up the knot by pulling tightly.

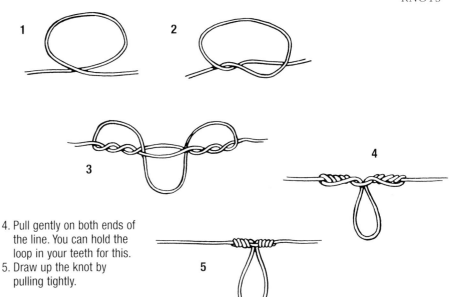

Bimini twist

This is the system used by many professional charter skippers to tie doubles in their lines. It is best tied by two people. Ensure the finished double line, including the knot, meets IGFA length requirements: up to 10 kg tackle maximum of 4.57 m (15 feet); over 10 kg 9.14 m (30 feet).
1. Take double the length of line needed and twist it for about 50 cm, holding the line and tag end firmly.
2. While one person holds the two strands of the loop firmly, wrap the tag end tightly around the twisted line.
3. This is what the partly formed knot should look like, with the wraps evenly spread.
4. When the twisted part is fully wrapped, put a half-hitch on one side of the loop, and repeat on the other side.
5. Add a half hitch around both strands of the loop and wind it back several times inside the half-hitch, and pull tight.
6. Finished knot. Trim tag end so it will pass through roller guides on the rod.

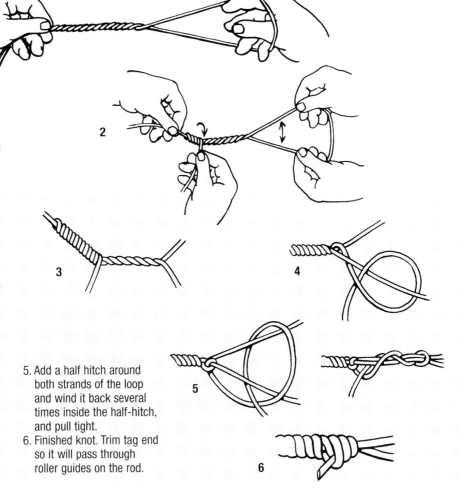

Spider hitch

A quick and easy way to tie a double in tackle up to about 25 kg breaking strain.
1. Measure the length of the double you want, then form a small loop and pinch with thumb and forefinger.
2. Wind the doubled line around your thumb and the loop five times.
3. Pass the rest of the long loop back through the small loop.
4. Pull it gently so the hitch comes off your thumb loop by loop.
5. Pull on both ends of the knot so there are no loose loops, and tighten.

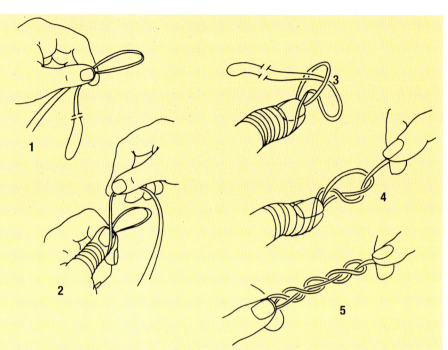

Offshore swivel knot

Used for securing the swivel to the end of your doubled game fishing line.
1. Pull the end of the double line through the eye of the swivel.
2. Twist the end loop a half turn and pull the loop back over the swivel.
3. Hold the end of the loop and the doubled line with one hand and rotate the swivel inside the doubled loops.
4. Continue to rotate the swivel through the loops six times or more.
5. Secure the swivel with pliers, and push the loops down towards the eye and pull tight.

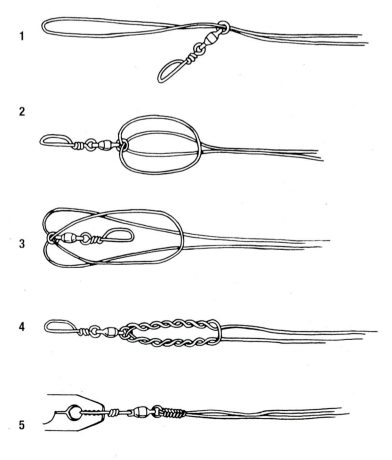

Blood knot

The most popular knot for joining line to line. It is two unlocked clinch knots tied back to back.

1. Lay the two lines against each other, overlapping by about 15 cm, and wrap the end of one line around the other five times, then bring the end back to where it is held between the two lines.
2. Repeat with the other line and also bring the end back between the two lines. The two tag ends project in opposite directions.
3. Pull gently on both lines, taking care the tag ends do not slip out.
4. Draw the knot up tightly and pull on tag ends if necessary. Trim ends.

1

2

3

4

Albright knot

Specifically used for joining a heavy leader to a light main line or two sections of line of different diameter.

1. Make a loop in the heavy leader (solid line). Pass the end of the light line through it and round and under the base of the loop.
2. Bring the light line around and continue to wrap it round the loop in the heavy line.
3. If using a single line make ten or twelve wraps, but if using a doubled main line make only seven wraps. Having completed the wraps, thread the tag end of the light line down through the end of the loop in the heavy line.
4. Reduce the size of the end loop by pulling the short end of the heavy line back through the wraps.
5. Tighten knot, but do not trim tag ends until the knot is fully tightened.

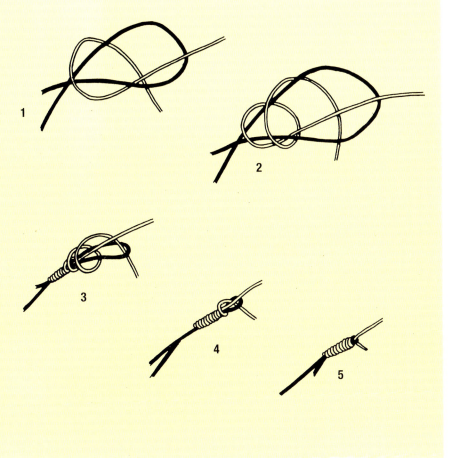

GLOSSARY

adipose fin   small, fleshy fin between dorsal and tail fins, found on salmon and trout.
air bladder   see swim bladder
anadromous   fish which spend part of their lives in freshwater and part in the sea.
anal fin   fin behind vent leading into peduncle.
armour spring   plastic coated wire spring which protects mono leader material, usually used over small loops.
artificial   any lure which represents an item of fish food.
backlash   see over-run
bail arm   half circle of wire which controls movement of line on and off a fixed-spool reel.
barbel   whisker-like feeler on lower jaw of some fish like catfish, gurnard and red cod, used to locate food.
bead chain   two metal beads used for eyes on trout nymphs for added weight and attraction.
benthic fish   fish that live on the sea bed or in rock crevices.
berley   food fragments and oils used to attract and excite fish; also called chum or groundbait.
bird's nest   colloquial term for over-run.
bluewater   term describing offshore ocean fishing.
bobby cork   float for suspending baits.
carapace   hard exterior shell-like skeleton.
cartiliganous   type of fish which have no backbone, notably sharks and rays.
caudal fin   tail.
caudal keel   small hard fin or keel on peduncle of fast-swimming fish like tunas.
choker   noose of heavy rope or chain used to secure big gamefish by looping over head and behind pectoral fins.
christmas tree   small lure used when trolling for tuna, with metal head and multi-coloured tinsel body.
crimp   metal sleeve which is squeezed with special crimping pliers in place of knots to secure heavy mono line or wire.
demersal   bottom-dwelling fish.
denticle   spiny scale found in skin of sharks and rays; also called placoid scale.
dorsal fin   fin on the back of the fish.
double line   section of doubled line at end of game line for added strength. Also called 'double'.
double strike   two fish hooked at same time.
double taper   fly line which tapers equally at each end, for delicate presentation of a cast.
downrigger   device with a winch, wire cable, heavy metal ball and breakaway system to troll lures or baits at deep levels.

drag   amount of pressure required to overcome preset tension and activate clutch mechanism on a reel.
dropback   time between fish taking bait and angler striking. Also refers to the slack line involved.
dropper   side loop or short line for attaching hooks or lures.
dubbing   mixed fibres twisted around fly tying cord and wound onto hook to create body of an artificial fly.
dun   newly hatched adult mayfly.
emerger   hatching fly in surface film.
EPIRB   acronym for Emergency Position Indicating Radio Beacon.
extension butt   often detachable, short length extending below reel.
false cast   action of casting a fly line so it does not touch the water; used to extend the distance.
fast taper   rod where the diameter tapers so that the action (or bend) is in the top section.
feather   to add tension to a reel by lightly pressing fingers on the spool or its rim.
ferrule   sleeves used to join parts of a rod.
filter feeders   family of marine creatures like shellfish which filter plankton from the water.
finning   action of a fish swimming near surface and showing dorsal and tail fins.
flying gaff   gaff which detaches from handle.
forged hooks   hooks which have been pressed and flattened for extra strength.
foul   colloquial term for area of reef or broken seabed.
foulhooked   fish which has been hooked other than in the mouth.
free gaff   to gaff a free swimming fish that is not hooked.
gearing   of a reel: determines the ratio at which it recovers line.
gimbal   a cup with a locking pin for seating the rod.
gimbal nock   fitting with crossed slots on the end of the rod which locks into the pin in the bottom of the gimbal or rod holder.
global positioning system   satellite-linked electronic device for establishing position of a boat or person.
gozzers   maggots.
GPS   acronym for global positioning system.
green   or fresh; term to describe a fish which has not become exhausted and has plenty of fight left in it.
greyhounding   term for gamefish jumping repeatedly across surface.
grip   moulded rubber called duralon or hyperlon which has replaced cork on just about all rods except trout fly rods.

gunwale   the upper edge or side of a boat.
gut   deep, narrow crevice in a rock or reef.
hackle   ruff of fine fibres around head of a trout fly; also feathers from saddle at back of neck of a cockerel.
handline   length of line often wrapped around a moulded plastic handle or piece of wood.
harling   to troll a fly for trout, or to gather line in hand to slowly retrieve a fly.
harness   gear worn by angler to support rod while fighting a fish.
harness lugs   fitting on top of reel where clips are attached.
haywire twist   knot for attaching wire.
hexhead   lure with angled, chromed metal head and skirted body.
horse   colloquial term for forcing a fish to come to the boat and not allowing it to take line.
IGFA   acronym for International Game Fish Association, the governing body which sets rules and keeps records.
indicator   small piece of floating material attached to line to signal strikes.
keel   device to prevent line from twisting.
kidney   line of blood under backbone in fish.
kirbed   hook where point is offset to the right.
knuckle buster   old-fashioned term for single action centrepin reel with revolving handles.
koura   freshwater crayfish.
krill   tiny red shrimp-like creatures which drift in dense concentrations, also called whale food.
lateral line   row of pores along flank of fish containing sensitive nerve endings.
leader   or trace; a section of heavier line carrying hooks or lure.
level line   fly line which is the same diameter throughout; usually used for trolling.
level wind   mechanism on some reels which automatically spreads line across face of spool.
lever drag   type of reel where the drag is operated by sliding a lever on the side of the reel.
line capacity   amount of line a reel can hold.
line class   another term for line weight, specifically when applied to catch records.
line twist   springing loops in monofilament line usually caused by revolving lures.
line weight   or breaking strain; the amount of pressure needed to break the unknotted line.
littoral drift   direction of tidal flow.
loaded   describes a rod which is under tension, either by casting or with a hooked fish pulling on the line.
locked up   when the drag on a reel is so tight that it will not give any line.
longline hook   hook with point bent back towards shank, usually associated with Japanese commercial fishing and used on set lines.
lure action   movement of a lure through the water in a manner which attracts fish.
meatball   school of baitfish concentrated into a dense mass by feeding predators.
minnow   small fish or small lure.
mono   abbreviation for monofilament line
NIWA   acronym for National Institute for Water and Atmospheric Research.
nymph   larval form of fly which lives in water; also describes artificial fly which simulates insect.
offset   hook where the point is angled away from the shaft, see kirbed and reversed.
otolith   bone from inner ear of fish; used to determine age.
outrigger   long pole attached to the side of a boat for holding the line out to one side.
over-run   explosion of coils of line out from reel spool, caused when spool rotates faster than the line is being pulled from it; particularly common when terminal tackle lands during casting and spool keeps spinning.
paravane   device to pull a trolled line down deep.
pectoral fins   pair of fins adjacent to gill plates.
peduncle   slender section, or 'wrist', of a fish's body which ends in the tail.
pelagic   fish that live in surface and midwater areas; usually fast swimming species including gamefish.
pickers   colloquial term for small fish which steal baits without becoming hooked.
pilie   abbreviation for pilchard.
plankton   zooplankton (animal), which include the young of many different species, and phytoplankton (plant organisms) are the base of the marine food chain.
plug   American term for a floating lure.
popper   floating lure which splashes and gurgles when retrieved.
pretest line   tournament or pretest line is guaranteed to break at or slightly under the rated strength.
pump   the act of lifting the rod to retrieve line on the downward stroke.
raise a fish   to attract a gamefish to a lure or bait.
recurve hook   see longline hook
reel foot   part of reel which fits into the reel seat.
reel seat   or winch fitting, which secures reel to rod.
refraction   bending of light rays as they enter water.
release clip   special clip used to secure line and release it when a fish strikes.
reversed   hook where the point is offset to the left.
rig   to assemble tackle; also used to describe a rod and reel combination.
rip   confluence of stream and lake; also where two currents meet.
rocket launcher   multi-rod holder, usually fitted over the windscreen or above the cabin of a boat.
rod action   refers to where a rod bends and is determined by the degree of taper.
rod bucket   leather or plastic pouch which holds the rod butt, usually attached to a rod belt.

rod guides small circular hoops attached to the rod through which the line runs from the reel to the rod tip.
rod power refers to the amount of force needed to bend the rod and is determined by the thickness of the shaft walls and overall diameter.
rod sensitivity the ability of the rod to transmit vibrations from the line through the tip and down to the hand.
rod making main materials used for rods are:
>solid fibreglass - for strong, robust cheaper rods;
>hollow fibreglass - most commonly used, and includes special S glass and E glass;
>graphite - or carbon fibre, is stronger, lighter and more sensitive than glass, but more expensive. Often combined with glass.

run action of a fish swimming away when hooked; also abundance of fish; tidal movement.
running sinker sinker sliding freely on line.
running line backing line designed specifically for casting behind a shooting head fly line.
salmonid family of salmon and trout.
set line usually with several hooks which is dropped from a boat or towed out by a kite, and left unattended.
shooting head shooting (10 m) fly line designed for distance casting.
shotgun lure set on an extra long line, usually in centre of pattern with the rod at a high position.
side pressure weight applied to a hooked fish by holding rod parallel to the ground.
sinker moulded weight which can be added to the line, usually part of the terminal tackle.
slack water when there is no tidal movement at top or bottom of tide.
smelt small thin fish similar to whitebait.
snake ring thin metal guide on a fly rod.
snood when line is tied around the shank of a hook rather than through its eye.
soft heads gamefishing lures with resin heads that do not crack.
sounding deep diving action of a hooked fish.
spawn the act of mating and laying eggs.
spinner dead adult mayfly.
spinning casting out and retrieving a lure.
split ring plated double ring connecting lure to hook or swivel.
split shot tiny lead balls that are squeezed onto line to add weight.
spoon revolving metal lure.
spreader a wide bar used to troll several lines at once; often used with teasers.
star drag type of reel where drag is operated by turning a knurled knob.
stinger see tagline
stopper knot or crimp on a line which prevents a float or sinker sliding.
sunset maximum drag setting on a reel.

straylining fishing unweighted baits.
streamer fly trout fly which represents a small fish.
strike action of pulling the rod or line firmly to drive the hook into a fish's mouth; also describes a fish taking bait or lure.
strip to pull in line by hand, especially trout flyline.
stripey colloquial name for a striped marlin.
stripping guide first guide up a rod, usually wider than other guides to gather the line.
superbraid new type of braided line of fine diameter which is super strong and non stretch.
swage to crimp, see crimp
swim bladder a gas bag under the backbone of the fish used to adjust buoyancy.
swimmer a dead bait which is towed under the surface.
tackle the combination of rod, reel and line, plus other add-ons, such as hooks, sinkers, etc.
tagline short line from outrigger line or gunwale which supports trolling line on a breakaway clip.
tail walking action of a marlin jumping vertically across surface of the sea.
teaser artificial lure with no hook used to attract and excite gamefish.
teleosk type of fish with a bony anatomy.
terminal tackle the business end of your tackle consisting of leader, weight, swivel and hook.
thermocline a narrow band of deep water sandwiched between layers of water of different temperatures.
thimble metal or plastic eyelet which fits inside a loop to protect the mono trace material.
ticer angled metal casting lure for salmon fishing.
tinnie colloquial term for an aluminium boat or can of drink.
tip wrap when line loops around the tip of a rod and jams.
top shot adding new line to existing line on a reel.
touch a gentle strike where the fish is not hooked.
trace see leader
transom the back of a boat.
ventral fins pair of fins at rear of belly; also called pelvic fins.
viviparous giving birth to live young.
weight forward line fly line which is thicker at the front to aid casting.
white water turbulent water in wake of a boat, or where waves break over rocks or a beach.
winch fitting reel seat.
wire a fish to grab leader by hand and pull fish to boat.
wobbler a type of lure that wobbles rather than revolves.
work-up feeding frenzy; see meatball
wrist strap loop of line on handle of a gaff for security.

INDEX

albacore tuna 141
anchovies 140
arbor knot 37

bait 53, 54, 61, 62, 63, 66, 68, 85, 87, 95, 96, 101, 110, 166; for big fish 110-11; butterfly 62; crabs 50, 63; mackerel 95; pilchard 85; piper 52; squid 78
bait board 70
baitfish 145; rigging 151
beach fishing 65-9; bait and berley 68-9; casting 68; casting rigs 68; reading the water 65-6; terminal tackle 67-8
berley 20, 23, 61, 68, 78, 96, 106, 155
bimini twist 297
boats, longlining in 164-6
bony fishes 19-20
brown trout (see trout, brown)
bullies 239, 253
butterfly bait 62

caddisflies 208, 209
Canterbury salmon fishing 258
Cascade River 277-80
casting techniques 45-9, 67; distance 47; fixed-spool 45-6; overhead reel 49; side-cast 45; spinfishing 46; surfcasting 46-7
catfish 271
Central Otago lakes 233
cleaning fish 286
coarse fishing, bait 269-70; rivers 272; stillwater 270, 272; tackle 268-9
coastal fishing 80-3; reading the water 80, 82
cod 84
crabs 50, 63, 110
crayfish 167-9
currents, East Auckland Current 119-20; East Cape Current 119-20; ocean 118-21

deep trolling, trout 189
deepwater reef fishing 104-7
distance casting 47
double overhand loop knot 296

double-hook rigs 131
downrigger system 148, 194
drag settings 119, 130
droplines 107

eel fishing 275-6
electronic depth sounders 193
evening rise 210

fighting gamefish 133, 136, 154
fish anatomy 19-20
fish body temperature 23
fish boxes 72, 284
fish food 13-16
fish organs 24-5
fish senses 20-4
fishing nypmhs 211, 220, 234
fishing over sand or mud 87
fishing structures 52-5; baits and lures 53-4; tackle 52-3
fishing wet flies 216
flies, for harling 187-8
floats 44
flounder 157-60
fly fishing 204-55; dry fly 222-4; lakes 224-7; nymph fishing 211-13; reading the water 204-8; Rotorua lakes 224; saltwater 107-10; South Island lakes 230; stream and rivers 211-24; tackle 240-1; Taupo 227; wet flies 216-20
fly patterns 241-2
freshwater crayfish 230

gaffs 138-9
gamefish, tagging 146-7
gamefishing, baits 142, 143-5, 151; drag setting for trolling 130; fighting the fish 133-4; the fish at the boat 136-9; game chair technique 136; land-based 155; with lures 121-7; ocean currents 118-21; safety 139, 148-9; spooling reels for 120; stand-up technique 135-6; tackle 145-6; the strike 130-3
gills 25
Globugs 220, 225, 238
grapnel anchor 76

handlines 35-6
hapuku 106
harbour and estuary fishing 74-80; high-current areas 77-8; low-current areas 78-80; reading the water 74-5; trolling 75
harling 180-96
hooks 42-4
improved cinch knot 295
inanga 252

jig fishing 88-91
jig flies 53
jigging, for trout 202-3
jigs 90, 92
john dory 54, 81

kahawai 76, 108
kingfish 15, 54, 76, 94, 99-104, 121; fighting the fish 104; live bait for 101-3; lures and baits 99-101
kite fishing 161-3
knots 78, 117, 125, 291-8; bimini twist 297; double overhand loop 296; dropper loop 297; improved cinch 295; longline 291; loop 294; nail or tube 293; offshore swivel 298; Palomar 292; plait 296; quick two-hook pilchard rig 292; spider hitch 298; uni 294
koi carp 268, 269
kontiki raft 161
koura 230

Laka Wanaka 200
Lake Aniwhenua 227
Lake Coleridge 230, 233
Lake Ferry 264-5
Lake Okataina 186, 189
Lake Otamangakau 237
Lake Rotoaira 237
Lake Rotoiti 182, 186, 187, 189, 201
Lake Rotoma 190
Lake Rotorua 182, 226
Lake Tarawera 189, 191, 202, 247-9
Lake Taupo (see Taupo)
Lake Waikaremoana 237
Lake Wakatipu 191
Lake Wanaka 232, 233

lakes, deep 190-1
land-based gamefishing 155
lateral line 21-2
leaders 40
lines 36-40; maintenance 282-3; monofilament 39-40; twist 38, 40
live bait 101-3, 148, 199; tanks 70
locating fish 56, 57, 58, 59, 64, 74, 77, 80, 81, 87, 120
locating trout 190, 193, 206, 223
longline knot 291
loop knot 294
lures, bibbed minnows 76; for gamefishing 121-3; for jigging for trout 202; Rapala 75; rigging for gamefishing 123-5; for spinfishing 199-200; spinning 201; for trout 184-5

mako shark 138
marlin 113, 116, 117, 137, 146, 147, 153; trolling live baits for 149
mayflies 208, 209, 210
measuring fish 74
Mohaka River 198
monofilament 62, 80
moon 287
mussels 170

nail knot 293
Nelson 200
netting 159-60
New Zealand Land-based Game Fishing Club 155
nylon lines, care of 39-40
nymphs 208, 209

outrigger tagline system 143
outriggers 146

Palomar knot 292
parore 69
paua 170
pelagic fishes 17-18
perch 268
pilchards 16, 85
pilchard rigs 78-9
piper 52, 53
plait knot 296
playing fish 63, 97, 104
playing trout 196

rainbow trout (*see* trout, rainbow)
Rapala lures 75
reading the water, beaches 65-6;
coastal fishing 80, 82; fly fishing 204-8; harbour and estuary fishing 74-5; rock fishing 58-60
reef fishing 83-5; baits 85
reels 31-5; baitcaster 35; centre-pin 31-2; closed-face 31; fixed spool 32-3; free-spool 33-4; maintenance 282; setting drag 38-9; spooling 37-39; spooling for gamefishing 120
releasing fish 284-5
rigging game lures 123
rock fishing 56-64; baits and berley 61-2; locations 64; playing the fish 63-4; reading the water 58-60; rigs 60; safety 60; tackle 60
rod holders 72
rods 27-31; maintenance 281-2; storing in small boat 72-3
Rotoiti trolling 186, 187
Rotorua 'big fish' programme 175, 246
Rotorua lakes 224-7
Ruakituri River 216, 217, 246
rudd 273

sabiki flies 53, 82
safety 73, 139, 148
salmon 174, 175, 257; Canterbury 258; Dunedin 263; fishing etiquette 266; fishing the surf 258-60; harbour fishing 263; harbour fishing, tackle 263-4; introduction to New Zealand 177; life cycle 257; river fishing 260-3; river fishing, tackle 262
Salmonidae 174
saltwater fly fishing 107-10
scales 21
scaling fish 285
scallops 169
sea-run brown trout 178-9
shellfish 169-70
short-billed spearfish 149
single hook rig 131
sinkers 41, 64
small boats, safety 73-4
smelt 181, 182, 251, 252, 253
smelting 181-6
snags 67
snapper 17, 57, 84, 92, 98, 111; bait for 95-6; fighting the fish 97; fishing in deep water 98; inshore 93-7; jigging for 88
South Island lakes 190
spider hitch knot 298
spinfishing, for trout 197-201

squid 78, 170-2
stand-up fishing 135
steelhead (*see* trout, rainbow)
surfcasting 46-7; tackle 67
swim bladder 24-5
swivel knot 298
swivels 40

tackle 26-44; maintenance 281-3
tagging fish 146
tagline 143
tarakihi 83-4, 107
targeting big fish inshore 92-7
Taupo 183, 190, 191, 201, 227-30
Taupo rivers 220-2
teasers 127-8
tench 268
terminal tackle 40-4
thermocline 190-1
threadlining 200
tides 59-60, 75, 92
traces 73
trolling 127; blue water 130; deep for trout 189-96; harbours 75; lures, sea 75, 76, 125; speed 128; speed for gamefish 128-30; for trout 180-96
trout 19, 229, 247; bait fishing 250-3; brown 174, 243; deep trolling for 189-96; food 208-10; introduction to New Zealand 176; licence areas 223; mounting 243, 247; netting 229; playing the fish 199; rainbow 174, 175, 179, 234, 245; releasing 195, 219; the strike 227; trophy 242-50; window 204
trout fishing, lakes 181-2; lures 184-5; jigging 202; spinfishing 197-201; trolling and harling 180-196
tuna, bluefin 118; yellowfin 118, 142
turbot 159
two-hook pilchard rig 292

uni knot 294

Waikato River 200
weather 287-9
wharf fishing 50-2
whitebait 277-80
wire lines 192
wobblers 200